A POLITICAL BIOGRAPHY OF
RICHARD STEELE

Eighteenth-Century Political Biographies

Series Editor: J. A. Downie

Titles in this Series

Forthcoming Titles

www.pickeringchatto.com/politicalbiographies

A POLITICAL BIOGRAPHY OF RICHARD STEELE

BY

Charles A. Knight

LONDON
PICKERING & CHATTO
2009

Published by Pickering & Chatto (Publishers) Limited
21 Bloomsbury Way, London WC1A 2TH

2252 Ridge Road, Brookfield, Vermont 05036-9704, USA

www.pickeringchatto.com

© Pickering & Chatto (Publishers) Ltd 2009
© Charles A. Knight 2009

BRITISH LIBRARY CATALOGUING IN PUBLICATION DATA

Knight, Charles.
A political biography of Richard Steele. – (Eighteenth-century political
biographies) 1. Steele, Richard, Sir, 1672–1729 – Political and social views.
2. Politicians – Great Britain – Biography. 3. Journalists – Great Britain – Biography. 4. Great Britain – History – Anne, 1702–1714 – Biography. 5. Great
Britain – History – George I, 1714–1727 – Biography.
I. Title II. Series
941'.071'092–dc22

ISBN–13: 9781851969135
e: 9781851966813

This publication is printed on acid-free paper that conforms to the American
National Standard for the Permanence of Paper for Printed Library Materials.

Typeset by Pickering & Chatto (Publishers) Limited
Printed in Great Britain by the MPG Books Group, Bodmin and King's Lynn

CONTENTS

For Chris, Nathaniel, Jenny and Lucy

ACKNOWLEDGEMENTS

Any literary and historical biography such as this rests on a large body of previous work, and I hope I have made my debts to that work sufficiently clear in my annotation. But two scholars need to be singled out. Alan Downie invited me to write this book, and writing it has entertained me through several years of retirement. But his own work on the connections between literature and political history in the early eighteenth-century has been both a model and a source of considerable information. Calhoun Winton has been a much more specific source. I have turned repeatedly both to his two-volume biography of Steele and to his doctoral dissertation on Steele as a political writer. Although I have not discussed the present project with him, his general encouragement of my work on Addison and Steele has been most helpful. When I was planning my annotated bibliography of Addison and Steele, I told him I was beginning after Steele's death so as to avoid the mass of controversial material published during his lifetime. Winton expressed mild disappointment that I was not looking at the earlier work, but I insisted that doing so would involve a different project entirely. At least the Steele part of that project (by far the larger one, given Addison's shyness about public fights) is represented by this book, where I have tried to see Steele's politics in the context of a multi-voiced political dialogue.

One of the pleasures of living in eastern Massachusetts is the access it allows to truly wonderful collections of eighteenth-century materials. Most of the work for this study was done at the Houghton and Widener Libraries at Harvard, but I have also used the Boston Public Library, the Boston Athenaeum, and the libraries of the Boston Library Consortium, especially Boston College and Boston University. Outside of Boston, I have profited from the resources of the British Library, the New York Public Library, the Library of Congress, and the Folger Shakespeare Library. Librarians seem to be genetically polite and resourceful, and I am most grateful for their help. Online research has been a further help, and I am particularly grateful to the Spectator Project, to Eighteenth-Century Collections Online, to the English Short Title Catalog, and to the 18th Century Interdisciplinary Discussion List.

A scholar whose children have long since left home need not negotiate the different demands of research and parenting, but I can testify to the success of those negotiations by dedicating this book to two sons and two daughters. My wife Kathy has been left to put up with my long days at the library and at my computer. More important, her commitment to the politics of the present has freed me to spend as much time as I have on the politics of the past. Roscoe, my Siberian Husky, has led me on long and frequent walks during which I have been able to work out writing problems. He knows no more about eighteenth-century politics than most, but although I have not thought of him as an audience for this book, I have tried to explain political contexts as best I can.

INTRODUCTION

A political biography of an author, as I think of it, overlaps considerably with both literary biography and personal biography, but it differs from both. Its defining characteristic seems to me its concern for the ways in which a particular author with a distinct personality uses writing as a way of understanding and influencing the political history of his time. A political biography will not be blind to its subject's love-life, marriage, children, friendships and places of residence, but, however much they serve to define the subject as a person, they will not be matters of major concern. But political ideas, influences, contacts, friendships and specific activities will be primary. While other biographies are characteristically tied to chronology, sometimes at the expense of narrative coherence, a political biography can be thematic, tracing the development of particular ideas and topics, elucidated historical contexts, and listening to active dialogues. This is the kind of limited biography I have tried to write here without seriously distorting Richard Steele in the process, either by neglecting his evident personality or by exaggerating his political originality. Steele was the subject of major biographies in the nineteenth and twentieth centuries. George Aitken's two-volume *Life of Richard Steele* is particularly useful in the documentary evidence it supplies and in the detail with which it looks at Steele's personal life and political contacts.[1] Its careful attention to Steele's chaotic financial situation will never be duplicated, but it pays relatively little attention to his writings. Calhoun Winton's two books on Steele's life correct Aitken's occasional errors, provide important new material and give a fuller picture of his life and work.[2] I think of the present study as a supplement to Winton's work that places Steele within the political discourse of his very political age.

Steele is a particularly appropriate subject for this approach. Known primarily as a sentimental dramatist and as half of the essay-writing team of Addison and Steele, he participated in the political world in a number of ways – as soldier, as Gazetteer, as dramatist, as essayist, as party propagandist, as Member of Parliament, and as writer on economics. He was expelled from Parliament in 1713 for seditious libel but, a year later, was knighted for the same propaganda. He came at a time when authorship was just developing as a profession and when the newly formed party system was not only dominating elections but also determining the composition of the ministry. Unlike Matthew Prior, whose roles as diplomat and poet were largely distinct, Steele combined his functions as author and as politician. Unlike Swift, who in 1710–14 advised behind the scenes and did not sign his political writings, Steele developed and projected a public persona as a political author. Over the years of his political activity this combination shifted from outright hackery to complex and principled consideration of constitutional issues. He saw a continuum from moral behaviour to political action, and he used his authority as a moral writer, an authority manifested in the highly popular *Tatler* and *Spectator*, to claim an analogous authority as a political writer. By running for Parliament and eventually becoming a knight of the realm, he tried to escape the common (and largely accurate) depiction of the political writer of short-lived periodicals and fugitive tracts as a badly paid hack. As a parliamentary participant in political debates, he could hardly be accused of ignorance; as a man given special recognition by the king, he could outface the insult that, as a man born in Ireland, he was not English at all. In literary terms his knighthood recognized his status as one of the few well-known public authors of the eighteenth-century.

His double identity as a public writer and a politician made him the target of focused and vituperative attacks that were often quite personal and often dishonestly so. If Steele sought to develop the example of the political writer, his opponents sought to discredit that public example as a warning to other writers. A key issue was the authority of writers, as writers, to speak of political matters. The government, some contended, had access to secret information or could see particular actions in the context of larger policies that it would be nationally dangerous to divulge. The opinion of mere scribblers would have no weight if set against the reliability of voices that it would be treason to question.

But Steele's carefully cultivated image also challenged the definition of what could be written about. In attacking the actions of the Queen's ministers, is one attacking the Queen or the country of which she is the living metonym? How far does the royal prerogative extend, and whom does it protect? In a period when cabinet government was still evolving, what were the relative responsibilities of ministers towards Parliament and towards the Crown? A similar set of questions emerges regarding the political power of the Church of England. If mere authors can write about matters of state, why cannot learned clergymen do so in the sanctity of their pulpits? Steele's editorship of the *Tatler* came during the most famous controversy on religion and politics – the trial of Henry Sacheverell for seditious libel. The relation between politics and religion was not merely abstract. Catholics were excluded for taking the crown, and when Queen Anne died childless in 1714, scores of nearer Catholic relatives were passed over before the Protestant Elector of Hanover assumed the throne. Catholics were severely limited in their civil rights, but Dissenters who did not take communion in an Anglican parish were excluded from public office. On one hand was the Jacobite danger that the Catholic James III would become king, with the support of France and Catholic Europe. On the other hand the movement of power away from the throne threatened to lead to a return of the Commonwealth. This last threat was remote, but it remained a possibility that propagandists could use to scare support away from Dissenters. Even more extreme than Dissenters were freethinkers and Deists who exploited the new freedom of the press made possible by the expiration of the licensing act (1695) to publish non-Trinitarian religious tracts that the mainstream Church regarded as atheist.

The expiration of the licensing act also meant that all of this was discussed in a variety of tracts and pamphlets, periodicals and tomes. Steele's efforts, evolving over time, to identify himself as an acknowledged political writer only set out one course to political participation, amid an onslaught of anonymous publications or publications identified with significantly characterized personae. But Steele's model is now the norm: the acknowledged author who takes public responsibility for what he has written and who can point to his own experience and character as grounds for his authority. Steele's major periodicals, the *Tatler* and the *Spectator*, are sometimes thought of as reflecting a consensus on issues of social morality, but they might equally be thought of as efforts to define, elicit, or impose such a consensus in a period of dynastic rivalry, war, religious contention and political uncertainty.

Steele's emergence as a political writer came at a time when authorship was moving from a patronage model to a commercial one. Steele, as we shall see, had rather unfortunate experiences with patronage in his early days and wrote about it harshly in the *Tatler* and *Spectator*. Jacob Tonson, the printer of Dryden and other Restoration authors, was what might be described as a close acquaintance of Steele, and he became one of the printers of the *Spectator*. He was also the Secretary of the Kit-Cat Club, an assembly that included on one hand the important Junto Lords, who were the leaders of the Whig party in the early years of the century and, on the other hand, important authors. The Kit-Cats were particularly interested in the theatre, and Steele became known to them initially as a playwright. As Whig magnates with strong literary interests, they became significant sponsors of political writers, although they were less strongly organized than the Tories were to be under Robert Harley. They represented a third stream, between literary patrons and commercial publishing, by which authors could be rewarded. Other groups of writers and influences were important during Steele's development as a political writer. In March 1712 Addison's servant Daniel Button opened Button's Coffee House, which quickly became a gathering place for Whig writers and politicians. After the *Spectator* closed, Steele seems to have developed a cadre of Whig propagandists. In a sense, then, the term 'political writer' also meant a participant in a school where ideas were discussed and papers drafted, refined and published. Steele's cultivated public image made him both a leader and a standout among the unknown and temporary stable of Whig political writers.

The process of Steele's politicization – his movement from student to soldier, soldier to playwright and playwright to Gazetteer – is the major topic of my first chapter. The second chapter focuses on his work as Gazetteer and, particular, on the politics of Isaac Bickerstaff, the persona of the *Tatler*. The *Tatler* began as a prime supporter of the Whig government then in power, but it reported foreign news, almost entirely news of the war, and organized its various comments on literature, theatre and society in departments identified by coffee-houses. It ended as rather a different paper, dropping the news entirely and extending its short perceptions into full paper-length essays, now identified by the general rubric 'From my own Apartment'. But during its run the government changed to from Whig to Tory. Steele decided, or was pushed to decide, to close the *Tatler* and start another paper, one that utilized more fully the talents of his friend Joseph Addison and that emphasized the *Tatler*'s pattern of political discourse through indirect implication. The *Spectator* in particular used the family and the virtuous merchant as model figures of Whig society. The society of the *Spectator* is the subject of Chapter 4.

The *Spectator* ended suddenly, partly perhaps because of the death of Arthur Maynwaring, who had been active as the chief Whig propagandist. His role was eventually filled by Steele. The *Guardian*, which replaced the *Spectator*, operated at the outset on much the same pattern. But Nestor Ironside admits that he will, from time-to-time, notice political affairs, although in a neutral way. The paper is, in its first months, as free from overt politics as the *Spectator*. All of this changed when the *Examiner*, the Tory mouthpiece, went after Lady Charlotte Finch for 'knotting' in church. The attack was meant to embarrass her father, the Earl of Nottingham, but Steele felt strongly that the *Examiner*, in mocking a woman and the child of an opponent, had crossed the line. It was not long before he crossed it himself with a sharp attack on Swift and Mrs Manley, neither of whom had written that particular paper but both of whom had written for the *Examiner* in the past. Steele's attack resulted in a prolonged dispute with Swift in which neither party acquitted himself well. Steele resigned from his remaining government positions and ran successfully for Parliament. On his return to the *Guardian* he took up the issue of the French failure to demolish the port of Dunkirk, as promised in the Treaty of Utrecht. He took it up in the *Guardian* but also in political tracts which were answered by Defoe, Swift and others. Steele saw the Dunkirk problem as evidence of the failure of the treaty of Utrecht, as an indication of French perfidy and as a sign that the ministry was cooperating with the French. His opponents saw his concerns as an attack on the royal prerogative and hence on the Queen herself. The *Guardian* represents a shift from the indirect politics of the *Spectator* to an open partisan warfare, during which Steele moved from an interested observer to a parliamentary participant, intending to use his position in Parliament as a source of propaganda and to use his propaganda to support the Whigs in Parliament. The changes represented by the *Guardian* are the subjects of Chapter 4.

Soon after his return from the hustings, Steele changed his periodical from the socially oriented *Guardian*, which occasionally took up political topics to the *Englishman*, which seldom abandoned them. He also shifted his major concern from the Treaty of Utrecht to the Protestant succession, called into question by the ill-health of the Queen and threatened by James III and the French. Chapter 5 traces the repeated and growing argument of the *Englishman* and its advertisement of *The Crisis*, in which Steele collected a variety of laws establishing the succession of the house of Hanover and argued that nonetheless that succession was in danger. *The Crisis* appeared almost a month before the opening of the Parliament to which Steele had been elected, and the government moved quickly to expel him for seditious libel. The Tories had gained seats in the recent election, and the outcome of Steele's trial in the House was predictable, despite able and important speeches by Steele himself, by Robert Walpole and by others. After his expulsion Steele shifted his periodical work in the direction of the *Tatler*, but continued to write political tracts, the most important of which was his defence of the right of Dissenters to educate their children. But the Tory ministry was breaking apart and the Queen died on 1 August 1714. The arrival of the King in September brought the Whigs back to power and brought a series of rewards for Steele. He was made one of the managers of Drury Lane Theatre, was given a variety of sinecures at court, was returned to Parliament, and was knighted.

Chapter 6 focuses on his experience at Drury Lane and its political implications. Steele was not only appointed manager (by the Crown) but also given a patent to run the company, a gesture he hoped would strengthen its independence from the Lord Chamberlain's office. But the Lord Chamberlain was the Duke of Newcastle who had allowed Steele to run for Parliament in a constituency which he controlled and who had presented Steele to the King to be knighted. Newcastle felt that theatre's lack of moral reform was a result of a lack of adequate supervision by his office. Although Steele was appointed as a reformer, he recognized the importance of professional judgement in determining which plays would be performed and by whom. Newcastle was an imperious man who would not stand the insubordination he felt was being shown by Steele. To make matters worse, Steele opposed the government in Parliament on the Peerage Bill, and Newcastle retaliated by excluding Steele from the management of Drury Lane. Newcastle had a point: Steele had been appointed to reform the stage, but the theatre was performing the same scandalous plays it had always performed, including some that Steele himself had specifically attacked. Very few new plays were being performed, and authors were being treated by the actor-managers with scant respect, a pattern that particularly enraged the splenetic author and critic John Dennis. When Steele was excluded, the actor-managers began to pay themselves a salary out of his share of the profits, and the pattern continued after he returned as a result of the collapse of the ministry. The dispute eventuated in a lawsuit which Steele, as was usually the case in his legal battles, especially regarding money, lost. But before matters deteriorated to the lawsuit, Steele did one more favour for his fellow-managers. His play *The Conscious Lovers*, which one might now regard as an interesting failure, brought in more money that any previous opening run. The basic issue that drove Steele's battle with Newcastle concerned the control of the stage. Does the stage, as Newcastle argued, fall properly under the control of knowledgeable and moral evaluators acting for the government, or does it exist as a product of a free market where demand is measured and met by professional theatre people? The issue was, for several centuries, resolved by the Licensing Act of 1737.

The final chapter looks at the disputes that consumed the final decade before Steele's retirement to Wales, largely for health reasons, in 1724. The decade began with a Jacobite rebellion in 1715 and ended with a more minor rebellion in 1722. Steele condemned the 1715 rebellion in the strongest terms, but when the rebels were defeated and a group of Scottish lords was brought to trial, Steele urged clemency, a position that was not popular with the government. Nonetheless, Steele was appointed to a parliamentary Commission for Fortified Estates, a position to which a substantial salary was attached but which required him to go to Scotland every year. (He often did not.) After some initial hesitation he wrote tracts and spoke in Parliament on behalf of the Septennial Bill, which extended the Parliamentary term from three years to seven, thus reducing the burden of elections and making Members at least marginally less dependent on the magnates whose influence put them in Parliament. He took a major role, although not the leading one, in opposing a government plan to limit the power of the King to create new members of the House of Lords. Steele felt that it was an unnecessary and unreasonable limitation of the royal prerogative and that it would have the effect of making the closed House of Lords into an oligarchy that would be more powerful than Commons. It would, of course, also limit the chances of able and ambitious commoners to be rewarded with a peerage. The debate engaged big constitutional questions about the relative power of the branches of government, but it was also an effort to take power away from the Prince of Wales, who had quarrelled with his father. The bill easily passed in the House of Lords, but when it came to the House of Commons it met stiff resistance. Steele published a pamphlet attacking the bill on the morning of the debate and vote in Commons, and opened the debate for the opposition. Robert Walpole closed it with a ringing speech, and the bill was defeated.

One final campaign involved Steele in the unexpected position of financial expert. His own finances were perpetually a shambles. He got into debt by giving money to others, by investing in big but unsuccessful projects and by borrowing money to pay off his other debts. He had invested heavily in a project to bring live fish to London in a 'fish pool' and had floated a stock company to finance the venture. The South-Sea Company, formed during the War of Spanish Succession to trade with Spanish America, successfully proposed to take over the large national debt that had accumulated during the War and to refinance the long-term annuities that had been granted at interest rates that now seemed too high. Steele recognized that the Company was not actually trading with the South Seas and that its rapidly rising stock prices were being used to provide returns to earlier investors. It was, in short, a bubble waiting to burst. Steele also objected to the company's offer to investors in government annuities to refinance at a lower interest rate. The government's only obligation, he argued, was to pay back the loans at the agreed-upon rate. Steele made these arguments in the winter of 1720, when the stocks were still rising. After they fell in the following autumn, the arguments seemed prescient indeed. Steele supported Walpole's successful plan to have the Bank of England and the East-India Company take over a substantial portion of the failing South-Sea stock. What was now left was revenge and, as in the case of the 1715–16 Jacobite rebels, Steele urged clemency.

When Steele first ran for Parliament in 1713, he felt that he could take advantage of the overlap between authorship and parliamentary membership. He could use his position in Parliament to report on speeches and debates, essentially breeching Parliamentary confidentiality. But he could also use his skills as an author to build public support for the positions he supported. Steele's major interventions after 1714 show that this pattern worked successfully. Steele consistently supported the revolution principles of a balanced government, free trade and religious toleration. He was not an original political theorist but was a practical political actor. His political writing got him into trouble: he was expelled from Parliament in 1714, and he was denied his proper place as Drury Lane manager in 1720. He seemed willing the take a great deal of personal abuse, and by signing his name to most of his tracts, he asked for it. But he effectively transformed the political writer from a lowly hack into a respectable member of British society who participates openly in the public arena.

1 PREPARING FOR POLITICS

Richard Steele, Irishman

Early in October 1713, the essayist, playwright, and political propagandist Richard Steele began a new periodical that he called the *Englishman*. It was the fifth periodical in seven years for which he acted as editor and principle writer, and it was the most political. It was the immediate successor to his *Guardian*, and its persona or eidolon claimed to have purchased the *Guardian*'s goodwill from Nestor Ironside, its fictional editor. Ironside dramatically reinforced the need to move from a periodical of manners to a periodical of politics.

> It is not, said the good Man, giving me the key to the Lion's Den, now a Time to improve the Taste of Men by the Reflections and Railleries of Poets and Philosophers, but to awaken their Understanding, by laying before them the present State of the World like a Man of Experience and a Patriot: It is a Jest to throw away our Care in providing for the Palate, when the whole Body is in Danger of Death; or to talk of amending the Mein and Air of a Cripple that has lost his Legs and Arms.[1]

More specifically, the *Englishman* was established to counter the effective propaganda of the *Examiner*, which the Tory ministry sponsored, and to answer the claims made by non-juring and other clerics on behalf of the Pretender's claim to succeed Queen Anne. Ironside ends his speech to his own successor with the exhortation to '*Be an* ENGLISHMAN'. Of course, the Hanoverians, whom Parliament established as Anne's successors by the Act of Settlement in 1701 and whose succession Steele defended in 1713, were not English. However, James III, who had lived all his life in France, could hardly claim to be English either. A further paradox, which Steele's political opponents quickly noted, was that Steele himself was born in Dublin. The pattern of an Irishman pretending to be an Englishman, they argued, typified the mendacity of Steele's political journalism.

Steele never denied his Irish background. He wrote a letter to the *Englishman*, signed with his own name, in which he proclaimed that 'I am an *Englishman* born in the City of *Dublin*'.[2] His Irish background did not prevent him from telling jokes on Irishmen as illustrations of wrongheaded, or obstinately foolish people in *Theatre*, no. 5 (16 January 1720). In February, 1720, in the course of a debate on classifying Irish cloth as foreign manufacture, he asserted that 'I was begot in Dublin by a Welsh gentleman upon a Scots Lady of Quality', a confession that led his modern biographer Calhoun Winton to the rueful comment that 'the statement raises interesting questions for a biographer'.[3] The only verifiable fact in the statement is that Steele was born in Dublin.

Richard Steele was born in Dublin in 1672, probably on 12 March, the date on which he was baptized at St Brides.[4] Captain Richard Steele, his grandfather, had been a merchant adventurer in the early seventeenth century. By the 1630s, he acquired land in Ireland and settled his large family in Ballinakill, but continued to serve as a courtier to Charles I. In 1641 an Irish rebellion besieged the castle and, in 1643, after long and bitter fighting, forced its inhabitants to flee to Dublin. Captain Steele died in 1658, still a significant property-holder in Ireland, and his family dispersed. The children who were most important to Richard Steele the essayist were his father, also Richard Steele, and his Aunt Katherine, who married Sir Humphrey Mildmay, an elderly widower. After his death in 1666, she married Henry Gascoigne but kept her title as Lady Mildmay.

Richard Steele, the author's father, became a lawyer and acquired minor civil positions, largely through the influence of James Butler, Duke of Ormond, who had known the first Richard Steele. In 1672, the year of his son's birth, he became subsheriff of County Tipperary. His position required the unpleasant task of collecting unpaid taxes, and proved to be unremunerative. (Given the author's financial record, it seems an irony of family history that his father should have been a debt collector.) He had married Elinor Symes in 1670. She was Elinor Sheyles, the widow of Thomas Symes, by whom she had three children. She may have been Irish in background, rather than a Scottish 'Lady of Quality', as Steele claimed, but her family name is found in Scotland as well as Ireland. Steele may have had more solid grounds for thinking his father a gentleman, if not a Welshman. Not only was he a lawyer, he was descended from a man of property. But financially and perhaps socially Richard Steele the father lived on the margins and struggled to survive. Katherine Steele, the essayist's older sister, was born in 1671, so that Richard's birth in 1672 meant that his father had two children of his own to support, as well as Elinor's three. Tax-collectors were liable for the revenues they were supposed to collect, and the elder Richard Steele was unable to meet that liability. He had to petition the Dublin courts for relief from his obligation, and his petition was supported by the Duke of Ormond.[5]

In addition to his financial burdens, the task of collecting unpaid taxes in a relatively distant county took its toll on his health. He died in 1676 or 1677, although the date of his death is uncertain. In *Tatler*, no. 181, Isaac Bickerstaff, the paper's eidolon, describes an early grief that has traditionally been seen as Steele's at the loss of his father.

The first Sense of Sorrow I ever knew was upon the Death of my Father, at which Time I was not quite Five Years of Age; but was rather amazed at what all the House meant, than possessed with a real Understanding of why no Body was willing to play with me. I remember I went into the Room where his Body lay, and my Mother sat weeping alone by it. I had my Battledore in my Hand, and fell a beating the Coffin, and calling Papa; for I knew not how I had some slight Idea he was locked up in there. My Mother catched me in her Arms, and transported beyond all Patience of the silent Grief she was before in, she almost smothered me in her Embrace, and told me in a Flood of Tears, Papa could not hear me, and would play with me no more, for they were going to put him under Ground, whence he could never come to us again. She was a very beautiful Woman, of a noble Spirit, and there was a Dignity in her Grief amidst all the Wildness of her Transport, which, methought, struck me with an Instinct of Sorrow, which, before I was sensible of what it was to grieve, seized my very Soul, and has made Pity the Weakness of my Heart ever since. [6]

However nondescript he may have been in life, the death of Richard Steele apparently made a profound impact on his son, and however limited his financial legacy may have been, the capacity to share the sufferings of others seems to have been his major bequest. Elinor Symes Steele seems to have disappeared soon after, along with Steele's Symes half-siblings. But some years later, perhaps 1713, perhaps 1708, as Rae Blanchard speculated, Steele wrote to his wife that 'since the Death of my Poor Mother I find a growing melancholy encrease upon me'.[7] If the traditional date of 1713 is correct, the mother to whom Steele refers may actually be his wife's mother. If the date is as early as 1708, she may be his own mother. We know virtually nothing of her after the death of her husband, despite Bickerstaff's references to her beauty, nobility and dignity. We are hardly better informed about Steele's sister Katherine. She and her brother both became wards of Henry Gascoigne and his wife, Katherine Lady Mildmay. Tradition has it that she suffered from some mental disability, and the only reference to her in Steele's letters comes in 1721, when he sends her to William Aynston, the husband of his illegitimate daughter Elizabeth Ousley, along with an annual sum of £30 for his sister and £10 for her maid.[8]

Steele's aunt Katherine had married Henry Gascoigne in 1675, a year or so before the death of Steele's father. The Gascoignes adopted the Steele children and were responsible for their education. Henry Gascoigne was private secretary to James Butler, first Duke of Ormond. Ormond had been a friend or at least an acquaintance of the first Richard Steele, had appointed the second as subsheriff of Tipperary, and had recommended the remission of his uncollected taxes. He became Viceroy again in 1677 and continued until the death of King Charles in 1685. He died in 1688, but Gascoigne remained private secretary to the second Duke until 1693. Steele's connection to the Ormonds continued significantly for another generation. Gascoigne's position made him an important and wealthy civil servant, noted for his efficiency, tact and prudence. But responsibility for Steele's upbringing was shared by his rather eccentric aunt. She was, by all accounts, a warm and generous woman, if rather vain of the high social status into which she had married. Steele's first extant letter, charmingly obsequious, was written to her, presumably from Charterhouse.[9] Gascoigne's position required considerable travel, and in 1682 the Gascoignes moved to London, where they accompanied Ormond.

Steele's residence in Ireland thus ended when he was ten, but he retained not only an accent but stereotypically Irish characteristics. Like so many stage and real Irishmen, he became a soldier, although on the opposite side from the Jacobite 'Wild Geese' who fled to France to fight for the Pretender. Like other Anglo-Irish writers (one thinks immediately of Toland, Swift, Burke and Sheridan), his interests focused on politics. He was charming and gregarious; he was notoriously irresponsible in financial matters. He was a heavy drinker who did not hold his liquor well. (One of his social functions was to drink with the shy Addison, but by the time Addison was ready to talk, Steele may have been sliding beneath the table.)[10] More significant for a political biography of Steele is his attempt, by referring to his Irish birth, his supposedly Welsh father and his possibly Scottish mother, to locate himself on the borders of Britain, in contrast to his obedience to Ironside's injunction to 'be an Englishman'. This double location, at the patriotic core and at the borders, seems to mark a central paradox in Steele as a political writer. He was, on one hand, an outsider, struggling for financial, social, and personal security and power without achieving the stability acquired by other men. But, on the other hand, he became a baronet, a Member of Parliament, a manager of the Drury-Lane Theatre, and an admired author. On one hand he was a loyal Whig propagandist, but on the other, he took his own path on a number of political issues. On one hand, he wrote the book on responsible middle-class culture for eighteenth-century England, but on the other he hardly represented that culture in his personal life. Although he advocated moral drama in his periodical essays and, somewhat less forcefully at times, in his own plays, as a theatre manager he continued to produce the wonderfully offensive plays of the Restoration. The double vision impelled by being at the edge but writing from the centre gives Steele's political writing its characteristic edge.

The Education of Richard Steele

Steele was enrolled at the Charterhouse school in November 1684, at the age of twelve. The Charterhouse was a seventeenth-century charitable foundation for old men and young boys that was located in the relics of the dissolved Carthusian monastery near Smithfield in London. Steele was sponsored by the Duke of Ormond, who was also a patron of Thomas Burnet, the author of *Sacred Theory of the Earth* (*Telluris Theoria Sacra*, 1681) and the school's headmaster. The extent of Burnet's influence on Steele is hard to determine, but it seems fitting that he was educated by a controversial, pseudoscientific, low-church Master. Steele quotes *Theory of the Earth* in *Spectator*, no. 143 and, in *Spectator*, no. 146, refers to Burnet as 'that Admirable Writer'. (The standard view of Burnet is that his writing was excellent but his reasoning faulty.)[11] After Burnet's death in 1715, Steele campaigned to succeed him as Master of Charterhouse, writing several letters and even petitioning the King. Since the position was traditionally held by a clergyman, Steele was in this case pushing his political favour too far.[12] Burnet's possible effect on Steele was overshadowed by the impact of the friendship with Joseph Addison that he developed at Charterhouse.

Although Addison was the same age as Steele, he did not come to Charterhouse until 1686, when he was fourteen, and he left for Oxford in May 1687. Steele went to Oxford in 1689, so his sojourn at Charterhouse was considerably longer than Addison's. The relation of Addison and Steele was fictionalized by Thackeray in *Henry Esmond*, and it is difficult to separate that fiction from reality, although the novel is filled with historical errors. Steele clearly admired Addison and felt deep devotion to him. Although they were the same age and Addison was a relative newcomer to Charterhouse, Addison's personality and his more secure social status made him seem older than Steele. Addison was the son of the Dean of Lichfield Cathedral, Lancelot Addison. He had two brothers and a sister. His mother had died in 1684. Steele was living with his sister in the Gascognes' rather cramped quarters in Fulton. There are several reasons, therefore, why an invitation for him to spend a vacation with the Addisons would have been welcome. In *Tatler*, no. 235, Steele paid tribute to his rather idealized recollections of Lancelot Addison and his achievements as a father who raised his children by encouraging them to emulate each other in their mutual kindness.

> It was an unspeakable Pleasure to visit or sit at a Meal in that Family. I have often seen the old Man's Heart flow at his Eyes with Joy upon Occasions which would appear indifferent to such as were Strangers to the Turn of his Mind; but a very slight Accident, wherein he saw his Children's Good-Will to one another, created in him the Godlike Pleasure of loving them, because they loved each other.

Years later, after the death of Addison and the edition of his works by Thomas Tickell, Steele published Addison's anonymous play *The Drummer*, which Tickell had not included. Steele's dedication to William Congreve recalled Lancelot Addison and his own place in Addison's family:

> Were things of this nature to be expos'd to publick View, I could shew under the Dean's own Hand, in the warmest Terms, his Blessing on the Friendship between his Son and me; nor had he a Child who did not prefer me in the first place of Kindness and Esteem, as their Father lov'd me like one of them; and I can with great Pleasure

say, I never omitted any opportunity of shewing that Zeal for their Persons and Interests as would become a Gentleman and Friend.[13]

Even allowing for nostalgia or for the exaggeration necessary to create an ideal father, Steele's descriptions speak of his affection for Addison and his family and of the central place that affection came to occupy in his idea of the family.

Before he came to Charterhouse, Addison had been a student at Lichfield Grammar School; Steele had been privately tutored. At Charterhouse their studies certainly focused on Latin and, to a lesser extent, Greek. They would certainly have read a great deal of Cicero and Horace, who were major literary influences on both, and Virgil, who was particularly important to Addison. They would have read Plato and the New Testament in Greek, and perhaps Lucian. Steele received a practical lesson in politics as well as the classical languages. In 1687, Charterhouse became the first institution to resist the Catholic micromanagement of James II. James sought to have a particular student admitted, perhaps no great departure from the patronage that usually led to admission. But in this case the student was a Roman Catholic, and James asked Charterhouse to waive the Anglican oath required of all students. James's purpose seemed to be to test whether the King could, in matters of religious practice, override the will, and indeed the law, of Parliament. The Governors of the school, led by the Duke of Ormond, refused to admit the student.[14] James's efforts to influence Oxford were still more strenuous. In December 1686, he appoint James Massey, a Roman Catholic, as Dean of Christ Church, Oxford, despite the reluctance of the college's other officials to go along. In 1687, John Hough was elected President of Magdalen College, despite James's insistence that the fellows elect Anthony Farmer. Hough was physically removed from his office by three troops of cavalry. The stage was being set for rebellion as Steele was finishing his years at Charterhouse, where he remained a student until 1689.

The first Duke of Ormond died in July 1688 and was succeeded by his twenty-three-year-old grandson. The second Duke was primarily a military man, and Steele had substantial contact with him in that capacity in later life. More important to Steele now was Ormond's prompt election as Chancellor of Oxford. Ormond immediately declared himself a supporter of William III and appointed Henry Gascoigne as his private secretary, the position he had held under the first Duke. William landed at Torquay with a force of Dutch troops and waited in the west of England while various groups, including large segments of the royal army, joined his side. Deserted by so many, James II panicked and fled, only to be recaptured and allowed to flee again by a government that did not know what to do with him. James had vacated the throne, and in the normal scheme of things he would be succeeded by his infant son. But James III was a Catholic, and all sides were, for the most part, agreed that on one hand they did not want a return to the Commonwealth and on the other they did not want a Catholic monarch. William III had a remote claim to the throne, but his wife Mary, as James's (Protestant) first child, had a much stronger one. So it was agreed that William and Mary would jointly reign, a convenient myth was concocted to justify the succession, and a Bill of Rights was pushed through that established the ground rules of cooperation between the monarch and Parliament. However ad-hoc these arrangements may have seemed at the time, they took on the force of principles, especially in the mind of Richard Steele.

The period of Steele's university education included crucial years of change in English politics. James II landed in Ireland with French supporters in 1689, and an Irish Act of Attainder was passed requiring 2,000 named persons, including the Duke of Ormond, to surrender by August. But Steele spent William's Irish campaigns in Oxford, where he signed the entry book at Christ Church College in December 1690. He transferred to Merton College in August 1691, and probably left Oxford in the Spring of 1692, when he joined the 2nd Troop of Life Guards, under the command of the Duke of Ormond.[15] The Revolution Settlement established a pattern, if a vague one, for the conduct of future politics. The Battles of the Boyne and Aughrim and the consequent treaty of Limerick brought an end to the Jacobite rebellion in Ireland and to the practical chances that James II would return to the throne. Locke's *Essay concerning Human Understanding* and *Two Treatises of Government* were published in 1689 (the latter dated 1690). Locke himself was an Oxonian, and the sudden appearance of what seemed a philosophical justification for the events of 1688–9, even though written in response to the Exclusion Crisis of the early 1680s, must have stimulated considerable discussion among Whigs, like Steele, at the university. (It was reported in 1695 to have made 'a great noise' there.)[16] Locke's *Two Treatises* were too radical for the rather cautious compromise of the Glorious Revolution, and Steele almost never cited them, however much they may have influenced his political thinking. He may have been more strongly influenced by the political implications of influential low-church clergymen such as John Tillotson, Isaac Barrow, and Gilbert Burnet. At Oxford in the early 1690s, he would surely have been aware of the ferment of ideas and events around him. What he shared with Locke in particular were the ideas that civil authority is not divinely ordained but derives its power from secular forces, that, although tradition may be among those forces, history is not an immutable determinant, and that although respect for constitutional authority, including the authority of the monarch, is important, exigencies may, if very rarely, require change.

Steele's tutor at Christ Church was Welbore Ellis, a divinity student already connected to the Ormonds. In his 'Preface' to *The Christian Hero* (1701), his first major literary effort, Steele pays particular tribute to Ellis as the person who taught him that happiness derives from virtue.

> For I was long ago inform'd where only it was to be had, by the Reverend Dr. *Ellis*, my ever Honour'd Tutor; which Great Obligation I could not but Mention, tho' my Gratitude to Him is perhaps an Accusation of my self, who shall appear to have so little Profited by the Institution of so Solid and Excellent a Writer, tho' he is above the Temptation of (what is always in his Power) being Famous.[17]

Ellis became Chaplain to the 2nd Life Guards the year after Steele joined it, and he acted as Chaplain to the Duke of Ormond's Household from 1700 to 1705. He subsequently became Dean of Christ Church, Dublin and Bishop of Kildare and Meath. His intellectual impact on Steele is not as clear as his moral impact, and that, as Steele rather sheepishly admits, was less effective than it deserved to be.

In 1713 Steele's alter ego in the *Englishman* pays a business visit to Oxford.

> The Sight of that College I am more particularly obliged to, filled my Heart with unspeakable Joy. Methought I grew younger the Moment I stepped within the Gate, and upon my entering the Hall in which I had so often disputed, I found my Logick come afresh into my Head, and that I could have formed Syllogisms in Figures whose very names I had not once thought of for several Years before. The Libraries, Quadrangles, and Grove, all renewed in my Mind, an hundred little pleasant Stories and innocent Amusements, though in the last place I could not help observing with some Regret the Loss of a Tree, under whose Shade I had often improved my Acquaintance with Horace.[18]

Richard Steele has become a political alumnus in his periodical persona, and that persona records his conversation with a Senior Fellow who seems to have stepped out of the pages of C. P. Snow to report that faculty politics is intense, and 'we sometimes make our Quarrels supply the Place of Business'. Isaac Bickerstaff, the putative author of Steele's *Tatler* is similarly impressed by an Oxford visit: 'Here only is human Life! Here only the Life of Man is a Rational Being!' (*Tatler*, no. 39).

The College that the Englishman visits is almost certainly Merton, for Steele transferred there from Christ Church in August 1691. He entered as an endowed scholar (*portionista*) and thereafter thought of himself as a Mertonian. Addison was now at Magdalen, which had resisted James's efforts to control administrative appointments even more strongly than Christ Church had. But all was now well at both colleges, and Henry Aldridge was now Dean of Christ Church College. Steele's studies continued, not without probable interruption, at Merton, and there he is reported to have written (and destroyed) a comedy.[19] That Steele should have gone down from Merton without a degree is not surprising. As its most recent historian reports about Christ Church,

> to students from wealthy or socially prominent backgrounds, a liberal education was one thing, and was obtained by attending the course of studies at Christ Church, but a degree was an unnecessary qualification and perhaps even a badge of servitude.[20]

Steele was not a distinguished student (as Addison was), but he was not a failure either. If, like many of his compatriots, he sometimes drank too much and sometimes gambled, he left no record of debauchery. He acquired some learning, exercised an able mind, and looked back on the experience with fond nostalgia.

Steele as Soldier

Although it was clear that Steele would not be a clergyman, what his vocation actually would be was uncertain. He was, despite his excellent education and the support of his uncle, an Irish orphan with no independent source of income. His first effort at establishing himself was to follow his uncle's patron, the Duke of Ormond, into the Life Guards. Thus in March 1692, four months after the taking of Limerick, Steele enlisted in the Second Horse Troop of the Life Guards. Although William had successfully defeated the Jacobites in Ireland, he had even more pressing continental interests. He was perhaps the leading political figure in Holland, trying to keep the United Provinces united in the face of French expansion from the south. A principle reason why he was so interested in accepting the invitation of various Englishmen to invade England was to secure it as a protective ally against the French. Thus a key issue in English foreign policy since the Restoration – whether England's principle enemy was Holland or France – was resolved by the accession of its Dutch prince.

Writing of himself in the third person many years later in *The Theatre*, Steele claims that by joining the Guards 'he lost the Succession to a very good Estate in the County of *Wexford* in *Ireland*', and failed to recognize his vocation as a writer, much less a successful political writer:

> When he cock'd his Hat, and put on a broad Sword, Jack-Boots, and Shoulder-Belt, under the Command of the unfortunate Duke of *Ormond*, he was not acquainted with his own Parts, and did not then know he should ever have been able (as he since appear'd in the Case of *Dunkirk*) to demolish a fortify'd Town with a Goose Quill.[21]

Steele went to Flanders in June 1692, during a period of great hardship for William and the allies. James's characteristic flight after the Battle of the Boyne meant that William was free to throw his army against the French.

For William, battling the French meant fighting in Flanders. There was recurring debate in England as to whether the island nation should rely on its navy to protect the channel and to safeguard its merchant shipping or whether it should wage a land war against France in the low countries so as to prevent the French from obtaining the force of both its own and the Dutch fleets to oppose England. William the Dutchman strongly favoured the alternative of war in Flanders, but in 1692 that war was going badly. The French had captured the important fortress of Mons in April 1691, and in June 1692 they had taken

Namur. By July 40,000 English troops were in Flanders, possibly among them Richard Steele. Stung by the loss of Namur in early July 1692, William was anxious to engage the French again. He was not only angry but fearful that wasteful defeat would make it difficult for him to gain the financial support of Parliament to continue the war. England's interest in the conflict was considerably diminished by the defeat of James II in Ireland.

The summer of 1692 was very rainy, making it difficult for troops to move and for their commanders to find promising fields of combat. As the allied army moved westward in search of forage, it ran across the French army commanded by the duc de Luxembourg at the small town of Steenkirk. The wooded ground, scarred by narrow valleys that lay between the forces, was not favourable to a major battle. Nonetheless, William decided to attack. To complicate matters, William's deposition of his troops was awkward and, in disobedience of his orders, cavalry advanced to the fore where the infantry should have been. The broken, wooded ground was inappropriate for cavalry action, and the topography made the movement of troops awkward in any event. But in this case the advance had to take place across a distance of several miles, a distance which made it impossible for the Dutch reserves to come to aid of their English allies. The attack was defeated with very heavy casualties, and a retreat was managed over difficult ground. The Second Horse Troop limped back to England at the end of the summer to repair its losses.

The process of repair was not too unpleasant for Steele. The Horse Troop was stationed at Whitehall during the Winter of 1692–3, and Steele had the help and, presumably, shelter of the Gascoignes. This may have been the Army life for which he had bargained: guard duty in London, the recollection of valour even in defeat and the prospect of an interval in which valour would not be required. Nonetheless, the war continued. When Parliament met in November, it continued to complain about the campaign in Flanders and to push for a direct assault on France, supported by England's naval superiority in the channel. But it was ultimately won over by the domino theory that if Holland fell, England would have to face the fleets of two nations rather than one. Steele remained in London during the summer of 1693; the Duke of Ormond did not.

Although all parties were growing tired of the war, and the French had suffered from bad harvests, the war continued in 1693, and Louis pushed for what he hoped would be a major victory that he could bring to the negotiating table. But much of 1693 was spent in manoeuvering until, in late July, the French, under Luxembourg, caught William in a disadvantageous position and the battle of Landen ensued. It was a defeat for William but not the decisive victory that Louis XIV had wanted. Casualties were heavy on both sides. William himself was almost captured. The Duke of Ormond was wounded and captured. But James Fitzjames, Duke of Berwick, the illegitimate son of James II and Arabella

Churchill, the Duke of Marlborough's sister, and an important soldier for the French in both the Nine Years' War and the War of Spanish Succession, was captured himself and exchanged for Ormond. The capture of Huy and Charleroi strengthened the French frontier and gave them control of the Sambre and Meuse rivers.

Steele's soldiering took a minor literary turn in the winter of 1694, when he wrote a conventional Valentine's Day poem for Mrs Selwyn, the wife of the Colonel of the Second Regiment of Foot. In the spring Steele was back in the Low Countries. The campaign of 1694, on the part of the English, largely involved marching and foraging. Foraging was particularly poor in the area of the Brabant and the Meuse, where much of the fighting had taken place in the previous years. William was successful in pinning down Luxembourg's forces in Flanders, and while they did so, the Allies were able to recapture Huy, on the Meuse, an important stepping stone to the retaking of Namur. Steele probably returned to London with William in the autumn.

In December 1694 Queen Mary died of smallpox, a loss that was harmful to William politically and devastating personally. William was a cold and reserved man, a mediocre general but an effective leader. He had a strong sense of general purpose and what was needed to accomplish it, and a willingness to persist despite setbacks, often of his own making. He was Dutch, and when he invaded England, it was a Dutch army that went with him to London. He kept some significant Dutch advisors in key positions. He himself was out of England, fighting in the Low Countries, from spring to fall. Queen Mary was young (only thirty-two when she died), a daughter of James II, and beloved by her people. She was the bridge between William and the English. Her presence as joint-monarch, notwithstanding her public declaration that she would leave decisions to her husband, gave a sense of English dynastic continuity. At her death the public demanded a state funeral, but the weather prevented one from taking place until early March 1695. It was celebrated by Purcell's extraordinary 'Music for the Funeral of Queen Mary' and, among many other outpourings of grief, by Richard Steele's first publication: *The Procession: A Poem on Her Majesties Funeral*. The poem, which was published anonymously, is a florid description of the funeral procession, emphasizing the grief of the mourners, some of them people from whom Steele might seek favours. The poem was dedicated to John Baron Cutts, then thirty-four and the commanding officer of the 2nd Regiment of Foot Guards, Coldstream Regiment.

Steele's continental fighting was over, but the war itself went on. The 1695 campaign was particularly notable for the retaking of Namur, a major fortress on the Meuse. Although the victory was a notable one, it did not bring the war to a decisive end. But it did assure the French that the best outcome they could hope for was stalemate. The financial situation of both sides was desperate, and the

war in Flanders in effect ground to a halt. The 1696 recoinage in England had
the temporary effect of weakening confidence in the currency.[22] On 24 February
King William announced to an astonished Parliament that a plot to assassinate
him had been uncovered. Sir George Barclay, acting as an agent of James II, had
organized the plot, apparently without James's knowledge and approval, and
its revelation caused revulsion against the Jacobites and support for William.
If the currency crisis prevented England from financing significant attacks in
the Netherlands, the revelation of the Jacobite plot prevented the French from
invading England, since they planned to do so only in concert with a rebellion
on James's behalf. With the signing of the Treaty of Ryswick in 1697, Louis XIV
recognized William as the rightful King of England.

Steele's dedication of *The Procession* to John Baron Cutts either followed or
anticipated his transfer to Cutts's regiment in the Cold Stream Guards. Cutts
was, like Steele, an Irishman, and he had gained particular prominence as a
courageous, even foolhardy soldier. He distinguished himself at the Boyne, was
wounded at Limerick, which surrendered to him in 1691, was wounded at Eng-
heim and Steenkirk in 1692 and at the Brest expedition in 1694. He did signal
service at the siege of Namur in 1695, where he personally led the charge, with
drawn sword, at the head of his troops, earning the title of 'The Salamander'.
He played a major role in Marlborough's victory at Blenheim (1704). Jonathan
Swift, whose attitude towards military men was often unsympathetic, described
him as 'brave and brainless as the sword he wore'.[23] In addition to gaining him his
barony, Cutts's military exploits led to his appointment as governor of the Isle of
Wight. His second in command – that is, the person who did the actual governing – was Joseph Dudley, from Massachusetts. Cutts was gallant and charming,
a minor literary figure himself, but thin-skinned, testy, and ambitious. His friend
General Hugh Mackay described him as 'pretty, tall, lusty and well-shaped, an
agreeable companion, with abundance of wit, affable and familiar, but too much
seized with vanity and conceit'.[24] Dudley shared some of these qualities, certainly the interest in power. The Isle of Wight sent a half-dozen representatives
to Parliament, and one of Dudley's jobs was to make sure that the right men
were elected. In 1701 Dudley was elected to Parliament himself, and in 1702
he returned to Boston as Governor of Massachusetts. Steele's observation of the
electoral manipulations of Cutts and Dudley may have been his first practical
political experience. As Cutts's private secretary, he would also have become
acquainted with the world of court. Cutts was a favourite of William III and
spent a good deal of time in his company when not on military campaigns.

As a member of the Second Regiment of Coldstream, Steele stayed in London to guard various royal residences, while the First Regiment went to war. In
1697 he became an Ensign (the third in command after Cutts and Dudley) and
acquired the honorary title of Captain. Cutts and members of Coldstream were

valiant (but unsuccessful) in their efforts to put out the fire at Whitehall in 1698. In the meantime, Steele's financial situation became seriously confused, as was to be the case for most of his life. Although he would go on to write eloquently and responsibly, as we shall see, about economic life, his own domestic economy was decidedly irresponsible. He was the eternal sanguine, expecting every day a substantial return on his investments. In 1705, Steele wrote to Cutts asking him for payment, as promised, for the service he had rendered. Cutts denied that he had ever promised him payment in money and found it odd that he should be expected to pay several years after Steele had left his service without asking for such payment. Cutts's tone moderated between cordiality and exasperation, and nothing came of the disagreement, as Steele admitted that he had come into money from his wife's estate and thus did not need any help. Cutts's letter confirms that Steele left his service sometime before 1705 (1702 is perhaps the most probable date). But the major irony is that Cutts himself was notoriously in debt, as Steele must have known full well. One can suspect that Steele's equally notorious mismanagement of money may have been stimulated by Cutts's example. But in 1705, Cutts was made Commander-in-Chief in Ireland by the Duke of Ormond, and Steele may have sought to exploit that connection rather than to get money directly. Cutts's letter makes it clear that Steele was not paid as his secretary other than what he would have received as an officer in the regiment. The value of the position lay in the opportunities it might open. Cutts died in Dublin in 1707, worn out by war and his wounds but also, perhaps, by debt and the struggle to survive. He was a minor poet, and Steele published lines of his poetry in *Tatler*, no. 5, as written by 'Honest *Cynthio*'.

The nature and extent of Steele's connection with Addison during the 1690s is unclear. They were at different Oxford colleges. Steele had left for the wars, but Addison stayed on, developing a local reputation as a Latin poet and moving in the circle of wits and writers that surrounded Dryden, until 1699, when, at the urging (and with the financing) of Charles Montagu and other Whig leaders, he left for France, where he studied the language at Blois and moved in intellectual circles in Paris. At the end of 1700, he went to Italy, where he mapped the topography of Latin poetry and observed the injustices of Catholic power. He acquired linguistic skills and the Whig perspective, based on Protestantism and the lessons of classical, republican Rome, to begin a political and diplomatic career as well as a literary one. He reported his findings in his poem 'Letter from Italy' (1703) and, more extensively, in his *Remarks on the several Parts of Italy, &c. In the Years 1701, 1702, 1703* (1705). He made his way over the Alps and up the Rhine to Holland, where he met John Baron Cutts and doubtless gossiped about Steele. By 1703 there was a great deal to gossip about. In late February 1704, Addison returned to England.[25]

Steele's Christian Hero

The ultimate indication of the power of Steele's desire for money and the distortion of reality to which it would lead was an investment in alchemy that nearly ruined him. Alchemy was on the border between science and greed, and it had a number of otherwise rational adherents, among them Isaac Newton. Steele's major support in his alchemical venture was Delarivière Manley, a colourful and brilliant women, who did not live with her husband (in fact with either of her husbands), but was living with John Tilly, the warden of the Fleet prison.[26] In addition to Tilly and Manley, the alchemical venture included a fellow Mertonian, William Burnaby, who was now trying to write plays. They sought to do business with an alchemist named Sir Thomas Tyrrel. Just who among these investors were the cons and who the gulls is not easy to determine, but it is clear that Steele was a prime gull. Delarivière Manley, some years later, described the situation in *The New Atalantis*:

> Well, a House is taken, and furnished, and Furnaces built, and to work they go; the young Soldier's little ready Money immediately flies off, his Credit is next staked, which soon likewise vanishes into Smoke ... Still the Furnace burnt on, his Credit was stretch'd to the utmost; Demands came quick upon him, and became clamourous; he had neglected his Lord's Business and even had left his house, to give himself up to the vain Pursuits of Chymistry.

Despite Manley's efforts to help, '*Monsieur* was forc'd to abscond, all he could preserve from the Chymical-Shipwreck was his Commission.'[27]

Mrs Manley did not only publish her famous *roman à clef* but also anonymously published, in *The Unknown Lady's Pacquet of Letters* (1707), a series of letters apparently written, in the late 1690s, between Steele and herself. These refer obliquely to the chemical experiments, to the death of an apparently illegitimate child referred to as 'Miss Temperance', to a country mistress, to the author's activities on the Isle of Wight (where Steele was doing business with and for Lord Cutts). Steele's letters are filled with florid praise for their recipient, but one cannot prove more than a flirtatious friendship between the two authors. One can, however, assert more tangible relations between Steele and other women. What happened to Miss Temperance and the identity of her mother are unknown, nor is it known whether the mother is the 'pretty wild young Country Mistress' Steele describes in Letter no. 18. But a great deal is known about his illegitimate daughter Elizabeth.

Her mother was Elizabeth Tonson, the niece of Jacob Tonson the bookseller. Whatever the family's reaction to the affair might have been, it did not prevent Tonson from being one of Steele's principle publishers. The child was called Elizabeth Ousley, perhaps from the family that brought her up, and was well cared for by Steele throughout his life. According to legend, several years later, at his wife's insistence, she was brought into his family, but the legend is probably untrue. Apparently intended, at one time, to be the wife of Richard Savage, she succeeded in avoiding that fate and married William Aynston in 1720. She is the only of Steele's children to have surviving children herself. The notoriously cantankerous Thomas Hearne referred to Steele as 'a rakish, wild, drunken Spark',[28] but Samuel Johnson, who heard scandalous Steele stories from Richard Savage, told Boswell that 'Steele, I believe, practiced the lighter vices'.[29] Steele may have been a wild young man, but he was not an unfeeling one. The death of one illegitimate daughter and the birth of another must have given him some pause.

An even more serious cause for reflection was the duel he fought in June 1700 with a Henry or Harry Kelly or Keally, an officer in the Queen's Dragoons. The standard account of the story, summarized by John Nichols in his edition of the *Tatler* and quoted by Blanchard is that Kelly told Steele that he intended to challenge a fellow officer, and Steele, who thought duelling improper, sought to dissuade him.[30] Kelly saw this effort as a defense of the man who had offended him and challenged Steele. Steele resisted the challenge but, as an officer and a gentleman, could hardly refuse it, whatever his private feelings about duelling might be. He rationalized the duel on the grounds that he might succeed in teaching the impetuous Kelly a lesson. But the lesson was more severe than Steele had bargained for. In the course of defending himself, Steele wounded his antagonist severely, and for some time his life was in danger. Cutts defended Steele warmly, but, of course, duelling was a Cuttsian thing to do, and Steele's wish to shine in the eyes of his patron may have been a motivating factor. Kelly survived, and Steele became a lifelong campaigner against duelling. The duel established a repeated pattern in Steele's public moral life: a significant and troublesome personal flaw becomes the object of Steele's direct and repeated moral attack, whether Steele has been successful in conquering the danger himself (as in the case of duelling and, apparently, sexual misconduct) or (as in the case of spending more than one takes in) has failed.

One more thread needs to be woven into the pattern of Steele's *The Christian Hero*, and that is his growing participation in the London literary scene. Steele's poem *The Procession* (1695), on Queen Mary's funeral, is a carefully observed description of the funeral procession itself as it makes its way to Westminster Abbey (or Steele may have used the *London Gazette*'s account of the funeral).[31] Steele moves from the description of groups of mourners to individual mourners whose personal grief represents that of Mary's subjects in general. There is nothing striking about the verse, and the sentiments, however sincere, are hardly original. But the procession structure gives an air of actuality, and the opening section on the plight of the poor women and widows who led the procession shows how strongly Steele shared the Queen's sympathy for suffering. Steele continued to write occasional poems of love or commendation, most probably now lost, but his next appearance in public print was as part of a joint response to Sir Richard Blackmore's *Satyr against Wit* (1700). Blackmore was a physician and the author of several pseudo-epic poems. Hence *Satyr* has a medical subtext, and imagery of sickness and contagion, especially associated with Dr Samuel Garth, the author of the *The Dispensary*, a popular satire, runs through the poem. Wit is the primary infection plaguing England, and the centre of such contamination is Will's Coffee-House, whose most prominent patron was John Dryden. Blackmore's attack allows him to insult a wide range of contemporary authors, including Joseph Addison, whose few poems had been praised by Dryden:

> But wit as now 'tis managed would undo
> The skill and virtues we admire in you.
> In Garth the wit the doctor has undone,
> In Smalwood the divine: Heav'ns guard poor Addison. (ll. 157–60)[32]

The wits at Will's responded with a composite poem titled 'Commendatory Verses', edited by Tom Brown. Steele's contribution consists of verses (parodying Blackmore's opening) in defence of Addison:

> Must I then passive stand! and can I hear
> The Man I Love, abus'd, and yet forbear?
> Yet much I thank thy Favour to my Friend,
> 'Twas some Remorse thou didst not him commend.
> Thou dost not all my Indignation raise,
> For I prefer thy Pity to thy Praise.

Steele goes on the insult Blackmore in two more stanzas, concluding with the prediction that he may be cured and forgiven by the very physician and divine he insulted.

Steele's contribution is decidedly minor, and the insult to Blackmore hardly warranted response. (Blackmore wittily expressed some surprize at 'the Noble Captain, who was in a Damn'd Confounded Pet, because the Author of the *Satyr against Wit* was pleased to pray for his Friend'.)[33] But behind the tomfoolery was a more serious issue. Blackmore's poem was part of a movement to censure the stage in particular and wit in general for immorality. The accusation was that literary men were self-conscious mockers of moral principle, moral behaviour, and religious practice, and Blackmore was part of a broader call for reform. That call did not originate with Jeremy Collier's *Short View of the Immorality and Profaneness of the English Stage* (1698), but Collier's screed caught middle-class revulsion against the wits of the Restoration and all their works. Hence when William Congreve's *The Way of the World* was first acted in 1700, it appeared before an audience that insisted that the play did not represent its world at all. Congreve, who had himself been attacked in Blackmore's poem, was Steele's friend, and however much Steele sympathized with the moral reformers, he wrote a poem to defend Congreve's play. Although he was one of Congreve's few defenders and despite the tradition of anonymous publication, he signed the poem. It does not address *The Way of the World* directly but praises Congreve more generally. It distinguishes between true discerners and 'Well-dress'd Barbarians' who are incapable of appreciating the meaning in his mirth. The realism of his scenes and the appropriateness of his language create real emotions and thus 'check unjust Esteem and fond Desire, / And teach to Scorn, what else we should admire'.[34]

Congreve presented a problem for Steele, and it is one he wrestled with the rest of his public career. Steele sympathized with Collier's position. He was himself a reformer, if a more graceful, less coercive one than Collier and many members of the reform societies established at the turn of the century. But he admired the artistry and humour of Congreve's play, and he was a personal friend of Congreve himself. Moreover, he was himself closer in his own behaviour to a Restoration rake than to a man of probity. He sought to resolve the threatening contradiction by arguing that Congreve's plays were in fact moral, and that the lukewarm reception of *The Way of the World* on moral grounds merely indicated the lack of critical sophistication in its audience.

The conflict that Congreve posed for Steele is even more pronounced in *The Christian Hero*, Steele's first major work. He described the personal origin of the work in his 1714 *Apology*, speaking of himself in the third person, as he imagined a witness at a trial might do.

> He first became an Author when an Ensign of the Guards, a way of Life exposed to much Irregularity; and being thoroughly convinced of many things, of which he often repented, and which he more often repeated, he writ, for his own private Use, a little Book called the *Christian Hero*, with a design principally to fix upon his own Mind a strong Impression of Virtue and Religion, in Opposition to a stronger Propensity towards unwarrantable Pleasures. This secret Admonition was too weak; he therefore Printed the Book with his Name, in hopes that a standing Testimony against himself, and the Eyes of the World (that is to say of his Acquaintance) upon him in a new Light, might curb his Desires, and make him ashamed of understanding and seeming to feel what was Virtuous, and living so quite contrary a Life.[35]

Steele is here responding to Delarivier Manley's description of his early life and the function of his religious tract. She reports that

> his Morals were loose; his Principles nothing but pretence, and a firm Resolution of making his Fortune, at what rate soever, but because he was far from being at ease that way, he covered all by a most profound Dissimulation, not in his Practice, but in his Words, not in his Actions, but his Pen, where he affected to be extremely religious, at the same time when he had two different *Creatures* lying-in of base Children by him.[36]

The problem of Steele's looser vices was that reform seemed hypocritical. What kept it from being so was not that Steele's language led to a change in his behaviour but that his language was so sincerely intended.

The intention of Steele's first tract is readily apparent from its subtitle: *The Christian Hero: or, No Principles but those of Religion Sufficient To Make a Great Man*. He establishes the Christian hero by military analogy. He writes as a soldier to an audience that includes military men. Men of wit, as contrasted to men of business, are attractive, eloquent and entertaining, but in railing against religion, they are apt to lead one astray. Philosophers, with their dry antidotes to temptations they never felt, are not much better in the other direction. Steele modestly hopes that his short tract will help people, especially his fellow soldiers, who are in need of valourous virtue. The Christian hero takes the place of the military hero of the classical world. The valour assured by a confident faith is the central military virtue around which others are organized, and the outcome of Christian principles is 'to make a great man'. Steele's explicitly religious tract is implicitly political. It suggests less a conduct book – that is, a guide to personal behaviour – than a religious analysis of the qualities that make a good leader. Above all, it is an assertion of the importance to seeing religion as the central and overriding force in life.

Without religion, Steele argues, one is ultimately the victim of the flaws of one's own personality, a point that he makes by the contrasting examples of Caesar and Cato in life and death. Caesar was, in addition to being a brilliant general and eloquent writer, an affable, generous and forgiving leader. Cato (and Steele's Cato is far from the serene philosopher of Addison's later play) is rigidly virtuous and envious of Caesar. It is thus at least an open question whether his suicide was a political protest against the fall of the Republic or an act of personal frustration at Caesar's success. What is clear is that Cato thereby rejected his friends and family, and that his suicide itself was violent and impassioned. The conquest of reason and friendship by misplaced passion is similarly evident in Cassius and Brutus. Here, as in his treatment of Cato and Caesar, Steele follows the familiar outlines of Plutarch. Steele sees natural goodness as inadequate to control individual emotions.

The Roman heroes contrast to Christian ones – Jesus in Chapter 2 and St Paul in Chapter 3. Steele's Christ, drawn primarily from the Book of Matthew, is presented as a redeemer, a point developed by a vivid if unoriginal telling of the fall story, and as a teacher and exemplar, emphasizing particularly 'a Sense of our Inability, without God's assistance, to do any thing Great or Good'.[37] For Steele, Christ exemplifies the world of spiritual truth, contrasting to the political world that surrounds him and puts him to death. That political world is the world of Rome and its Empire, and Steele's depiction of it in terms of Christ's death is the extreme example of the inability of reason and nature to achieve goodness. But Steele wants to make this argument without denying the value of the active, political life. He insists that Christian principles do not conflict with any particular form of government, a thrust at those who insist that God ordains absolute monarchy. Nonetheless, he needs to bring the political and spiritual worlds together, and the first step in that process is represented by St Paul.

Steele is not interested in St Paul as a theologian and only somewhat in his role in establishing and developing the Christ movement. It is tempting to describe Chapter 3 of *The Christian Hero* as 'the adventures of Paul'. Steele is interested in St Paul's character and in that character as it is manifested in moments of threat. The central characteristic that Steele wants to emphasize is Paul's meekness but, as his examples illustrate, that meekness is combined with intense concentration, clarity of priority and concern for other people. Steele particularly narrates Paul's confrontations with authority: his farewell to the Ephesians, his imprisonment and trial in Jerusalem, his journey to Rome and bravery in adversity, which is contrasted to Scipio and Seneca.

Steele recognizes that he needs to 'talk of Motives which are common to all Men, and which are the Impulses of the ordinary World, as well as of Captains, Heroes, Worthies, Lawgivers, and Saints'.[38] This shift requires a change from narrative to analysis. Steele argues that fame and conscience are the springs of action. Fame is the principal motivator but it must be controlled and directed by conscience, which is in turn instructed by religion.

> And what more glorious Ambition can the Mind of Man have, than to consider it self actually Imployed in the Service of, and in a manner in Conjunction with, the Mind of the Universe, which is for ever Busie without Toil, and Working without Weariness.[39]

The mind of the master is what attaches us to other people, prompting charity even when it will have no return, and causing us to serve our enemies as well as our friends. Steele moves from these rather unoriginal sentiments to exemplify them by a contrast of Louis of France to William of England: 'Both animated by a restless Desire of Glory, but pursue it by different Means, and with different Motives: To one it consists in an extensive undisputed Empire over his Subjects, to the other in their rational and voluntary Obedience'. Steele goes on to praise William in fulsome terms. 'All the Circumstances of the Illustrious Life of our Prince seem to have Conspir'd to make him the Check and Bridle of Tyranny'.[40]

Steele's style is sometimes awkward, especially in the theoretical sections of the tract, but his narrative movement is strong and gives a sense of power and thrust to his argument. That argument is unoriginal, but Steele has not claimed to write original theology – only a private meditation now made public for the use of others. And others apparently used it throughout the century. The English Short Title Catalogue lists eighteen editions in the eighteenth century, and all or part of the tract was included in collected editions.

Steele as Playwright

Unusually, for such religious works, *The Christian Hero* was signed by its author. Unconsciously or ironically, Steele exemplified his observation that the love of fame is a prime motivator of human action. But the nature of the fame, in this case, may have been unwelcome. His friends, aware of his wild life, labelled him a hypocrite; his fellow soldiers no longer regarded him as a good fellow but saw him as an insufferable moral prig. It may have been to readjust his image that Steele spent the summer of 1701 in Wandsworth, where he worked on a play. Equally, he may have been hiding from his creditors and turning to the theatre as a means of restoring, or at least alleviating, his financial condition. *The Funeral*, the result of this effort, was accepted by Christopher Rich in October for performance at Drury Lane Theatre, and that performance took place in early December 1701.[41] Steele's relations with his fellow soldiers seemed to have become more cordial, as might be expected from his emergence as an acknowledged playwright. He packed the opening house with soldiers, as the Prologue indicates. (Steele was to acquire considerable practice in packing houses over the years.) But the artificial audience was not really needed, as the play was a genuine, if not spectacular, success. It continued to be acted regularly for the next seventy years.[42] Both David Baker Erskine and Charles Dibdin in their eighteenth-century histories of stage refer to it as Steele's best play.[43]

The play appealed to its preponderantly military audience in other respects beyond authorship. The two male aristocratic heroes are officers, and their soldiers play significant roles in the action. There are many references to recent military campaigns, and the play is chock-full of chauvinistic sentiments, especially towards the end. But beyond its military attraction, it is a funny and reasonably well-plotted play, not dependent on previous plays for its general shape, as Steele's later plays were. It begins with a sharply satiric treatment of undertakers, a term and profession reasonably new in England.[44] The funeral in question is that of Lord Brumpton, who, however, is not dead, a fact he is anxious to conceal from his wife. Inspired by his faithful steward, Trusty, the secret plotter of the play, he wants to use the fact that he was mistaken for dead to spy on his young wife, with whom he is infatuated. But Trusty knows that she is interested only in his money and therefore quite happy to be a widow. A further complication is that his wife has misrepresented the behaviour of his son, Lord Hardy, to such a degree that Brumpton has disinherited him. Hardy has done what any disinherited son would do – join the army.

His close army friend Campley assists him in the plot, as does his loyal servant, Will Trim. Hardy and Campley are in love with the two wards of the supposedly deceased Brumpton – the sweetly demur and modest Lady Sharlot and the lively Lady Harriet. There are a number of eccentric minor characters, but the basic plot flows directly from the interrelation of the wicked step-mother, the naive father, the worthy but disinherited children and the plotting servants. Once Lord Brumpton finally comes to life in the last act, he spouts such tub-thumping moral and patriotic sentiments at the other characters that a modern audience might well wish him dead again. But in the contemporary context the death of James II in September 1701 and the recognition of James III as England's king by Louis XIV, in violation of the Treaty of Ryswick, portended a resumption of war with France and made the military posturing and patriotic sentiments of the play germane and popular. The major theme of the play is appropriate, sustained and repeated in diverse segments of the plot: the profession of mourning is the faking of an emotion that ought to be natural and heartfelt. The good characters of the play are those that are sincere and sympathetic, however tricky the plots of their servants may be; the bad characters are those that are self-centred and pretentious.

Among the patriotic sentiments that close the play is high praise for King William. It is certainly possible to read the play as a conscious effort to promote support for William's military activities. After Steele's extravagant praise of William in *The Christian Hero* and his celebration of him in *The Funeral*, Steele had reason to hope that the King would make some return. Moreover, the published play (20 December 1701, dated 1702) was dedicated to the Duchess of Albemarle, a Dutchwoman who had recently married William's friend Arnold Joost van Keppel, Earl of Albemarle. Steele had now come to the attention of the King. But William died in early March 1702, before he could do as much for Steele, as perhaps he had planned. Nonetheless, on 10 March 1702, Steele was commissioned as Captain of the 34th Regiment of Foot, a newly established corps, commanded by Robert Lord Lucas. In accordance with contemporary custom, Steele was required to recruit and train his troops as part of the expanded army set to fight. Steele had to borrow money to go recruiting. At the same time, in April and May of 1702, Queen Anne was recruiting a new cabinet, one that included Sidney Godolphin as Lord Treasurer and John Churchill Duke of Marlborough as Captain-General (essentially taking the military place that had been occupied by William himself). But there were nine Tories in the cabinet and only three moderate Whigs. In the General Election of July 1702, a Tory majority was returned.

In May, Steele's troops were assigned to guard Landgate Fort near Harwich. He remained there for at least the next two years, and thus did not ride to glory at Blenheim or any of Marlborough's other more-or-less glorious victories. It is possible that he was more highly valued as a writer than as a soldier, and it is possible that his recently recruited and untested troops were more appropriate to home than continental service. But Harwich was an important debarkation point for English troops and others heading to the continent, and it was a vulnerable point of invasion. Landgate Fort was thus a significant defensive emplacement, certainly in need of troops. Unfortunately it was also in need of considerable repair. In September Steele wrote to the Board of Ordinance about

> the ill condition, the Barracks and all parts of this Garrison, is in, as to our Windows and Tyling; There are Sick Men of the Company here (whereof I am Captain) lye in their Beds exposed to all the injuries of the Weather ... I cannot expect the continuance of other men's health, if the Remedy be defer'd till the Weather advances further upon us.[45]

Steele made what repairs he could and drilled his soldiers into a proper military form. The duties gave him plenty of time, and the isolation of the fort gave him little to do except writing and, as it turned out, politics.

Steele accepted a commission from Christopher Rich for another play, doubtless taking advantage of interest in the recent election, called 'The Election of Gotham'. Steele also accepted £72 but never wrote the play. His failure to do so resulted in one of the more tangled cases among his usually tangled financial transactions and led to a lawsuit in 1707 that was dismissed without finding.[46] But Steele was involved in more immediate, less literary electoral matters. John Ellis, the brother of Welbore Ellis, Steele's tutor, and, like Welbore, involved in the household of the Duke of Ormond, had been elected MP for Harwich. As a resident in the neighbourhood, Steele could keep Ellis informed of the relevant actions and opinions of the townspeople. He also, in 1704, sought Ellis's influence with Ormand to get him command of 'a Troop in a Regiment of Dragoons' that Ormond was raising, but nothing came of the application.[47] Steele's activities on Ellis's behalf certainly acquainted him with the degree to which politics are local, and he came to understand the relationship of a Member of Parliament to his constituency.

Although Steele did not write 'The Election of Gotham', he did write, withdrawing for that purpose, according to local legend, to a farmhouse in the neighbourhood,[48] *The Lying Lover*, which opened at Drury Lane in early December 1703. If *The Funeral* was a modest success, *The Lying Lover* was a modest failure. It ran six nights, so that Steele got two benefit nights. (The proceeds of every third night were usually given to the author and constituted his major remuneration from the play.) But it did not remain in the repertoire because it was not a good play. Steele was trying to find the proper balance between moral reform and witty entertainment. In *The Lying Lover* the balance weighs heavily on the side of morality.

The Lying Lover derives, at times directly, from Corneille's *Le Menteur*, probably in its French iteration rather than its English translation.[49] Steele added to the French play the hero's friend Latine, who is, as the name suggests, a classically-endowed Oxonian; throughout the play, he pretends to be the servant of the mendacious hero Bookwit. Latine is a relatively clever addition, but a more serious change to Corneille is the completely rewritten ending. The play offers the familiar balance of three men and two women. The third of these men is Lovemore, apparently a decent fellow but quite literal-minded and also quite jealous. He is in love with Penelope, who is the more flighty and superficial of the two women. She and her friend Victoria are in conflict over Bookwit for much of the play, until the complicated action concludes with Penelope in love with Lovemore and Victoria in love with Bookwit. The play revolves around the tall tales through which Bookwit tries to live in an alternative reality. He and his friend Latine have just come down from Oxford to London, where they are primarily seeking a social life with women.

To achieve this end, Bookwit concocts elaborate stories about being in the army and serving in William's campaigns. He meets his friend Lovemore and tells him a story about entertaining women at great expense, and particularly Penelope, who, even though he did not entertain her at all, is rather taken with him and his stories. Lovemore, in a jealous fury, challenges Bookwit to a duel which, at the time, no one seems to take seriously. But by the fourth act, Bookwit is rather drunk and in the vicinity of Penelope's lodging, where he meets the jealous Lovemore. They duel, and Lovemore falls to the ground, apparently dead. After a rather good scene at Newgate, Bookwit sleeps only to wake with the realization that he has killed his friend. The efforts of the loyal and concerned Latine to comfort him are unsuccessful, and he is racked with remorse. The play in turn is racked not only by the sudden shift in tone but by a movement to the heightened rhetoric of tragedy. The shift in itself would be bad enough, but it is compounded by the fact that, although Steele could write successful comedy, his tragic language, inappropriate in the first place, is hollow fustian. Lovemore, of course, turns out to have only a minor flesh wound, and the right males get connected to the right females, but the tonal shift to a happy ending, although welcome, seems almost as severe as the tonal shift to tragedy. A major problem is that the characters are so thinly characterized that we do not much care what happens to them.

Although *The Lying Lover* is a failure by any measure, it is an instructive one, and in senses not covered by the play's didacticism. It is the first major expression of Steele's long and passionate campaign against duelling. Its depiction of a collegian who tries to establish a social identity by comic role-playing deserves a better vehicle. But the play's uncomfortable shift of tone seems to represent Steele's impatience with the traditional Restoration comedy of manners. The comedy of manners is a play about play. The characters act out artificial roles expressed in self-consciously witty language. But Steele insists that such multilayered role-playing is not reality. In the real world young male bravado leads to duels and death; seduced maidens are made pregnant, abandoned, and left to prostitution.

Reality, for Steele, is friendship, love, duty and pain. The movement of the play from the artificiality of wit to the steely reality of death shows where the comedy of manners fails. But Steele's problem is that the reality of death and the tortures of a guilty conscience are expressed in language that is, if anything, more artificial than self-conscious wit. And, since the dead man turns out not to be dead, the reality of death is not real at all. Steele's criticism of Restoration comedy requires a more subtle and resourceful playwright to be effective.

Between the opening of the play in early December 1703 and its publication in late January 1704, Queen Anne issued a proclamation that 'Nothing be Acted in either of the Theatres contrary to Religion or Good Manners'.[50] In his 'Preface' to the play (which was published by Bernard Lintott, rather than by Jacob Tonson, as were his other plays), Steele admits that the pathetic scenes of the fifth act

> are, perhaps, an Injury to the Rules of Comedy; but I am sure they are a Justice to those of Morality: And Passages of such a Nature being so frequently applauded on the Stage, it is high time that we should no longer draw Occasions of Mirth from those Images which the Religion of our Country tells us we ought to tremble at with Horrour.[51]

The sentiment might have come directly from Collier. The campaign for the reformation of the stage had made it to the highest levels, but the Queen's approval of Steele's theatrical principles did not make his play any better or more successful.

In a real sense his career was at a crisis. He could expect no advancement in his present military situation, and hence the urgency of his request to the Duke of Ormond, to whom *The Lying Lover* was dedicated, for a position in the Regiment of Dragoons he was raising. The relative failure of *The Lying Lover* did not promise well for his career as a playwright, and such a career could hardly be regarded as a stable source of income. But he continued to be heavily in debt. During the Hilary term of 1704 (the end of January and beginning of February) he was brought to court for £60 by a creditor and lost. More serious suits would soon follow.

One positive sign was the return of Addison in February from his continental travels, although Addison had his own course to set and could not provide much immediate help. He was much better connected with the Whig power-brokers than was Steele, and his continental travels had given him political and social sophistication. But even so, he had to explore the possibilities of employment, and had established himself in a garret in Haymarket to do so. He had known Jacob Tonson from the days when he contributed to Dryden's *Miscellany Poems* (1693, 1694). Charles Montagu, Earl of Halifax, had plucked him from Magdalen College and sent him on his European tour. Both were members of the powerful Kit-Cat Club, whose other members included the leaders of the

Whigs (among them Somers, Sunderland, Marlborough, Godolphin, Walpole and Maynwaring) and such important literary figures as Garth, Vanbrugh, and Congreve. According to John Macky, the size of the club was limited to thirty-nine members.[52] With the sponsorship of Halifax and Tonson, Addison joined in 1704. Addison cultivated his connections in both political and literary circles, among them Richard Steele. Matters were to break more quickly and dramatically for Addison than for Steele.

The Duke of Marlborough's strategy in the War of Spanish Succession showed more flexibility and imagination than William's in the Nine Years' War. William seemed content to hold the French to a stalemate by battles and sieges in the Low Countries, most of which he lost. In May 1704, concerned about a combined French and Bavarian army moving to take Vienna, which was already preoccupied with a Hungarian revolt, Marlborough, without informing his Dutch allies, whom he knew would interdict the strategy, marched his army down the Rhine, joined Prince Eugene's Imperial army, turned towards the Danube, defeated a French and Bavarian army at Schellenburg, destroyed hundreds of villages in an effort to persuade the Bavarians to change sides, and finally engaged and routed the Franco-Bavarian army at the village of Blenheim.[53] According to Winston Churchill, 'on the field of Blenheim also sank the fortunes of the House of Stuart'.[54] Although the war dragged on for another eight years (and the Stuart cause for longer still), Louis, after Blenheim, was seeking a graceful exit with as much political advantage as he could gain, and that advantage did not include the restoration of James III. The 1704 campaign was a brilliant manoeuver, capped by an outstanding, although not decisive, victory, and it demanded appropriate celebration in England. Sidney Godolphin, the Lord Treasurer, at the suggestion of Halifax, sent an emissary to Addison's Haymarket garret with a commission to provide the most public and celebratory poem he could. Godophin approved the rough draft, and Addison was consequently named a Commissioner of Appeal in Excise, a sinecure that had been held by Locke until his death in October.[55]

The forthcoming poem was well advertised in advance, not least by Richard Steele, whose 'Imitation of the Sixth Ode of *Horace* ... Supposed to be made by Capt. R. S.' appeared in *The Diverting Post*, no. 2 (4 November). Addressed to Marlborough, it praises Addison, Marlborough through Addison, and Queen Anne through Marlborough:

> Should Addison's Immortal Verse,
> Thy Fame in Arms, great Prince, Rehearse,
> With Anna's Lightning you'd appear,
> And glitter o'er again in War:
> Repeat the Proud Bavarian's Fall!
> And in the Danube plunge the Gaul!

Steele admits that, in contrast, his own gift is for moderate social satire:

> From the gay Noise affected Air,
> And little Follies of the Fair,
> A slender stock of Fame I raise,
> And draw from others Faults, my Praise.[56]

Addison's *Campaign* appeared in December 1704 and was an instant and resounding success. Commendatory verse is not a genre that survives for long, but *The Campaign* lasted longer than most. Its signature image is that of Marlborough, like the angel of bad weather, calmly and deliberatively directing the chaos of the battle: 'And pleas'd th' Almighty's orders to perform, / Rides in the whirlwind, and directs the storm'.[57] The image was to become a commonplace in the eighteenth century, and more than celebrating Marlborough's victory, it assured Addison's political career. In return, perhaps, for Steele's puffing of his poem, Addison helped Steele with his next play.[58]

Steele's commander Lord Lucas died in January 1705, and Steele left the army within months. His play *The Tender Husband* opened at Drury Lane on 23 April. Although it is the best of Steele's plays, it only ran for five nights in its initial run, thus giving Steele only one benefit night. But it stayed in the repertoire and was often performed during the next forty years.[59] In contrast to *The Lying Lover* and even *The Funeral*, it is an unsentimental comedy of manners that derives in part from Molière's *Le Sicilien*, and probably, to a lesser degree, from *Les Précieuses ridicules* and *L'Avare* as well. At the centre of the plot are two contrasting brothers – Clerimont Senior and Captain Clerimont. (Speech prefixes in the printed version are somewhat confused and straightened out by the probable conjectures of modern editors.) Clerimont is the bad older brother; Captain Clerimont is a more sympathetic character. Both are deceivers, but Clerimont is a corrupter as well. He has taken his wife to Europe and corrupted her taste with continental artifices. More seriously he has corrupted Lucy Fainlove, who is now his kept mistress. He disguises Fainlove as a man and wants her to try to seduce his wife. Captain Clerimont, who rather resembles Captain Steele, is a penniless soldier who seeks to improve his fortune by marrying an heiress. Unlike Steele, he is a veteran of the Blenheim campaign.

The heiress in question is Biddy (Bridget) Tipkin, who is the ward of her aunt and uncle. She is a central figure in the array of contrasts through which Steele organizes the play. The Tipkins are merchants who live in the East End; the Clerimonts are fashionable people who live in the West End. A third representative family consists of Tipkin's country brother-in-law, Sir Harry Gubbin and his son Humphry, who is proposed as a suitable husband for Biddy Tipkin. Biddy, who rebels against the plainness and boredom of life with the Tipkins, moves in the world of romance and is a female Quixote. She therefore finds the country-yokel talk of Humphry Gubbins appalling. She and Humphry are so united in their mutual hatred that they seem like lovers. Captain Clerimont quickly picks up Biddy's romantic proclivities and, being a literary man himself, can quite readily speak the language of romance. Steele has thus set up a comic interplay of diverse dialects, expectations, and ways of thinking.

Captain Clerimont manages to break out of Biddy's romantic cage by a further disguise as a painter that allows him to woo her successfully. His brother does indeed catch his wife in what she supposes to be the masculine arms of Fainlove, but she succeeds in pretending repentance in the face of his anger. Fainlove manages to find fortune in the otherwise rustic and ridiculous form of Humphry Gubbin. At the end Clerimont invites everyone to dinner, but it is, for many of the guests, a very grudging feast, and the resolution of the plot has hardly reconciled the different attitudes and values of the various characters. Steele wrote that he draws his praise from the faults of others, and that certainly seems a description of *The Tender Husband*. The very title is ironic, and Steele has successfully deployed contrasting social stereotypes in a way that anticipates the social satire of the *Tatler* and *Spectator*.

In May 1705 Steele's personal life seemed to take on the quality of social comedy. His play, produced at the end of the season, had earned him little. The 34th Foot Regiment, of which he was no longer a member, sailed for the Mediterranean. In April or May he married Margaret Ford Stretch, a widow from Barbados whose brother John was captured by pirates and died in captivity, leaving her with a very substantial estate. Almost nothing is known of this marriage, except that it did not last long, for Margaret Stretch Steele died in December of the next year. We do not know if she was old and ugly or young and beautiful. Was the marriage only a financial transaction for the sentimental Steele, or did he love her deeply? He left hundreds of letters to his second wife, but no letter to his first survives. Was she illiterate, did she simply fail to keep his letters, or is his silence a hidden sign of pain or an indication that he did not care to remember?

Steele was sued for a debt of £600 by John Sansome, who had loaned it to him three years earlier, presumably to support his recruiting. Steele admitted that he had no liquid assets and could not pay. (Possibly his fruitless effort to get money from Lord Cutts was an effort to pay off the debt to Sansome.) In fact, Steele had no employment. He had left the army, his profits from *The Tender Husband* were meager, and he had no further play ready for production. The only things he wrote between the production of *The Tender Husband* in April 1705 and his appointment as Gazetteer in April or May of 1707 were a Prologue for Sir John Vanbrugh's play *The Mistake* (December 1705) and a 'Prologue to the University of Oxford' (June or July 1706). The prologue for Vanbrugh alludes to the fact that he built and managed the Haymarket Theatre as well as writing the play now performed in it. The Oxford prologue, for the visit of a theatrical troop performing at the tennis court near Merton College, acknowledges his return to his alma mater. Both are not embarrassing but undistinguished verse. Steele lived on his wife's inheritance, which gained him, he later told the mother of his second wife, an income of £850, minus a debt on the estate, the interest of which was £180.[60] Steele gained further money from the sale of his military commission.

Steele lost several further suits for debt in 1706, but had acquired two significant if not immediately remunerative honours. He was elected a member of the Kit-Cat Club, probably in 1705, and probably with the sponsorship of Addison and Tonson.[61] The Kit-Cats, famed, if for nothing else, for their portraits by Geoffrey Kneller, now hanging in National Portrait Gallery, were luminary Whigs, who admitted into their company important writers, especially playwrights. The club was instrumental in supporting Vanbrugh's Haymarket Theatre, which was begun in 1703. But Vanbrugh's interest in writing plays waned after be began work as the architect of Blenheim Palace, in 1705. Congreve no longer wrote for the stage. Addison, although he had four acts of *Cato* completed, was still years from appearing as a playwright. The most active playwright in the club was now Richard Steele. Theater and literature more generally were seen as a vehicle of support for Whig interests. A fairly immediate consequence of Steele's membership in the Kit-Cat Club was his appointment in August 1706 as Gentleman-Waiter to Prince George of Denmark, Queen Anne's husband, 'with a sallary', he explained to his future mother-in-law, 'of one hundred pounds a Year not Subject to taxes'.[62] The job had virtually no duties until, after George's death in October 1708, Steele had to keep watch over the catafalque one night in three during the two weeks that the Prince lay in state. But it was a source of income, and it testified to Steele's movement in court circles.

Margeret Steele's death, late in December 1706, is as mysterious as the quality of her marriage. At her funeral Steele met a Welshwoman, Mary Scurlock, whom he began to court in the following August. Between those dates, politics had improved his life and financial situation and made him a more marriageable widower. Marlborough and Godolphin, with the help of Robert Harley, as Speaker of Commons from 1702 to 1705 and as Secretary of State from 1705 to 1708, tried to govern independent of parties (although they, particularly Harley, were initially sympathetic to the Tories). The strong influx of Tories in 1702 required some sympathy for landed efforts to protect the established order. But there was a war to finance, and Tory efforts to pass an Occasional Conformity Bill failed in the House of Lords. The parliamentary election of 1705 saw a surge of support for the Whigs, who used their power to pass the Regency Act, which provided for an orderly succession, and the Act of Union, which assured that the English monarch would be a Scottish one as well. Whig leaders became cabinet members, among them the rather controversial Earl of Sunderland, Marlborough's son-in-law, who became Secretary of State for the North. Joseph Addison continued as Under-Secretary of State, with considerable responsibility for the daily operations of the office. In spring of 1707, Steele became Gazetteer, reporting to Sunderland and Addison, at a newly enlarged salary of £300. The position was hardly a sinecure. In the summer 1707, his uncle and foster-father Henry Gascoigne died; Lady Mildmay had died somewhat earlier. Steele may well have decided it was time to seek a new wife.

What Steele's relation to Mary Scurlock was between his wife's funeral in December 1706 and the time of his first surviving letters to her in August 1707 is hard to say. Perhaps they saw each other at mutual friends. She was, if Sir Godfrey Kneller's 1715 portrait of her is an accurate representation, an attractive woman with delicate features.[63] Steele's first letter is the moment at which he no longer is merely a friend but becomes a suitor. He wrote twenty-one letters to her before they were married on 9 September 1707. A week after receiving Steele's first letters, Mary wrote to her mother in Wales asking her approval of a marriage. Steele's letters shift through a variety of tones and genres – some self-consciously playful, some rather rhetorical, some straightforward and sincere, and some religious. Some are quite short and seem to have only a phatic function. Steele thought highly enough of some of them to include them, somewhat altered and with carefully concealed authorship, in *Tatler*, no. 35 and *Spectator*, no. 142. He continued to write to her frequently throughout her life, and their correspondence offers a direct and, despite his obvious faults and excesses, an endearing picture of his private life. The story of his relation to 'Prue', as he came to call her, belongs elsewhere in this study, but it represents, along with his appointment as Gazetteer, a movement towards definition in his private and public life.

In 1707 Steele was thirty-five, and if he stopped at the proverbial mid-point of his life to look back he might have seen a linear movement to bring him to his position as writer for the Whig establishment. What, at the time, seemed random and undirected now seemed purposeful. Steele became politically involved because his life was shaped by his interaction with pressing political issues and exigencies. He looked at the world around him from the vantage point of his family, his education, and his experience as a soldier and a dramatist. Born the son of a struggling lawyer in Ireland's Protestant ascendancy, he became an orphan by the time he was five. The determining event of his childhood was his aunt's marriage to a man of power and influence who moved in Whig circles. As a result, Steele attended an excellent school with decided Whig tendencies, where he became close friends with Joseph Addison. From the vantage of his school, he watched the 'bloodless revolution' of William of Orange. From the vantage of Oxford, he read Locke and watched William defeat the Jacobites in Ireland. He joined the army under Ormond and, in the course of three years, participated in two campaigns and, possibly, one major battle in the Low Countries, as well as serving guard duty in London. He shifted to the Coldstream Regiment under Cutts, to whom he dedicated his first literary work, and served as his private secretary, gaining specific electoral experience by helping Cutts and Dudley manage elections on the Isle of Wight. He socialized with literary figures, lost his money in an alchemical scheme, sired at least one illegitimate child, and nearly killed a man in a duel, but he turned those experiences into a popular religious tract and three plays.

That literary transformation was guided in part by Steele's interest in moral reform, inspired both by his own experience and by his awareness of the tenor of the times. The transformation was guided as well by his sense that literature can play an important role in that reform, an inversion of Collier's position that literature was responsible for the vices that needed reformation. In the meantime he transferred from Cutts's Coldstream Regiment to Lord Lucas's regiment of foot soldiers, which was posted to a dilapidated fort on the Essex coast. There he acted as the eyes and ears of John Ellis, MP, whose brother had been his tutor. Leaving the army on the death of his superior officer, he married a widow whose Barbados estate kept him afloat for several years, while he moved in London Whig society, welcomed his friend Addison's return from the continent, and joined the Kit-Cat Club of Whig grandees and Whiggish writers. After his political friends, including Addison, assumed important positions as a result of the 1705 election, Steele was appointed Gazetteer.

Throughout this period he remained a committed Whig. He held William III in very high regard, despite William's general unpopularity. He was a man of powerful but not necessarily complete loyalties – to William, to Ormond, to Cutts, to Marlborough and to Addison. His relatively new interest in moral reform sat somewhat uneasily with his gregarious, easygoing, tolerant, ambitious and self-indulgent personality. But his mixture of moralism and personal warmth gave a human character to his political writing at its best. What gave his political writing his most striking personal character was his unusual willingness to sign his name to much that he wrote. Whether this was merely egocentricity or a public acknowledgement of personal responsibility, it was to cause great trouble for him and also to bring him great rewards. But these would lie in the future. For now, his work as Gazetteer would serve as the first step in a campaign to create a new culture that propagated, embodied and extended Whig attitudes towards the social world.

2 CREATING WHIG CULTURE: THE *GAZETTE* AND THE *TATLER*

Political Contexts of Steele's Gazette

Steele was appointed as Gazetteer in the spring of 1707, almost certainly at the nomination of Joseph Addison. Queen Anne preferred moderate Tories in general, and Robert Harley in particular, but the need to maintain broad support for the war and to counter the dangerous influence of extreme Tories made it desirable to include Whigs among her ministers. Moreover, John Churchill, Duke of Marlborough, England's great military leader, and his Duchess Sarah, along with Sidney Godolphin, the Lord Treasurer, urged the appointment of Marlborough's son-in-law Lord Sunderland as Secretary of State for the Southern Department. Addison became his Assistant Secretary, and Steele, as Gazetteer, reported to him.

The shift that led to Steele's appointment was a byproduct of perhaps the most volatile decade of early eighteenth-century political history. A key element of the settlement that accompanied the accession of William and Mary was the provision of triennial elections for the House of Commons. During the reign of Anne, elections were held in 1702, 1705, 1708, 1710, 1713 and, after her death, in 1715. The frequency of these elections meant that parties came to wage an intense and growing propaganda debate over major issues. By the election of 1710 both parties had assembled a fairly reliable stable of writers – the Tories, quite successfully under Harley, the Whigs more loosely under the leadership of Arthur Maynwaring.[1] After the death of Maynwaring in November 1712, both Addison and Steele, in different ways, became more sharply partisan writers.

Although substantial groups of voters were permanently committed to one party or the other, there were enough floating voters to make issues and propaganda about issues significant factors in the outcome of elections. James O. Richards found this particularly the case in the election of 1705, which he described as 'one of the most ideologically rancorous and warmly contested elections of the reign'.[2] Some elections were dominated by particular issues: the High

Tory effort to 'tack' a measure against occasional conformity to money bills in order to prevent Dissenters from meeting minimal requirements to hold public office dominated the election of 1705 and was largely responsible for the significant loss of Tory seats; the Trial of Dr Henry Sacheverell for a seditious sermon stimulated Tory cries of 'the Church in danger' in 1710 and contributed to the substantial Tory victory, although weariness with the war was another significant factor. But even the important issues in particular elections derived from the several large concerns than run throughout the public debate in the reign of Anne.

A number of these issues were subsumed in the nexus of the War of Spanish Succession. Whether Spain should be ruled by a Bourbon or Hapsburg heir was a significant factor in the balance of European power, but, however abstract it may have seemed to an Englishman, the idea of 'succession' also had a particularly English character. On the death of James II in September 1701, Louis XIV recognized his son as the rightful king of England, thus violating the Treaty of Ryswick he had signed four years before. England had determined the succession of the house of Hanover and, after the death of William in March of the following year, Anne Stuart became Queen rather than her brother, the Pretender. The possibility that James III might become King, either instead of or, more likely, after Anne seemed a distinct threat, and there were enough English Jacobites to make the threat serious. An aborted French and Jacobite raid on Scotland in March 1708 was a strong factor in the 1708 election.[3] The issue of the Hanoverian succession remained a central feature of the Whig propaganda arsenal, even after the war was over and George I in fact became King.

Despite its apparent defence of a properly Protestant monarchy, the war was controversial because of an inveterate distrust of continental alliances. It had not been very long since the Dutch rather than the French had been England's wartime opponent and some, such as Swift, saw the Dutch as a major maritime rival.[4] Swift, of course, exploited residual anti-Dutch sentiment in *The Conduct of the Allies* (November 1711), which argued that Holland (and the Marlborough family) sought to prolong the war at British expense. The residual distrust of the Dutch paralleled a longstanding preference for naval wars over campaigns on land, the so-called 'blue waters' policy, and it was bolstered by basic English distrust of standing armies, a suspicion that extended back to the Commonwealth. The question of how the war was to be funded distinctly divided the parties. The war was financed by direct taxation and by bonds on the recently-formed Bank of England. But these in turn would be paid by taxation. Merchants and others in a position to lend to the government were beneficiaries of the war and likely to be Whigs; landholders who paid the bulk of taxes were hurt by the war and likely to be Tories. It would be unfair to suggest that Whigs wanted the war prolonged for their personal benefit, although Tory propagandists made that claim, but they certainly were willing to prolong it until all its goals were accomplished.[5] Many Tories, on the other hand, had opposed it from the outset and wanted it ended as soon as possible. The war, the Hanoverian succession, the nature of Britain's continental involvement, and the burden of financing the war were dominant issues of propaganda during Anne's reign. Although Britain gained significantly from the war in its colonial possessions and rights, colonialism was hardly an issue in propaganda for the war.

One other issue, however, was of major importance. The Church of England, as it trumpeted, occupied a middle position in the religious topography, and the middle position is open to attacks from both sides. On one side, the Jacobites stood not only for the perpetuation of the House of Stuart but also for the Catholic religion that James and his son espoused. On the other side, the Dissenters stood for the authority of individual conscience and the democratic principles that flowed from it. Throughout Anne's reign, with varying degrees of intensity, debate raged regarding the practice of Occasional Conformity. Public office and various other privileges of society were reserved for members of the Anglican Church, and membership in the church was determined by receiving communion once a year. Some individuals who spent fifty-one Sundays each year at Meeting felt no real compunction about taking communion from an Anglican priest on the fifty-second. High Church Anglicans were offended by the practice and saw it as subversion of the religious test. Efforts to pass an Act eliminating occasional conformity were successful in the Commons but not in the Lords, where Whigs blocked it. It was passed in 1711, with Junto support as part of a deal made with the Earl of Nottingham, but quietly repealed after the accession of George I.

The rank-and-file clergy were decidedly Tory, and the pulpit remained an important locus of propaganda, especially in the election of 1710. But the Bishops were predominately Whig, and their presence in the House of Lords was an important source of Whig strength. The political force of Anglican extremism became apparent after Dr Henry Sacheverell preached a sermon, 'The Perils of False Brethren', before the Lord Mayor at St Paul's. The sermon defended absolute monarchy, and asserted that 'Atheism, Deism, Tritheism, Socinianism, with all the hellish principles of Fanaticism, Regicide, and Anarchy, are openly professed and taught'.[6] It attacked Godolphin personally and virtually demanded prosecution. The Sacheverell trial in the Whig-dominated House of Lords was the sensation of 1710 and predictably ended in a vote that he had been guilty of sedition. But the margin was narrower than expected and he was sentenced to three years of silence from the pulpit. This modest sentence and Sacheverell's triumphant progress to the living he had gained by the sermon aroused Tory sentiment and signalled to the Queen that the time had come to change her ministry.

Where there is hot air there may be fire, and Sacheverell's hysterical proclamation of 'The Church in Danger' combined a general sense that public morality
had reached a low point in the reign of Charles II with the publication of tracts
by such Low-Church and, from the point of view of Sacheverell and his sympathizers, freethinking or even atheistic writers as John Toland, William Whiston,
Matthew Tindal, Charles Blount, and Anthony Collins. These writers were
unleashed by the repeal of the Licensing Act in 1695, and the freedom of the
press to promulgate unorthodox ideas was anathema to High-Church Tories.
Running through such works was a tendency to question authority, whether that
of the monarch or the church. The Whig position that one might even resist the
monarch, although enacted successfully in the Revolution of 1688, seemed to
combine in a sinister way with the Dissenting view that salvation is an individual
matter rather than the result of obedience to the Church.

Whigs as a practical matter stood for the rights of Dissenters. Most Dissenters were Whigs, although few Whigs were Dissenters. This was not an active,
positive position during the reign of Queen Anne but a reactive, defensive one.
The previous century had been preoccupied across Europe with wars fought
on the basis of precisely the kinds of principles that High Tories, at their most
extreme, espoused. Latitudinarian theologians and Low-Church Whigs not
only advocated toleration but sought a religious common denominator that lay
in Christian moral teachings. This was the position that Steele adopted, and it
was particularly useful for the author of periodicals seeking moral reformation.
A particular manifestation of such toleration was the attitude of many Whigs
towards the Palatines. These emigrants from southwest Germany, an area hard
hit first by the Thirty Years War and, more recently, by the movement of French
troops, came to England in 1708 and, in greater number, in 1709. They appealed
to the sympathies of Queen Anne and the Whigs on the grounds that they, like
the Huguenots, were Protestants fleeing from the religious persecution of the
French, although in some cases the reasons for their flight may have been economic rather than religious. Their presence engaged both English xenophobia
and Protestant fellow-feeling.[7] A Bill for the Naturalization of Foreign Protestants passed in February and March 1709. But some 13,000 came to England
in 1709, many of them gathering at a camp in Blackheath. Most were sent to
Ireland, America, the West Indies, or back to Germany.[8]

One further political issue received scant partisan attention in England,
although it received plenty in Scotland. In 1707 the long-awaited and long-
delayed union between England and Scotland took place. Among the English it
was primarily a footnote to the problem of Hanoverian succession. England and
Scotland had the same monarch under the Stuarts (a Scottish family, after all),
but there was no assurance that both countries would recognize the Hanover
dynasty. The prospect of the Scots inviting a Stuart king had enough likelihood

to be threatening. The threat was intensified by the aborted French-Jacobite raid of March 1708 and later repeated by Scottish involvement in the feeble uprising of 1715. English relations with Scotland were to have a significant impact, as we shall see, on the later life of Sir Richard Steele, but at this point they are important because they forced a redefinition of the nation in a time of war. One of the functions of the *Tatler* was to articulate national unity, and national unity in support of the allies and in opposition to France. It did so in a variety of ways, one of which was an inconsistent but significant reference to the inclusive 'Great Britain'. In *Tatler*, no. 241 Steele printed a letter by 'Scotto-Britannus' asserting that a proud man who claimed he kept 'the best House of any Man in *England*' should amend his language so as to become 'the wisest of any Man in *Great Britain*'. *Tatler*, no. 258 contained a letter from J. S., M. P. and N. R. who reported dining with Mr South-British and Mr William North-Briton, previously known as Mr English and Mr William Scott. The writers run similarly through a variety of puns, stopping short only of North-British whisky. They were Jonathan Swift, Matthew Prior and Nicholas Rowe, who thought they were having a joke on Steele until Steele, apparently against their intentions, published the letter.[9] Behind the joke lay the efforts of the *Tatler* to articulate an inclusive society.

Although the union, the church and the war and its implications generated a great deal of passion expressed in a considerable amount of print, there was, especially in the first half of Anne's reign, a feeling that government could be run from the middle, or even that governing did not require political parties. The Whigs and the Tories, after all, had come into being during the Exclusion Crisis of 1679–81, were vague and approximate in definition, and had not developed the organizational structures that are now associated with political parties. Three important figures who shared this centrist view of metapartisan government were Robert Harley, Sidney Godolphin and John Churchill, Duke of Marlborough. Robert Harley, a moderate Tory, a country squire and a bibliophile, became Speaker of the House in 1702 and was a master of Parliamentary procedures and personalities. He withdrew from the ministry in 1708, only to return as Lord Treasurer in 1710. He was affable, expert in exploiting his connections (especially his close connection to the Queen), ambitious and perhaps devious and cunning. He was certainly given to secrecy and intrigue. He developed mechanisms for gathering intelligence and cultivated a stable of important writers, including Defoe and Swift.[10] Godolphin, the Lord Treasurer until 1710, had considerable administrative skills, which he used, as best he could, to finance the War of Spanish Succession. Marlborough was, like Godolphin, a moderate Tory, but his Duchess was a strong Whig. His repeated successes in battle made him rich and gained him a reputation as a brilliant general but an avaricious man. Godolphin and Marlborough moved closer to the Whigs in later years because the Whigs supported the war and, more to the point, Godolphin planned to finance it. As they grew closer to the Whigs, they grew further from the Queen, and their unwillingness to make peace with France ran counter to the war-weariness of the people.

The Whig Junto, a quintet of aristocratic leaders who held office under William, did not hold office under Anne until Whig electoral strength brought them into the ministry in 1708. John, Baron Somers was perhaps the most able jurist and astute politician of the era and a man of great personal charm. Thomas, Earl of Wharton was a powerful politician, with strong influence in the North. His notorious womanizing and staunch Whiggery earned Swift's contempt.[11] He was the Lord Lieutenant of Ireland when Addison was Secretary there. Edward Russell, Earl of Orford, became First Lord of the Admiralty in 1709, a position he had held earlier and would hold again. He was one of the signers inviting William of Orange to England in 1688. Charles Montagu, Earl of Halifax had been William's First Lord of the Treasury and was ambitious to return to similar eminence. Although he was rather thin-skinned, he was able in economics and a patron of the arts, and was particularly close to Addison. In 1710 he became godfather to Steele's son Richard. Charles Spenser, third Earl of Sunderland was the youngest and, perhaps, the least attractive of the Junto Lords. An aggressive personality and a doctrinaire Whig, he was strongly supported by his more moderate father-in-law Marlborough and by Godolphin. Hence he became Secretary of State for the Southern Department and therefore Steele's supervisor in his role as Gazetteer. The Whig Junto met frequently, usually at the Rose Tavern in Covent Garden, especially during the 1690s, and constituted the closest the period could come to an effective political organization. Steele dedicated volumes of the *Spectator* to Somers, Halifax, Wharton and Sunderland, thus proclaiming the real politics of that ostensibly neutral periodical.

The Format of the Gazette and the News of the Tatler

Richard Steele's role as Gazetteer was quite modest. The paper itself had in recent years been regarded as sometimes inaccurate, and it was sometimes scooped by the *Daily Courant* and by the three papers that appeared thrice weekly – the *Post-Man*, the *Post Boy* and the *Flying-Post*.[12] Steele's job, for which he was paid a salary of £300, minus a tax of £45, was to make the *Gazette* more timely and more accurate. He collected reports that were transmitted by British officials abroad, usually as these were screened by Addison, the under-secretary of state, and by Sunderland. Steele routinely consulted with Addison and Sunderland regarding what news to include and how to present it. On one hand the job was relatively mechanical and hardly required Steele's skills as a writer. On the other hand, the determination of material often required a tactful and informed understanding of how it might be read and who might be offended. One of the relatively few letters relating to Steele's editorship of the *Gazette* is his defensive reaction to the complaint of Prince George, the Lord High Admiral, that an account of popular enthusiasm at the arrival of a convoy implied that the convoy was late in arriving.[13] Steele insisted to Sunderland that he included the information at the express command of Addison, on Sunderland's orders. One of the problems of the *Gazette* was that the chain of command was not clear and that officials in various offices might issue conflicting orders as to what should be included.[14] Years later, Steele put a description of his role in the *Gazette* in the mouth of a supposedly impartial witness:

> His [Steele's] next Appearance as a Writer was in the Quality of the lowest Minister of State, to wit, the Office of Gazetteer, where he worked faithfully according to Order, without ever erring against the Rule observed by all Ministries, to keep that Paper very innocent and very insipid.[15]

Steele was well aware of the difficulties of the *Gazette* in collecting news and distributing it in a timely fashion. He proposed four steps to a solution: (1) that 'all the Ministers in each Province' should 'send a circular Letter every Post of what passes in their respective stations', (2) that these letters should be sent via the flying packet, (3) that they can be kept from other newswriters, and (4) that the *Gazette* be published on Tuesday, Thursday and Saturday.[16] Tuesday, Thursday and Saturday were postal days, and the days on which the *Tatler* would later be published; publication on those days assured more expeditious distribution outside of London and reduced the likelihood that the *Gazette* would be scooped by the private newspapers. Steele's later apologetic description and his earlier recommendations combine to suggest his frustration at the limitations of his job.

Whatever impact the *Gazette* may have had on his later political adventures, it had a demonstrable impact on the format of his later periodicals.[17] The *Gazette* was designed to achieve maximum economy of space. It was printed on two sides of a folio half-sheet, with two columns on each page, separated by a vertical rule. The double column meant that less space was left at the ends of paragraphs and, in general, the format could produce the most words at the least cost in labour and material. 'The rearrangement of the layout of *The London Gazette* was of greatest importance to the printer, because it halved the amount of presswork'.[18] In addition to saving presswork, the format minimized the amount of paper needed for each number. This economical format became that of the *Tatler*, the *Spectator*, and the *Guardian*. The Stamp Act of 1712 led to modifications in this format, so that periodicals often appeared in a folded sheet-and-one-half format to avoid the tax, even at the cost of using more paper. The folio half-sheet allowed some flexibility in the length of issues, depending on how much space was used by advertising. *Tatler* material ranged in length from about 1,000 words to 3,000 words.[19] The inexpensive format of the *Gazette*, its ease of production, and its immediacy of distribution (especially after adopting Steele's recommendation that it be published on postal days) made that paper a model for later periodicals.

Some sense of what the news was like in the *Gazette* can be gathered by what it was like in the *Tatler*. Richmond P. Bond compares the treatment of news in the *Gazette* and *Tatler* and concludes that they are quite similar, that Steele tended to distribute the news reports evenly, and that he had a somewhat freer editorial hand in the *Tatler*, especially since news and politics could be treated in other departments of the paper as well as 'St. James's Coffee House'. Steele was also influenced by the more frequent appearance of news in the *Daily Courant*.[20] Robert Walter Achurch and Louis T. Milic find Steele's *Tatler* style more colourful than the style of the *Gazette*, and Milic compares the *Tatler*'s style to that of Defoe's *Review* and Swift's *Examiner*.[21] Bond, Achurch and Milic do not emphasize the substance of the news that the *Tatler* reports, my major interest here.

The news that the *Tatler* presents, like that of the *Gazette* was a summary of dispatches. Indeed, its status as summary gives its reporting an authority beyond rumour or coffeehouse chatter. News is characteristically reported from St James's Coffee House, whose chief waiter, Humphrey Kidney, serves as a kind of bureau chief for Isaac Bickerstaff and others who gather there to hear the news. All of the *Tatler*'s reports dated 'St. James's Coffee-house' attribute the news to letters or advices from a specific place, often on a specific date (usually New Style). The first such report, in *Tatler*, no. 1 begins 'Letters from the *Hague* of the 16th, say, that Major General *Cadogan* was gone to *Brussels* ... ' The variety of places from which these letters are sent suggests the continental scope of the War of Spanish Succession; news reports in no. 7, for example, come from Vienna, Rome, Berlin, Copenhagen, the Hague, Paris, and Spain. This geographical spread combines with an obscure specificity, sometimes amounting to little more than names and places, so that one understands why Toby Shandy had to resort to building models in order to make sense out of military reports from the same war. The obscurity created by lists without contexts is extended by pronouns without reference and by vague generalities that mask the incomplete information available in the dispatches. The inclusion of a variety of news in a department of only a few paragraphs means that the reports are very concise and in indirect discourse. This highly restrained voice and its presentation of the material in indirect discourse contrast noticeably with the loquacious and speculative style of Isaac Bickerstaff, the paper's eidolon or persona.

The *Tatler* began on 12 April 1709. Its initial news announcement about General Cadogan pointed out that he had orders for the gathering and deposition of troops for the ensuing campaign. Marlborough's armies, like those of William III, usually fought from May to October, when the ground was hard enough to support battles and marching armies. The 1709 campaign during those months was strong and arguably significant (perhaps in its failure to be decisive either in battle or in negotiations), and watching it unfold in the reports of the *Tatler* has a certain fascination, One particularly significant event in the spring and summer background was the march of Charles XII of Sweden towards Moscow, a march that, of course, concluded in the Russian triumph at the battle of Poltova and in Charles's exile. A main reason for the *Tatler's* interest in Charles was that his defeat would divert Danish attention from the Northern War to the War of Spanish Succession, and the Danish King is one of the monarchs whose whereabouts are tracked the *Tatler*. The resounding defeat of Charles contrasts with the rather dogged successes of Marlborough, his chief rival as the great general of the era.

Lord Somers's motion on 'No Peace without Spain' had carried in December 1707, and succession in Spain by a Hapsburg rather than Bourbon King remained a central feature of Whig policy on the war. Campaigns in Spain were more uncertain than the succession of Marlborough's victories in the Low Countries. Not the least important factor was that the Spanish themselves favored the Bourbon Duke of Anjou, while the Portuguese favored the Austrian candidate Charles. *Tatler*, nos. 6 and 7 noted the vacillations of the Pope on the question of Spanish Succession. *Tatler,* no. 9 noted the arrival in Portugal of Henri de Massue, Earl of Galway (a French Huguenot who had fought in William's Army), followed in no. 19 by a detailed account of the battle of the Caya, which the Portuguese, against Galway's strong advice, insisted on fighting. The Portuguese defeat was saved from rout by the successful engagement of Galway's forces on one wing, but at the cost of many prisoners. The *Tatler* praised 'the Capacity and Courage of my Lord *Galway*', but the battle encouraged the stubbornness of the French in negotiations. The other major Spanish battle of 1709 reported in the *Tatler* (nos. 30 and 31) was the Spanish and Portuguese fighting over Olivenza, then, as now, a disputed city. News that the Spanish abandoned the blockade of Olivenza (no. 51, 4 August) ended the *Tatler's* treatment of Spain in 1709.

Although the *Tatler* occasionally takes up successes of the navy – the capture of French privateers in no. 15, for example, and reports on troop movements elsewhere in Europe, its major emphasis is on the warfare in the Low Countries. In 1709 (when all but six of the reports on continental news take place) the plot of the war can be seen in three acts – the failure of negotiations, the successful siege of Tournai and the Battle of Malplaquet and subsequent taking of Mons. In retrospect, these events seem to have marked the campaign of 1709 as a turning-point in the war. After their defeat at Oudenarde in 1708, the French were clearly interested in achieving a negotiated peace, and the arrival of Marlborough on the continent in May marked the beginning of negotiations (nos. 13, 14, 16). The Tatler gave great credit to the fact that the moderate M. Torcy was a primary French negotiator (nos. 9, 13, 16). Desperate economic conditions made peace desirable from a French point of view, but the fact that troops were ordered to the frontier (nos. 14 and 17) made peace uncertain. *Tatler*, no. 20 reports that a treaty has been agreed, and although it has not been published, its terms are summarized in detail according to general understanding. The French yielded a great deal, but the sticking point, as the allies probably expected, was the Spanish succession. Article XXXVII insisted that 'in case the Duke of *Anjou* shall not retire out of the *Spanish* Dominions, he [Louis] shall be oblig'd to assist the Allies to force him from thence' (summary in *Tatler*, no. 20). Deposing his grandson by force was not an obligation that Louis XIV was prepared to accept, and accordingly he refused to sign the treaty, as no. 23 reports.

In consequence, military activities began in late June with the siege of Tournai. The news in *Tatler*, nos. 35 and 36 reports the movement of troops around the city, and *Tatler*, no. 37 speculates on the number and deposition of troops involved. The next paper adds that gunboats on the Scheld and miners (who turn out to be particularly important later in the siege) joined the forces. The *Tatler* continues to report the progress on the siege until the paper for 21 July (no. 44) announces that, after hard resistance and heavy casualties, the town is taken. But French troops withdrew into the more heavily fortified citadel. Resistance was complicated by Louis's refusal to surrender the citadel until a general peace had been negotiated. The assault on the citadel required complex and extensive tunnelling, mining and countermining, so that the fighting seemed to have shifted underground,

> where every Step is taken with Apprehensions of being blown up with Mines below 'em, or crush'd by the Fall of the Earth above 'em; and all this acted in Darkness, has something more terrible than ever is met with in any other Part of a Soldier's Duty (No. 59).

The besiegers nonetheless persevered, and the final surrender is announced in *Tatler*, no. 62 (1 September 1709).

But the taking of Tournai turns out to be only a prelude to the more dramatic battle of Malplaquet and taking of Mons. Reports on the siege of Mons begin even as prisoners from Tournai are exchanged (no. 62), and they are immediately followed by sketchy reports of an allied victory in a major battle (no. 63). *Tatler*, no. 64 narrates the battle, unusually, in Bickerstaff's voice and from his point of view, rather than through the narrow medium of reports. Bickerstaff's attendant spirit Pacolet gathers data that emphasizes the difficulties and uncertainties of the battle, states the casualties in vague and general terms, and celebrates the heroic generalship of Marlborough. Going to St James's the next day, in expectation of celebration over the victory, Bickerstaff finds complaints and quibbles until 'Sir George England' asserts that even if details are unclear, Malplaquet is a great victory that would have been celebrated with a triumph in Roman times.

Tatler, no. 66 admits that casualties were higher than originally thought, and no. 67 provides a report of specific statistics: the loss of 8,000 among the States-General, 1,500 among the English, and 5,000 among the others, a total that agrees roughly with other contemporary reports.[22] (Later compilations from the casualty lists suggest a much higher total – 20,000–24,000, about twice the number of French casualties.)[23] The siege of Mons continues until the brief announcement in no. 83 (20 October) that it has been taken and, in no. 88 (1 November), an equally brief announcement that Marlborough is returning to England.

Steele's reports of continental news from St James's Coffeehouse grew less frequent during 1709. On 20 June 1709, the *Gazette* announced that it would begin appearing three times each week (Tuesday, Thursday and Saturday) rather than on Mondays and Saturdays. This change meant that Steele was responsible for producing news for the *Gazette* on one extra day, and that the publication schedule of the *Gazette* coincided with that of the *Tatler*. Other factors may have contributed to the decline in the *Tatler's* news, but the possible increase in advertising, the competition for space with other departments, and the participation of Addison, who had returned from Ireland on 9 September 1709 were all dismissed or downplayed as factors by Richmond Bond, who saw the coincidence of publication dates with the *Gazette* as the major reason.[24] Steele certainly began the *Tatler* with the expectation that he would use his position a Gazetteer to get a jump on other newspapers, and that he would use his inclusion of news as a major attraction to a periodical designed to cover a variety of issues, designated by the coffeehouses from which departments were dated.

The early issues often contained a department from St James's. The first eleven *Tatler*s contain reports from the continent. *Tatler*, no. 11 announces that 'Politick News is not the principal Subject on which we treat', perhaps a response to criticism of the allegorical praise of the Junto Lords in no. 4. The frequency of reports from St James's Coffeehouse decreases by one in each set of ten issues, from ten in the first ten to six in the fifth decade, followed by seven between *Tatler* nos. 51 and 60, and seven between nos. 61 and 70, until four between nos. 71 and 80, two between nos. 81 and 90, and finally one in no. 96, and no more thereafter until no. 136, at which point there are two (nos. 136 and 137) on the negotiations at Gertruydenberg, two (nos. 174 and 175) on the siege of Douai, and, finally, two overly optimistic reports on advances in Spain (nos. 210 and 225). The shape of the reports suggests that Steele was fairly committed to following military and diplomatic matters during the 1709 campaign, and the substance of his reports reflects the major events of that campaign. But he, no doubt in consultation with others, seems to have made a definite decision not to include such material in 1710, with very rare exceptions.

1709 was a turning-point in the War of Spanish Succession, and the news events reported in the *Tatler* trace the rotation, without being quite aware that it is doing so. For example, *Tatler*, no. 10 (3 May 1709) comments on the widespread famine in France, on the shortage of bread and the consequent rise in its price, and on the food riots that resulted. But it does not realize that hunger is forcing larger numbers of male peasants into the army, where they will have a better chance of getting food.[25] As a result, the French army was in better shape by June or July, when the actual campaigning began in the Netherlands, than it had been in 1708, despite the serious loss at Oudenarde. The first months of the season, as the *Tatler* reports, were devoted to negotiations, and here the positions of the French and the Whig ministry were irreconcilably opposed. British intransigence in their unreasonable position on the Spanish succession made negotiations impossible in 1709. The alternative would have been to take advantage of French military weakness after 1708 to sweep down to Paris. But the delay caused by fruitless negotiations allowed the French to put a substantial army in the field, to fortify the La Bassée lines between the Lys and Scarpe rivers, to hold out longer than expected at the siege of Tournai, and to achieve a virtual stalemate at the costly battle of Malplaquet. Unlike the rout at Blenheim, the French army withdrew in good order from the field at Malplaquet and with considerably lower casualties than the allies. With stalemate at the negotiating table, with disappointing progress on the battlefield, and with stark awareness of the cost of the war in human life, support for the war diminished in England, despite the periodic efforts of the *Tatler* to rally support.

The *Tatler* and Whig Identity

By the early spring of 1709, Steele must certainly have seen his position as Gazetteer as something of a dead end. He had been doing the job for two years, and the initial excitement would have been replaced by a sense of dull routine. His hopes of replacing Addison as Under-Secretary of State when Addison was appointed as Wharton's Secretary in Ireland had come to nothing. The *Gazette*'s concentration on continental news and its restrained tone must have seemed confining. Beyond that personal and professional restlessness, the Junto lords and their allies may have seen the value of a paper that, drawing on the resources of the *Gazette*, combined news with entertaining reflections on theatre and literature and on manners and morals, and that did so from an established political identity. It is important to note about Steele's political writings and those of his contemporaries that they are facets in an array of Whig propaganda messages, written by diverse writers and distributed both to a general audience and to a number of discrete ones. Although it would be a stretch to describe the *Tatler* as a political periodical, it was a periodical that, among its other functions (and often in relation to those functions) played a significant political role.

The *Tatler* is Whiggish in politics and Whiggish in culture. These two respects are often in conflict – or at least each serves as the counterweight to the other. At times the paper is overtly and strongly political, and hence it earns strong rebuke from Tory writers. Steele does not want the political commitments of the *Tatler* to drive away Tory readers or to identify his paper as narrowly political. But he does want readers to recognize that, however it may lurk in the background, politics is a significant element of the *Tatler*'s identity. Indeed, such identification is important to the cultural purpose of the *Tatler*. When individuals say that they are a member of a political group, they are not merely saying that they agree with the political philosophy of a party or the practical political measures it advocates. They identify themselves with the groups that are associated with the party, whether they be family, class, occupation, region or religious faction. The *Tatler* celebrated behaviours, values and attitudes that it associated with Whigs, and it made fun of behaviours and attitudes that might be thought of as Tory. But it did so with a genial good nature that was attractive to all.

The task of balancing these political and cultural functions is effected through the *Tatler*'s fictional apparatus, comprising the self-conscious author Isaac Bickerstaff, his sister, more distant family members, attendant spirits, friends and fellow members of the Trumpet Club and a wide range of letter-writers of both sexes, from all walks of life and various religious and political persuasions. Steele borrowed Isaac Bickerstaff from Swift's popular mock-astrological tracts predicting (among other things) the death of the astrologer Partridge and testifying (falsely) that his death had occurred. Steele's Bickerstaff lacks the cool irony of Swift, but comes across as more personable and genial, using the astrological device less frequently than Swift. He combines his function as the paper's principle reporter and sole editor with his role as astrologer and his personal life as an old bachelor whose family is extended and extensive.

Bickerstaff's position as an elderly man who has seen it all before and as an astrologer who can see a future that others cannot combines experience with vision. It also places him rather on the margins of society, a position that Steele liked to establish as the vantage point for social observation. But much of the *Tatler*'s moral and social commentary is quite conventional, and the eccentricity of Bickerstaff's character and position thus gives the familiar a cast of newness. The adoption of Swift's Bickerstaff figure, like the adoption of the *Gazette*'s news, gives the *Tatler* a recognizable personality at the outset. In due course Bickerstaff takes on the personality of Richard Steele, but one of his recognizable characteristics is that he is, so to speak, self-consciously fictional. His character can therefore shift in substance and emphasis without betraying any real integrity. He can speak with the voices of social wisdom (the role of the astrologer is, after all, to discern the order of things) and of personal feeling. Perhaps his most important characteristics, political as well as personal, are his moderation

– his dislike of extreme and excessive behavior – and his interest in social reform. These characteristics, like the interplay of convention and eccentricity, modify each other. Hence his social reform lacks the rigidity of Collier and others but is carried out with toleration and good humour. His toleration is not amorality, and his good humour does not lack seriousness. Steele's effort to find a middle course between the shallow liberties of the Restoration and the rigid repression of the reformers is embodied in the figure of Bickerstaff.

Bickerstaff, like Mr Spectator after him, is an observer of others, and hence a figure of a sort of mock-terror. Of course, eighteenth-century Londoners, like their modern equivalents, were observed all the time by all sorts of people, and Bickerstaff, as a social spy, could only observe random individuals for brief moments. He was more reliable, on one hand, with friends or family members or well-known public figures, and, on the other, with composite abstractions. The advantages Bickerstaff has over regular observers are that he can publish his observations, thus posing a threat to the most obvious offenders, and that he can divine the future, although he is discreetly silent, for the most part, about his predictions. That policy of silence is particularly useful in Bickerstaff's reporting on the evils of gaming.[26] At one point Bickerstaff threatens his readers and demands a bribe:

> I expect Hush-Money to be regularly sent for every Folly or Vice any one commits in this whole Town; and hope, I may pretend to deserve it better than a Chamber-Maid or Valet de Chambre: They only whisper it to the little Set of their Companions; but I can tell it to all Men living, or who are to live. Therefore I desire all my Readers to pay their Fines, or mend their Lives (*Tatler*, no. 26).

Bickerstaff is considerably aided in his investigations by his guardian angel Pacolet, whom he meets in no. 13. Pacolet is not only a perceiver and protector, although often an unsuccessful one, but an encourager of Bickerstaff's effort at reforming society. In No. 15 he explains that guardian angels are the spirits of infants who have died before experiencing life and who therefore experience it vicariously by angelic observation. Pacolet's main function in the *Tatler* is to collect information that Bickerstaff would otherwise be unable to get; Bickerstaff, despite the supernatural aid, remains the *Tatler's* primary moralizer. Pacolet is particularly useful in collecting information on duelling and gaming, two of Bickerstaff's principle targets, and on one occasion (no. 64) he travels to the woods and fields of Malplaquet to report on the outcome of the battle. In no. 129, Bickerstaff receives a letter from Pasquin, an eponymously satirical spirit, who sees Bickerstaff's functions as parallel to his own:

> Your Reputation has passed the *Alps*, and would have come to my Ears by this Time, if I had any. In short, Sir, you are looked upon here as a *Northern* Drole, and the greatest Virtuoso among the *Tramontanes*. Some indeed say, That Mr. *Bickerstaff* and *Pasquin*

are only Names invented to father Compositions, which the natural Parent does not care for owning.

Pasquin provides satiric materials on the Roman Church that suggest possible parallels with British politics. He refers to Whigs and Tories as different religious orders. In no. 187 Pasquin writes again, providing a distant perspective on the *Tatler*'s satiric successes.

Another kind of assistance to Bickerstaff comes from his much younger half-sister Jenny Distaff. She first emerges in no. 10 as a substitute for Bickerstaff and, perhaps more significantly, as an alternative to his patriarchal point of view. Her creation of the paper out of the notes and comments of her brother explains its mixed topics. Jenny, like Bickerstaff himself, is a self-consciously fictional character, and a female character clearly created by a man. Bickerstaff, as her much older brother, has a fatherly relation to her. She is, within the bounds of the family's moderation, an independent and assertive woman. Bickerstaff finds her a worthy husband (that is, a husband whose worth she herself recognizes, *Tatler*, no. 75), gives her a wedding dinner (no. 79), and lectures her on the appropriate behaviour of a married woman (nos. 85, 104, 143). She writes one further paper (no. 247), in which she asserts that 'the Perfidiousness of Men has been generally owing to our selves, and we have contributed to our own Deceit'.

The real threat posed to one's privacy by periodicals such as the *Review*, *Tatler*, and *Spectator* is not that the paper's editor will observe one's misdemeanors but that one's friends and neighbours – or even spouse – will write to the *Tatler* asking what to do about one's case. The same people who gossip to the neighbours may gossip to Isaac Bickerstaff. Letters, of course, are the periodicalist's easy way to produce papers – by pulling a letter out of the drawer, making a few grammatical and stylistic corrections, and adding a paragraph or so of context. But they are far more useful in multiplying the range of social observation and the voices of those who write. They are a primary vehicle by which the writer engages with his society.

It is probably a dangerous oversimplification to equate the writers of letters with readers of the *Tatler*, but they certainly reflect the diversity of that audience. Here, as elsewhere, Steele's essential task was to achieve an appropriate balance. Most of the papers in the *Tatler* addressed a range of readers, often overlapping, so that papers on domesticity addressed to women might appeal to unmarried men as well. A number of papers dealt with topics that could be grouped under the heading of 'domesticity' and the status of women, virtually always considered in terms of a patriarchal family. Bickerstaff generally avoids direct advice, but indulges in general reflection, illustrative narratives (as in the saga of his sister Jenny and her husband Tranquilus), satiric attacks on general types such as coquettes and prudes (no. 126), and scolding wives (nos. 217 and 221), and exercises in exemplary pathos (for example the death of his friend's wife in no. 114). Numerous papers take up the topic of courtship from both male and female perspectives. Comments on clothes and dress recur fairly frequently, the most famous being Addison's attack on the hoop-petticoat (no. 116).[27] One playful device of social analysis is to literalize a commonplace metaphor and to extend that literal meaning. Thus Addison represents social harmony as a consort of musical instruments who, in turn, stand for classes of people. Drums are noisy, overbearing people; the lute is soft and sweet and seldom heard in companies of more than five; the trumpet is pleasing in a very limited range, as are pleasant but shallow men. Violins are lively with wit and imagination, but unwelcome when one does not want to hear music. The bass-viol repesents quiet men who 'sometimes break out with an agreeable Bluntness, unexpected Wit, and surly Pleasantry', in short 'every sensible, true-born Britain'. Rural wits are hunting-horns; people who repeat stories are bagpipes. Harpsichords are men who can talk well on all subjects (*Tatler*, no. 153). Such classification is a primary means of social analysis in the *Tatler*, and it is often hidden under comic figures.

Men too are analysed through comic figures and fictitious categories, but the devices for such analysis are broader and more inclusive. Coffeehouses were exclusively male, and *Tatler* organizes the major categories of its materials by the coffeehouses in which they are collected and written.

> All Accounts of *Gallantry, Pleasure*, and *Entertainment*, shall be under the Article of *White's Chocolate-house*; *Poetry* under that of *Will's Coffee-house*; *Learning*, under the Title of *Graecian*; *Foreign* and *Domestick News*, you will have from St. *James's Coffee-house*; and what else I have to offer on any other Subject, shall be dated form my own *Apartment* (*Tatler*, no. 1).

The complex function of the coffeehouse as a public place with the conversational atmosphere and defining purpose of a private gathering made it a particularly appropriate parallel for the informal and communicative *Tatler*.[28] Although the coffeehouse designations ultimately became insignificant, the initial choice to identify the periodical's structural elements this way gave the *Tatler* an inevitably patriarchal cast. The emergence of Jenny Distaff as an alternate speaker in *Tatler*, no. 10 seems to reflect Steele's recognition that he needed a way to incorporate his female audience in the structure of the paper. Most of Bickerstaff's commentary on women's issues comes from his own apartment or from letters.

Another class of excluded readers lives in the country, rather than London. In no. 31, Bickerstaff receives a letter from a supposed cousin, probably from Swift, who reports that countryfolk do not know what a 'toast' is and have not heard of the *Tatler* either. 'Thus, Cousin, you must be content with *London* for the Center of your Wealth and Fame; we have no Relish for you'. But one of the functions of the *Tatler* is to explain the strange ways of London to an otherwise ignorant country readership. The *Tatler* engages dual audiences. Papers addressed to the country readership (the target audience) are actually intended for their avid city readers (the audience of witnesses). Similarly, women may be a target audience and men the witnesses. Each element of this dual audience will be aware of the presence of the other audience and may, indeed, conjecture the responses of that other audience. The distance between the two audiences may become a source of irony, and the use of self-consciously double audiences becomes a further device of the *Tatler's* indirection. The country audience stands, more broadly, for those who, for reasons of class, age, gender or geography need to be introduced to the cultural life of London. This introductory purpose excuses the *Tatler's* traversal of familiar territory. It overlaps usefully with Steele's reformist mission and the usual placement of his moral and satiric targets within sharply delineated categories.

Perhaps the most famous of Steele's moral campaigns in the *Tatler* and else-where (especially *The Lying Lover* and *The Conscious Lovers*) is his attack on duelling. Duelling was a practice frequently condoned by society at large and virtually mandatory among aristocrats and military men.[29] A letter from a young woman in *Tatler*, no. 25 initiates the series. Her lover has been wounded in a duel, and Bickerstaff reflects on the silliness of the phrase 'giving a man satisfaction'. Bickerstaff provides a model letter of challenge:

> I will meet you in *Hyde-Park* an Hour hence; and because you are want both Breeding and Humanity, I desire you would come with a Pistol in your Hand, on Horseback, and endeavor to shoot me through the Head, to teach you more Manners.

In *Tatler*, no. 26, Pacolet, in the afterlife, meets a man who as died as a second in a duel the cause of which he did not know. Socrates points out that the duellist knew whom he gave his estate to but not what he gave his life for. In no. 28 Bickerstaff advises that calling someone a 'smart fellow' is not grounds for a duel, but notes that duels are fought for trivial reasons. Tom Switch writes a letter in no. 29 in which he argues that the causes of duelling depend on custom, convention and a concern for reputation, especially reputation among ladies. Bickerstaff, in response, imagines a letter to his beloved from a duellist in love: 'Whoever says he dies for you, I will make his Words good, for I will kill him'. The history of duelling in various nations is reported in no. 31, and is elaborated in a lengthy contributed conversation in no. 39. Steele's attack on duelling runs counter to his attack on gambling, for gamblers threaten to kill him, and in consequence Isaac Bickerstaff reports that he has taken up fencing. In his final paper, Steele thanks three military friends for their readiness to protect him.

The set of papers and passages on duelling reflects the diversity of Steele's approach to moral campaigning. Some sections are straightforward, but many are ironic. Some are written by Bickerstaff, some are contributed by others. Some of these others, including the woman whose letter in no. 25 initiated the series, seem to be real people, while others (Tom Switch in no, 29) are pseudonymous. And there are the fake letters that Steele has written in nos. 25 and 29. There is very little serious appeal to moral principles. The immorality of duelling is well known and hardly needs to be argued. Steele emphasizes instead the silliness of duelling. The duellist will hardly be prevented by the charge of immorality, but he can be stopped if he is made to feel that he is being fatally ridiculous. For such a feeling to work, the target of Bickerstaff's comic and ironic treatment of duelling must be not only the would-be duellist but the broader society that is encouraged to see his actions as foolish. The replacement of direct moralizing with ironic mockery and the use of multiple devices to convey the message are typical traits of the *Tatler*'s campaigning and reasons for its success.

Steele collects various kinds and levels of social misbehaviour into mock-significant fictitious categories, which he usually delineates in a sequence of related papers, only to replace one category by another. There is no sense that the replacement is due to the deficiencies of the first category, but the metaphorical implications of the second can extend the possibilities of the first. In no. 96, Isaac Bickerstaff announces his concern for the dead:

> In short, whoever resides in the World without having any Business in it, and passes away an Age, without ever thinking on the Errand for which he was sent hither, is to me a Dead Man to all Intents and Purposes; and I desire that he may be so reputed. The Living are only those that are some Way or other laudably employed in the Improvement of their own Minds, or for the Advantage of others; and even among these, I shall only reckon into their Lives that Part of their Time which has been spent in the Manner above-mentioned.

He thus creates a zombie-like class of people that includes many. The dead come trooping by or walking in. In *Tatler*, no. 106 Jeffrey Groggham announces that he is dead and has been since he was born. Bickerstaff insists that he remain alive as an example to others. The 'Upholders' (or undertakers) express dismay that among so many deceased so few have turned themselves in: 'But so it is, Sir, that of this vast Number of dead Bodies, that go putrifying up and down the Streets, not one of them has come to us to be buried' (*Tatler*, no. 99). In no. 109, the 'Upholders' announce that some of the dead have been disorderly, and Bickerstaff holds a court to adjudicate them in no. 110. The Court, here as with other court cases, focuses on individual comic people. In no. 113, Bickerstaff sets aside various areas of the town where, at various hours, the walking dead can appear to each other. Bickerstaff concludes (no. 118) by observing that the wives of dead men have not appeared in mourning, as would be appropriate, and he prints a letter, dated 'From the Banks of Styx', from John Partridge himself, the great archetype of the walking dead. Partridge finds the life, or rather the non-life, of meaningless activity quite congenial.

Soon after Steele buries his dead, he turns his attention to confining the mad, a project which he may have adopted and extended from Swift's *A Tale of a Tub*. But his starting point, in no. 125, is Cicero's observation that Rome is a city of lunatics. Rome had an island to which mad people were sent to recover, and Bickerstaff proposes a similar enlargement of Bedlam in which the many mad of London who suffer from excess of imagination or excessive self-regard can be lodged and cured. Readers are invited to bring in coffeehouse politicians and freethinkers. Madness, he goes on to say in no. 127, is the superstructure of folly based on pride, and he describes several of his patients, many of whom have taken on titles. He returns to madness in no. 174. Having disposed of lazy, worthless people by pronouncing them dead, Bickerstaff will turn to the falsely active, who are mad and fit for his hospital in Moorfields. Other astrologers will take care of the fools, he will tend to the mad. He begins to canvass the varieties of mad people and to concentrate on the rich. He distinguishes between the madness of men and women. But Steele seems to be casting about for a fish to land with this particular line, and the appropriate stream turns out to be politics. If Don Quixote was driven mad by romances, so that he could not tell illusion from reality, modern coffeehouse Quixotes are driven mad by newspapers.

> What I am now warning the People of is, That the News-Papers of this Island are as pernicious to weak Heads in *England* as ever Books of Chivalry to *Spain*; and therefore shall do all that in me lies with the utmost Care and Vigilance imaginable to prevent these growing evils. (*Tatler*, no. 178).

The prime example is Bickerstaff's friend 'the political upholsterer', a character created by Addison, whose madness lies specifically in his fixation with Charles XII but who exemplifies more generally those whose personal experience has been replaced by their reading of the news.

Having disposed of his Upholsterer and other political madmen in his Moorfields asylum, Bickerstaff proposes a 'Court of Honour', another device developed by Addison for the satiric analysis of society. The Court is introduced by Addison in *Tatler*, no. 250, and all of the relevant papers thereafter are jointly composed by Addison and Steele.[30] Its purpose, following other court devices used in the *Tatler* is to adjudicate 'Injuries and Affronts, that are not to be redressed by the common Laws of this Land' (*Tatler*, no. 250). The court provides the mechanism for presenting individual comic cases. The *Tatler* characteristically uses devices such as the lazy dead, the deluded mad and the Court of Honour to focus Bickerstaff's moral satire over a sequence of papers. But each device disappears and is replaced by another.

This shifting is more broadly typical of the paper as a whole, which seems to try out a series of organizing tactics – the coffeehouse departments, the various members of the 'Staff' family, the assisting spirits such as Pacolet and Pasquin, the ubiquity of letters, submitted or imagined, and the changing characteristics of Bickerstaff himself as astrologer, theatregoer, collector of news, family advisor, observer of society, censor of Great Britain, playful satirist and serious moralist. This diversity of intertwined structural elements makes it possible for the *Tatler* to reach a variety of audiences and to canvass a range of topics. As one modern critic has observed, 'Bickerstaff's many definitions and classifications make his periodical into a reference book of social folly'.[31] What holds the paper together is its politically significant tone. Although Bickerstaff can be satiric, he is, for the most part, an exemplar of the good-natured toleration and the moderation that he urges on others. The very breadth of the *Tatler*'s subjects and Bickerstaff's concern derives from this moderate toleration, the rejection of extremism in behaviour and in politics and religion as well. The society described by Bickerstaff is fashionable society, perhaps fashionable by virtue of the fact that Bickerstaff has described it. Steele creates a fictional world where comic gestures confirm and enhance the reader's proper place in the real world.

Steele does not cite scripture to develop his moral advice. He does not base his teaching on religious authority, although he respects religious authority. His moral views derive, ultimately, from the common opinion of reasonable people; his celebration of consensus dominates his sense of the importance of conformity in behaviour. To be an honest trader, a kind husband and a good citizen is to live in conformity with the morals and customs of the British community. Steele's version of moral reform is not the enforcement of moral laws. His purpose is to explain to his readers what the common principles and practices are, and to do so in a way that makes moral behavior attractive. This is a pre-eminently Whig position, in contrast to the authoritarian and sectarian rigidity of High-Church-men such as Blackall and Sacheverell. The sermon and the periodical enunciate very different understandings of political and religious life.

The Politics of the *Tatler*

The connection between Steele's moral and social comedy and his Whig politics is made clear by the specifically political references in the paper. As the *Spectator* was later to do (*Spectator*, no. 3), the *Tatler* inserts an early paper which, despite the indirection of allegory, unmistakably establishes its political character. In *Tatler*, no. 4 Bickerstaff describes the Island of Felicia (Britain), which is ruled by 'the ablest and best Men of the Nation, to carry on the Cause of Liberty, to the Encouragement of Religion, Virtue, and Honour'. As these worthy individuals are described, their similarity to the Whig Junto is clear: the chief minister represents Godolphin, Camillo represents Somers and Verono represents Wharton. The significance of other characters is less certain.[32]

The connection of Whig politics to the conduct of the war and hence to the character of Marlborough runs through the paper and gives a political edge to its reporting of the news. Bickerstaff has praised the Junto in no. 4; in no. 5 he describes the Duke of Marlborough:

> It is, methinks, a pleasing Reflection, to consider the Dispensations of Providence in the Fortune of this Illustrious Man, who in the Space of Forty Years, has pass'd through all the Gradations of Human Life, 'till he has ascended to the Character of Prince, and become the Scourge of a Tyrant, who sate in one of the greatest Thrones of *Europe*.

In the next paper, Marlborough and Prince Eugene, 'the present great Captains of the Age', are compared to Alexander and Caesar. Steele (probably) writes a similar paper, *Tatler*, No. 130, in honour of the Queen's forty-fifth birthday. She is honoured because she has assembled such a worthy group of leaders: the General (Marlborough), Treasurer (Godolphin), Speaker of the House (Somers), Lord Chancellor (Cowper), head of the Admiralty (Orford), and governor of 'a distant Kingdom (Wharton in Ireland). These leaders are set in a exaggerated historical context:

> Methinks a Man cannot, without a secret Satisfaction, consider the Glory of the present Age, which will shine as bright as any other in the History of Mankind ... We have seen Kingdoms divided and united, Monarchs erected and deposed, Nations transferred from one Sovereign to another; Conquerors raised to such a Greatness as has given a Terror to *Europe*, and thrown down by such a Fall, as has moved their Pity.

Although the *Tatler* contains news reports and has a clear political identity, it dissociates itself from newspapers, political writing and curiosity about news. The prospects of peace in the spring of 1709 led to the first of Addison's contributions to the *Tatler*. In no. 18 he paints the distresses of newswriters, who 'have taken more Towns, and fought more Battles' than the army itself. He identifies these warriors in print by name and suggests an addition 'to the Hospital of *Chelsea*, for the Relief of such decay'd News-Writers as have serv'd their Country in the Wars'. But he is exempt from such distress because 'my chief Scenes of Action are Coffee-houses, Play-houses, and my own Apartment'. Bickerstaff is as hard on the consumer of news as he is on its writers (or inventors). The Political Upholsterer (nos. 155, 160, 178, and 232) exemplifies misplaced attention to reports of external events. News becomes an alternative form of madness, in which one's personal reality is replaced by unreliable reports and rumors of public events. The *Tatler*'s attention to the real experience of individuals and its social contexts marks it as the antidote to a deluded and sickly concern for false events. Steele extends the attack on newswriters by attacking libellers (*Tatler*, no. 92) – implicitly criticizing the Tory writers who have slandered the Duke of Marlborough, Mrs Manley in particular. Pasquin urges the expansion of Bickerstaff's madhouse because 'Heroes in your Service are treated with Calumny, while Criminals pass through your Towns with Acclamations' (*Tatler*, no. 187). The hero in this case is Marlborough, the criminal is Sacheverell. The paradox of the *Tatler*'s journalism lies in its insinuation that the factual representations by Bickerstaff's fellow journalists are mostly fictions but the fictions of the *Tatler* are true to experience as its readers know it. Nonetheless, the *Tatler* continues to report the news, although less frequently as the paper continues.

Thus, although the paper continues to praise Whigs and attack Tories, its praise and attacks are always hidden, sometimes thinly, under a fictional mask, and it does not attack often enough to define itself as a political or party journal. One trick of non-partisan political propaganda is to present the commentary as the appropriate response of patriotism. Marlborough was in fact a moderate Tory, but at this point owed his military position to the support of Whigs. The *Tatler* does not present him as a figure of Whig policy but as a great military leader, the pride of the nation. He is explicitly compared to Caesar in *Tatler*, nos. 6, 37, 64, and 137; in the last of these papers the comparison triangulates among Marlborough, Caesar and Henry V. At the other extreme, *Tatler*, no, 193 is a decidedly but complexly unsympathetic treatment of Robert Harley. It seems to be a paper about the efforts of Christopher Rich to take control of the theatre. At the outset, Bickerstaff dismisses the accusation that he has dabbled in political matters for sordid mercenary reasons.

> It is apparent that my Motive could not be of that Kind; for when a Man declares himself openly on one Side, that Party will no more take Notice of him, because he is sure; and the Set of Men whom he declares against, for the same Reason are violent against him.

Having made that declaration, he goes to Will's Coffeehouse, where the actor Thomas Doggett gives him a letter from old John Downes the prompter, who complains that 'a Gentleman of the Inns of Court, and a deep Intriguer', with 'restless Ambition, and subtle Machinations' had become sole manager of the theatre and sought to impose foreign dancers and singers. However, his superiors detected his schemes and withdrew their favour. Unfortunately, the schemer has now managed to return with inferior actors and plays. The schemer in question is, of course, Robert Harley, who was dismissed as minister in February, 1708, ostensibly because of the spying of his clerk. By the date of this paper (4 July 1710), he had used his friendship with the Queen to begin replacing the Junto lords and their allies in the ministry, but his victory was not yet complete. Steele later disavowed authorship of the letter (*Guardian*, no. 53), but he probably wrote it and, more important, included it.[33]

The *Tatler* had remained relatively silent on political matters, especially personal attacks, since its opening papers, preferring the varieties of indirection I have discussed. But Whig fortunes had suffered a series of setbacks. Military operations in the Low Countries had still not opened a clear route to Paris. The mild sentence imposed on Rev. Henry Sacheverell for his seditious sermon was regarded by High-Church Tories as a victory. The Duchess of Marlborough had been replaced as the Queen's confidante by Abigail Masham, an ally of Harley, who himself was moving clearly to topple the Godolphin ministry and replace it with his own. Matters were moving towards an election in the autumn that would be, in effect, a referendum on a now unpopular war. In response the *Tatler* sought to divert political passions and to deride Harley in particular. The result was a series of papers culminating in *Tatler*, no. 193. Pasquin, the satiric spirit, writes in No. 187 that Bickerstaff's madhouse should be extended to the entire kingdom, crazed as it is by violent celebrations for Sacheverell, and he articulates the comparison of Marlborough to Hannibal later developed by Arthur Maynwaring.[34] In no. 190 Bickerstaff defends his involvement in politics:

> But as there is no Character so unjust as that of talking in Party upon all Occasions, without Respect to Merit or Worth on the contrary Side, so there is no Part we can act so justifiable as to speak our Mind when we see Things urged to Extremity, against all that is Praiseworthy and valuable in Life, upon general and groundless Suggestions.

He follows this reflection with a letter from a Quaker that parodies Quaker style and argument through biblical references, and hints at governmental changes to come. The next letter patently refers to the Hanoverian succession. The writer has inherited an estate which previous heirs, now living abroad, demand be returned. Bickerstaff had characterized the point of this letter as so clear that no further discussion was needed. Bickerstaff concludes the paper with a short letter to Louis XIV complaining that French writers only report about one party.

Tatler, no. 191 turns specifically to the character of Harley, here figured as Polypragmon, who

> makes it the whole Business of his Life to be thought a Cunning Fellow, and thinks it a much greater Character to be terrible than agreeable ... It is certain *Polypragmon* does all the Ill he possible can, but pretends to much more than he performs.

Contemporary readers saw Polypragmon as Harley, but Steele claimed in *Guardian*, no. 53 that Polypragmon was a general portrait of ambition. That claim and the fact that Steele and Harley were still ostensibly friends led Calhoun Winton to doubt that *Tatler*, no. 191 was meant to attack Harley. But it is hard to believe that a propagandist as sophisticated in his sense of audience as Steele would not have recognized that readers would be aware of the closeness of his description to Harley's character. Steele followed his statement of political concern with specific attack, but that attack itself appears initially as general moral comment against the dangerous tendency of 'this Age' to emulate behaviour that is contemptible. The negative comment allows Bickerstaff to reiterate the central principles of the periodical and its politics: 'Simplicity of Manners, Openness of Heart, and Generosity of Temper'.

Tatler, nos. 192 and 194 are not significantly concerned with political matters. *Tatler,* no. 193, as we have seen, extends the attack on Harley by mocking his efforts to form a new ministry. In No. 195, Bickerstaff takes on the issue of political writing directly. He replies to those who 'have but a very mean Opinion of me as a Politician' with the assertion that 'the first and essential Quality towards being a Statesman is to have a publick Spirit'. This defence introduces a letter from Cato Junior, who is obviously a Tory and quite possibly Jonathan Swift. Cato refers to the Whigs as 'the Staggering Party' and warns Steele that he is offending 'the better Half'. Bickerstaff dissents from Cato's representation of Whigs and Tories but promises to dedicate his paper for the rest of the month (it is only 10 July) to 'the Service of the Fair Sex'. He has, in effect, withdrawn from direct political polemics in favour of the general creation of Whig culture that has characterized his paper.

A further expression of the *Tatler*'s political moderation is its treatment of religion. At the end of an attack on infidels, 'whether distinguished by the Title of Deist, Atheist, or Free-thinker' (*Tatler*, no. 111), Isaac Bickerstaff proclaims his religious moderation:

> As a Protestant, I do not suffer my Zeal so far to transport me, as to name the Pope and the Devil together. As I am fallen into this degenerate Age, I guard my self particularly against the Folly I have been now speaking of. And as I am an Englishman, I am very cautious not to hate a Stranger, or despise a poor *Palatine*.

The Palatines were Protestant but not members of the Church of England; they were, in essence, war refugees from Germany. They also arrived in considerable number in 1709 (*Tatler*, no. 111 is dated 24 December 1709). High-Church Tories thus turned against them for several reasons, and Bickerstaff's refusal to despise them thus reminds readers of his Whig toleration, at the same time as he attacks freethinkers. If he wins the lottery, he says, he will provide a pension for a family of Palatines (*Tatler*, no. 124). Steele and his colleagues continue their occasional attacks on 'freethinkers' throughout the *Tatler*, and in the *Spectator* and *Guardian* as well. Addison's contributions on a 'Political Barometer' (no. 214) and 'Church Thermometer' (no. 220) reinforce the centrist position that the *Tatler* seeks to represent. In *Tatler*, no. 220, Addison concludes that 'the terms *High-Church* and *Low-Church*, as commonly used, do not so much denote a Principle, as they distinguish a Party'. The ultimate attack on religious differences is to claim that they have no meaning, and such an attack deprives Tories of a major supporting base.

Given that position, it seems odd that the *Tatler* had virtually nothing to say about the trial of Rev. Henry Sacheverell, whose Gunpowder-Plot sermon, delivered on 5 November 1709 at St Paul's, on 'The Perils of False Brethren', led to his impeachment in the House of Lords on charges that he had attacked the revolution of 1688, that he attacked toleration and liberty of conscience, and that he insisted, contrary to Parliamentary resolution, that the Church was in danger and endangered particularly by the Queen's government.[35] The trial lasted from 27 February to 20 March 1710 and was the sensation of the season. It resulted in Sacheverell's conviction, but the very light sentence (suspension from preaching for three years and burning of the sermon) amounted to a defeat for the Whigs. Public opinion supported Sacheverell, seriously rioting during the trial and celebrating, in a manner hardly less violent, Sacheverell's triumphant progress to his living after the trial. This noisy support created an atmosphere in which Harley and the Queen were emboldened to take measures to replace the Whig ministers. Steele reacted against the first steps of replacement with the vitriolic sequence of *Tatler*s nos. 189–95, but his reaction to the Sacheverell trial was quite different. On 2 March (*Tatler*, no. 140) he devotes his paper to correspondents on the grounds that the eyes of his audience are trained on 'greater Matters'. In *Tatler*, no. 141 a group of petitioners from a fictionous parish ask that their preacher be confined to Bickerstaff's new madhouse on the grounds that the terms 'orthodox' and 'heterodox' cause him to 'fall into Ravings and Foamings, ill becoming the Meekness of his Office, and tending to give Offence and Scandal to all good People'. *Tatler*, no. 142 notes the effect of early attendance at the trial on the life of fashionable London. As an astute observer and 'Censor of Great Britain', Bickerstaff could hardly avoid paying some attention to the Sacheverell case, but, in light of popular support for Sacheverell, Steele may have felt reluctant to engage with the issues. He therefore contented himself with implying that interest in the case was another example of the foolishness of superficial people and with attacking Sacheverell's extreme language and rhetoric.

But he had earlier engaged the issues, with playful metaphorical indirection, in the case of a parallel controversy. In March 1709, Offspring Blackall, Bishop of Exeter delivered a sermon before the Queen in which he defended the divine authority of a hereditary magistracy and hence the duty of passive obedience, a position with which Anne, as the last of the Stuarts, sympathized but which implicitly, and often explicitly, denied the validity of the 1688 deposition of James II. Blackall, like Sacheverell, was a loud advocate of a narrow state Church, and he shared with Sacheverell a style marked by angry vituperation. Rev. Benjamin Hoadly, a rising Whig clergyman and friend of Steele, but not yet a Bishop, responded that the right to resist an impossible monarch derived from the widely accepted right of self-defence.[36] On one level the dispute was a philosophical one between disciples of Filmer and Locke; on another level it was a clash between the stylistic excesses of Blackall and the conversational reasoning of Hoadly. Steele engaged the issue by equating Blackall with a puppeteer named Martin Powell, who first appears (*Tatler*, no. 16) in Bath, where his puppets perform a controversial version of *Genesis*. He reappears in *Tatler*, no. 44 as an attacker of Bickerstaff. Steele exploits the metaphorical connections between Powell the puppet-master and Blackall the Bishop and between the control of a puppeteer over his puppets and that of a monarch over his people: 'I know well enough your Design is to have all men *Automata*, like your Puppets; but the World is grown too wise, and can look through these thin Devices'. Powell replies in *Tatler*, no. 50, in an ironic letter obviously written by Steele. He accuses Bickerstaff of 'sowing the Seeds of Sedition and Disobedience among my Puppets', and asserts his 'paternal Right to keep a Puppet-Show'. The whole letter is written in a comic parody of Blackall's style, as well as his ideas, and it extensively compares the principles of government to those of puppetry. Steele returns to Powell and his malicious puppets in *Tatler*, no. 115.

Steele's puppet-politics connection is an instance of the larger theatre-politics connection that runs through the *Tatler*. At the outset reports about the stage were a regular feature, dated from Will's Coffeehouse. The first number includes a report of a benefit performance, for the veteran actor Thomas Betterton, of Congreve's *Love for Love*, one of the plays that a reformer such as Collier would find objectionable. A benefit performance of the same play for Thomas Doggett is announced in *Tatler*, no. 120 and Bickerstaff describes his reaction to its performance in *Tatler*, no. 122. Steele's reflections on Betterton's funeral at Westminster Abbey describe him as a man 'from whose Action I had received more strong Impressions of what is great and noble in Human Nature, than from the Arguments of the most solid Philosophers, or the Descriptions of the most charming Poets I had ever read' (*Tatler*, no. 167). The stage was a particularly Whig project, and analogies between politics on the stage and politics in the real world were commonplace.[37] The stage-politics connection emerges specifically in several papers. In *Tatler*, no. 90, Bickerstaff chances to look at the last act of Shakespeare's *Richard III*, and the scene leads him to reflect on the contrast between that evil monarch and both William III and Queen Anne: 'We now see as great a Virtue as ever was on the *British* Throne, surrounded with all the Beauty of Success'. Marlborough embarking at Harwich for another campaign season in the Low Countries is compared to Shakespeare's Henry V embarking for France with famine, sword and fire 'Leashed in, like Hounds'.[38] The comparison leads Bickerstaff, by process of association, to recall Antony's description of 'the dogs of war' in *Julius Caesar*[39] and Virgil's description of the Temple of Janus in which Fury is Chained.[40] Bickerstaff hopes for a similar peace as a result of Marlborough's efforts.

Political discourse in the *Tatler* operates almost entirely through indirection. The only direct manifestation of politics comes in the form of patriotism, and

Steele takes advantage of the fact that during the run of the *Tatler* his propaganda was allied to the faction in power, so that celebration of the achievements of one's country becomes praise for the people in power. Thus praise of Marlborough, certainly a highly political topic, takes the form of patriotic celebration, and reports of often-exaggerated successes of the army advance Whig interests. Like the theatrical connections of *Richard III* and *Henry V* with contemporary Britain, historical analogues often provide ways of commenting indirectly on politics. The *Tatler* shares the age's propensity for political argument from historical and biblical analogy. One purpose of such arguing was to transfer the authority of historical fact or biblical revelation to the immediate political situation, and it is one reason why religion overlaps significantly with politics throughout the period. Other forms of narrative, such as the allegorical dreams that Addison in particular writes, provide sometimes obvious devices for political commentary. Static allegorical descriptions such as that of the Island of Felicia in *Tatler*, no. 4 are particularly useful as devices of indirect praise.

Characters such as Polypragmon (*Tatler*, no. 191) introduce an enticing ambiguity into personal political attack. He may be Harley, or he may, as Steele claimed, be a general type (of which Harley may be an instance). The fictional name and the description of qualities that may or may not belong to the actual figure lodge responsibility for the identification with the reader and allow authors such as Steele to claim innocence of personal attack. They also transform the actual target into a mythic figure, whose defining qualities may be exaggerated and distorted. A similar result is possible for classes of figures, as when Bickerstaff compares sharpers to curs: 'I cannot represent those Worthies more naturally than under the Shadow of a Pack of Dogs; for this Set of Men are like them, made up of Finders, Lurchers, and Setters' (*Tatler*, No. 59). Not only does the rapacious hunting of sharpers after their prey resemble the work of dogs of various breeds and functions, the discovery of new sharpers adds to the pack that Steele attacks. The sharper-dog equation is rather more abstract that the Harley-Polypragmon equation and thus throws the satiric weight on the behaviour that admits one into that class rather than on the personal characteristics of an individual. The treatment of lazy and inconsequential people as dead and of falsely energetic people as mad shares a similar abstraction. More abstract still are unspecified general statements, the reference to general qualities from which the reader may deduce political applications.

Such devices of indirection are not unusual in early eighteenth-century political discourse. In addition to creating deniability for the author, they allow a variety of authors to hide behind a single persona, as Addison did in the case of the *Tatler*. They create a code through which readers can look to find political meaning, whether intended by the writer or not, thus making the reader complicit in creating the propaganda. Once the basic political sympathies of the periodical are established, it does not make much difference if the reader is inserting a private meaning, since any meaning consistent with the governing ideology is a propaganda gain. Just as the distinction between author-meaning and reader-meaning dissolves in the acid of satiric indirection, other distinctions disappear as well. The *Tatler* was founded on the organizing principle that different coffeehouses would supply the location for discrete bodies of material. But as the paper developed its sense of direction and audience, 'From my Apartment' became the dominant department, and single-essay numbers became commonplace. Similarly, as the *Tatler*'s political identity became known (surely by no. 4) the hard distinctions between politics, on one hand, and the observation of social behaviour and culture, on the other, broke down. The permeability of categories became an important feature of the *Tatler*, which refused to define its function in fixed terms but felt free to range over subjects from the battle of Malplaquet (*Tatler*, no. 64) to the fantastic passions of two old ladies (*Tatler*, no. 266). These diverse topics cohere in the idea that moderation, tolerance, industry and patriotism, principles that Steele associates strongly with Whigs, are those of a British gentleman, and that deviation from those principles is a major source of humour.

> If the *Tatler* and *Spectator* are not themselves especially 'political', the cultural project they represent could nevertheless be sustained only through a close traffic with political power; and if they were not especially political, it is in part because, as I have argued, what the political moment demanded was precisely 'cultural'.[41]

In *Tatler*, no. 271 Steele drops the mask of Bickerstaff and announces that the publisher has told him there are now enough issues to make up four volumes. Since the chore of writing has, he says, grown irksome, and since his identity is generally well known, undermining the advantages of anonymity, which lie in the ability to speak of morals without compromising his advice by his own faults, he has decided to end the paper. He admits that 'the most approved Pieces' were written by others and that 'the finest Stokes of Wit and Humour' are due to an anonymous friend (Addison). John Gay, in *The Present State of Wit*, testifies enthusiastically about the excellence and popularity of the *Tatler*, but is puzzled as to why it closed. He reports that the Town speculated that Steele was out of material, 'that he lay'd it down as a sort of Submission to, and Composition with the Government for some past Offenses', or that he stopped in order 'to appear again in some new Light'.[42] The claim that Steele may have lacked material is inconsistent with the suggestion that he wanted to reappear in another form, and reappear is precisely what he did, since only two months elapsed between the closing of the *Tatler* and the opening of the *Spectator*.

But most scholars who have commented on the close of the *Tatler* have followed Gay's speculation about Steele's relations with the government. The reasons, then, are both political and personal. As a committed Whig, Steele could hardly expect to continue as Gazetteer once Harley and the Tories came to power. The job of the Gazetteer, after all, is to narrate the government's version of events. But in January 1710, Steele had become Commissioner of the Stamp Office, with a salary of £300. Despite his salary from the Gazette, his salary from the Stamp Office and his earnings from the *Tatler*, Steele continued to spend more than he earned and to be the prey of creditors. He apparently was briefly arrested for debt in early May 1709.[43] His political *Tatlers* had been sharply attacked by the Tory *Moderator* in early July 1710 and by the *Examiner*, which began in early August. He had been attacked in several pamphlets. In mid-October, he resigned his position as Gazetteer and met with Harley, possibly with the help of Swift. The upshot of that meeting was that Steele continued at the Stamp Office and brought the *Tatler* to an end. What roles Harley and Steele may have played in arriving at this course of action is unclear. It is quite possible that Steele and his advisors felt that a less partisan periodical along the lines of the *Tatler* was quite possible and that it might well serve their own interests, as well as compensating for the revenue lost by closing the *Tatler*.[44]

The political characteristics of Isaac Bickerstaff had made him a clear political target, not least of Delarivière Manley. In May, 1709, the first volume of the *New Atalantis* appeared, with its reminiscence of Steele's alchemical folly, among other attacks. Manley's scorn was directed at Whigs in general and at the Marlboroughs in graphic particular, so that Steele was a passing shot. But Steele responded on 3 September (*Tatler*, no. 63) by recording a college for women, one of whose instructors was Epicene, a writer of *Memoirs from the Mediterranean*, whose skill with odours has both killed many and wakened the dead. Mrs. Manley perceptively took this as an attack on herself and wrote him angry letter to which he made a moderate response.[45] He came to her defence on her arrest and brief imprisonment in October 1709 for the publication of the second volume of *New Atalantis*, but she took his strong attack on libellers (*Tatler*, No. 92), implicitly libellers of Marlborough, such as Mrs Manley, as an attack on herself and ironically dedicated the third volume of *New Atalantis* to Isaac Bickerstaff.

Further attacks on Steele-as-Bickerstaff testify to his emergence as a political writer, especially after the spring of 1710. *The Character of the Tatler*, a one-sheet folio, makes fun of the *Tatler*, and asserts that it has a whimsy machine that changes serious things into frivolity. Members of the society that work it 'oblige themselves to call every Thing by a Wrong Name, take every Thing in a Wrong Sense, and put False, and Rude, New and Unheard-of, Interpretations upon Nature, Manners, and Religion'. Isaac Bickerstaff himself is 'an Author who is everywhere and nowhere'. An anonymous author calling himself 'Censor Censorum' (censor of censors) compares the self-appointed Isaac Bickerstaff to the elected Roman Censor, conflates him with the actual Richard Steele, and berates him for not avoiding the vices he censored. Bickerstaff has been arrested for debt, a problem every man with a good family and a decent income ought to be able to avoid. The author recommends Bickerstaff's use of an 'Oeconomical Barometer', modelled on the barometers of the *Tatler*.[46] William Oldisworth, a Tory and recent defender of Blackall against Hoadly, wrote a two-volume set of *Annotations on the Tatler*, allegedly translated out of the French of Monsieur Bournelle by William Wagstaff.[47] Wagstaff was an actual Tory writer, but probably did not write this. His name connects him to the Staff family of the *Tatler* and to Swift's contributions under the name of Humphrey Wagstaff. In the preface, the alleged translator describes 'Monsieur *Bournelle*'s new method of *Panegyrick by Banter*', but most of the comments are negative and most of the banter is forced and niggling. *Examiner*, no. 11 (12 October 1710) answers Bickerstaff's figurative remarks on his enemies by condemning his arrogance and abuse and by dismissing his similes as inappropriate. The most comic simile is the comparison of his duns to a great man's equipage: 'I have heard of a certain Illustrious Person, who having a *Guard du Corps*, that forced their Attendance upon him, put them into a Living, and maintained them as his Servants', an anecdote that, in one form or another, made its way through eighteenth-century accounts of Steele.[48] Henry St John placed the *Tatler* clearly among the Whig journals and praised the newly-founded *Examiner* as providing 'a Weekly Antidote to that Weekly Poison, which by the President and Inferior Members of a *Factious Cabal*, is so profusely scatter'd thro' the Nation'.[49] Lord Cowper responded with *A Letter to Isaac Bickerstaff, Esq* which sets out quite clearly the political programme and propaganda tactics adopted by the *Tatler* and, later, by the *Spectator*: Bickerstaff's purpose is

> to insinuate gradually into the Publick, that as acting with all the noble Simplicity of Nature and common Reason carries a Man with Ease and Honour thro all the Scenes and Offices of ordinary Life; so the same Principles, which in Friendship, Love, and common Converse and Society, go to the Composition of a Person, whom both Sexes agree to call by the name of *the generous honest Man*, must necessarily contribute to the forming of the best Servants of a Prince, and the Truest Patriots.[50]

Bickerstaff also emerges in 1710 as a Harleian moderate, not specifically connected to the *Tatler*; he argues against a high-flyer and a Low-Churchman that both the Tory principle of non-resistance and the Whig assertion of the right to resist are untenable.[51]

What emerged from much of his political squabbling was a double image of Bickerstaff and Steele. On one hand, Isaac Bickerstaff was the genial, learned, gracious and humane observer and instructor of social life; on the other hand, Richard Steele was a party hack, a political writer who would say anything his bosses wanted, as long as they paid him. In later years the split was between the *Tatler* and Steele's directly political propaganda. The claim was that Steele was fine as the jolly spokesman of social truisms but beneath contempt as an analyst of modern politics. Within the *Tatler* the social comment is associated with Bickerstaff but the political papers with Steele. This dissociated double image is what Steele seems to have had in mind when, in his final *Tatler* paper, he tried to insist that 'the Points I alluded to are such as concerned every *Christian* and Freeholder in *England*; and I could not be cold enough to conceal my Opinion on Subjects which related to either of those Characters' (*Tatler*, no. 271). The double image of Steele and Bickerstaff strikes particularly at Steele's apparent intention not only to create a gentleman but to imply that a gentleman is, by necessity, a moderate Whig.

As the final *Tatler* paper points out, not only was Bickerstaff a persona for Richard Steele, but Steele himself was a mask for a number of other writers, so that the authorship of the *Tatler* was a composite affair, of which Steele was organizer and chief writer. He wrote about 200 of the *Tatler*'s 271 papers.[52] His primary collaborator was Joseph Addison, who wrote, the consensus is, forty-seven papers and collaborated with Steele on twenty-two others. Swift contributed his 'Description of the Morning' to *Tatler*, no. 9 and 'A Description of a City Shower' to no. 238. In no. 31 he impersonated Bickerstaff's country cousin who complains that country folk have not heard of the *Tatler* and cannot understand its London ways. He wrote a long letter for no. 230, and a short one, signed with his initial and those of Nicholas Rowe and Matthew Prior, for no. 258. (Swift complained to Esther Johnson, probably not seriously, that 'Steele, the rogue, has done the impudentest thing in the world' in publishing the letter, which made fun of a letter in *Tatler*, no. 241.)[53] Steele's friend John Hughes, the poet, playwright and musician, wrote a letter on wit in no. 64, a letter on gamesters in no. 73, and a letter on the inventory of a beau in No. 113. (Since Hughes later edited Spenser, it is tempting to attribute to him the paper on Spenser, no. 194.) Others contributed letters, parts of papers, and ideas for papers: William Harrison, Heneage Twysden, Ambrose Philips, Edward Wortley Montagu, Samuel Pargiter Fuller and James Greenwood.[54]

Papers formally recognized by these attributions may be at least equalled in importance by the network of coffeehouse conversations and personal suggestions out of which the *Tatler* emerges. On October 8, 1709, Steele wrote Swift, then in Ireland, about a dinner at Lord Halifax's at which Swift was highly praised. 'The company that day at dinner were Ld Edward Russel [Lord Orford], Ld Essex, Mr. Maynwaring, Mr. Addison, and myself'.[55] Such an august gathering probably would not have been called to discuss the *Tatler* or to make suggestions of specific topics for papers, but it might have suggested useful directions or the coordination of the *Tatler* with other propaganda efforts. Steele spent considerable time meeting with friends, creditors, patrons and business associates, and the *Tatler* itself testifies to his keen awareness of the social scene as it revealed itself in clubs, coffeehouses, taverns and the theatre. Not only friends but ordinary citizens could, recognizing Steele as Bickerstaff, suggest topics, sentiments, and anecdotes, and if they did not actually do so, Bickerstaff implies that he draws his material from the suggestions of audience members, especially in letters, as well as from his observation of them.

But the principle suppliers of 'hints', as Swift calls them, were Addison and Swift, and their influence on the paper depended upon their presence in London. Addison left London on 9 April 1709, a few days before the publication of the first *Tatler* on 12 April. The closeness of the dates casts doubt on Thomas Tickell's claim, in the 1721 edition of Addison's *Works*, that Addison was unaware that the *Tatler* was forthcoming.[56] The early *Tatler's* were more directly influenced by Swift, whom Steele thanks generously and perhaps ironically in the preface to Volume IV of the Collected Edition of the *Tatler*:

> I have in the Dedication of the First Volume made my Acknowledgments to Dr. *Swift*, whose pleasant Writings, in the Name of *Bickerstaff*, created an inclination in the Town towards any Thing that could appear in the same Disguise. I must acknowledge also, that at my first entring upon this Work, a certain uncommon Way of Thinking, and a Turn in Conversation peculiar to that agreeable Gentleman, rendered his Company very advantageous to one whose Imagination was to be continually employed upon obvious and common Subjects, though at the same time to treat of them in a new and unbeaten Method.[57]

Swift left London on June 14, 1709; Addison returned from Ireland in September, and his renewed influence was apparent soon after. On Saturday, 1 October, *Tatler*, no. 75, the first paper-length essay (except for no. 48) narrated the marriage of Jenny Distaff and Tranquillus; it was jointly written by Addison and Steele. Swift is generally credited with the hint for Steele's 'Tables of Fame' in *Tatler*, nos. 67 and 68, but Addison develops at length the 'Vision of the Temple of Fame' in no. 81. The 'Vision' paper was a characteristic, though not exclusive, genre of Addison. Steele adds two sentences to the effect that the dreamer was wakened by the firing of guns at Mons, which, like the firing from Flanders in World War I, sounded across the channel. The combination of Swift's hint, Addison's 'vision', and Steele's connection of the war and hence of fame to Marlborough, embodies the collaboration that went into the making of the *Tatler*. Without much evidence, Addison is seen as responsible for the *Tatler's* transition to single paper-length essays rather than the individual departments of the early papers, and perhaps also for the disappearance of the news. The abandonment of Steele's persistent motto, Juvenal's 'Quidquid agunt Homines nostri Farrago Libelli',[58] for different mottoes for each essay is often attributed to Addison's classical bent. Whether Addison or Steele was responsible, new mottoes are appropriate to a series of individual essays, and the earlier motto from Juvenal serves a paper in which each issue is made up of separate essays and reports.

Addison may well have been responsible for some or all of the changes in the *Tatler*. But Steele did not need to rely on Addison for classical mottoes (presumably he found his own for his *Spectator* papers), and the natural movement of frequent publication is towards single essays. At the outset the possibilities of material may have seemed endless and the paper could evolve in the direction of audience interest. But the task of keeping tabs on a variety of areas and writing about them with some regularity became burdensome, especially if readers were more interested in Bickerstaff's whimsical reflections and ethical advice. It became easier to write a paper-length essay on a single subject rather than a series of different essays and reports. The structure remained open enough to accommodate letters, notes and other contributions.

More important than the particular changes, topics and hints that might have been suggested by Swift and Addison is the openness of the *Tatler* itself. Steele developed, out of the pieces of earlier periodicals, a series that was malleable, shifting, encompassing and experimental. It could adopt a variety of genres, address a wide range of subjects and speak in a number of different voices. It could be written by different authors and was attractive to various audiences. It can be viewed as a series of experiments – some of which were dropped or neglected as the paper's identity became clearer. Among the experiments that returned at different times and in different ways was Steele's defence of Marlborough as a great British hero and of the Whig ministry as an able and worthy government. The *Tatler* was interesting in material and attractive in tone throughout, and some of its best and most memorable papers were not surpassed by later periodicals.

3 THE *SPECTATOR'S* POLITICS OF INDIRECTION

Much of the recent commentary on the *Spectator* has emphasized one or more of three overlapping approaches. The *Spectator* is seen as the prime example of Jürgen Habermas's concept of the 'bourgeois public sphere', with particular attention to the effect of print and to the institution of the coffeehouse. A second tendency of some criticism has been to read the *Spectator* against the grain, finding it advancing ideas that it renounces and illustrating practices that it rejects. A third tendency, far more prevalent, has been to mine the *Spectator* for material on a particular topic, or set of topics, of interest to modern readers. None of these approaches can be dismissed out of hand, and all have produced interesting results, but none, alas, is of particular use to the political biographer, whose approach is skewed by concern for a person and for the specific nature of his politics.

The connection of the *Spectator* to the bourgeois public sphere was first made in English by Terry Eagleton in 1984.[1] 'The bourgeois public sphere', Habermas wrote,

> may be conceived above all as the sphere of private people come together as a public; they soon claimed the public sphere regulated from above against the public authorities themselves, to engage them in a debate over the general rules governing relations in the basically privatized but publicly relevant sphere of commodity exchange and social labour.[2]

The 'bourgeois public sphere' is an intellectual construct that postulates connections among the development of capitalism, the emergence of new methods of transmitting information and of social institutions that allowed access to it, and shifts in the configuration of class structure. In England, during the reign of Queen Anne, the bourgeois public sphere was effected by the democratic access to discourse practised in coffeehouses and recorded in literary periodicals, pre-eminently the *Spectator*, which 'worked toward the spread of tolerance, the emancipation of civic morality from moral theology, and of practical wisdom from the philosophy of scholars. The public that read and debated this sort of thing read and debated about itself'.[3]

Although references to the bourgeois public sphere have become something of a cliché of scholarship on the *Spectator*, some recent scholarship has sought to modify, correct or even deny the concept. J. A. Downie looked at a series of key pronouncements by Habermas about the eighteenth-century public sphere, every one of which he found insubstantial or simply wrong. He asserts that Habermas antedates the arrival of the industrial bourgeois, and that he is seriously mistaken in his assertion that periodicals and coffeehouses provided an open association regardless of wealth, rank and status.[4] Brian Cowan similarly refutes the utopian qualities of the bourgeois public sphere: 'Properly understood in the mental world of the *Spectator* project, the coffeehouse was not the practical realization of the Habermasian public sphere, it was rather the seat of a whole host of anxieties about proper behavior in that public space'.[5] The formal association of topical papers in the *Tatler* with London coffeehouses indicates the degree to which by the early eighteenth century coffee houses had become specialized in their functions and clientele, rather than functioning as an open, classless, unrestricted space for exchange.[6] Erin Skye Mackie expresses reservations about the factuality of the bourgeois public sphere but seeks to retain it as a useful construct nonetheless.[7]

The bourgeois public sphere has become a vague idea that tends to disappear on closer inspection but that remains temptingly useful when one wants to move from specific historical or literary detail to larger generalizations about a period or about the historical changes associated with that period. In many cases alternative constructs may be available, and the public sphere may be a mask that hides the more rapid, more complex, and more various changes that are actually taking place. The concept seems particularly ill-suited to political biography, which requires greater precision and which must trace frequent – sometimes daily or weekly – changes in events, issues and reactions, both in personal life and in political writing.

A further interpretive possibility, independent of the bourgeois private sphere but sometimes combined with it, is to read the *Spectator* against the grain, to see it as representing ideas and values that are precisely those that it explicitly denies. This procedure is not as irrational as might first appear, for the movement of ideas is driven by social forces that individual authors do not control and sometimes do not recognize. This approach is developed with particular force and sophistication by Erin Mackie.

> *The Tatler* and *The Spectator* ultimately seek to manage the world from a perspective at once in and out of the world. And, to be sure, the papers, like Mr. Spectator himself, exist both inside and outside of the world of commerce. For although many objects of their reform are products of the commercialized markets of culture and fashion, and although they seek to reform the values and behavior that a commercialized society seems to encourage, the papers also derive much of their success from

their status as best-sellers on the periodical market. They are themselves fashionable life-style magazines and win their place as the most prestigious arbiters of taste and manners by virtue of successful marketing. Thus they depend upon the very commercialization and commodification they warn against.[8]

Setting aside the tendency towards tautology masking as causality (the papers are successful because they are bestsellers), and the habit of describing eighteenth-century periodicals in question-begging modern language (as 'fashionable life-style magazines'), the argument presents a seemingly inescapable paradox. The *Spectator* insists that following popular fashions is an irrational exercise in superficiality, but it seeks to become a popular fashion itself and to make fashionable the behaviour it urges. But this is a paradox only because two different senses of fashion are being conflated: fashion as the expression of consensus on moral values and fashion as the superficial display of publicly identifying behaviour or commodities. The *Spectator* exemplifies the first and warns against improper manifestations of the second. Reading against the grain interprets the *Spectator* as an example of values and practices it rejects and has as its subject those values and practices rather than the *Spectator* itself.

Many of the topical approaches to the *Spectator* are illustrated by the essays collected in *The Spectator: Emerging Discourses*. In addition to Erin Skye Mackie's essay on the public sphere cited above, Terence Bowers sees the *Spectator*'s public sphere as an extension of Shaftesbury's ideas of sociability and politeness, as these are elucidated by Lawrence E. Klein.[9] But the *Spectator*'s politeness is redefined from Renaissance courtliness to become an expression of inner virtue. This concept of politeness, Bowers contends, enlarges the audience enfranchised (socially if not politically) by the *Spectator*'s moral instruction and explains its continued popularity in the eighteenth century.[10] The *Spectator* has been most fruitfully explored for its self-consciousness in addressing an audience that included women, for its efforts to speak to them about domestic topics, and for its inability to shed its patriarchal character in doing so.[11] Brycchan Carey analyses the *Spectator*'s various representations of the colonial world.[12]

Two problems of these approaches face the political biographer. (1) Most obviously, the *Spectator* is mainly characterized by the range of its topics, the variety of voices it includes, and the rapidity with which it shifts from topic to topic and voice to voice. Singling out particular topics, however useful in itself, is less valuable in characterizing the *Spectator* as a whole, unless means can be found to connect such particularities to broader ideas and attitudes. Moreover, the reign of Queen Anne developed a variety of codes to hide, reveal and insinuate political meaning, and the *Spectator*, I shall argue, utilized such codes beneath the pretense of avoiding political discourse altogether. (2) Biography is the elucidation of changes limited by and to the lifetime of an individual. For much of the time, therefore, it operates on a much smaller scale than that of cultural generalizations. Concepts such as the 'bourgeois public sphere' need a larger frame of reference than the difference between 1713 and 1715, although that difference turns out to be quite significant in the life of Steele. The effects of time minutely measured are important for texts as well. The *Tatler* changed quite significantly over the 21 months of its appearance. The *Guardian*, as we shall see, changed as sharply, if for different reasons. These personal, political and literary shifts need to be measured by more exact instruments than the large generalizations, useful as they may be in other respects, that Steele's periodicals have been asked to serve by recent scholarship. But the *Spectator* did not undergo the radical evolution of the *Tatler* and *Guardian*, and its stability must have derived from a broader and more effective process of planning after the *Tatler* closed.

One can easily imagine that the two months following the close of the *Tatler* were spent in wide and intense deliberations about the shape and nature of the *Spectator*. Whatever arrangement Steele might have made with Harley about the closure of the *Tatler*, it is likely to have shaped the *Spectator*. Steele may well have suggested to Harley that he would drop the *Tatler* in favour of a new, less overtly political paper, coauthored by Addison, and focusing on manners, morality and literature rather than politics. Harley might have welcomed such a periodical as a counterweight to the High-Church, ultra-Tory position associated with Sacheverell and supported by St John. In the period following the supposed conversation between Harley and Steele in mid-October, a Parliament with a decidedly Tory majority was returned, Swift became editor of the Tory *Examiner* but was opposed by the *Medley*, edited by Arthur Maynwaring, for the Whigs.[13] Harley began secret peace negotiations with France (running counter even to Tory propaganda) and, still more important, news reached London of General Stanhope's defeat at Brihuega in Spain, seriously undercutting Whig hopes for 'No Peace Without Spain'. Harley's efforts to arrange a centrist ministry operating from a broad consensus were frustrated, and in February 1711 the ultra-Tory October Club began what amounted to a campaign against the moderate Harley position. In the context of the difficult line he was seeking to walk, Harley may well have encouraged a general Whig periodical that was not so much non-partisan as anti-partisan.

Addison and Steele would have sought Whig advice as well. They certainly would have consulted Arthur Maynwaring, a principal political advisor to the Duchess of Marlborough and the primary organizer, writer and reviser of Whig propaganda.[14] They probably would have talked as well with his assistant John Oldmixon. Maynwaring and Oldmixon had, in early August, begun the *Medley*, a Whig paper designed to respond to the *Examiner*, and Maynwaring superintended, wrote and edited a flurry of pamphlets in the summer and autumn of 1710, particularly *Four Letters to a Friend in North Britain*, which defended Parliament's case against Sacheverell, attacked Sacheverell's high-flying position, and deplored the consequences of the trial.[15] Francis Hare, Marlborough's Chaplain, produced a series of four 'management tracts', the first dated 23 November, 1710, that defended Marlborough's conduct of the war by answering Tory claims that peace could have been concluded much earlier, that Spain had been neglected, that Flanders was an ill-chosen theatre of war, and that Marlborough prolonged the war for his own interest.[16] Heinz-Joachim Müllenbrock points out that Whigs sought to establish the correctness of present war policy by reference to parliamentary resolutions and similar documents.[17] Addison and Steele may have talked as well with members of the Whig Junto and other leading Whigs to whom volumes of the collected edition of the *Spectator* were later dedicated: John, Lord Somers; Charles Montagu, Lord Halifax; Henry Boyle; the Duke of Marlborough; Thomas, Earl of Wharton; Charles Spenser, Earl of Sunderland; Paul Methuen. They would have talked with Samuel Buckley and Jacob Tonson, who were prominent Whig booksellers and the *Spectator's* publishers, and other literary associates of Addison and Steele – some potential contributors, others keen observers of the literary, theatrical and political scene.[18] Although the exact scope and nature of consultation is a matter of speculation, two points are clear: the *Spectator* was a part of a full arsenal of Whig propaganda, and it was in several respects a cooperative enterprise. It had two principle writers and a number of secondary ones; it invited and embraced participation, usually in the form of letters; and it represented the interests of political leaders. The connections between Whig politicians and Whig writers embodied by the Kit-Cat Club and revivified by Addison's establishment of Button's Coffee House in March 1712, were joined and expressed on the pages of the *Spectator*.

One can only infer the results of such consultations from the actual nature of the *Spectator* itself. Unlike the *Tatler*, which seemed to evolve as topics and approaches proved successful or as Steele's interests shifted and developed, the *Spectator* remained fairly constant throughout. It thus seemed the result of conscious planning rather than evolving discovery, as was the *Tatler*. The *Tatler* was a relative failure as a political paper, however successful it may have been in other respects. On one hand, it was not sufficiently focused on specific political controversy to have much impact, but, on the other hand, it attracted opposing criticism that undermined its cultural functions. The *Tatler's* function to support the ministry and, specifically, to celebrate the triumphs of Marlborough meant that much of its political propaganda took the form of patriotism – the celebration of national achievements. In contrast, the *Spectator* had to function from a position of relative political powerlessness. It could not control the political agenda, and the genial conversational tone, speaking from a moral consensus, that the *Tatler* had established as a defining characteristic was hardly appropriate to the kind of reactive attacks that a party out of power needs to make. But Whigs already had an effective attacker in the person of Maynwaring and an informed defender of Marlborough's policies in Francis Hare. The *Spectator* was one half of an apparent split in the Whig propaganda machine – the specifically political half belonging to Maynwaring and his colleagues, and the generally cultural half belonging to the *Spectator*.

It is likely that discussions among Addison and Steele and their allies in the winter of 1710–11 established the tone and direction of the *Spectator* as anti-partisan and politically indirect, and determined that the responsibility for the subtly generalized treatment of politics should, for the most part, rest with the circumspect Addison rather than the impetuous Steele. Addison and Steele must have agreed in the months between the termination of the *Tatler* and the inception of the *Spectator* that they would roughly share the substantial burden of providing papers for a periodical that appeared six times each week, and that each would supply a substantial series of papers during periods when the other was busy with other matters, so that the burden would be shared equally without tying either editor down to a regular and unrelieved schedule. But a pattern of alternative days developed that corresponded to the two printers (Tonson and Buckley) who were needed to produce the papers. Out of the first run of 555 numbers, Addison wrote 249 and Steele 251.[19] They must also have contacted other potential contributors – Eustace Budgell, John Hughes, Thomas Tickell and Alexander Pope. Other contributors emerged as the periodical developed. Still, the bulk of the papers were by Addison or Steele. (The first substantial contribution seems to be Budgell's paper on dancing, *Spectator*, no. 67.) In addition to writing political papers, Addison famously wrote the serious and theoretical literary criticism and his series of 'Saturday sermons' and other moral or philosophical papers. These contributions gave a depth to the periodical and its eponymous spokesman that, in turn, established his authority to speak about other topics. Steele wrote papers on the theatre, on manners and on various social oddities and characters. He also put together a number of papers based on letters, often real but sometimes concocted by the editors themselves. These were a particularly useful way of introducing topics and problems that were ostensibly rooted in the actual experience of readers. Thomas Tickell claimed, plausibly enough, that Addison and Steele worked independently, not showing their papers to the other before sending them to be printed.[20] But, of course, each could respond to the other's paper after printing. It was a cooperative arrangement but not a collaborative one, and it worked well for producing a long and intensive series of essays of high quality.

The Framework of the *Spectator*

The framework of the series rested on two fictional supports. The first, and most important was the character of the eidolon, or fictional conductor of the paper, Mr Spectator himself. His lack of a proper name suggests his function as the embodiment of the paper rather than a mask of its two authors, although he possesses the short face of Steele and the taciturnity of Addison. His inability to talk in company compels him to communicate in print and to use the devices of booksellers, of hawkers, of subscriptions, and of coffeehouses to reach a public far greater than he could by speech. The character of Mr Spectator is introduced by Addison in the first paper. Coming from a 'small hereditary Estate', educated at the University, learned in foreign languages, extensively travelled ('I made a Voyage to *Grand Cairo*, on purpose to take a measure of a Pyramid'), he now lives in London, where he frequents coffeehouses, theatres and other places of business and entertainment, all the while remaining silent.

> Thus I live in the World, rather as a Spectator of Mankind, than as one of the Species; by which means I have made myself a Speculative Statesman, Soldier, Merchant, and Artizan, without ever medling with any Practical Part in Life.

He adds that 'I have never espoused any Party with Violence, and am resolved to observe an exact Neutrality between the Whigs and Tories, unless I shall be forc'd to declare my self by the Hostilities of either side'. Addison begins the periodical by describing a character who combines attractive eccentricity with a capacity to absorb and reflect on the great variety of learning and experience. In fact, that breadth of absorption is Mr Spectator's major and defining eccentricity.[21]

Steele was responsible for describing the 'club' in *Spectator*, no. 2. He provides no context, other than what Addison had provided in no. 1. He begins by announcing that 'the first of our Society is a Gentleman of *Worcestershire*' and ends his description of the unnamed clergyman by admitting that 'these are my ordinary Companions'. Steele describes six members of the Club: Sir Roger de Coverley, the bumbling but good-natured Tory squire who is the most prominent, most featured and most loveable of club members; the unnamed Templar who ought to be studying law but actually studies the London theater; Sir Andrew Freeport, a Whig merchant whose sensible enthusiasm for the value of trade speaks for the *Spectator* itself; Captain Sentry, a retired military officer perhaps modelled on Steele, who had himself been a sentry; and finally an unnamed clergyman. These characters have various possible functions. One can think of them as authors of papers, or at least as contributors to them. One can think of them as the envisioned audience of papers. One can think of them as standing for the categories of material that the *Spectator* will cover: the Templar for papers of criticism and theatrical review; the clergyman for Addison's 'Sunday sermons', Will Honeycomb (if somewhat improbably) for papers on women and courtship. Captain Sentry seems to stand for the moderate and appropriate exercise of manly virtues; he discusses the nature of military courage in no. 152. His presence suggests a sentry-like watchfulness against enemy encroachments.

(*Spectator*, no. 165, complaining of the overuse of French words in military descriptions suggests Captain Sentry as an interested member of its audience. In no. 350 he discourses on the relation of courage to magnanimity.)

The most important members of the club are Sir Roger and Andrew Freeport, and their introduction establishes a dominant mode of political discourse in the *Spectator* – dialectic rather than diatribe, discussion rather than dissertation. Dialogue was often utilized as a political genre in the debates that marked the 1710 election and the negotiations of peace.[22] What differentiates the dialogue of the Club from these more direct political dialogues is that indirect political controversy is covered, checked and modified by the interaction of characters who represent groups of people without being reduced to the flat qualities that identify those groups. They are more complex, and they care for one another, despite their political differences. Roger de Coverley and Andrew Freeport are not Jack High and Will Low. But they are ideal vehicles for a periodical that wants to continue the political argument while insisting upon civility.

Deliberations of the full club are rarely reported, and when they are, it is Addison who reports them. The members gather in no. 34 to consider the appropriate targets of satire, in response to reader complaints about the *Spectator*'s attacks. The members predictably insist that the class or category they represent should not be mocked. Mr Spectator finds that 'every Subject of my Speculations was taken away from me by one or other of the Club'. Fortunately, the Clergyman insists that 'Vice and Folly ought to be attacked wherever they could be met with', especially if they are encountered 'in high and conspicuous Stations of Life'. The Club meets again in no. 99, where they discuss the topic of honour (courage in men, chastity in women), but the club is only used as a device to introduce the topic. The club and its members also function as a potential chorus commenting on events or behaviour. The dropping-away of its various members signals the close of the periodical itself: the Clergyman meditates on his illness and approaching death in no. 513, and the death of Sir Roger is reported in no. 517. No. 530 climaxes the *Spectator*'s series of papers on marriage by announcing the marriage of Will Honeycomb and his retirement to the country. Sir Andrew Freeport also retires to the country, where he announces he will cultivate his estate by the mercantile principles of investment in labour and careful utilization of resources (no. 549). The close of the *Spectator* comes with the death or disappearance of club members in ways that reinforce some of its main thematic concerns: the wise follies (or foolish wisdom) of Tories, the essential consonance of good economic and good agricultural practices (a natural husbandry that governs both Addison's papers on horticulture and Steele's on economics), and the importance of marriage, not only as a basic institution of society but as an essential personal relationship.

Particularly in the early papers the Spectator Club serves as a model for similar clubs. Addison describes a variety of these in *Spectator*, no. 9. Steele introduces
the Ugly Club in no. 17 in a letter from Alexander Carbuncle, who describes the
'Quearity' of aspect and 'Gibbosity' of physique required for membership. Mr.
Spectator himself is invited to join the Ugly Club (no. 32), and in no. 52 letters
from the Ugly Club propose a marriage for him with his personal opposite – a
long-headed garrulous Pictish woman (referring to women who paint their faces,
as did the ancient Picts). An Ugly Club emerges at Cambridge, and other clubs
make their presence felt – an Amorous Club at Oxford (no. 30), the Loungers
at Cambridge (no. 54), Addison's 'Everlasting Club' (no. 52), a She-Romp Club
(possibly by Budgell) in no. 217, and Steele's Lazy Club in no. 320.

More important than the proliferation of clubs is the extension of the
Spectator Club's dialectic through the frequent insertion of letters, a tactic the
Spectator derives from the *Tatler* and, more remotely, from such journals as
Defoe's *Review* and John Dunton's *Athenian Mercury*. [23] The letters cover a wide
variety of material. Some simply suggest topics, present relevant personal anecdotes, or ask questions that stimulate Mr Spectator's answer. Some provide essays
more-or-less similar to those of Mr Spectator. Many serve as effective vehicles for
the fiction of the paper, presenting interesting characters – sometimes rounded
and sometimes exemplary – and narrating compelling stories.[24] Greg Polly sees
the relation of letters (and therefore readers) to Mr Spectator as analogous to the
political contract between citizens and rulers.[25] Letters enable and extend the
Spectator's dialogue with its readers, and they give those readers a sense of actuality that strengthens the paper's credibility and authority. Eve Tavor Bannet, in a
thoughtful discussion of letters as conversational models and vehicles for instruction, points out that 'letters could be written on any topic about which a person
might discourse while he or she was present, in any style considered appropriate
to the topic or topics she or he chose'.[26] Addison takes up the topic of letters late
in the run, admits that Mr Spectator is the author of many of them, and gives five
reasons for this way of doing things. (1) He wants to try out material without
admitting its authorship. (2) He wants to 'extort a little Praise from such who
will never applaud any thing whose Author is known and certain'. (3) He wants
to introduce 'a great variety of Characters'. (4) He wants to avoid responsibility
for 'ludicrous Compositions'. (5) He wants to use letters to introduce 'additional
Reflections' (*Spectator*, no. 542; see also no. 271).

These three elements constitute the vehicle for *Spectator*'s presentation: Mr
Spectator is the silent observer and the embodiment of print, the club represents
the range of readers and the broad categories of topics, and letters extend the
scope of authorship and serve as the vehicle connecting the periodical and its
readers. These three elements are accompanied by an occasional but informative
self-consciousness that helps to define the paper further and to remind read-

ers of its essential moral function. Since the topics of its essays are so various, these reminders are a useful guide to the process and purposes of reading. *Spectator*, no. 10 makes Addison's famous claim to his readers that he has resolved 'to refresh their Memories from Day to Day, till I have recovered them out of that desperate State of Vice and Folly into which the Age is fallen' and that he is 'ambitious to have it said of me, that I have brought Philosophy out of Closets and Libraries, Schools and Colleges, to dwell in Clubs and Assemblies, at Tea-Table, and in Coffee-Houses', a statement that is notable both for its lofty goals and for its slightly comic pretension. Addison goes on to categorize his readers with a similar humour. Ironic overstatement seems characteristic of Addison's comic style, just as affable good-humour is typical of Steele's.

Addison is the author of most of the *Spectator*'s self-conscious or programmatic papers. In No. 124 he describes the nature of the essay, contrasts essays with books, and notes, about his '*rural Speculations*', that readers have 'made up separate Sets of them, as they have done before of those relating to Wit, to Operas, to Points of Morality, or Subjects of Humour'. No. 179 describes the audience of the *Spectator*, with its Mercurial and Saturnine readers, and the various papers appropriate to it. No. 221 explains the opening mottoes and is whimsically misleading about the closing initials. In no. 262 Mr Spectator congratulates himself on including no news, no politics or 'Stroke of Party', no obscenity, no inappropriate ridicule and satire, no scandal and no defamation. He explains, in no. 355, the considerations that allow him to resist personal attacks on others in response to their attacks on him and adds, somewhat cattily, 'that the Work wou'd have been of very little use to the Publick, had it been filled with Personal Reflections and Debates'. In *Spectator*, no. 451 he pursues and intensifies the argument: scurrility and calumny are rampant, and 'every dirty Scribler is countenanced by great Names, whose Interests he propagates by such vile and infamous Methods'. The result is the degradation of literary polemic: 'Our Satyr is nothing but Ribaldry and *Billingsgate*. Scurrility passes for Wit; and he who can call Names in the greatest Variety of Phrases, is looked upon to have the shrewdest Pen'. Readers of such trash share the blame not only with the writer but the government that allows it. In the next paper Addison complains about the curiosity of the public for news that is concocted by half-a-dozen writers who all receive the same dispatches from abroad, and this complaint introduces a letter from an unnamed author (actually Alexander Pope) suggesting that this curiosity might as well be satisfied by local village trivia as by foreign news. In no. 445 Addison reflects whimsically on the new tax on paper and its consequent effect on the price of periodicals. He accurately anticipates the demise of many of his rivals and insists that he will stay in business, noting that the tax on the half-sheets on which the *Spectator* is printed will substantially support the government.

It may have been another of Steele's mysterious devices to conceal Addison's authorship, but after the series of self-conscious authorial remarks by Addison, it is Steele who makes the final comment of the original run and signs his own name to the paper. He is careful, however, not only to acknowledge Addison's participation (in terms so clear as to point directly to him) but to specify the particular papers he wrote:

> All the Papers marked with a C, an L, an I, or an O, that is to say, all the Papers which I have distinguished by any Letter in the name of the Muse *CLIO*, were given me by the Gentleman, of whose Assistance I formerly boasted in the Preface and concluding Leaf of my *Tatlers*. (*Spectator*, no. 555).

He goes on to credit the other contributors, to brag about the *Spectator*'s circulation and to thank his readers for their support. Despite the fact that he now takes credit for the periodical, it was Addison who all along articulated its nature and goals, but in doing so he doubtless followed a set of principles that emerged from the discussions of the two authors between the close of the *Tatler* and the opening of the *Spectator*.

Neutrality and Generalization

The appropriate role for the *Spectator* as an excluded organ of propaganda was non-partisan, or, more specifically, anti-partisan. Following the line taken in the *Tatler*, it argued that political controversy, with its inevitable personal attacks, was unworthy of rational people and less important than concern for art, literature, theatre and morality. Like the *Tatler*, the *Spectator* saw Whiggism as an intrinsic element of the public and even private values it articulated. Given the age's ambivalence about the private discussion of politics, an ambivalence manifested by the *Tatler*'s mockery of public interest in newspapers, the *Spectator* sought to give greater weight to matters of social behaviour, but it did so in ways that engaged political elements. Just as the age was seeking, and Steele's social periodicals are examples of this, a way to talk publicly about private and even intimate aspects of life, it sought ways to extend political dialogue beyond name-calling, unverifiable arguments about the facts, and selective readings of an opponent's argument.

> While the *Examiner* was revealing the peculations of the Duke of Marlborough and attacking the unreliability of the allies, the *Spectator* proposed a less contentious mode of discourse, extolled the advantages of trade, and subtly suggested that the major danger to the Church was not the impeachment of Sacheverell but the hypocritical piety of worshippers.[27]

One tool of the consequent indirection was the political exploitation of the club. The disagreements of Sir Roger and Sir Andrew are a relatively direct manifestation of political difference, but Sir Roger himself, as has often been noted, is a lovable Tory whose intelligence and personality does not equip him to govern.[28] Mr Spectator, who writes but does not speak, becomes an image of this indirection and an invitation to readers to see the more specific political application of his general points. This indirection seems particularly appropriate to a party out of power, especially one that, like the Whigs, had established close connection with the Queen's likely successor. Harley initially sought to govern from the middle but was forced to the right by St John and the October Club. The *Spectator* sought to insinuate itself into that middle ground by claiming to renounce politics and political faction while referring frequently to political matters but at an apolitical level of generality.

This method of indirection works effectively for attacks on individuals, who need not be named but merely described. Addison and Steele surely knew that a major writer for the Tories was their friend Jonathan Swift, but it is unclear at precisely what point their suspicions became confirmed knowledge. His authorship may not have been apparent until May or June 1711.[29] But on 27 March Addison claimed that

> There is nothing that more betrays a base, ungenerous Spirit, than the giving of secret Stabs to a Man's Reputation. Lampoons and Satyrs that are written with Wit and Spirit, are like poison'd Darts, which not only inflict a Wound, but make it incurable. For this Reason I am very much troubled when I see the Talents of Humour and Ridicule in the Possession of an ill-natured Man (*Spectator*, no. 23).

Contemporaries saw the paper as a 'Character of Dr. Swift', although the *Spectator* certainly did not say it was.[30] Having established the pattern of unnamed but effective attack, Mr Spectator, in another unmistakable reference to Swift, claims that 'Nothing that is not a real Crime makes a Man appear so contemptible and little in the Eyes of the World as Inconstancy, especially when it regards Religion or Party' (*Spectator*, no. 162). Swift's satire and his political inconstancy are both indications of disrespect for personal and political integrity and suggest a lack of commitment to the truth. But, as Swift probably recognized, the attacks were at such a general level that they could not be answered.

On the positive side, a similar indirection characterizes the *Spectator*'s defence of the Duke of Marlborough. Marlborough was under blatant attack in the summer and autumn of 1711, most blatantly in Swift's *The Conduct of the Allies*.[31] In *Spectator*, nos. 125 and 126, on the evils of political factions, Addison applies his argument specifically but indirectly to Marlborough when he complains of 'wild *Tartars*, who are ambitious of destroying a Man of the most extraordinary Parts and Accomplishments', such as the 'great Man' about whom Will Wimble has heard 'strange stories' (*Spectator*, no. 126). In *Spectator*, no. 139 Steele points more clearly at Marlborough when he claims that greatness requires 'the

Prince's favour', and is enhanced by 'Sovereignty over some Foreign Territory'. (As a reward for his Blenheim victory, Emperor Leopold gave Marlborough the Principality of Mindelheim.) After this indirect toying, Steele makes the identification clear: 'these Sketches and faint Images of Glory were drawn in *August* 1711, when *John*, Duke of *Marlborough* made that memorable March wherein he took the *French* lines without Blood-shed'.[32] The *Spectator* does not undertake the difficult task of responding to Tory charges of Marlborough's peculation but introduces a careful understatement of his reputation and most recent brilliant achievement.

In *Spectator*, no. 262, which significantly appeared on 31 December 1711, the date on which Marlborough was dismissed and Queen Anne created twelve new peers to assure passage of the Treaty of Utrecht in Lords, Mr Spectator points out that the paper 'draws Mens Minds off from the Bitterness of Party', and that he is 'so very scrupulous in this Particular of not hurting any Man's Reputation, that I have forborn mentioning even such Authors as I could not name with Honour'. Mr Spectator seeks to focus on broad questions of personal and public behaviour rather than the nasty details of political attack. 'The strategy was to outflank the opponent and to threaten an encounter on a higher ground of one's own choosing. The *Spectator*'s manoeuvering, like Marlborough's military tactics in 1711, sought to achieve victory without the expense of battle'.[33]

The Fiction of Consensus

Addison directly articulated the *Spectator*'s social purpose – to reform society through good humour, exemplary discourse and the spread of knowledge – and more subtly implied its political function – to combat the rancour of partisan politics while suggesting its own Whig alliance, taking a whiggish position on a number of social and economic questions, and suggesting that the polite and useful member of society must also be a Whig. He defined the genre of the periodical essay by describing its circulation, its means of distribution, its place at coffeehouse and tea-table (*Spectator*, no. 10), and by discussing the mixture of method and spontaneity, of written and oral culture, that formed the nature of the essay (*Spectator*, no. 124). He identified the saturnine and mercurial elements of the audience to whom such essays were addressed and instructed them on their roles in perceiving connections, grouping and collecting essays, responding to them by letters that he might print and by carrying out the advice that they contained. The *Spectator* developed the characteristics of genre and production that enabled it to comment on a widely diverse body of material and to distribute it to an unusually heterogeneous audience.

The superficial impression given by the *Spectator* is that this audience is harmonious – prosperous gentlemen laughing in the coffeehouse at the minor eccentricities of their neighbours and genteel women smiling at the foolish husbands Mr Spectator describes and nodding their heads at his advice. But the notion that the *Spectator* speaks of and to an audience which, despite its differences, is united in most of its values, so that eccentrics are forced to the margins, is itself a fiction that is created and maintained by Addison and Steele. It is useful to think of the *Spectator* as a response to the events immediately preceding it and the events that took place during its run – to the trial of Henry Sacheverell, to the riots accompanying it and the celebrations that followed, to the election of a Tory majority in Commons and a subsequent change of ministry, to the defeat of British troops in Spain and to the death of Joseph II of Austria, with their effects on British foreign policy, to the progress of the war and the politics of the peace.[34]

The Tories rode to victory on the cry of 'The Church in Danger', despite the misgivings of some Tory politicians, Harley in particular, about the fanaticism that the motto expressed. The primary fear of the Sacheverellites, particularly those who were not out-and-out Jacobites, was that his conviction would mean the end of the church's ability to speak independently and forthrightly about the major issues of the state and hence would mean the silencing the church on those issues where religion and politics overlap (or could be pushed together). It is hard for a modern secularist to understand the depth of emotion that the 'Church in danger' stimulated, but it becomes easier if one sees the phrase as covering a sequence of connected fears that pose threats more deeply unsettling. The appeal of Sacheverell's position becomes more apparent if one sees it as a defence of patriarchy, especially the idea advanced by Sir Robert Filmer in the seventeenth century that order and hierarchy in human (and divine) society is characterized at a number of levels by the relationship of father to child. God is our father and we his children; we are the inheritors of the sin of Adam, the father of humankind. The monarch is the father of his people, who must obey him and cannot replace him, any more than they can replace their biological fathers. The strength of this notion lies in the power, emotional if only analogical, with which it connects and justifies most social relations. But it relies particularly on the authority of the father within the ordinary family. It was precisely this authority that was being undermined both by changes in theories of government and by shifts in the experience of families.

A number of immediate concerns are expressed in the extensive pamphleteering of 1711 and 1712. (1) On one hand was concern for the prolongation of the war, with its expenses in lives lost and taxes paid; on the other was concern that a convenient peace would allow France to keep Spain and its dominance of Europe, thus wasting ten years of military effort. Tracts and pamphlets, many stimulated by Swift's *The Conduct of the Allies* for the Tories and by Hare's *The Management of the War* for the Whigs, focused on the Treaty of Utrecht and on the attendant charges that the allies, particularly the Dutch, had acted dishonourably and that Marlborough had acted rapaciously. (2) On one hand was fear that the doctrine and discipline of the Church were being undermined by freethinkers, latitudinarians, and dissenters; on the other hand was the sense that the freedom to worship according to the dictates of one's conscience was being prevented by a narrow and self-interested clergy. The Test-Act was a measure that was unsatisfactory to both sides – allowing easy hypocrisy in the eyes of the Church but imposing on conscience in the eyes of dissenters. (3) The problem of succession presented both sides with uncomfortable paradoxes: James III was a direct heir of the Stuarts, but he was Roman Catholic; the House of Hanover (at this point still headed by the Electress Sophia) was comfortably Protestant but even more foreign than even William had been. George, Sophia's successor, spoke little English. Both sides sought the support of Queen Anne, who recognized the parliamentary establishment of Hanover but was understandably reluctant to discuss a successor. On one hand passive acceptance of the absolute power of the monarch was necessary to the good order of society, which would otherwise split into competing interests; on the other hand the power to resist the monarch was necessary to prevent the eccentric tyrannies of an arrogant King, tyrannies that the reign of James II amply illustrated. (4) Finances for the war depended to a large degree on the managerial skill of Sidney Godolphin, and with his replacement fears for public credit gripped the financial community. Tories, in defence, argued that '*Publick Credit* is the Consequence of honourable, just, and punctual Management in the Matter of *Funds*, and *Taxes*, or *Loans* upon them', and that responsibility for protecting public credit rests not only with particular ministers but with the Queen and Parliament.[35] But fear is an emotion not easy to dispel, and the Officers of the Bank of England appealed to the Queen directly, unusually and unsuccessfully to keep Godolphin in office.

The Indirection of Metonymy: The Family

Deeper uncertainties, often not articulated in the pamphlet wars, lay beneath the surface of the patriarchal theory articulated by Sacheverell. One problem was that of the family itself. Restoration rakery, especially as celebrated by the plays of Wycherley, Etherege, Vanbrugh and Congreve, espoused (if that is the appropriate term) the notion that few women are any better than they should be and many men are anxious to make them worse. But this is hardly the male–female relationship envisioned in proper patriarchal theory of male dominance. It blurs the proper lines of inheritance, as exemplified by the inability of the Duke of Monmouth to succeed Charles II and the suspicion that James III was not the son of James II. But if the proper relation of a father to his family is not defined by the relation of God to his Church or the Monarch to his subjects; what prevents the family, like the unpatriarchal state, from become a chaos of conflicting interests and unbridled lusts? If the role of the wife is not merely childbearing and domestic servitude, what is it? Is the alternative to a strict patriarchal society a quasi-matriarchal one, in which domestic inheritance and political power remain with the husband but domestic affairs and the education of children are the exclusive duties of wives?

These uncertain domestic structures of power and authority are paralleled by a broader uncertainty of social structure, class and manners. The sequence of events of the last seventy-five years – the civil war and execution of the King, the unruly commonwealth, the Restoration, with its changes in manners and culture, the failed plots against Charles, the divisive reign of James and the invasion that brought it to an end, with its uneasy constitutional compromise, followed by twenty years of almost unceasing and interminable war with France – all created the sense that the basic structures of life lacked reliability.[36] If one sense of public instability lay in the intensity of conflicts among social and religious interests, another was the uncertainty created since the Commonwealth by the relatively rapid shifts in cultural, political and military events, policies and attitudes. This uncertainty was most immediately felt in the area of politics, and particularly succession, where the rival claims of inheritance and Parliamentary will were not fully resolved, but it was felt in private as well as public life. If inheritance, and hence patriarchy, loses its force as the justification of succession and the defining principle of monarchy, what happens to the authority of the father in the family? Without denying the religious source of patriarchal authority, the *Spectator* stresses the affective nature of family relations. What emerges is no less centred on the father and husband but has a very different quality.

Two rather different manifestations of the relation of marriage to the position of women occur in papers by Addison, and they define the *Spectator's* understanding of the politics of domesticity in ways that are in turn amplified and extended by Steele.[37] In no. 81, Addison's Mr Spectator, writing with characteristic whimsy, observes women arrayed in facing sideboxes of the Haymarket Theatre who have patches similarly arrayed on one side of their faces or the other. The location of these patches reflects the politics of their wearers. Mr Spectator takes great pleasure in the possibility that a committed partisan might actually have a mole on the politically incorrect side of her face. But the *Spectator's* major concern, here as in the past, is 'to expose this Party Rage in Women, as it only serves to aggravate the Hatreds and Animosities that rage among Men, and in a great measure deprive the Fair Sex of those peculiar Charms with which Nature has endowed them'. He goes on to insist that 'Female Virtues are of a Domestick turn. The Family is the proper Province for Private Women to Shine in' (*Spectator*, no. 81). This position was perhaps a delicate one to maintain, since the most virulent female partisan of the age was probably the Duchess of Marlborough, who was a principal and well-known supporter of the Whigs and Whig propaganda. But Steele echoes it some ten months later:

the utmost of a Woman's Character is contained in Domestick Life; she is Blameable or Praise-worthy according as her Carriage affects the House of her Father or her Husband. All she has to do in this World, is contained within the Duties of a Daughter, a Sister, a Wife, and a Mother. (*Spectator*, no. 342)

Politics is properly a masculine world, the *Spectator* contends, not because women cannot do it but because doing it distorts the essentially domestic nature of women as the servants of men.

But for men the nature of the domestic world is as essentially political as any follower of Filmer might hope. Addison's second defining paper of domestic politics comes late in the initial run but epitomizes the *Spectator's* celebration of male-dominated domesticity. In *Spectator*, no. 500, Philogamus specifically compares the joys of fatherhood to those of monarchical power.

You must have observed, in your Speculations on Human Nature, that nothing is more Gratifying to the Mind of Man than Power or Dominion, and this I think my self amply possessed of, as I am the Father of a Family. I am perpetually taken up in giving out Orders, in prescribing Duties, in hearing Parties, in administring Justice, and in distributing Rewards and Punishments ... In short, Sir, I look upon my Family as a Patriarchal Sovereignty, in which I am my self both King and Priest. All great Governments are nothing else but Clusters of these little private Royalties, and therefore I consider the Masters of Families as small Deputy-Governors presiding over the several little Parcels and Divisions of their Fellow Subjects.

His family gives him an outlet for his emotions and allows him to serve as the centre for the attentions of others. Philogamus takes pleasure in contemplating the various middle-class trades and professions by which his numerous sons will raise the status of the family. Addison has, in effect, turned the Filmerian analogy on its head: rather than the monarch resembling the First Father, reigning not only over Eve but over all nature, the father resembles the monarch in his controlling the destiny of his family and in reaping the rewards of his powerful position. But governments are only 'Clusters of these little private Royalties'.

A number of implications flow from this analogy. The affective life of the family, as ideally conceived – the love of spouses, the love of parents and children, but, most important, their mutual respect and concern for each other's well-being – becomes a close parallel to the ideal life of the state, with mutual (although, as in the case of families, not necessarily similar) respect among its constituent parts. The pleasure that Philogamus takes in his family and its prospects makes the familial model of the state seem attractive as well. And as the family grows and develops, its increasing fortunes are based on education and endeavour rather than inheritance. A wife and children are satisfying to men in ways that profligacy is not. 'I have very long entertained an Ambition to make

the Word *Wife* the most agreeable and delightful Name in Nature', Steele writes
late in the series (*Spectator*, no. 490). He goes on:

> Two Persons who have chosen each other out of all the Species, with Design to be each
> other's mutual Comfort and Entertainment, have in that Action bound themselves
> to be good-humour'd, affable, discreet, forgiving, patient, and joyful, with Respect to
> each other's Frailties and Perfections, to the End of their Lives.

The *Spectator*'s campaign for marriage resembles a political campaign, and like
a political campaign it stresses not only the advantages marriage brings but the
enemies of its proper functioning.

One of the many connections between the *Spectator*'s campaign for loving
and virtuous domesticity and its campaign for the rational and appropriate use
of wit comes in Steele's attack on George Etherege's *The Man of Mode* and especially on its central character, Dorimant. *Spectator*, no. 65 follows immediately
on Addison's series of papers on wit and seems to be a continuation of it. Steele
will turn to the theatre, he says, as 'the Seat of Wit' which 'has as strong an Effect
on the Manners of our Gentlemen, as the Taste of it has upon the Writings of
our Authors'. Etherege's play is considered 'the Pattern of Gentile Comedy'. But
Steele criticizes the characters for dishonest behaviour and uncouth language.
He denies

> that it is necessary to the Character of a Fine Gentleman, that he should in that man-
> ner trample upon all Order and Decency ... This whole celebrated Piece is a perfect
> Contradiction to good Manners, good Sense, and common Honesty; and as there is
> nothing in it but what is built upon the Ruin of Virtue and Innocence, according to
> the Notion of Merit in this Comedy, I take the Shoemaker to be, in reality, the Fine
> Gentleman of the Play.

In no. 75, Mr. Spectator admits that he has been attacked for calling Dorimant
a 'clown', and in his defence characterizes in general terms the real and positive
qualities of the fine gentleman: 'What is opposite to the eternal Rules of Reason
and Good Sense, must be excluded from any Place in the Carriage of a Well-
bred Man'. He concludes that 'to be Fine Gentleman, is to be a Generous and a
Brave Man'. A letter in no. 154 seems on the surface to dispute that judgment.
It recounts the story of the writer, a virtuous man who 'was forced to wench,
drink, play, and do every thing which are necessary to the Character of a Man
of Wit and Pleasure, to be well with the Ladies'. His fortuitous marriage to a
young woman of 'Innocence and Beauty' returns him to the life of happy virtue.
Two papers later, Steele contrasts the 'Woman's Man' to the 'Man of Sense' on
one hand, and the Fool on the other. The Woman's Man is distinguished by his
singularity, and his function is to entertain. He has 'that sort of good Breeding
which is exclusive of all Morality, and consists only in being publickly decent,

privately dissolute' (*Spectator*, no. 156). Steele, in paper after paper, proposes the life of domestic virtue as superior to that of the falsely reputed 'fine gentleman', and in so doing he elevates middle-class respectability above upper-class debauchery.

But middle-class values are not without drawbacks of their own. Too often the love of money triumphs over romantic love. The most famous instance is that of Inkle and Yarico (*Spectator*, no. 11), which is proposed by the virtuous Arietta as a counterweight to the story of the Ephesian matron in Petronius. Inkle is a young merchant in the West Indies whose ship is wrecked on an unexplored island. He is saved from the angry locals by the Indian woman Yarico, who eventually becomes his mistress. Eventually he is taken off the island by Europeans, and when he is back among the colonizers, his attitude towards Yarico, who is now pregnant, shifts. Where before she was his kindly rescuer and lover, she now becomes his commodity, and he sells her into slavery. Unlike the Ephesian matron, who was faithless, the Indian maiden was faithful. Money not love conquers in this case, and in others as well.[38]

In *Spectator*, no. 199, 'Statira' writes on 'the mercenary Practice of Men in the Choice of Wives'. She is in love with a man whose fortune is greater than her own, and she includes a letter expressing her love for him and giving him, in the first place, the imagined choice between having her as his mistress and having her as his wife. In the second place, she compares herself as wife to a much richer woman who also interests him. The mistress–marriage choice, setting aside the effects of her likely abandonment on herself, presents a contrast defined by the effects of time. The permanence of marriage allows her husband, she claims, to have access to deeper elements of her personality, particularly her gratitude and consequent loyalty, that her temporary encounter as a kept mistress would not allow. Marriage to a richer woman would merely shift the inequality of wealth from one gender to the other:

> She is in all things to have a Regard to the Fortune which she brought you, I to the Fortune to which you introduced me. The Commerce between you two will eternally have the Air of a Bargain, between us of a Friendship.

Here as elsewhere the balance of Steele's affectionate marriage favours the man, who is elevated by the gratitude of the woman for marrying her in the first place and by the superior fortune he brings to the match.

Statira raises the alternative of becoming a kept woman and thus introduces the issue of prostitution. Steele sees prostitutes not, primarily, as a threat to the relationship between husband and wife but as instances of the exploitation of women. The first major appearance of prostitutes in the *Spectator* occurs in no. 190, where Rebecca Nettletop, who describes herself as 'a poor strolling Girl about Town', writes a remarkably literate letter in which she contrasts the consequences of illicit sex among men and women: 'to the eternal Infamy of the Male Sex, Falshood among you is not reproachful, but Credulity in Women is infamous'. She narrates her seduction by the heir of a great house, her betrayal by a bawd, and her consequent life as 'the common Refuse of all the Rakes and Debauchees in Town', including 'the greatest Politicians of the Age' (taken, in the eighteenth century, as a reference to Henry St John).[39] Steele returns to the issue of prostitution in Mr. Spectator's voice in no. 266, where he describes his meeting with a very beautiful but obviously cold and hungry young woman, who he speculates is new to the streets. He recalls his observation of a bawd suborning a woman newly arrived from the country. In no. 274 he considers 'the impotent Wenchers and industrious Haggs, who are supplied with, and are constantly supplying new Sacrifices to the Devil of Lust'. In *Spectator*, no. 383 Addison takes Sir Roger de Coverley to Spring Garden, where he wishes 'there were more Nightingales, and fewer Strumpets'. In *Spectator*, no. 410, Sir Roger's artless letter urging a prostitute to leave off her vanities and join him in the country earns him the mockery of his fellow club members and earned Steele the disapproval of Addison.[40]

Steele's embarrassment at Addison's disapproval parallels Sir Roger's embarrassment at having apparently invited the company of a prostitute he only hoped to help, and both Sir Roger's and Steele's embarrassments reflect the *Spectator*'s awkwardness in approaching the subject. On one hand the *Spectator* shares the condemnation of prostitution by mainstream morality, but, on the other, it tries to take a sympathetic view of prostitutes themselves, whom it sees primarily as victims of male sexual aggression and the unprincipled avarice of bawds. Prostitution is a significant instance of the social tendency to regard women as sexual objects and as commodities. The major issues that emerge from the *Spectator*'s treatment of prostitution are primary elements of its treatment of marriage as well, and they are prime weapons in Steele's campaign to replace the male-centred practice of 'keeping' with the more egalitarian idea of marriage in which the dominant husband and father takes pleasure in responding to the needs of the family below him.

For Steele the issues raised by prostitution are those of dominance or authority as a characteristic of personal relationships and of money as a false value replacing the true ones of personal love or communal good. Authority and wealth define his attitude towards the family in terms both of the gender relationship between husband and wife and the generational relationship between parents and children. The husband is the dominant member of the family, and his ultimate reward is the love and respect of his wife and children as a result of his concerns for them. But children also, if given the education proper to their status and their hopes for advancement, increase the wealth of the family and its position in society. This increase of wealth within a bourgeois family contrasts to the mere transmission of wealth in an aristocratic one. Marriage re-emerges as a major way in which wealth can be transferred, increased, and preserved. The economic function of marriage reintroduces the issue of authority. To what degree does the father have the right to determine his children's choice of mate? In the *Spectator*'s world of negotiated compromise, neither has an absolute authority. The child owes respect and obedience to the father, but ideally those emotions flow from the affection which has stimulated the father's behaviour towards the child.

Addison's *Spectator*, no. 181 comments on a letter from a woman who married at an early age without her father's consent. Although the marriage worked out well, the father remained vehemently unreconciled, much to his daughter's distress. Steele took up the sequence in no. 189 by publishing a letter that had been forwarded to Buckley, the *Spectator*'s publisher, in which a father rails at his son, disowning him for offences that do not seem to deserve such severity. But although Steele publishes the letter as an example of monstrous vice, he speculates that the son may possess the father that he deserves. He expands that speculation to apply in general to his treatment of generational differences and to familial politics.

> I must confess, in all Controversies between Parents and their Children, I am naturally prejudiced in favour of the former. The Obligations on that side can never be acquitted, and I think it is one of the greatest Reflections upon Human Nature that Paternal Instinct should be a stronger Motive to Love than Filial Gratitude.

He goes on to assert the familial nature of government: 'The Obedience of Children to their Parents is the Basis of all Government, and set forth as the measure of that Obedience which we owe to those whom Providence hath placed over us' (*Spectator*, no. 189). Valuable as children are in preserving and increasing the wealth of a family, they preserve and memorialize the characteristics and virtues of the father. Mr Spectator contrasts the family of Ruricola, where the virtuous father has produced a drunken and dissolute son but a beautiful and modest daughter, to the family of the Cornelii, eminent traders, where father and sons share 'Friendship, Good-will, and kind Offices' (*Spectator*, no. 192).

Happy families in the *Spectator* tend to be stereotypical Whig families – their wealth coming from the enterprise of several generations, their unity coming from shared affection and mutual esteem. The *Spectator* is trumpeting a new paradigm for marriage, based on affection as the cement of personal relationships. But this new pattern changes relatively little: husbands lead their wives, and parents govern their children, even if the character of that leadership and that governance has shifted to a greater flexibility and openness. Running through the *Spectator*'s treatment of marriage, the family, children and servants are concern for the proper mode of authority (authority by the right people, exercised in the right way) and for the proper balance between the acquisition of wealth and service to the community.

The relationship between the *Spectator*'s treatment of the family and its politics can be looked at in two ways. On one hand the family serves as a code for political relationships. The God-monarch-father analogy provides the key to interpreting that code. The family serves as a model for the state. The limited authority of the father, whose decisions must be guided by his concern for the wishes and intentions of other family members and by his sense of the well-being of the family as a whole, parallels the authority of the monarch, whose decisions are limited by the actions of Parliament. Mr Spectator's natural predisposition is to take the side of parents rather than children, but that predisposition needs to be tested against the reality of particular cases. Neither parental nor monarchical authority is absolute. On the other hand Steele exploits the psychological force of this family analogy. By attaching the dynamics of family relationships to deep and virtually universal feelings and values, Steele creates a source for proper political opinion, opinion that recognizes the compromises necessary among conflicting values, and creates as well the force that makes it attractive.

> Child orientation, then, acquires a second meaning apart from trying to meet the child's essential concerns: the child-oriented family also functions as a stabilizer in a social structure whose balance is maintained through orientation toward the child who is placed at this center.[41]

Mr Spectator's families and his politics are based on moderation and mutual respect, not on the emotional extremism of Tories such as Sacheverell. But the connection of broad Whig politics to the relationships among family members gives them an emotional force of an altogether different kind. And Steele creates this force by expropriating the familiar analogy between the family and the state that is associated with High Tory propaganda. The general effect of the family analogy is to comfort the anxiety that readers might feel at the dynastic uncertainties of the succession and at the diminution of monarchical authority.[42]

The Indirection of Metonymy: The Moral Trader

The *Spectator*'s treatment of familial wealth as a product of education rather than inheritance identifies the paper's Whig proclivities as clearly as Addison's papers on Public Credit (no. 3) and on the Royal Exchange (no. 69). In the *Spectator*, as in the *Tatler*, Steele sought to join aristocratic and bourgeois interests by redefining the concept of the gentleman in terms of behaviour rather than birth or even status, hence Steele's crack in *Spectator*, no. 65 that the real gentleman of *The Man of Mode* is the shoemaker. The combination of social charm and moral goodness that defines the gentleman runs parallel to the mixture of the accumulation of wealth with sympathy for others that restrains the exercise of avarice. The economic order provided Addison and Steele with a secular basis for moral behaviour that restrained the free operation of the marketplace and subordinated individual gain to the common good.[43]

The financial revolution that funded the war gave considerable power to those who had invested significantly in public credit, but, with the dismissal of Godolphin and the Tory victory in the 1710 election, the financial community became agitated at the prospect that lack of confidence would diminish the value of government bonds. The Tory victory resulted in the passage of the 'Landed Property Qualification Bill', which required land ownership worth £600 (or £300 for representatives of boroughs) for membership in Parliament, a measure that was less effective in limiting Parliament to the squirearchy than both parties supposed in 1711.[44] The Bill certainly reflected a Tory reaction against the political efforts of moneyed interests and may have been a motive for the *Spectator's* positive treatment of merchants and credit.[45] The stability of public credit and the basis of that stability became a significant subject of pamphleteering during the years of the *Tatler* and *Spectator*. Whigs such as Maynwaring and Hoadly argued that there was a Tory campaign against the system of public credit that largely financed the war and that the replacement of Sidney Godolphin with Robert Harley as Lord Treasurer would undermine the confidence of investors whose support was necessary to the strength of the public economy.[46] Whigs argued that credit was essentially a matter of trust, directed towards responsible individuals. Credit thus depended on personal competence and integrity. Tories argued that public credit pertained to the nation rather than individuals, and that the nation as a whole could function to assure the stability of credit and the competence of financial management: '*Publick Credit* is the Consequence of honourable, just, and punctual Management in the Matter of *Funds*, and *Taxes*, or *Loans* upon them.'[47] Addison's contribution to the debate took the form of an allegorical vision in which the female figure of public credit is threatened by tyranny and anarchy, bigotry and atheism, the Commonwealth and the Pretender, but revives at the approach of liberty and monarch, and moderation and religion, thus rooting public credit not in the person of Godolphin but in the ideological keywords of Whig politics (*Spectator*, no. 3).[48] The instability of Public Credit in Defoe and Addison, as J. G. A. Pocock pointed out, 'symbolized and made actual the power of opinion, passion, and fantasy in human affairs'.

> Credit is now being translated into virtue, in the entirely moral and societal sense of that word. The precondition of her health is the health of all society and the practice of all the moral activities which society entails; and she is being endowed with a faculty of perception sufficient to inform her whether these conditions are being met.[49]

Steele was particularly interested in the figure of the trader as an instance of these manifold social and moral activities. Trade manifested the energy, exchange, expansion, and transformation that, in Steele's mind, typified the economic order. It contrasted to the stable but less productive agency of property. The force and movement of economic exchange made it the heart of the urban life that the *Spectator* described. Addison's famous visit to the Royal Exchange in no. 69 reveals its activities as having an international scope and a national importance, making merchants the most useful members of the commonwealth: 'They knit Mankind together in a mutual Intercourse of good Offices, distribute the Gifts of Nature, find Work for the Poor, add Wealth to the Rich, and Magnificence to the Great'. Steele makes a quick visit to the Royal Exchange as part of his whirlwind, one-day ramble through London. He regards the activities there with what might be called a mercantile sentimentalism: 'I, indeed, look'd upon my self as the richest Man that walked the *Exchange* that Day; for my Benevolence made me share the Gains of every Bargain that was made' (*Spectator*, no. 454).

The dynamism of exchange has its negative implications, as Mr Spectator is reminded when he passes a debtor's prison where an old acquaintance begs money from him at the grate (*Spectator*, No 82). Steele reflects in harsh terms on a subject with which he was personally quite familiar – the shamefulness of the debtor. He sees debt as a problem of landowners, who mortgage their estates in hopes that their sons will pay the mortgage with money from their future wives. He goes on to contrast Sir Andrew Freeport, who was never sued for debt, to Jack Truepenny, who is always in debt as a result of his tendency to give money to friends whose capacity for repayment is even worse than his own. Contemporaries recognized Jack as a portrait of Steele himself.[50] Steele returns to the quandaries of poverty and debt in *Spectator*, no. 114, where an ill-natured guest at Sir Roger's table exemplifies the anxieties of one who lives in debt rather than reveal his financial condition by selling part of his estate. The contrasting examples of Laertes, who is ashamed of poverty, and Irus, who is afraid of it, lead to reflections on the consequences of those emotions: 'Usury, Stock-jobbing, Extortion and Oppression, have their Seed in the Dread of Want; and Vanity, Riot and Prodigality, from the Shame of it'.

Eubulus, the wealthy and respected merchant whom Steele observes as a coffeehouse regular in *Spectator*, no. 49 could make considerable profit in the public stocks but invests instead in the needs of his friends: 'He does not consider in whose Hands his Mony will improve most, but where it will do the most Good'. Like Sir Andrew Freeport, he combines generosity with prudent investment and seeks to enrich others by enriching himself. The economic contrast dominating the lesser contrasts within the *Spectator* and giving them their most significant political direction is between the merchant, embodied by Sir Andrew Freeport, and the landed aristocrat, represented by Sir Roger de Coverley. In *Spectator*, no. 174, Sir Roger attacks merchants as parsimonious rather than generous, relying on their narrow figures to cheat those who relied on memory, gaining their ends without regard to the morality of their means. Sir Andrew replies with a spirited defence of frugality and bookkeeping as ways to assure that generosity is possible. 'Sir Roger gives to his Men, but I place mine above the Necessity or Obligation of my Bounty'. As he goes into his rural retirement, Sir Andrew promises to manage agriculture with the same principles he used in pursuing trade (*Spectator*, no. 549). In *Spectator*, no. 346, Steele cites Cicero to argue that 'all Liberality should have for its Basis and Support Frugality'. The trader alone can be liberal without 'the least Expense of a Man's own Fortune'. But Steele also insists that 'Benignity is essential to the Character of a fair Trader'.

The *Spectator*'s commercial principles not only provide for the management of land and money, they envision wealth in human terms as well. Addison (*Spectator*, no. 21) comically notes that there are more clergymen, lawyers, and doctors than the market can bear, but the market is almost infinitely open in the area of trade. Eustace Budgell reiterates the accessibility of trade, almost to the point of absurdity: 'I think I may lay it down as a Maxim, that every Man of good Common Sense may, if he pleases, in his particular station of Life, most certainly be Rich' (*Spectator*, no. 283). A treatise in *Spectator*, no. 200, probably by Henry Martyn, uses the calculations of political arithmetic to argue that the real riches of a land lie in the industry of its people and that even the poor contribute to the taxes of a king.

A stark alternative to the life of benign and prosperous investment is the life of patronage, and in criticizing that life, Steele joins a classical tradition notably represented by Horace (for example, fortune-hunting in *Satires* II.5) and Juvenal (*Satires* 1 and, especially, 5).[51] But it was also a life painfully familiar to him from his military and early political experiences with the Duke of Ormond and Lord Cutts. Steele had complained about patronage in *Tatler*, no. 196, but his bitterest and most extensive description of this pain occurs in *Spectator*, no. 214, on the futility and waste of attending great men in hopes of reward. Steele estimates roughly that one-third of the nation is made up of clients and patrons, although most clients lack merit and most patrons lack the means to reward it. Steele's complaint about the patronage system is double-barrelled: it is demeaning to clients, but it is artificial in any case – a toying with appearances of praise and reward that are insincere or nonexistent, false flattery met by false promises. Clients may devote years to the pursuit of that unreality, while patrons are quick to absorb flattery or react with anger. The life of patronage is a hollow intrusion on the proper functioning of merit and labour in society, but, as Steele knew well, it remained a central feature in the organization of political life.

The dynamic qualities associated with commerce needed to be restrained by forces of personal morality and social responsibility. Avarice, like sexuality, is a human force that needs restraint, and just as spousal love replaces unbridled lust, an emotional concern for the benefit of others restrains avarice and transforms personal gain into public good. The properly altruistic merchant becomes a prime example of practical morality. He does so because general social and national benefit is an inevitable result of the exchange of goods, services and money, and because the properly motivated man of commerce seeks ways to use his wealth in order to benefit others. Steele is well aware of the possibility, even the likelihood, that unrestrained capitalism may do social harm, and it certainly does harm to the individual whose personality is distorted by its devotion to gain. Altruistic behaviour, Steele argues in *Spectator*, no. 248, is within the capacity of all but downright paupers: 'The great Foundation of civil Virtue is Self-Denial; and there is no one above the Necessities of Life, but has Opportunities of exercising that noble Quality, and doing as much as his Circumstances will bear for the Ease and Convenience of other Men' (*Spectator*, no. 248).

The alternative to such altruistic behaviour is exemplified in the personality of Ephraim Weed, whose letter on money in no. 450 is one of the few places where the irony of Steele approaches that of Swift in satiric force and effect. Weed argues, almost in parody of Steele's position on the beneficial effects of commerce, that the foundation of virtue is the love of money. He begins by asserting that love of money is more important than self-preservation and, indeed, than honesty itself. But he turns around, dismisses that argument as 'Scholastick' talk, and launches into an account of his own life. He is condoled for the loss of his wife and children in the plague by the considerations that they had not represented a major investment, that some of her fortune was left, and that he can now live more cheaply. In fact he marries twice more and both wives cuckold him, probably because, as he confesses, 'I cannot call to Mind, that in all the Time I was a Husband, which, off and on, was about twelve Years, I ever once thought of my Wives but in Bed'. He concludes that 'the Love of Money prevents all Immorality and Vice; which if you will not allow, you must, that the Pursuit of it obliges Men to the same Kind of Life as they would follow if they were really virtuous'. Although Steele celebrates the economic, social, and personal benefits of the life of commerce, he admits that it is not without its problems.

Conclusion

As a result of whatever agreement Steele might have reached with Harley in their meeting of October 1710, the *Spectator* was not an overtly political magazine. Its covert status may have resulted as well from the more direct Whig propagandizing of Maynwaring, Hare, Hoadly, Boyer and anonymous others, leaving clear room for an alternative approach – broader, more subtle and devious – not only to Whig propagandizing but to political discourse itself. The *Spectator* therefore took a deviously neutral and indirect approach to politics, one that was layered through a variety of often-overlapping devices, topics, methods and arguments. (1) Although the *Spectator* repeatedly proclaimed a political neutrality and condemned the passions of party, occasional papers took up specifically political topics or made specifically political statements – Addison's paper on Public Credit (*Spectator*, no. 3), for example, and Steele's publication of the Preface to the Bishop of St Asaph's sermons (*Spectator*, no. 384). Beyond their usefulness in discussing particular issues, these proclaim the Whig identity of the *Spectator*, and hence give a Whig cast to whatever else the periodical may do. (2) Authorized by this identification, the *Spectator* utilizes an indirect political language that discusses matters of controversy at a level of generality that is higher than that of the controversy itself. (3) An important instance of this technique is its treatment of the Duke of Marlborough, who was under continued and intense attack, exemplified by Swift's *The Conduct of the Allies*.[52] In the *Spectator*, as in the *Tatler*, references to great men, to historical figures such as Alexander and Caesar, and to envious attacks on a great man almost always refer to Marlborough.

(4) The most important continuing device for general and occasionally topical political comment is the Spectator Club, with its typically significant characters, dominated by the bumbling but decent and kindhearted Tory squire and the hardnosed but generous (and successful) Whig merchant. The Club allows a treatment of specific issues on occasion but throughout pursues the ideological difference between an economic activity that contributes to the wealth and advancement of the country and an agricultural inactivity that, however commendable in its relations with its immediate community, is hardly reliable in its general social utility and political acuity. But the Club also represents a critical alternative to the political discourse represented by the active press. The characters of the club respect each other, in spite of their political differences. Their discussions reveal clearly defined differences but are conducted with civility and even geniality. The Club offers an oasis of straightforward discussion that allows ideas to shine through the veil of eccentricity.

(5) While the *Spectator* tends to express its explicit politics by generalities that imply a distinct political application, it seeks to create a broad and attractive Whig culture through metonymy. Over the 555 papers of its initial run, the *Spectator* canvasses a wide variety of topics, some of which (literature, for example) carry implicit political – even partisan – significance. As insistent as this variety may be in its political implications, it cannot address specific issues on a regular basis, and it cannot make totalizing conclusions about its disparate material. But it does emphasize certain topics that it associates on one hand with the Whig culture it seeks to enunciate and, on the other hand, with contemporary political controversy – the sentimental family and the moral trader.

The effect of this multilayered effort was to extend Whig culture beyond London merchants and the financiers of the war and to show its relevance to all walks of life. It sought to reassure anxious citizens that the changes brought about by the war, by the likelihood of a German dynasty assuming the British throne, by the ideas of Locke, and by the new political prominence of money did not pose a threat to the existing order but reformulated and reinforced traditional political, religious and literary ideas. The consensus which, in retrospect, the *Spectator* seemed to reflect was, in many respects a consensus that the *Spectator* created.

The role of Steele in this double act of creation (the creation of the *Spectator* and the creation of the attitudes that the *Spectator* presented) was collaborative. Few of Steele's ideas were original; they derived on one hand from literary tradition (as reflected, for example, in Latin mottoes that began each paper) and on the other from a perceptive reading of the spirit of the times. But his most significant act of collaboration was his cooperation with Addison. Although they contributed separate papers, for the most part to separate publishers, the concept of the periodical, of its nature and of its dynamic relations to its readers was jointly arrived at. As a collaborative literary periodical, the *Spectator* was unsurpassed. In the course of the century there were certainly other jointly-composed periodicals – the *Connoisseur* for example – but the *Spectator* was unique in the quality of its achievement over an unusual length. Never again in their careers would Addison and Steele achieve such collaborative quality.

Addison's papers tended to be more serious, more organized and more intellectual, but many show a humourous social observation. Steele's are more various, often made up of letters, often with a sentimental tone modified by whimsy. The territories of Addison and Steele overlapped considerably, but the differences in their emphasis are apparent in their treatment of Sir Roger de Coverley. Steele initially describes him in *Spectator*, no. 2 in rather contradictory terms. He is 'very singular in his Behaviour, but his Singularities proceed from his good Sense'. He is 'rather beloved than esteemed'. Addison extended and developed the tensions in his character, and sharpened both his lovable nature and his political backwardness. Steele's Roger is a reformed rake, rumoured to have sexual relations with beggars and gypsies, but Addison cleaned up these coarser elements. When Steele returned to Sir Roger during Mr Spectator's country visit (where most of the papers are by Addison), he narrates his unrequited love for a neighbouring widow with whimsical sentimentality. For all his eccentricities, Sir Roger is a character who is large enough to subsume both Addison's complex political and social satire and Steele's sentimentality.

The *Spectator* was not the target of many political attacks, and the few attacks that appeared with the opening numbers of the paper in 1711 tended to focus on its intrusion into private life. In *The Spectator Inspected* a soldier, claiming to write from camp, complains about the *Spectator*'s unauthorized use of a letter he wrote on military matters. He goes on to launch a general attack on the *Spectator*:

What is more odious in *England* than the Name or Memory of an Usurper or Tyrant: What can be a greater Usurpation, upon the Magistracy and Government of the chief City of the best constituted Nation in the Universe, than for a fantastical, splenatick, discontented Wretch to assume to himself the Authority of a Censor, to expose every thing that disagrees with the humour which happens to be uppermost, while he is writing for his daily bread? What can be a greater Tyranny upon the Subject, than to have a constant Spy upon their actions, to publish, in a false light, family conversations, harmless mirth, and other trivial incidents, which would never be thought faults, if they were not by his Talent improv'd into such.[53]

The bulk of the paper is an often mocking discussion of the use of borrowed words in English, especially when these involve technicalities.

A Spy Upon the Spectator, published by the Tory bookseller John Morphew, asserts that the *Spectator*'s effort to combine morality and wit only succeeds in imposing the shadow of morality. He goes on to examine the opening numbers and similarly characterizes the *Spectator* as invasive, a judgment he couches in terms of a comparison to other periodicals:

So I find that this silent Man, with his *profound Taciturnity,* is resolv'd to invade every ones *Province.* He will furnish more Prattle than the very *Tatler*; for that came out but thrice a week, but this Daily; When he says, *that all Breaches against the Noble Passion Love, the Cement of Society, shall be strickly* Examined: He seems to intrude upon the Post of the *Examiner,* to which his Style and Judgment are in no manner equal: But when he tells us, That *we shall not find him an idle, but a very busie Spectator,* he sinks down to the *Medley*; to which as his Humour seems more inclinable, so his Parts and Learning are more justly adapted.[54]

The *Spectator* reappears briefly in a 1712 Whig paper (possibly by Addison) misleadingly entitled *Thoughts of a Tory Author, Concerning the Press* that defends the anonymity of authors and notes that the *Spectator*, *A Tale of a Tub*, and *Law is a Bottomless Pit* would never have been published if their authorship were not anonymous.

What concerns the authors who accuse the *Spectator* of spying and the defenders of authorial anonymity is the age's uncertainty regarding the scope and nature of personal privacy. The seriousness of *Spy*'s concern for the *Spectator*'s invasion of privacy is somewhat mitigated by its playful punning with the names of other intrusive periodicals. The serious element of the *Spectator*'s intrusions into private life was a groping towards a literary form that was capable of representing as well as commenting upon (moralizing about) those elements of the private lives of individuals and families that normally were hidden from public scrutiny. Here too was a political divide – between those who sought to safeguard the privacy, even the secrecy, of the individual and those who wanted to open that secrecy to an awareness of other people and to the possibility of moral advice. Some such dichotomy was evident even the authorship of the *Spectator* itself, with the very private Addison writing alongside the extroverted Steele. The lines between privacy and community were still unclear, and the issue was shortly to affect Steele directly in the specifically political form of parliamentary confidentiality. But for now the *Spectator*'s capacity to discuss private family matters was essential to its efforts to root a Whig point of view in the experiences of ordinary life.

Steele beyond the *Spectator*

During the course of the *Spectator*'s run, Steele published little that anticipated his later role as a major producer of political tracts. His contribution to *Medley*, No. 23 (5 March 1711) virtually coincided with the opening of the *Spectator*. To make the distinction between Envy and Emulation it tells the story of clean sailors and dirty colliers together at a ball in Wapping. The colliers jostle with the sailors until they become equally dirty. The story is applied to the *Examiner*: 'such an Inventor of groundless Falsehoods, such a Reviver of confuted Calumnies, who has no regard to the Dictates of Truth, nor even the Sentiments of common Humanity'.[55] In the following January, in response to the dismissal of the Duke of Marlborough from his command, Steele, always a Marlborough enthusiast, wrote a broadside entitled 'The Englishman's Thanks to the Duke of Marlborough'. It looks like a rejected *Spectator* paper, with fulsome thanks expressed in purple prose: 'Your Actions have exalted you to be the Chief of Your Species; and a continued Chain of Successes resulting from Wise Counsels, have denominated You the First of Mankind in the Age which was Bless'd with Your Birth'.[56] Steele evidently thought enough of the piece to include it in his *Political Writings* (1715). Although these are the only contributions that can certainly be attributed to Steele, they are perhaps not his only political efforts during the run of the *Spectator*. John Oldmixon, in his life of Maynwaring, reported that Steele 'frequently attack'd those hated Ministers with his Pen, under other Names, when he did not thing fit to make use of his own, while he was Commissioner of the *Stamp-Office*'.[57]

On 17 September 1712, Steele wrote his wife from Hampton Court (the Steeles then lived in Bloomsbury Square) telling her that he was dining there with the Junto leaders Halifax and Somers and would go thereafter to Watford to speak with the Solicitor-General Sir Robert Raymond. In her note to this letter, Rae Blanchard suggests that the conversation 'was related to politics – possibly political writing'.[58] The Junto leaders had much to discuss with Steele. Arthur Maynwaring was on his deathbed; the Tories had succeeded in passing the Treaty of Utrecht, with the assistance of Tory peers appointed at the last minute by the Queen; a more controversial barrier treaty was in the offing, as was a Parliamentary election (in 1713). The time had come to develop a new propaganda campaign, one element of which was to be Addison's *Cato*, another was to be a periodical, edited by Steele, that would be similar to the *Spectator* but more open to political discussion and attack. Sir Roger de Coverley died on 23 October and, accordingly, in November, Addison and Steele sold their rights to the collected volumes to the booksellers Buckley and Tonson for £575 each half-share. The marriage of Will Honeycomb was announced on 7 November. On 29 November readers were notified of Sir Andrew Freeport's retirement. The process of closing the paper was finished, and the paper itself ended on 6 December, having succeeded in imposing an appearance of stability on an unstable age.

4 THE *GUARDIAN*, PARLIAMENT AND DUNKIRK

Father, Debtor and Entrepreneur

Between 1709 and the first months of 1713, the period of the *Tatler* and the *Spectator*, Steele's activities and accomplishments were not confined to the literary periodical, however taxing that work must have been. His growing family certainly added significant responsibilities. His first daughter, Elizabeth, was born on 26 March 1709 – shortly before the beginning of the *Tatler* (12 April 1709). His son Richard was born on 25 May, 1710; he died at the age of six. Eugene was born on 4 March 1712. Mary was probably born at the end of January, 1713, under difficult circumstances. Mary Scurlock, Prue's mother, had come to London to visit the family but took ill and died. The young Irish clergyman and philosopher George Berkeley, who had first met Steele in January, reported that Mrs Steele had given birth to a son on the same day as her mother died. Most biographers suspect that Berkeley was mistaken as to the gender of the baby, but Aitken speculates (on no real evidence) that a son may have died soon after, and Mary may have been born at the end of the year.[1] In addition to these four children, Steele remained responsible for his illegitimate daughter Elizabeth Ousley.

On the death of Mrs Scurlock, Steele gained an annual income of £500 from her Welsh property. Berkeley notes Steele's kindness to his wife on this occasion and goes on to describe the happy situation of the Steeles:

> Before she lay down the poor man told me he was in great pain and put to a thousand little shifts to conceal his mother's desperate illness from her. The tender concern he showed on that occasion, and what I have observed in another good friend of mine, makes me imagine the best men are always the best husbands. I told Mr. Steele if he neglects to resume his writings, the world will look on it as the effect of his growing rich. But he says this addition to his fortune will rather encourage him to exert himself more than ever; and I am apter to believe him, because there appears in his natural temper something very generous and a great benevolence to mankind. One instance of it is his kind and friendly behaviour to me (even though he has heard I am

a Tory). I have dined frequently in his house in Bloomsbury Square, which is handsome and nearly furnished. His table, servants, coach and everything is very genteel,
and in appearance above his fortune before this new acquisition. His conversation is
very cheerful, and abounds with wit and good sense.[2]

Berkeley's description makes Steele's Bloomsbury Square house seem a middle-class domestic idyll, but if that picture was true at all, it was true for a very
short time. Steele's relationship to his mother-in-law was respectful but not
quite affectionate. Her final illness prompted a series of letters from Steele in
Autumn 1712, in which he urged Mrs Scurlock to settle the bulk of her estate
on his son Eugene. He pointed out that he and his wife had been supported,
even if uncertainly, on the results of his own labours. A bequest to his children
would alleviate his nervousness that he could eventually provide for them. Since
he was himself a substantial beneficiary of her estate, his efforts seem to have
been successful. His wife also inherited from her mother, and in March 1713,
shortly after the inception of the *Guardian*, she wrote a letter to her husband
which essentially agreed with his own plans for the estate but reserved the right
to bequeath £3,000 as she saw fit. Steele quickly agreed.

Steele wrote to his wife frequently – some sixty letters in the period between
the birth of Elizabeth in March 1709 and his wife's letter regarding her estate in
March 1713. Surely he wrote more that have been lost. These letters are almost
infallibly short, written on the fly, and concerned with matters of logistics
– where Steele was at the time of writing, how long he was going to stay there,
why he could not get home for dinner, and how much rather he would be home,
except that business kept him where he was. There are frequent expressions of
affection, both in the salutation and the body of letters. An equally frequent
apologetic tone suggests that Mrs Steele took umbrage at relatively minor matters, but in fact she had a great deal to try her patience, despite Steele's obvious
affection and desire to please. Steele had much work to do and was often away,
perhaps from inclination as well as work. Still more worrying was his financial
irresponsibility. Steele was generous with his money when he had it, but lurched
from debt to debt, borrowing from one to pay off the other. Mrs Steele, in her
husband's absence, had to face the unanswerable demands of creditors and their
agents.[3] Not only was she aware of his serious financial difficulties, she also knew
that he had gone through his first wife's estate. She did not want him to impover-
ish her as well. Hence her mother's death seems to have created tension between
them. Her letter sought to keep her estate independent of his debts and, insisting
upon her right to give £3,000 as she saw fit, she asserts that 'I intend not to Enter
into Argument least (in Passion) I may be answer'd as severly in writing as I have
been by Speech'.[4] Mrs. Steele was clearly an apprehensive person, and Steele's
comforting and apologetic letters were probably addressed to these apprehen-
sions. But he must also have had the guilty awareness that her fears were only

too well grounded. That they continued to be as open as they were about their feelings and the details of their daily lives seems commendable.

The Steeles had lived in the house in Bloomsbury Square for only a few months when Berkeley first visited there in January 1713. Steele wrote to his wife on 15 July 1712, telling her that 'You cannot conceive How pleased I am that I shall have the prettyest house to receive the Prettyest Woman who is the Darling of [signed] Richard Steele'.[5] On 8 August he wrote to his mother-in-law from Bloomsbury Square.[6] Until they moved to the Bloomsbury house, they had lived, since shortly after their marriage, in a house in Bury Street. Steele purchased a second house in Hampton Wick in 1708, and this house may have been the subject of Samuel Johnson's report that Addison had sold Steele's house to pay a debt and to teach Steele a lesson about thrift. Modern commentators are inclined to view the story skeptically.[7] Steele spent June 1712 alone in a house in Haverstock Hill, near Hampstead, and there is some possibility that the family used it often.[8] The house had been owned by the poet Charles Sedley, who died there. Eventually the house in Bloomsbury Square was advertised 'for let' on 20 July 1714. The instability of the Steeles' domestic life is represented by the sequence of their houses during the first half-dozen years of their marriage. But the major source of instability was not infidelity or lack of affection but Steele's financial irresponsibility, despite his adequate income.

The detailed extent of that irresponsibility was traced in George Aitken's 1889 biography, and to my knowledge no one has undertaken the thankless task of retracing it. The record of the years leading to the publication of the *Guardian* is daunting enough. Steele was arrested on 2 May 1709 and perhaps imprisoned for a debt of £120 at the suit of Stephen Creagh.[9] On 27 May he borrowed £140 from George Tilden, for which Tilden sued him in Easter term of next year. Apparently in response to the 2 May suit of Creagh, he wrote a letter to Halifax begging £150 to rescue him from 'the most Afflicting Circumstances' that were putting him 'in danger of being torn to pieces'.[10] Steele's financial situation was presumably improved when he became one of the Commissioners of the Stamp Office, at a salary of £300 per year in January 1710. It may therefore have been careless forgetfulness that led to John Wright's suit against him for the relatively paltry sum of £18.10s. Not so paltry was George Doddington's suit for £1,000 in April. There is some evidence that Steele was briefly imprisoned at the end of the summer.[11] In October his loss of the *Gazette* as a result of the recently elected Tory ministry deprived him of £300 per year. In Hilary term 1710–11 he was sued for £270, apparently by his butcher,[12] and in Easter term he was judged to have defaulted on a debt of £230. In May 1712, Stephen Stretch, presumably a relative of his first wife, sued him for £580, and in June 1712, he borrowed £100 from John Warner. In August of that year he borrowed £3,000 from Benjamin

Ashhurst, who sued to recover the debt in October. Another action was brought that summer by Edward Vernon for £24.

Aitken's record of Steele's economic woes, of which I have given a partial list from May 1709 through 1712, was drawn from available legal documents, and hence does not reflect the compromises and informal settlements that may have accompanied the court cases. Richard Savage's famous stories about Steele writing a pamphlet in a tavern and having Savage sell it to a bookseller so that Steele could pay his dinner bill and about Steele using his duns as servants to wait on his dinner guests, who then discharged his debt, are almost certainly apocryphal, although the liveried-bailiff story has its origin in *Examiner*, no. 11 (12 October 1710).[13] Untrue as they may be, they suggest a realistic picture of Steele's character. Although his financial irresponsibility may have been inconsistent with the economic propriety he celebrated in the *Spectator*, it seems to have resulted from forgetfulness, generosity and carelessness rather than from any attempt to deceive or defraud. He was like individuals who have gotten into the habit of continually borrowing from one credit card to pay the other, thus distributing rather than paying their debts.

One further problem that might have caused his wife discomfort was his drunkenness. 'Dear Prue', Steele writes (26 October 1708), 'If you do not hear of me before three tomorrow afternoon believe I am too fuddled to take care to observe your Orders but however know me to be Y[ou]r Most Faithful Affectionate Husband and Ser[va]nt Richard Steele'.[14] The early eighteenth century was a period of high alcohol consumption, and Steele moved in literary and political social circles where drinking was common and excessive. The problem for Steele was compounded by the fact that he did not hold his liquor well. Since Addison required significant alcoholic stimulation to reach his conversational best, Steele would sometimes be out of commission by the time Addison got there. One effect of Steele's consumption of alcohol may have been the gout, which plagued him in 1713 and thereafter. Gout was virtually the first characteristic of Steele mentioned by Berkeley in his 26 January letter to John Percival:

> The first news I had upon my coming to town was that Mr. Steele did me the honour to desire to be acquainted with me: upon which I have been to see him. He is confined with the gout and is, as I am informed, writing a play, since he gave over the 'Spectators'.[15]

The play is almost certainly *The Conscious Lovers*, which Steele seems to have begun, impelled in part, perhaps, by his sympathetic treatment of merchants in the *Spectator*, but which he set aside upon beginning the *Guardian*. His gout plagued him sporadically for the rest of his life. William Whiston, in a rather unsympathetic characterization of Steele, reported accusing him of inconsistency on the South-Sea Bill, to which Steele replied, 'Mr. Whiston, you can walk on foot, and I cannot'.[16] Dr John Woodward includes Steele among the cases he successfully treated. Steele was apparently disabled by the gout in the winter and spring of 1715 and again in July 1720. Although he was initially 'wholly disabled and helpless', he recovered as a result of Woodward's treatment, despite overeating and drinking.[17]

One domestic adventure involving both Steele and his wife occurred in August 1712. Edward Wortley Montagu, a cousin of the Earl of Halifax, was a close friend of Addison and Steele. In fact, he lived with Addison during the winter of 1711–12. He had been involved in a long courtship of Lady Mary Pierrepont, whose aristocratic father opposed their marriage. The negotiations were largely financial, but the financial uncertainties may have stood for personal reservations as well. The courtship was played out in part in the pages of the *Tatler*. Wortley contributed substantial passages to *Tatler* nos. 199 and 223, both of which complain about the crass mercenary motives of families who marry off their daughters for money.[18] The second volume of the *Tatler* was dedicated to Wortley (July 1710), and he was godfather to the Steeles' daughter Elizabeth. Lady Mary was or became a friend of Mary Steele, and the couple used the Steeles' Bury Street house as a meeting place. The couple finally eloped on 18 August 1712. Lady Mary contributed an essay to Addison's continuation of the *Spectator* (no. 573) and, after the death of her cousin, Henry Fielding, in 1754 compared his character to Steele's:

> There was a great similitude between his character and that of Sir Richard Steele. He had the advantage both in learning and, in my opinion, genius: they both agreed in wanting money in spite of all their friends, and would have wanted it, if their hereditary lands had been as extensive as their imagination; yet each of them was so formed for happiness, it is a pity he was not immortal.[19]

On 7 March 1713, Berkeley wrote to Percival to announce Steele's forthcoming publication of the *Guardian* but adds a description of his latest entrepreneurial enterprise:

> He is likewise projecting a noble entertainment for persons of a refined taste. It is chiefly to consist of the finest pieces of eloquence translated from the Greek and Latin authors; they will be accompanied by the best music suited to raise those passions that are proper to the occasion. Pieces of poetry too will be there recited. These informations I have from Mr Steele himself. I have seen the place designed for these performances: it is in York Buildings, and he has been at no small expense to embellish with all imaginable decorations. It is by much the finest chamber I have seen, and will contain seats for a select company of 200 persons of the best quality and taste, who are to be subscribers.[20]

Steele planned a venue for high culture, directed at a small and select audience, and presenting heterogeneous material drawn from various genres and media. It was modelled on the Academies of Europe and, to a lesser degree, England.[21] The expense of renting and refurbishing the house where the great room was located would have been a considerable drain on Steele's precarious expenses. Classical recitations were to be held there, often accompanied by music, serving as an alternative to the theatre. Or musical performances, with or without text, would become a rational person's alternative to opera, the excesses of which preoccupied Addison particularly in the early numbers of the *Spectator* (see, especially, no. 18). Steele's misfortune was to connect with the English composer Thomas Clayton, who had written several English operas but was driven off the stage by the arrival of Handel. He wrote the music that sank Addison's English opera *Rosamund*. Steele was involved at some level in the production of Clayton's setting of Dryden's *Alexander's Feast*, which was performed at the York Room on 24 May 1711. Shortly before the performance Steele wrote the poet and musician John Hughes, who had arranged the text of Dryden's poem for Clayborn's setting, and asked about the music. Hughes's response was concise, cogent and negative.[22] Clayton probably rented the York room before Steele did, and the failure of his concerts allowed Steele to take it over.

The York room seems also to be designed as an Athenaeum, where lectures and scientific demonstrations would be given to a select audience of subscribers. William Whiston, the eccentric and heterodox clergyman and scientist, gave a series of astronomical lectures, sponsored, perhaps, more by Addison than by Steele, at Button's Coffee House in August 1713. Steele advertised further lectures by Whiston in the *Englishman*.[23] Finally, a lecture by Whiston in the Consortium was recorded in the *Daily Courant* of 16 March 1716. Steele apparently sought to expand the audience of the Censorium to include Tories as well as Whigs and to present culture as transcending partisanship. According to Berkeley's 27 March letter Steele 'talks as if he would engage my Lord Treasurer in his project, designing that it shall comprehend both Whigs and Tories'.[24] The intense political writing in which Steele was a principal figure in 1713 may have dashed his hopes for a non-partisan cultural institution, as Loftis suggests.[25] He returned to the Censorium in another reign and a different political situation.

Another area of Steele's entrepreneurship in 1712 and 1713 was the theatre. *The Distressed Mother*, a mediocre adaptation of Racine's *Andromaque* by Ambrose Philips, opened at Drury Lane on 17 March 1712, with a Prologue by Richard Steele. Its first performance was preceded by Steele's fulsome puff in *Spectator*, no. 290 (1 February 1712). Partly as a result of the *Spectator*'s praise and partly as a result of Steele's success in packing the house, the play had a good run of eight performances. The response to Philips's play in turn encouraged the diffident Addison to finish his *Cato*, four acts of which he had brought back with him from the continent in 1704. Steele, Colley Cibber, Pope and others had read the unfinished play, and there was some doubt as to whether it was stage-worthy, regardless of the wisdom of its ideas and the poetry of its language. But the play was filled with Whig sentiments and, in a period of weak propaganda for the Whigs, its production would assert the spirit of republican liberty. Addison therefore finished the play and consulted with a number of literary advisors, including Pope (whom Addison asked to show the play to Oxford and Bolingbroke), Lady Mary Wortley Montagu, Berkeley, the actors and others. Tonson purchased the copyright for a handsome sum while the play was in rehearsal.[26]

Steele's relation to the play was much the same as his relation to *The Distressed Mother*. He described his role much later in the 'Dedication to William Congreve' that prefaced Addison's posthumously published play *The Drummer*.

> All the Town knows how officious I was in bringing it [*Cato*] on; and you that know the Town, the Theatre, and Mankind very well, can judge how necessary it was to take measures for making a Performance of that sort, excellent as it is, run into popular Applause. I promis'd before it was acted, and performed my Duty accordingly to the Author, that I would bring together so just an Audience on the first Days of it, that it should be impossible for the Vulgar to put its Success or due Applause to any hazard.[27]

Accordingly, he packed the house with Whigs and Kit-Cats and, four days later published a brief appreciation in the *Guardian*, emphasizing the moral virtues not only of Cato but of other characters, and added the 'Prologue' by Pope and 'Epilogue' by Garth. He contributed some rather awkward lines to a collection of commendatory poems that Tonson printed in the seventh edition of the play. His commitment to Addison's play stemmed from a joining of personal friendship and gratitude for the help Addison had provided to him, going back to his contribution to *The Tender Husband*, with an anxiety to make the most of what he saw as an important political moment. *Cato* was an enormous success, but its politics somewhat backfired. At the first performance Bolingbroke summoned Barton Booth, who played Cato, to his box and presented him with fifty guineas for 'defending the cause of Liberty so well against a perpetual dictator'.[28] Caesar, the dictator in question, was often taken, even by Whigs, to stand for the Duke of Marlborough.

Steele's literary reputation made him a useful figure as the editor, publisher or even titular author of books. In December 1713 (dated 1714), Jacob Tonson published *Poetical Miscellanies, Consisting of Original Poems and Translations. By the best hands. Publish'd by Richard Steele*. The volume contained poems by Pope, Swift, Gay, Tickell, Parnell, Wharton, Eusden, Philips, Budgell and William Harrison and was dedicated to William Congreve. Steele thus included major Tory authors as well as the usual run of Whigs. The inclusion of Swift flies in the face of the fact that in late 1713 his relations with Steele could hardly have been worse. It may have been a goad on the part of Steele, whom Swift had recently attacked in *The Importance of the Guardian Considered*. In October 1714, Tonson issued *The Ladies Library. Written by a Lady. Published by Mr. Steele* in three volumes. Steele dedicated the first volume to Juliana Countess of Burlington, the second to 'Mrs. Catherine Bovey (or Boevey)', a beautiful and intelligent philanthropist who was reputed to be the model for the perverse widow who disappointed Sir Roger de Coverley in the *Spectator*. The third volume he dedicated to Mrs Steele, partly perhaps, as Paul Hyland suggested, in order to refurbish his domestic image in the face of personal attacks.[29] The dedication is filled with the loving hyperbole that characterized Steele's domestic moods:

> That ingenuous Spirit in all your Behaviour, that familiar Grace in your Words and Actions, has for this seven Years only inspired Admiration and Love, but Experience has taught me, the best Counsel I ever have received, has been pronounced by the fairest and softest Lips, and convinc'd me that I am in you blest with a wise Friend, as well as a charming Mistress.[30]

The volumes consist of extracts from various devotional and other instructive works, collected by a woman, possible Mary Lady Wray, and forming, as advertised, 'general rules of conduct in all the circumstances of the Life of Women'.[31] But the unattributed passages got Steele into a controversy regarding copyright. Royston Meredith, a descendent of Jeremy Taylor's publisher, asserted that Steele's publication of passages from Taylor violated the copyright that Meredith claimed belonged to him, and demanded restitution. Neither Tonson nor Steele was convinced by Meredith's rather belligerent letters, and all that Meredith could do was publish them as *Mr. Steele Detected or the Poor and Oppressed Orphan's Letter to the Great and Arbitrary Mr. Steele* (London, 1714).[32] Despite Meredith's intervention, *The Ladies Library* sold well during the eighteenth century. The seventh edition appeared in 1772.

The diversity of Steele's interests – domestic, financial, theatrical and literary – in the period when he was primarily engaged in writing the *Tatler* and *Spectator* suggests his venturesome character and his active intellectual curiosity, his openness to a variety of cultural activities. But these characteristics well suited his role as the compiler, editor and author of broadly defined literary and social journals. Among these journals the *Guardian* seems peculiarly unstable – the shortest, the most diverse in authorship and content, and the most uneven. Written in a time of intense political pressure, it marks Steele's transition from a good-humoured social commentator to a blatant political spokesman.

The *Guardian* and the Quarrel with Swift

The *Guardian* began publication on 12 March 1713 and concluded its run on 1 October of the same year. Like the *Spectator*, it appeared six times a week, totalling 175 numbers by the end. As in the case of the *Spectator*, Steele had responsibility for producing the daily papers, but the *Guardian* had a broader range of contributors. Of the 175 numbers, eighty-two were by Steele, according to G. A. Aitken.[33] But the *Guardian*'s most recent editor, John Calhoun Stephens, more conservatively credits Steele with sole responsibility for fifty-seven or fifty-eight numbers and shared responsibility for six more.[34] In 'The Publisher to the Reader', which appeared in the first (1714) collected edition of the *Guardian*, Steele gratefully acknowledged his debt to the anonymous Addison, 'a Gentleman who has obliged the World with Productions too sublime to admit that the Author of them should receive any Addition to his Reputation, from such loose occasional Thoughts as make up these little Treatises'.[35] Addison was, of course, heavily involved in the preparation of his *Cato*, which premiered on 14 April and may not have been projected as a *Guardian* author at the outset. His first contribution, no. 67, an appreciation of the poet Tom D'Urfey, appeared on 28 May. He contributed only occasionally during the following weeks, but with no. 96 (1 July), he took over for an unbroken string of essays that ended with No. 124 (3 August). The string resumed on August 14 and ran through 21 August. Beginning with no. 152 (4 September), he reeled off a further fifteen essays, with only one interruption, before becoming silent for the final eight numbers of the periodical. After Steele decided to run for Parliament, Addison virtually replaced him on the *Guardian*.

'The Publisher to the Reader' goes on to list twelve further contributors. Eustace Budgell, who contributed only two essays; Alexander Pope, whose ironic mockery of Ambrose Philips's pastorals is one of the highlights of the series, and whom Steele credits with a further six essays (he probably contributed more); John Gay (two essays); Henry Martyn, whom Stephens credits with three essays articulating Whig issues; Ambrose Philips (four essays); Thomas Tickell (five essays on pastoral poetry, mocked by Pope in no. 40); 'Mr Carey' (either Henry or Walter), whose contributions are unidentified, as are those of Robert Ince; Laurence Eusden (two translations and perhaps other contributions); John Hughes (one essay and perhaps more); and Thomas Parnell (two dream visions). Berkeley made a major contribution, about a dozen essays, largely attacking free-thinking, but definitive attribution of some essays is hard to determine.[36] By the end of the *Guardian*'s run, Steele seems to have collected and even housed a stable of apprentice writers. An October 1713 letter to Oxford asserts that he

> hath 8 or 10 Persons, if not more that Lodges and Diats in his owne house in York buildings, and are Students in Oxford and Cambridge ... these Schollers were bright culled out men ... and were assisting to Mr. Steel and all upon Mr. Steel's Charge.[37]

Although by the end of the *Guardian* Steele seemed to collect a coterie of Whig propagandists, the collection of writers contributing to the *Guardian* at the outset was notably multi-partisan. Pope, Gay, Berkeley and Parnell were all Tories or (in the case of Pope) Tory sympathizers. In the brief period of relative partisan calm that marked the beginning of the *Guardian*, Steele may have been cultivating a non-partisan group of writers.

Nestor Ironside, the name of the *Guardian*'s editor and spokesman (or 'eidolon'), of course betokens age and wisdom – the proverbial Nestor of Homeric epic – but it represents as well a gradual movement towards the real Richard Steele. For the *Tatler*, Steele had borrowed Isaac Bickerstaff from Swift. Mr Spectator is a shared persona, with Addison's taciturnity and Steele's short face. Ironside denotes an armoured hero, prepared for battle, and thus an appropriate 'guardian', but it suggests as well the name and nature of Steele. In his first paper Ironside lays our his programme for the periodical:

> The main Purpose of the Work shall be to protect the Modest, the Industrious, to celebrate the Wise, the Valiant, to encourage the Good, the Pious, to confront the Impudent, the Idle, to condemn the Vain, the Cowardly, and disappoint the Wicked and Prophane. (*Guardian*, No. 1)

Such material will be of value to everyone, even 'Mechanick Hands'. 'As to these Matters, I shall be impartial, tho' I cannot be Neuter. I am, with Relation to the Government of the Church, a Tory, with Regard to the State, a Whig. The price of the paper will be two-pence., a half-penny more than other papers. Letters addressed to Nestor Ironside should be sent to Mr. Tonson.' He concludes, 'My Design, upon the whole, is no less, than to make the Pulpit, the Bar, and the Stage, all act in Concert in the Care of Piety, Justice, and Virtue'. (*Guardian*, no. 1)

Ironside's perplexing promise to be impartial but not neutral seems to separate his personal political leanings from his public analysis of party-statements. The statement seems to parallel his use of both Tory and Whig writers, and it leaves Steele free to pursue his own political agenda. But the first forty numbers of the *Guardian* are, if anything, more apolitical than was the *Spectator*. Thus Steele seems to open a space for political discourse that remained unoccupied for over six weeks. Instead, Steele and his colleagues provide a series of papers on criticism, characters, the roles of women and the foibles of men, a sequence continuing the familiar topics of the *Spectator*. Some of these papers are connected to the Ironside's friends the Lizard family, whom he introduces in the second *Guardian* and thereafter.

Nestor Ironside was born in 1642, near Brandford, with a fortune sufficient only to provide the basics. He went to Magdalen College, Oxford, where he met and became friends with Ambrose Lizard, later Sir Ambrose. Ambrose was married at the behest of his father, but the marriage worked out well. Thereafter Ironside summered with the Lizards, until, in 1674, Sir Ambrose engaged his friend as tutor and guardian (hence the title) of his son Marmaduke. Both Sir Ambrose and Marmaduke are now dead, but their widows are still alive. Marmaduke's wife Aspasia now has children of marriageable age, and the family's conversations and behaviour will be the subject of many papers. 'The Members of this Family, their Cares, Passions, Interests and Diversions shall be represented from time to time, as News from the Tea-Table of so accomplished a Woman as the intelligent and discreet Lady Lizard' (*Guardian*, no. 2). Ironside returns to the characters of the Lizards in Nos. 5 and 6. The dowager of Sir Ambrose does not converse outside the family, but the family includes Ironside. She and he engage in sad but tender recollections of the past: 'there is a kind of Sorrow, from which I draw a Consolation that strengthens my Faculties, and enlarges my Mind beyond any thing that can flow from Merriment' (*Guardian*, no. 5). Aspasia, the widow of Marmaduke is still rather attractive and has an ample fortune. Therefore she is still much courted by lovers but is bent on passing down her fortune to the next generation. Her daughter Jane, now twenty-three, is in love with a worthy man of minor fortune but is sought after by less worthy men of great fortune. Her prudent mother wants her to marry one of these, but Ironside hopes it will not come to that. Her sister Annabella is a lively, sensible, beautiful girl but rather vain and careless. Cornelia is a great reader of romances, Betty is interested in 'what passes in the Town', while Mary, the youngest, is Ironside's favourite because she resembles her grandfather, both in her character and in her affection for Ironside.

In addition to this collection of daughters, the Lizards have four sons. The oldest, Sir Henry, is a moderate country gentleman, twenty-six years old, well-educated, at least in business matters, punctual in his payments (the Lizards are scrupulous economists), and a good rider but not a racer of horses. He has the capacities to manage his estate responsibly and well (*Guardian*, no. 6). Several papers concern his ongoing matrimonial prospects. Thomas Lizard, the second son, has the secret of being amiable without design and an easy deportment and sagacity that will do him well at court. His brother William is 'not of this smooth Make', but curious and inquisitive, so that he will make a good lawyer. Ironside has made sure that he speaks well. John, the youngest, now nineteen, is a fellow at Oxford. He is a sincere young man with a 'Sublime Vein in Poetry'. He is resolved to go into Holy Orders (*Guardian*, no. 13).

In the Lizards Steele has accumulated a rich group of characters, four sons and five daughters, with interesting enough characteristics to make them worthy of Jane Austen, although she would presumably change their name from 'Lizard' to 'Bennet' or 'Dashwood'. Given Steele's skill as a storyteller and his experience as a dramatist, one might expect him to develop interesting vignettes, as character sketches or anecdotes or dialogues. But a major disappointment is that here, as in the *Spectator*, a promising narrative situation is introduced with interesting characters but then not developed beyond the several papers devoted to possible wives for Sir Henry. The Lizards, as depicted, suggest a number of usefully Whiggish topics, rather like those developed in Steele's previous periodicals. The large family allows a range of domestic topics, especially as framed by a matriarchy. Henry Lizard's eventual matrimony allows for far more papers than the few devoted to it, and his sister Jane's choice between affection and affluence promises a family dispute with a predictable sentimental outcome. Other sisters imply still further marital topics. Henry's succession to the estate engages issues of proper estate management – economy, generosity and investment. Other sons represent law, literature and the proper nature and role of the clergy. These topics represent the talking-points of Whig culture, but they were not pursued because of the pull of Whig politics. In part the Lizards are left unfulfilled because Steele was engaged on other issues within the *Guardian* and certainly pursuing other matters outside of it, but also because his political agenda, hardly apparent when the paper began, finally took over. Sir Henry, the ideal country squire, did not run for Parliament in 1713, but Richard Steele did. After Addison took over the paper in July 1713, the Lizard family was essentially dropped, and its place was taken by the 'Lion's Head', a hollow, open-mouthed device located at Button's Coffee House, into which letters and other contributions could be placed. The Lion's Head, the device by which, actually and symbolically, the *Guardian* contacted its audience, survived the closure of Button's and persisted at various coffeehouses until, in the early nineteenth century, it passed into private hands.[38]

The first forty numbers of the *Guardian* continue the broad, apolitical character of much of the *Spectator*. But the relatively slight emphasis on the characterized persona, the multiplicity of authors and the variety of topics tend to blur the paper's focus, although many individual essays are virtually the equal of those in the *Spectator*. There are several well-written essays on religion by Berkeley, various descriptions of the Lizard family, respectable critical essays by Steele and others, and a self-conscious series of essays of pastoral poetry by Thomas Tickell (a series intended to advance the reputation and presumably the sales of the 'Pastorals' of Ambrose Philips, himself a contributor). It was this series which commanded the attention of another, more powerful and subtle contributor to the *Guardian* – Alexander Pope. Pope's *Guardian*, no. 40, which begins as if it were a continuation of Tickell's series, compares the 'authentic', shepherdlike pastorals of Philips to the refined, Virgilian pastorals of Pope, and moves into parody of Philips's crude aesthetic. The unanswerable question ever since concerns the reasons for Steele's publication of this essay, which certainly infuriated his friend Philips. Pope's essay is as cunning as it is cutting, but it is hard to believe that Steele would have been deceived by its irony. It is possible that he accepted it on Pope's authority and published it without even reading it. It seems more likely that he was quite willing to risk a friend's anger for the sake of a brilliant essay. He may, of course, have seen Pope's irony as more good-humoured than Philips did. (Philips kept a switch at Button's with which to beat Pope if he ever came in.)

In fact the very next number of the *Guardian* proved decisive in determining the identity not only of the periodical but of Steele himself. One of the possible functions of the *Guardian*, indeed of any Whig paper during the period, was to respond, when deemed appropriate, to the attacks of the Tory *Examiner*, earlier edited by Swift, later by Mrs Manley, but now by William Oldisworth. The *Guardian*'s title came to suggest that it protected the country against Tory slander. In its issue of 21–4 April (vol. 3, no. 44), the *Examiner* attacked Daniel Finch, Earl of Nottingham, long a Tory stalwart, but now regarded as a renegade because of his support for the Whig position on the war. That sort of political apostasy suggested as well a religious apostasy, of which the *Examiner* now felt it had an example in the irreverent behaviour of Lady Charlotte Finch, Nottingham's daughter, who

> is taken *Knotting* in St. *James's Chapel*, during Divine Service, in the immediate Presence of both *God* and *Her Majesty*, who were affronted together, that the *Family* might appear to be entirely come over. I spare the *Beauty* for the sake of her *Birth*; but certainly there was no occasion for so publick a Proof, that her Fingers are more dexterous in *Tying a Knot*, than her *Father's* Brains in *perplexing the Government*.

The equation of 'tying a knot' with 'perplexing the government' derives from the 'knotting-Nottingham' homonym, and the complexity of the pun may have been one reason why Steele suspected Swift, a notorious lover of puns, as the author. (Other reasons include his awareness that Swift had been, even if he was not now, an editor of the *Examiner* and Swift's well-known antipathy to Nottingham, as expressed in his poem 'An Excellent New Song' (December 1711) and his broadside 'A Hue and Cry after Dismal'.) Steele had welcomed the conversion of Nottingham and may have been courting his patronage.[39] But the issue that touched him off was the embarrassing personal attack on Nottingham's arguably imprudent but otherwise innocent daughter. It was an attack on a damsel in distress that a guardian armed in steel ought to avenge. Hence in an unsigned letter to *Guardian*, no. 41 (April 28, 1713), after a spirited defence of Nottingham, he turns to his daughter:

> The utmost Malice and Invention could go no farther than to forge a Story of her having inadvertantly done an indifferent Action in a Sacred Place. Of what Temper can this Man be made, that could have no Sense of the Pangs he must give to a young Lady to be barely mentioned in a Publick Paper, much more to be named in a Libellous manner, as having offended God and Man.

Steele pushes further to seek the identity of the *Examiner* author: 'Lady *Char—te*'s Quality will make it impossible, that this cruel Usage cannot escape her Majesty's Notice, and 'tis the Business of every honest Man to trace the Offender, and expose him to the Indignation of his Sovereign'.

Examiner, vol. 3, no. 48, in response, notes that another letter has been brought, recounting Steele's satiric attacks on individuals in the *Tatler*, urging the *Examiner* not to respond to the *Guardian's* scurrilities, and suggesting that it act with Tory generosity rather than Whig resentment by apologizing to Lady Charlotte. But the *Examiner* does not quite do so. Steele's response, in *Guardian*, no. 53 changed the conventions of political discourse, especially regarding the names of people attacked and of the people attacking them. Ironside introduces the letter by pointing out that the previous letter in *Guardian*, no. 41 was written by Steele, 'a very good sort of a Man', who 'does not understand Politicks'. On rereading the *Examiner*, Ironside infers that the reference to words near the royal stamp imply that the *Examiner* writer intended to turn Steele out of his office. In his letter Steele contends that it is silly for an anonymous author, such as the author of the *Examiner*, to attack individuals by name. For himself, his satire in the *Tatler* used fictitious names and was addressed at general vices, so that any offence taken must be proof of guilt. He notes the *Examiner's* weak apology to Lady Charlotte and offers an apology in return:

> However, I will not bear hard upon his Contrition; but am now heartily sorry I called him a Miscreant, that word I think signifies an Unbeliever. *Mescroyant*, I take it, is the old *French* Word. I will give myself no manner of Liberty to make Guesses at him, if I may say him; for tho' I have sometimes been told, by familiar Friends, that they saw me such a Time talking to the *Examiner*, others, who have rally'd me upon the Sins of my Youth, tell me it is credibly reported that I have formerly lain with the *Examiner*. I have carried my Point, and rescued Innocence from Calumny; and it is nothing to me, whether the *Examiner* writes against me in the Character of an estranged Friend, or *an exasperated Mistress*. (*Guardian*, no. 53)

Steele is upset by the *Examiner's* attacks on Marlborough:

> In particular, I beg you, never let the Glory of our Nation, who made *France* tremble, and yet has that Gentleness to be able to bear Opposition from the meanest of his own Countrymen, be calumniated in so impudent a manner, as in the Insinuation that he affected a perpetual Dictatorship'. (*Guardian*, no. 53).

Here, as in the *Tatler*, Steele has not named his antagonists but has managed to make their identity absolutely clear. Swift immediately and angrily wrote to Addison to complain: 'I found he had, in several parts of it, insinuated with the utmost malice, that I was the author of the Examiner; and abused me in the grossest manner he could possibly invent, and set his name to what he had written'.[40] Swift reminds Steele that the author of the *Examiner* denied Swift's participation in the paper, as Swift would have told him if he had asked him personally, and he claims that Steele's attack is ungrateful because, as Steele knows, 'my Lord Treasurer has kept him in his employment upon my intreaty and intercession'.[41] Swift's response, however sincerely intended (a quality hard to evaluate at this distance in time), is disingenuous in several respects. If Swift was not editing the *Examiner* now, he certainly did so in the past and continued to supply hints and ideas to William Oldisworth, its present editor, with whom he corresponded, if he did not know him personally. He may well have believed (or been led by Oxford to believe) that Steele owed his continued employment in the Stamp Office to Swift's support, but Oxford's broad and secretive manipulations included more than Swift knew. 'They laugh at you, if they make you believe your interposition has kept me thus long in my office', Steele wrote in reply, and pointed out that Swift did not directly deny his connection with the *Examiner*.[42] He goes on to congratulate Swift on his appointment as Dean of St Patrick's, a further dig, since Swift had hoped for much more. Swift did not take kindly to being laughed at behind his back, and Steele had implied several such laughers – Oxford and the Tories, and Steele himself. His 23 May letter to Steele thus is detailed in narrating Swift's efforts to arrange a meeting between Steele and Oxford, efforts that were frustrated by Steele's failure to attend the meeting that had been arranged, much to Swift's embarrassment. If Steele's surmises about laughter were true, Swift argued, he would have been the object of that laughter for Steele's sake, and hence Steele's attack is not only unjustified but ungrateful. He repeats that he had nothing to do with the *Examiner* and 'had never exchanged one syllable with the supposed author in my life'.[43] Swift, of course, had exchanged far more than one word with Oldisworth, and Steele had exchanged letters with Oxford, and probably words as well, without Swift's intervention. Steele responded to Swift that he has overreacted:

> For an allusion to you, as one under the imputation of helping the Examiner, and owning I was restrained out of respect to you, you tell Addison, under your hand, You think me the vilest of mankind, and bid him tell me so. I am obliged to you for any kind things you said in my behalf to the Treasurer.

With careful ambiguity Steele assures him that 'when you were in Ireland, you were the constant subject of my talk to men in power at that time'.[44] He writes calmly, after Swift's 'ill usage', out of respect for him. In the last letter of the exchange (27 May) Swift announces that he is going to Ireland and wants to clarify that he did not attack Steele merely because of an allusion.

> This allusion was only calling a clergyman of some little distinction an infidel; a clergyman, who was your friend, who always loved you, who had endeavoured at least to serve you; and who, whenever he did write any thing, made it sacred to himself never to fling out the least hint against you.

He insists that he had also toned down Tory attacks on Marlborough (although, of course, he wrote *The Conduct of the Allies*, where attacks on Marlborough are blatant).[45] He left for Dublin several days later, and when he returned to London, he resumed the attack with a different subject.

The hostility between Steele and Swift that is expressed in this exchange developed over a long period of time and involved a number of factors. Rae Blanchard argues that Marlborough was 'the crux of the estrangement between Swift and Steele'.[46] Certainly Swift's attacks on Marlborough, especially in *The Conduct of the Allies*, echoed and prolonged in the *Examiner*, most immediately in *Examiner*, vol. 3, no. 47 (1–4 May 1713), would have irritated Steele, whose loyalty to the Duke had been briefly but fervently expressed in 'The Englishman's Thanks to the Duke of Marlborough' (January 1712). Steele must have felt that the *Examiner's* continuing attacks on Marlborough, after he had been deprived of his command of allied forces, were excessive. But he was irritated as well by the fact that Marlborough had been attacked directly and by name, while the author of the *Examiner* remained anonymous. He saw such anonymous attack as dishonourable, hence his concern to argue that his *Tatler* attacks had not named their targets. His signing of his letter to *Guardian*, no. 53 is thus part of his real or pretended campaign to shift the nature of political discourse from anonymous to responsible attack.[47] If Swift were not the present author of the *Examiner*, Steele might surmise that his false identification as the author simply derives from his insistence on anonymity and that his charge that Steele should have recognized his style is weak.

Steele's response to the *Examiner's* attack on Lady Charlotte further raises a question about the limits of personal attack, about the legitimacy of attacking women at all and, especially, about the morality of attacking a woman by name. Given the position of the *Tatler* and *Spectator* that a woman's proper role is limited to private and domestic life, the *Examiner's* condemnation of a woman who, even if she was knotting in church, was carrying on an activity appropriate to a woman, as contrasted, perhaps, to writing the *Examiner*, seems to step across the line distinguishing protected, private life from public activity. Steele stands for the public (and hence named) identity of authorship and the unnamed (if not unrecognized) identity of satiric targets; Swift stands for the private and unnamed identity of the author practising salutary satire by attacking publicly identified individuals. Bertrand Goldgar argues that the friendship between Swift and Steele had begun to deteriorate several years before this incident, that after Swift's shift to the Tory party it was virtually inevitable.[48] The issue may not be when their friendship ended but when their open hostilities began. Here, I think, the inception of their bitterness may be dated: for Steele with the *Examiner's* attack on Lady Charlotte Finch (24 April 1713), for Swift with Steele's insinuation in the *Guardian* that the Reverend Jonathan Swift was the author of that *Examiner* and that the author was a 'fawning Miscreant' (*Guardian*, no. 41), a description Steele pretends to take back while reminding his readers that the term means 'Unbeliever' (*Guardian*, no. 53). Among the many goads that irritated Swift to passion, questioning his vocation, especially in the midst of his disappointment at missing a bishopric, was paramount.

While Swift and Steele were conducting the argument on a personal level and largely through private letters, the *Examiner* and the *Guardian* were fighting on the public front. The *Examiner* noted with amusement that Steele's signed letters to a periodical he was editing under an assumed name provide him the opportunity to carry on a conversation with himself. It chides Steele because 'he has endeavour'd to Rescue *one Innocent Lady* by Blasting *another*; and in so negligent a manner, as if he were sensible of the little Expense this piece of Scandal cost him, the loss only of his Honour, Vertue, and Gratitude'.[49] In standing up for the former ministry, it goes on to say, Steele is defending the indefensible. Steele's response unattractively recognizes the claim that his attack on his alleged mistress was in error: 'I can now make her no Reparation, but in begging her Pardon, that I never lay with her'. He repeats his attack on the *Examiner* for attacking Marlborough (*Guardian*, no. 63).

Steele has placed the *Examiner* squarely in the *Guardian*'s sights as a target for political responses. These are persistent but not frequent and sometimes minor. Although Stephens notes that 'the essay continues in humourous vein the very topics concerning which he had been tilting with the *Examiner*',[50] the prime allusions from *Guardian*, no. 64 to that combat are letters that refer to Ironside as '*Guardian* of good Fame', and 'Avenger of Detraction'. *Guardian*, no. 65 does discuss general misbehaviour that Ironside has observed in Church, as if to contrast this real disrespect to the minor foible of Lady Charlotte. Support for the Whigs is continued in no. 76, where Henry Martyn argues that trade returns money to the landed interests, so that an enmity between the City and Country is unreal.

The *Examiner* of 5–8 June complained that 'the *Whigs* indeed use the Government worse than a *Common Enemy*, and push the War at home with more Vigour than they formerly did that abroad', as instanced by the lukewarm celebration of the Peace of Utrecht by Whiggish clergymen, especially at St Paul's Cathedral. Steele reads this as disrespect toward the Church and suggests, again, that this disrespect derives from Swift: 'The *Examiner*, upon the Strength of being a received Churchman, has offended in this particular more grossly as any other Man ever did before, and almost as grossly as ever he himself did' (*Guardian*, no. 80, June 12, 1713). He prints a long letter demonstrating in detail the falsity of the *Examiner*'s characterization of celebrations at St Paul's. In no. 90, Steele prints a letter which he claims is genuine (but may not be) that defends the debunking of the life and miracles of St Wenefrede, one of Wales's more outlandish saints, in a book by William Fleetwood, Bishop of St Asaph. Fleetwood was a publicly Whig Bishop, whose volume of sermons was condemned by the

Tory Parliament the previous year, after its 'Preface' had been published by Steele in *Spectator*, no. 384. Steele wrote only two more *Guardian* papers, nos. 94 and 95, June 29 and 30, before turning editorial responsibility over to Addison for the month of July. When he returned, it was with a more defined political topic and a more avid partisan energy.

Politics and Parliament

In March 1713, before he had adopted the strategy of signing his tracts, Steele published a *Letter to Sir M. W. Concerning Occasional Peers*, signed Francis Hicks, and arguing against the creation of new peers to support the passage of contro-versial commercial clauses of the Treaty of Utrecht in the House of Lords.[51] 'Sir M. W.' is Sir Miles Warton or Wharton, who had refused to be made a peer when Queen Anne created new ones to pass the Treaty of Utrecht. The possibility of a repeat creation stirred Steele's fears that the constitution could be rewritten whenever the occasion warranted. 'Occasional' peers are compared to occasional conformists: 'It is amazing that such Care should be taken to prohibit an Occa-sional Conformist from being a Constable, and no Body takes it in his Head to prevent an Occasional Lord from being a Judge, nay, Legislator.'[52] Steele's tract earned a much longer response, which argued, by way of a rather elemental dis-cussion of mixed government and a historical review of the occasions when it had become unbalanced, that Steele's proposal that new peers should not vote for three years after their creation deprived the Queen of the prerogative to cre-ate peers and to make war and peace.[53] In the upshot the new Peers were not created on this occasion, and the commercial clauses, which were seen as giving inappropriate trade advantages to France, were narrowly defeated later in the spring of 1713. In the meantime the Treaty of Utrecht itself was signed on 11 April 1713.

On 4 June, Steele sent a letter to Robert Harley (Earl of Oxford since May 1711) announcing his intention to run for Parliament and, since he could not do so as a Commissioner in the Stamp Office, resigning from that position. The letter had been a difficult one for Steele to write because he owed Oxford some thanks for allowing him to continue in his lucrative sinecure at the stamp office, but they were separated by party, and Steele had written harshly of Oxford and his policies. An earlier draft of the letter, dated 23 May, in the midst of Steele's battle with Swift, notes that he had 'uttered expressions in the Guardian which I cannot but suppose would be something unacceptable to you'. He assures Oxford that he has 'the greatest abhorrence imaginable' for 'the opinions and prejudices of Party', but the vicious attacks of the *Examiner* on the Duke of Marlborough have required his responses, which he has offered 'from no other motive in nature but the Love of Truth'.[54] His rather awkward explanation of his possibly offensive writing takes up most of the letter, and his intention to run for Parliament seems to come as an afterthought. In the revised version that he actually sent, he begins with his 'Ambition to Serve in the ensuing Parliament'; neither Marlborough nor the *Examiner* is mentioned, although he again insists 'that Whatever I have done, said, or writ has proceeded from no other motive, but the Love of, what I think, Truth'.[55] He congratulates Oxford on his power and prominence and promises that should he lose them, he will find a friend and advocate in Steele, a promise that, as we shall see, he did not quite manage to keep. Steele was included on a 12 June list of appointments to the Commission, so that he wrote again on 30 July to remind Oxford of his resignation. He also resigned his position as Gentleman-Usher to Prince George of Denmark, Queen Anne's late husband. He was now without government employment – or salary.

But he was certainly getting money from the Whigs or various Whig patrons such as Wharton or Nottingham. Candidates for election were expected to spend freely or bribe widely to gain the support of their constituents. Steele had given up his profitable crown employments to run for Parliament, yet 1713 was a year of near financial security for him. Aitken reports only one action for debt brought against Steele in 1713.[56] The constituency in which Steele stood for Parliament was Stockbridge, Hampshire, not a pocket borough but one in which all local taxpayers had the right to vote. These votes must, of course, be paid for. Defoe describes Stockbridge as 'a poor sorry brought town, noted for its corruption in electing Members of Parliament, two of whom it returns'.[57] A local legend recounted in Richard Warner's *Collections for the History of Hampshire and the Bishopric of Winchester* (London, 1795) and retold by Calhoun Winton 'tells of Steele offering an apple stuck full of guineas to be given to the elector voting for him whose wife was first brought to bed of a child nine months thereafter'. The reward was said to be celebrated by women decades later.[58] Parliament prorogued on 27 July, and the election process officially commenced.

There were real issues to be addressed in the 1713 election. The Tories took credit for ending the war, along with the taxation and the loss of life that it caused, hence they won the election handily. But the Commercial clauses of the Treaty of Utrecht had failed in Parliament, and they provided the occasion for Whigs to speak of Tory insensitivity to England's commercial establishment. The Whigs decried the sacrifice of English lives for an inadequate peace and insisted that the Tories were handing the country to France by ruining the economy. The prime Whig issues were trade (the rejection of the commercial clauses) and the Jacobite succession. The argument was that the commercial clauses would create an unfavourable balance of trade with France and would impede trade with Portugal.[59] A particular issue that engaged Steele's attention was the failure of the French to demolish the fortifications at the port of Dunkirk, as required by the ninth article of the Treaty of Utrecht. That issue became a significant centre of Steele's propaganda efforts in the ensuing months, and those efforts were to unleash a storm of counterattack from the Tories. In the midst of the debate, Steele announced, in *Guardian*, no. 168, that he had won the Stockbridge election by a vote of fifty to twenty-one.

Steele's anxiety to enter Parliament, and the willingness of his Whig friends to finance his campaign probably derived from a plan for the conduct of Whig propaganda. As the Ministry was preparing its case for Steele's expulsion from Parliament, Daniel Defoe, who had joined the ranks of prominent debaters against Steele, wrote to Oxford regarding Steele's purpose in Parliament: 'The new champion of the party, Mr. Steele, is now to try to an experiment upon the Ministry, and shall set up to make speeches in the House and print them, that the malice of the party may be gratified and the Ministry be bullied in as public a manner as possible'.[60] Steele and his allies would not, of course, use the same language as Defoe in describing his propaganda intentions, but Defoe was correct in his insight that the Whigs were trying an experiment that would change the process of political discourse. Steele would become an embedded reporter, both an actor in political deliberations and a commentator on them. The standard ministerial retort to pamphleteers, that they could do no more than write out of ignorant supposition, could hardly be sustained if the author of such pamphlets were himself a member of Parliament. Steele's presence in the House and his willingness to write about what took place there threatened the confidentiality of parliamentary debates that ostensibly prevailed in the early eighteenth century. But before he had even entered Parliament, Steele called hostile attentions to himself by his writings regarding Dunkirk.

The Dunkirk Debate

The Treaty of Utrecht stipulated that Louis XIV

> should take care that all the fortifications of the City of Dunkirk should be razed, that the harbour be filled up, and that the sluices or moles which serve to cleanse the harbour be levelled, and that at the said King's expense, within the space of five months after the conditions of peace are concluded.[61]

By the late spring considerable concern had arisen, especially among the Whigs, as to whether this demolition was being carried out and whether the Ministry had any interest in enforcing this provision. That curiosity was sparked in particular by the Francophile character of the commercial clauses and by the general principle that the interests of France were the interests of the Pretender. In early July the Duc D'Aumont, who had recently been Governor of Dunkirk, had an audience with the Queen, and he was swiftly followed by M. Tugghe, one of Dunkirk's magistrates, who presented the Queen with a memorial urging that the harbour and port of Dunkirk not be destroyed. This address was roundly rejected by Bolingbroke but subsequently printed at the end of July. It became the occasion for Steele's response in *Guardian*, no. 128.

The substance of *Guardian*, no. 128 is a letter signed 'English Tory', presumably because the position of any English Whig would have been so clear that reading the essay would have been unnecessary. 'English Tory' begins with a negative comment that seems to signal the shift of the *Guardian* to more serious political topics. He rejects the concern for fashion that Erin Mackie finds characteristic of the *Tatler* and *Spectator*:[62] 'You employ your important Moments, methinks, a little too frivolously, when you consider so often little Circumstances of Dress and Behaviour, and never make mention of Matters wherein you and all your Fellow-Subjects in general are concerned' (*Guardian*, no. 128). He corrects M. Tugghe's assertion (or Bolingbroke's assertion as reported by Tugghe) that 'her Majesty did not think to make any Alteration in the dreadful Sentence she had pronounced against the Town'. In fact, he goes on, 'her Majesty has pronounced no Sentence against the Town, but his most Christian Majesty has agreed that the Town and Harbour shall be Demolished'. He insists 'That the *British* Nation expect the immediate Demolition of it'. The letter continues with a number of insistent clauses in the form of bullet points. These tend to coalesce into two major arguments. (1) England has suffered considerably as a result of the fortified harbor of Dunkirk, from which substantial fleets sailed during the recent war, from which the Pretender sailed on his unsuccessful 1708 foray to Scotland, and from which 'Runners' can spy on the shipping on the Thames and Medway. (2) The destruction of Dunkirk in effect moves France, or French shipping, several hundred miles further away – to Brest on the Atlantic coast. In the course of making these points, Steele's English Tory insists twice more 'that the *British* Nation expects the Demolition of *Dunkirk*', a phrase that was to become the subject of considerable recrimination on the part of Tory pamphleteers. Steele's point was clear: not only did the continued fortification of Dunkirk aid the French, it harmed the English and, in particular, provided a convenient launching-point for invasion by the Pretender. Destroying the fortifications would make Brest the nearest fortified harbour, and to attack from Brest, as Steele later wrote, it would be necessary to sail west into the Atlantic but then swing east and up the Channel – in effect sailing into the wind on one leg of the journey.

The Tories lost no time in counterattacking, but in doing so they paid scant attention to Steele's actual arguments. As I have argued elsewhere, the propaganda stirred up by Steele had relatively little to do with facts and issues but a great deal to do with the perceived authority of the arguers.[63] Defoe, here disguised as a country Whig, was the first to pile on (14 August) with the assertion that Steele, previously a moderate man who appealed to a variety of political opinions, had now 'made your Friends asham'd of you, made the moderate Men hate you, and the warmer Tories triumph over us in your Infirmity'.[64] The prerogative to make war or peace rests with the Queen, and if the Queen in her wisdom decides that the immediate destruction of Dunkirk is unwise, the nation has no right to 'expect' it. To make matters worse Steele has spoken to the Queen 'just as an Imperious Planter at *Barbadoes* speaks to a Negro Slave'.[65] Defoe, the Whig pretending to be a Tory writer who is now pretending to be a Whig, asks whether Steele is really a secret Tory, since he has betrayed the Whigs by addressing the Queen in language that is both offensive and unparliamentary. He hints that if elected (Steele was actually elected on 25 August), he could expect to be expelled: 'What think you, Mr. *Steele, Would* the People resent that Treatment of the Sovereign, and think those Men unworthy ever to represent a Loyal, Dutiful Nation any more, *Or would they not?*'[66] The *Examiner* of 14–21 August (vol. 4, no. 27) quickly took up the chorus. Steele's supposed insistence that the nation will resent the Queen if she does not see to it that Dunkirk is immediately destroyed amounts to a supreme insult. If Steele continues such insults as a Member of Parliament, he will 'obtain the *Honour*, as another of their haughty Leaders [Robert Walpole] has already done, *of being Expelled the House*'.[67] Four days after Steele was elected MP from Stockbridge, Swift left Ireland, where he had gone in order to be installed as Dean of St Patrick's Cathedral, for England. (He arrived on 9 September.)

Defoe returned to the attack in early September by pointing out that Dunkirk was in English possession and therefore of more use to the English intact than destroyed. It should particularly be retained if it has the importance that the *Guardian* suggests, but Defoe (or the anonymous English Protestant who, he claims, is writing the letter) suspects that Dunkirk has merely been captured by the Whigs as an issue of political propaganda. At some length, he accuses the author of the *Guardian* letter of insolence, falsehood, sedition and absurdity.[68] John Toland answered Defoe and extended the argument on the Whig side with an alarmingly-titled pamphlet: *Dunkirk or Dover; or, The Queen's Honour, The Nation's Safety, The Liberties of Europe, and The Peace of the World, All at Stake till that Fort and Port be totally demolish'd by the French*. He responds to Defoe's position that the British should keep Dunkirk or sell it back to the French. He insists that the Tories have too extensive a view of the Queen's prerogative: 'the Prerogative is no more a justification of concluding a disadventageous Peace, than beginning an unjust War'.[69] The ceding of Dunkirk provisionally to the British and its return to France after its fortifications were destroyed was the result of long negotiation and approved by the Queen and Parliament. If this clause of the treaty is not fulfilled, there will be no assurance that any provision will be obeyed.

Steele, by now, had gathered enough antagonism to warrant a careful response. *The Importance of Dunkirk Consider'd; In Defence of the* Guardian *of* August *the 7ᵗʰ. In a Letter to the Bailiff of* Stockbridge (London, 1713) prints M. Tugghe's published petition to the Queen (or at least the English translation of it), *Guardian*, no. 128, passages from *The Honour and Prerogative of the Queen's Majesty*, and passages from the two *Examiner* papers (21 and 24 August) on the subject. He begins his account of 'the Advantages the Nation might reap from the Demolition, which will appear by Considering what Part of our Trade has and may be annoy'd by *Dunkirk*' by a rather laboured extension of his *Guardian* discussion of the geographical advantage of Dunkirk to the French in interrupting British trade in the Channel.[70] He insists that M. Tugghe rather than he has been disrespectful of the Queen and proceeds to a point-by-point discussion of Tugghe's Memorial (famous for Swift's mockery of its elegant variation), concluding that 'It will be a great Act of Humanity to insist upon the Demolition of that Town, which has destroyed so many Thousand of her Majesty's Subjects and their Ships'.[71] He then turns to his 'Domestick Foes', who have falsely accused him of ungratefully quarrelling with the Queen while in her employment. He points out that he has given up all such employment to be an MP and therefore writes as a disinterested party. He notes that the Ministry has the power to silence the *Examiner* but for some reason has not done so despite the *Examiner's* repeated attacks on virtue and innocence.

Taking up the vague meaning of the term 'Royal Prerogative', Steele defines it in a sense more favourable to his argument: 'The true Meaning and Use of the Prerogative is to be interpreted and understood by the Rules of the joint Welfare and Happiness of Prince and People'.[72] Steele's move to include the welfare of the country under the prerogative of the monarch implies that his statement that the Nation expect the treaty to be followed cannot insult that prerogative. If the Royal Prerogative were used as a threat to silence the expression of honest opinion, the monarch, 'whatever Advantage his Ministers might make of his Prerogative, would himself have no Prerogative but that of being deceiv'd'.[73] Steele protests that he is acting as a private individual and that as a Member of Parliament he will act independently. In using the term 'expects', even if it were addressed to the Queen, which it was not, Steele is doing his duty by warning of a danger to the nation and hence to the Queen herself. Steele summarizes *A Letter to the Guardian about* Dunkirk, which supports his position, and answers Defoe's *Reasons concerning the Immediate Demolishing of Dunkirk*. He denies the imputation that he has 'secret Views of Supports' in running for Parliament and writing about the affairs of state. He insists once more that he is completely disinterested and provides a Spectatorial moral sermon on the value of such charitable behaviour: 'The greatest Merit is in having social Virtues, such as Justice and Truth exalted with Benevolence to Mankind'.[74] He contrasts this public spirit to the 'prostituted Pens' that attack him, whose malice he will endure patiently. Another person who possesses public virtue is the Queen. 'By Her great Example, Religion, Piety, and all other Publick and domestick Virtues, are kept in Countenance in a very loose and profligate Age'.[75] The tract thus ends with a panegyric on the Queen.

These attacks and responses of August and September 1713 lay out most of the major themes that were to be debated by Steele and his antagonists for the remainder of the year. They seek to define the nature of political discourse in a constitutional monarchy and the particular voice that Steele was trying to find within that discourse. *Guardian*, no. 128 appeared on 7 August; Steele was elected on 25 August. Steele's *Guardian* paper can therefore be viewed as a contribution to the election campaign, indeed to Steele's campaign in particular. The strength of the Tory electoral appeal lay in the fact that they had won a significant peace with France, a peace that had increased Britain's colonial power and ended a war that had been costly in lives and money. The only argument that Steele and the Whigs could make was the argument implied in *Guardian*, no. 128 and its successors – that the peace was a poor one (a) because it did not adequately protect Britain and its interests, particularly its trade interests, and (b) because there was no guarantee that the French, known for violating treaties in the past, would abide by the provisions of this one, and here the failure to demolish the Dunkirk fortifications was the prime example.

Tory reaction to Steele's bold assertion that the nation 'expects' the demolition of Dunkirk diverted the argument away from the issue of French adherence to the Treaty and onto the issue of the royal prerogative. Clearly matters of war and peace rested with the Crown. Implementation of a treaty became a somewhat cloudy issue, one of several that the debate over Dunkirk sought to resolve. The 'Royal Prerogative' is the power exclusive to the monarch, and because it is exclusive it is also beyond challenge. But the problem that needed definition was nature, scope and limits of that power. In particular, were actions of the ministry, taken in the name of the Queen, included in that prerogative? If so, what were the limits to such protected ministerial action? These questions remained unresolved after the agreements of 1689. They were not addressed in the abstract, however; the issue of the royal prerogative was engaged in particular cases, of which the demolition of Dunkirk was one. For Steele the royal prerogative included the will and welfare of the people. For the Ministry it was coterminous with their own will. The issue, like others involved in the Dunkirk debate, could shift depending on the historical circumstances. The royal prerogative was sacrosanct to Swift when he claimed Steele violated it in 1713, but it was a false claim of overweening ministerial power when he argued against Wood's half-pence in 1724.[76]

The problem of defining royal prerogative quickly shades into the broader question of who is authorized to discuss matters of state and what the grounds for such authority are. At one extreme everyone has a right to articulate an opinion and to do so publicly. But if everybody does so, there are no grounds for believing anyone. Granted that the cogency of an argument may be a reason to believe it, the authority of the arguer remains an issue. Even the most cogent argument must be read to be believed. The problem is complicated by the anonymity of pamphleteers. Steele's unusual move to sign his pamphlets and to write periodicals with transparent personae is an effort to assert the identity of the author as a basis for authority. In the absence of an authoritative author the political identity of a given periodical (the *Examiner* for the Tories, the *Medley* for the Whigs) supplies an identity while allowing actual authors to change over a period of months. Publishers of tracts and pamphlets (Morphew and Baker for the Tories, Buckley and Baldwin for the Whigs) suggest political leanings without revealing authorship. An important tract such as *The Conduct of the Allies* may establish a thread of political discourse tied clearly to the issues and positions it expresses. At the other extreme is the position that no one other than those with direct responsibility for government has the right to discuss matters of state. This draconian position underlies efforts by successive Tory and Whig administrations to suppress opposing writings on the grounds of seditious libel. It justifies the policy of keeping parliamentary debate confidential. It forms a significant motive for the Stamp Act of 1712. The government seeks to control the flow of information, and to do so it both distributes information formally (the *Gazette*) and informally (the *Examiner*) and it limits and represses the distribution of opposing views.

Steele sought to establish a position midway between these apparently antithetical extremes. By identifying himself as a political author, he was, unlike Swift and Oldisworth, and unlike Maynwaring and Addison, engaging information regarding his own life and experience as elements establishing his authority to be heard. He was, in effect, replacing the manufactured persona of the periodical – a persona that grew more transparent as it moved from Bickerstaff to Mr Spectator to Nestor Ironside and finally (as of early October) to Mr. Englishman – with the lineaments of his own features. He had served as Gazetteer and had held various court and political appointments. He was thus familiar with the political milieu in a way that some other writers were not. But familiarity is a weak claim to authority, and Steele's candidacy for Parliament was in part an effort to establish a solid basis for political writing by being both political actor and political commentator, by reporting both to his constituents and to the public at large. Hence *The Importance of Dunkirk Consider'd* takes the form of a letter to the Mr John Snow, Bailiff of Stockbridge.

By establishing his personal identity as a source of political authority, Steele, of course, opened himself to a variety of personal attacks that sought to question, ridicule or otherwise demolish that authority. The most important and effective of these attacks came in Jonathan Swift's *The Importance of the Guardian Considered* (London, 1713), published on 2 November 1713. Swift had returned from Ireland, partly to see if he could somehow reduce the friction between Oxford and Bolingbroke. On arriving he was quite happy to find that his enemy had written a book, or at least a political tract of rather uneven quality. Swift uses Steele's permission to treat him as a 'Brother-Scribbler' rather than as an 'honest Man' as the excuse to say almost nothing about the substance of Steele's argument but a great deal about Steele himself, his prose style and manner of arguing, and his inconsistencies. He shifts his own modes of argument rapidly, as though to demonstrate the ubiquity of Steele's foolishness. He too writes a letter to John Snow and seeks to correct the misleading statements in Steele's.

Writing as 'A Friend of Mr. St—le', an irony that once was true, Swift points out that the electors of Stockbridge, by virtue of their cultural distance from London, may not have known their elected representative very well. Swift will rectify that ignorance. He describes Steele as a man of some skill and accomplishment, but not very much: 'He hath no Invention, nor is Master of a tolerable Style; his chief Talent is Humour, which he sometimes discovers both in Writing and Discourse; for after the first Bottle he is no disagreeable Companion'.[77] But Swift emphasizes two faults in particular, both linked to previous personal disagreements with Steele – ingratitude and personal exaggeration. The first is exemplified at some length by Steele's failure to acknowledge that Oxford had significantly raised his salary as Gazetteer. Steele's claim to Snow that his importance is illustrated by the fact that he is 'spoken of more than once in Print' plays upon Snow's ignorance that half-a-dozen insignificant (or even fictitious) scribblers and artisans are similarly mentioned in print. When Steele spoke of laying the Dunkirk issue before the Ministry, he did not mean a formal document but a letter to a penny periodical.

Having chipped away at the foundations of Steele's character, Swift turns to his writing and especially his style. He has great fun with the various circumlocutions by which Steele refers, in *Guardian*, no. 128, to M. Tugghe and the various headings of his petition. He lists these and adds, 'I could heartily wish Monsieur *Tugghe* had been able to find Ten Arguments more, and thereby given Mr. *Steele* an Opportunity of shewing the utmost Variations our Language would bear in so momentous a Tryal'.[78] In taking up Steele's text more closely, Swift achieves an effective multi-vocal mingling of text and ironic commentary on it. Thereby Swift can transform Steele's reasonable statements into absurdities. For example, Steele argues that the assertions of Defoe and the *Examiner* make rational discourse impossible:

> But the Author of the Letter from the Country Whig, personates that Character so awkwardly, and the *Examiner*, without entering into the Point, treats me so outrageously, that I know not how to offer against such Adversaries, Reason and Argument, without appearing void of both.[79]

Swift removes the conditional clauses that justify the conclusion, and therefore forces Steele into an apparent contradiction:

> Well, but he tells you, he cannot offer against the Examiner and his other Adversary, Reason and Argument without appearing void of both. What a singular Situation of the Mind is this! How glad should I be to hear a Man offer Reasons and Argument and yet at the same time appear void of both![80]

Swift's commentary here, however entertaining, is itself devoid of reason and argument, at least in the philosophical sense. But he is more substantial when he pursues Tory talking points and identifies Steele's contradictions. He berates Steele for his defence of Marlborough and for his insistence that the Ministry, having closed down the *Flying-Post*, ought to close down the *Examiner* as well. He notes Steele's claim that as a private individual he has a right to instruct the Queen on what the nation expects but points out that the Whigs silenced a clergyman (Sacheverell) who sought to look at political matters from a religious perspective. 'If a Clergy-man offers to preach Obedience to the higher Powers, and proves it by Scripture, Mr. *Steele* and his Fraternity immediately cry out, What have Parsons to do with Politicks?'[81] Sacheverell's authority came from his learning and religious position, but Steele can hardly derive authority from publishing the *Tatler*. Does his authority to direct his monarch derive from 'his being a Soldier, Alchymist, Gazetteer, Commissioner of Stampt Papers, or Gentleman-Usher? No; but he insists it is every Man's right to find Fault with the Administration in Print, whenever they please'.[82] Ultimately Steele the self-interested scribbler hired by his party is contrasted to the thoughtful, dutiful and disinterested Queen whom he pretends to instruct.

Swift's attack was distinctly focused on Steele. It had virtually nothing to do with the wisdom of destroying Dunkirk, with the importance of holding France to its treaty obligations, or with the balance of power in Europe. Steele was attempting to shift the nature of political discourse from the irresponsible anonymity of the *Examiner* to the identification of authors who took public responsibility for what they wrote and whose personal identity included the accomplishment and experience to give authority to their arguments. For Swift, the absence of the author threw considerable emphasis on prose style and logical arguments, and these are key elements of Swift's attack in *The Importance of the Guardian Considered*. But Steele had, from Swift's point of view, committed the serious error of not only revealing but trumpeting his identity. If Steele's argument was that the integrity of the author's identity helped establish the authority of his argument and that an author who was also a Member of Parliament carried an enhanced authority, his personal integrity was open to attack and, in light of the shift he was seeking to effect, it was important to wage an attack. Thus Swift's arguments sought to eliminate any sense that Steele was a reliable source of information. In doing so he was also establishing a basis for the eventual prosecution of Steele by the Tories and for his expulsion from Parliament. Swift also must have felt some personal pleasure in the fact that by attacking Steele he had avenged himself on Steele's nastiness of the previous spring.

The tendency to attack the messenger rather than the message was loudly reiterated some ten days later in *The Character of Richard St—-le, Esq.; with some Remarks. By Toby, Abel's Kinsman*. Steele and others have thought the work was by Swift, but it was included in the *Miscellaneous Works of Dr. William Wagstaffe* which was published a year after Wagstaffe's death.[83] The argument is that Steele is a man of modest talents (derived, for the most part from others) but immense gall in addressing matters of war and peace and telling the Queen what the nation expects.

> Mr St—le, in short, has neither an Head, nor a Style, for Politicks; there is no one Political *Englishman* but contains either some notorious Blunder in his Notions or his Language; and he seems himself so well aware of this, that he is already run from his Purpose.[84]

By changing the conventions of political discourse by moving from anonymous to named authorship, Steele had made himself the personal target of propaganda attack. He did not have the advantage that Defoe and Swift exploited so successfully of shifting personae to engage a variety of perspectives. Instead he shifted his periodicals and with that shift he changed his topic. Dunkirk was something of a Potemkin village. The real threat it concealed was the threat of the Pretender.

The *Guardian* served as a transition from Steele's genial social commentary to his outspoken political activism. Although it is difficult to know exactly when Steele decided to make the shift and to run for Parliament, Steele's attack on the *Examiner* in *Guardian*, no. 41 (28 April 1713) for insulting Lady Charlotte Finch was the first public manifestation of the *Guardian's* political engagement. It was certainly the beginning of its paper war with the *Examiner*. It was also the beginning of Steele's personal battle with Swift, which was to continue until Steele was expelled from Parliament. Steele's movement from social commentary to politics was thus intertwined with personal rancour and propaganda. In all likelihood it was also motivated in part by financial considerations. Steele wrote to his mother-in-law on 25 October 1712 that his family was now 'supported only by my Industry', and much of that industry was the production of the *Tatler* and *Spectator*. With the *Guardian*, his financial situation was eased by the inheritance he received from Mrs Scurlock, but the remodeling of his space in the York Buildings was an investment that had not yet realized a return. The willingness of Whig magnates to fund his political writing and even his parliamentary career was a partial motive. The charge that Steele sought Parliament as a refuge from creditors is probably not a complete fabrication. Moreover, the situation of periodical publishing had shifted from the *Spectator* days. The tax on paper substantially reduced the circulation of periodicals, making them less attractive as a source of income.

But the personal rancour, paper war and financial need were perhaps less important factors than Steele's genuine alarm at the weakness of the Treaty of Utrecht, his fear that a Jacobite Succession was likely, and his anger at the calumnies directed at Marlborough, Godolphin (now dead), Wharton and other members of the Whig ministry (an alarm, fear, and anger generally shared by Whigs). In order to address a political environment that he saw as dangerous, he redefined the nature of political discourse and the relationship between political writers and government. Arthur Maynwaring had been a Member of Parliament who took on the task of writing and directing propaganda for the Whigs. Steele, his ultimate successor in propagandizing, reversed the direction by moving from being a writer to becoming an MP, with the clear design of writing about matters discussed in Parliament. A rather specialized glimpse of what might have resulted is possible in his *Apology*, in which his own speech in Parliament is surrounded by contextual information and attacks on Tories. Beyond political disagreements, Tories surely regarded this combination of politician and political writer both as offensive overreaching and as a serious affront to the confidentiality that protected political debate. The nature of the propaganda and the argument over such propaganda are evident in the *Englishman*, *The Crisis*, Steele's expulsion from Parliament, and the fall of the Tories themselves.

5 *THE CRISIS* AND THE SUCCESSION

The *Englishman* and the Debate over Succession

On Thursday, 1 October, *Guardian*, no. 175 recommended Rev. William Derham's *Physico-Theology*, a series of sermons on God and the physical universe. There was no indication that the series was coming to an end. On Tuesday 6 October, the *Englishman* published its first number. The fact that the periodical appeared thrice weekly rather than daily probably took some pressure off of Steele, although he had only written about half-a-dozen of the fifty or so *Guardian* papers that appeared in August and September. The motto of the first *Englishman* paper, Cato's famous imperative 'Delenda est Carthago', signals the sense of urgency that Steele imposes. The author of the *Englishman* claims to have purchased the writing equipment of Nestor Ironside, 'who has thought fit to write no more himself'. Ironside encourages his successor:

> It is not, said the good Man, giving me the Key of the Lion's Den, now a Time to improve the Taste of Men by the Reflections and Railleries of Poets and Philosophers, but to awaken their Understanding, by laying before them the present State of the World like a Man of Experience and a Patriot.

He goes on to urge his successor to '*Be an* ENGLISHMAN'.[1] The paper marks a clear shift away from the position articulated by the *Tatler* and *Spectator* that responsible readers should not concern themselves with political rumours but with moral and intellectual truths.

The change in persona is meant to underscore the urgency of the political context. As P. B. J. Hyland noted, in the eyes of Steele's contemporaries 'the explicit party logic of the *Englishman* represented a decisive break with the traditions of Steele's work, for the image of an impartial and thoroughly agreeable persona could no longer be observed'.[2] Nestor Ironside, the friend, companion and advisor of the Lizard family, could hardly serve as a spokesman against the calumnies of the *Examiner* or in defence of the Protestant Succession. He was created as a private figure rather than a public disputant. Nonetheless, he continued to appear in the *Englishman* as the author's friend and correspondent, and in the pamphlet literature surrounding the periodical and its controversies he functioned as a cognate for Steele himself. Ironside's occasional reappearance gave Steele another voice to add to those of Mr Englishman and himself (and, of course, the real or fictional writers of letters). Steele emerges in the first *Englishman* number, writing a long letter to an anonymous but clearly ministerial Lord (Oxford) to complain of the insults heaped on him by his servant (the *Examiner*). Steele's response does not seem much more than an exchange of insults (with particular digs at Swift), but it is a clear admission that Steele is the driving force behind the *Englishman* and that the *Englishman* is at war with the *Examiner*.

Rae Blanchard is probably right in her surmise that

> these moves were arranged within the councils of the Whig party – with the leaders of the old guard, Lord Halifax, Steele's personal friend, for one; with the younger genera-tion of Whig leaders, Walpole and Stanhope, lately returned from was service overseas; with the Hanover Club, organized avowedly to fight the dynasty battle to a finish; and with the trade-minded sponsors of the Whig anti-French commercial policy.[3]

But the danger of a Jacobite succession, which called into question the revolution principles that Steele associated with his hero William III, clearly ignited Steele's political passions.[4] The urgency derives in part from recent pamphlets, or pam-phlets known to be forthcoming, supporting the case for the Jacobite succession. *Seasonable Queries relating to the Birth and Birthright of a Certain Person, James Edward Francis Stuart*, reprinted the section relating to the Pretender from a book by the non-juror George Hickes. As its title suggests, it argues the legiti-macy and force of the Jacobite claim to the crown and begs the question of why such an argument is seasonable. One cause of its immediacy was the chronic ill health of the Queen, which was to become more acute in December. *Seasonable Queries* argues forcibly that James III was a legitimate and therefore undeniable monarch on the basis of hereditary descent.[5] In *Englishman*, no. 5 (15 October 1713) Steele argues that it makes no difference whether the Prince was truly legitimate or not, since he is excluded from the Crown by an Act of Parliament. The Ministry went on to disown *Seasonable Queries*. A far more pretentious and controversial Jacobite publication, also published in October, *The Hereditary Right of the Crown of England Asserted*, appeared in spacious folio format and set forth at considerable length the legal, historical and religious claims of heredi-tary monarchy in the English constitution.[6] 'Hannovero-Britannus' (Abel Boyer, the Huguenot propagandist for the Whigs) responded to it in *Englishman*, no. 20, quoting offensive passages, arguing against them, and concluding that the author has threatened the life, liberty, and property of any who have supported the 1688 revolution. The form of the argument in both *The Hereditary Right ... Asserted* and in the answers to it was that people who accept the antagonists' argument would have to accept some other, intolerable tenet as well.

Continuing the argument from history, no. 23, probably written with the help of William Moore, the lawyer who assisted Steele in preparing *The Crisis*, prints in both Latin and English King John's transfer of the entire kingdoms of England and Ireland to the Catholic Church, a document that seems to indicate both the dangerous power of Rome and the unreliability of historical precedents. In no. 31, the sad condition of French Huguenots released from the galleys and taken in by the inhabitants of Geneva testifies to the inhumanity of Catholic France; that description is followed by a letter describing the lack of progress on the demolition of the Dunkirk harbour. An allegedly eyewitness letter describing the poverty of France is printed in no. 40. In no. 46, Steele writes in his own voice as 'an *Englishman* born in the City of *Dublin*' to note the similarities of the English and Irish Constitutions, to defend the Irish Whig Robert Molesworth on what is now a rather obscure constitutional point, and to attack the *Examiner* for implicitly favouring the Pretender. A fictional Irishman writes in no. 50 to defend the habit of Irish Whigs to drink toasts to the memory of King William, a practice the Bishop of Cork condemned as an irreverent parody of the Eucharist. Later *Englishman* papers recommended publications defending the Hanoverian succession. The burning of the Pretender in effigy on the Queen's birthday (by the Hanover Club, of which Addison and Steele were members) is described in no. 55, which also contains letters recommending Sir John Willes, *The Present Constitution and the Protestant Succession Vindicated* and the forthcoming *An Alarm to Protestants or a short method with a papist*, attributed to John Battersby.

Steele's occasional references to the succession itself are set in the contexts of his broader attack on Catholicism in general and religious persecution in France in particular and of his theoretical and historical meditations on the nature and structure of government. In an age when religion and politics were closely intertwined, Steele, whose views tended toward the low Church, if not towards Deism, sought to gain the support of moderates in the clergy, and he saw anti-Catholicism as a weapon against the Pretender, against France and against the Tory ministry. Steele's quarrel with Catholicism centres upon the control exercised by its powerful clergy over the faithful. Religions, he explains in no. 14, have an 'Order of Men' who promulgate the rules for getting to heaven and avoiding hell, but this function gives them power to make their followers do horrendous things such as burning people to death. It is amazing that such horrific practices should be associated with Christianity, but a Popish successor to the British throne would follow in a tradition of cruelty. Steele lists historical 'Suggestions' as they occur to him: James II is the transition between a list of past cruelties and present or future examples and dangers.

Steele's treatments of Catholicism are often modestly ridiculous. The situation of English clergymen's wives, for example, presents a conundrum, since

Catholic priests are celibate. Such a wife writes in no. 44 and reports her husband's anxieties at the possibility of French invasion and hence of enforced Catholicism. This would mean that the clergy would have to give up their vocations or their marriages. A sixteenth-century order from Queen Mary regarding precisely this issue gives historical reality to these fears. At the other extreme of religious practice, a prostitute with the significant name of 'Obedience Passive' reports that a professional client gave her a number of papal indulgences that would forgive her sins. Since sinning is her business, the gift is quite valuable, or would be if the indulgences actually worked. The remission given by her confessor is no more effective than the cure prescribed by her physician. False or scandalous documents are further evidence of Catholic mendacity. No. 45 consists of 'A Declaratory Sentence of Pope Pius V' against Elizabeth the pretended Queen of England', and no. 53 prints a Catholic excommunication illustrative of the cruelty and superstition of Catholicism. It is, in fact the curse of Ernulphus, which Dr Slop reads to Obadiah in volume 3, chapter 11 of *Tristram Shandy*.[7]

Such attacks are fairly typical of anti-Catholic sentiment in the wake of the Revolution of 1688. What gives them currency in the fall of 1713 are the rumours of the Queen's ill-health, the Ministry's courtship of the Pretender, and fears of invasion from France. But they also allow Steele to emerge as an exemplar of Whig defense of the established Church, despite Tory claims to the contrary (e.g., *Examiner*, vol. 3, no. 44 (21–24 April 1713); vol. 4, nos. 4 (25–9 May) and 13, (26–9 June)). Thus he devotes several papers to appreciative remarks on the appropriate role of the Church and its clergy. A recently ordained clergyman writes in no. 6 to express his reasonable satisfaction at the condition of the clergy and to make the politically important point 'that the holy Oracles have described no particular Mode of Power and Establishment for the Civil Accommodation of Clergymen; but that that Circumstance is wholly left to the State, or Monarchy, where it happens that Christianity shall take place', a point which Benjamin Hoadly, Bishop of Bangor, was later to make to greater effect. In no. 12 one gentleman writes to another about their quarrel over religion and politics. The letter-writer, taking a Whig position, has been accused by his Tory friend of antagonism to the Church and its clergy. But he insists that the virtuous clergy are integral to society.

> It is therefore the most barbarous and unjust Insinuation imaginable, to form Opinions of that Order in general from the fantastical Behaviour of some Men of cold Imaginations and warm Complections, who entertain their Audiences with an Account of the Preacher's Passions, Hopes, and Politicks in this World, instead of instructing them in their Way to another.

Preachers such as Sacheverell, he implies, abandon their sacred duty.

The distinction between sacred and profane clergy is extended in no. 21, which includes a letter from a clergyman that congratulates the *Englishman* on its respect for the clergy and asserts that they cannot do their job of teaching virtue as long as the behaviour of some in their flock disgraces the whole order. The author is an Englishman as well as a clergyman and celebrates the union of Church and State. 'It was ever my Opinion, that should our happy Constitution in the State be in the least altered, the Church would soon totter, and by Degrees fall to the Ground'. Within the union, in short, the Church is contingent on the State. Three successive papers in late December 1713 and early January 1714 emphasize the dangers of Jacobitism: no. 37, in a letter from 'English Protestant', attacks a heterodox idea put forth by the Jacobite nonjuror Charles Leslie; Nestor Ironside visits in no. 38 to give an extemporaneous sermon on charity, based on 1 Corinthians 13, and turning at the end to condemn French persecution of the Huguenots; no. 39 contains a letter from a clergyman defending lay-baptism, a issue that had been raised by the *Examiner* (volume 5, no. 8, 21–5 December 1713) and was the subject of lengthy and laboured discussion in *Lay-Baptism Invalid*.[8]

The *Englishman's* treatment of the clergy draws towards a conclusion with two letters from 'Constant Churchman' (nos. 55 and 56). These in turn feed into the full pamphlet that serves as the *Englishman's* final paper and touches upon the variety of its concerns. Churchman's specific concern is with reactions to the Sacheverell trial and with the principle of passive resistence. He argues that the trial was resolved on solid legal grounds but was followed by 'Noise and Clamour ... with foolish Strains of Obedience without Reserve, and not allowing a Nation to defend itself against Tyranny and Oppression'. Preachers ought to argue from the pulpit against the fallacious doctrine of passive obedience rather than maintaining a discrete silence. Passive obedience is not a significant Church of England doctrine, and not a doctrine of other churches. It was abrogated in the case of James II, and would prevent resistance to the excesses of a future Catholic monarch. The implication is that propaganda that emphasizes passive obedience is propaganda for the Pretender.

The *Englishman's* concern for the proper stance of the clergy in response to the threat of Catholicism and the Pretender is paralleled by a series of general papers on politics that uses historical models to examine the origins and validity of power within the state. Steele uses the familiar model of a semi-mythical Rome to indicate not only the abstract characteristics of government but, more tellingly, the pattern of governmental change. Rome is contrasted to other models and ultimately replaced by a northern or Germanic model that is preserved only in Britain. The central historical-theoretical sequence (Nos. 25, 28, 32) asserts that the 'only Skill or Knowledge of any value in Politicks, was *the Secret of Governing All by All*' (*Englishman*, No. 25) and traces the discovery of that secret through a sequence of governments. The Romans were ruled by Kings until the time of the Tarquins, after which the executive power was share by the Consuls. As long as the Tarquins lived, nobles and people were united by a common enemy. When the nobility, freed from fear of the Tarquins, grew arbitrary, civil discord emerged until the nobility granted the office of Tribunes to the people. 'So that now the *Roman* Constitution seemed calculated for a long and happy Duration, having found out the Secret of *Governing All by All*, by giving every *Roman* personally, or by Representation, a Share in the Legislature'. Caesar's introduction of bribery into the political process corrupted it, and played one branch of the government off against the other, until he 'saw himself sole Lord of the *Roman* Empire, and saw the Laws and Liberties of his Country fall Victims to his Ambition'. The constitution was destroyed by bribery and corruption, qualities associated with Robert Harley, Lord Oxford.

No. 28 argues that the success of a nation depends on its constitution and its laws, and these in turn require liberty and property, a common Whig slogan. Those governments most conducive to liberty derive from Northern Europe. 'For wherever those People settled, they established a Government of Liberty, and shew'd themselves to be greater Masters of the great Secret of *Governing All by All*, than those Nations that had given them the opprobrious Name of *Barbarous*'. The origin of free participation in government lay with the military, with soldiers uniting to choose their generals. The need for balanced government was soon recognized, hence the distribution of power among the monarch, nobles, and people. This distribution became unsettled at different periods, most recently with the Civil War and Commonwealth.

> So that by what has been said it plainly appears, That though in *Great-Britain* only the Ancient, Generous, and Manly Government of *Europe* survives, and continues in its original Lustre and Perfection, and is a most exact Scheme of Politicks, yet it may be endangered by any one of the Branches of the Constitution invading the Province of the other.

No. 32 adopts the familiar analogy between the government of the state and the government of the family but uses the analogy very differently from the divine-right theorists. When the father acts in the interests of family members, he is respected and obeyed, but if he significantly prefers his own interests to those of the family, acting with cruelty and immorality, the family members will abandon him. In government this usually happens as a result of the bad advice of flattering ministers who allow the monarch to go beyond the bounds of wisdom or law, and had Charles I properly punished those who advised him so ill, he would have preserved his crown. Clearly, Steele is seeking to maintain the essential separation of the monarchy from the ministry, a separation that allows him to maintain his attacks on Oxford and Bolingbroke. Rome is specifically contrasted to Carthage at the beginning to the *Englishman* (no. 2) and again at the end (no. 52). In both papers, the great general Hannibal is opposed by the corrupt minister Hanno, whose refusal to support him was the major factor in the defeat of Carthage. Hannibal and Hanno were common historical analogues for Marlborough (the great general) and Oxford (the corrupt minister).[9] In general, Steele contrasts military virtues to political corruption: the Tory ministry, he implies, has turned its back on Marlborough, just as Hannibal was not supported in the Second Punic War.

The conflict between Oxford and Marlborough is echoed by lesser conflicts involving Steele. The *Examiner* is perceived not only as a paper supporting Oxford and the Tory ministry, but as a paper that is, in effect, under Oxford's direct control, so that he is responsible for its scurrilous attacks in Marlborough, Wharton and Steele himself. The *Examiner* for 2 November 1713 (vol. 4, no. 43), timed to appear with Swift's *Importance of the Guardian Considered*, launches a series of papers directly attacking Steele, but doing so in the context of attacks on Wharton and Marlborough.[10] (Steele responds in *Englishman*, no. 13; the *Examiner* continues its attacks in vol. 4, nos. 45, 46 and 48.) The political rivalry of Tory and Whig is echoed by the conflicts between the *Examiner* and the *Englishman*; the personal rivalry of Oxford and Marlborough is duplicated by the mutual hatred of Swift and Steele. Steele, probably wrongly, thought Swift responsible for *Examiner* vol. 4, no. 43, but Swift and the *Examiner* author wrongly thought Steele the author of Samuel Croxall's Spenserian allegory, *An Original Canto of Spencer: Design'd as Part of the Fairy Queen, but never Printed. Now made Publick, by Nestor Ironside, Esq;* (London, 1714 [November 1713]), which viciously attacks Oxford as the evil wizard Archimago. The *Examiner* (18 December 1713) was particularly offended because Oxford was, at the time grieving for the death of his daughter.

The parallelism of political, personal and literary antagonisms calls into question the anonymity of the *Examiner*, since it can launch untrue personal attacks on a real individual without taking responsibility for its dishonesty. Steele's willingness to sign his name testifies to his contrasting integrity. Steele answers an attack on Marlborough in *Examiner*, vol. 5, no. 7 (21 December 1713) by making a trinitarian appearance in *Englishman*, no. 36. As narrator of the paper, which is set in Button's Coffee House, he reports the analysis of *Examiner*, vol. 5, no. 7 by his alter ego Nestor Ironside. When Ironside is finished, a gouty Richard Steele limps in and is honoured by Ironside with a seat by the fire. Because of gout Steele was carried in a chair, where he was accused of laziness by passersby until he explained he was lame. At Button's he asserts that he could dispel the false personal attacks as easily, but

> it would be a great Arrogance to suppose the Publick have their Eyes so much upon me as to be entertained with what concerned only my personal Character. The Company was much pleased with the Modesty of so considerable a Man; and took much Satisfaction in observing the high Value Mr. *Ironside* put upon him.

The failure of Steele-the-narrator to distinguish the statement of Steele-the-character by setting it off in quotation marks seems appropriate to Steele's multiple and overlapping roles here.

The analogies among political, personal and literary spheres were extended in *An Invitation to Peace: Or, Toby's Preliminaries to Nestor Ironsides* [*sic*], *Set forth in a Dialogue between Toby and his Kinsman* (London [1714]), a dialogue between Toby (Swift?) and the author. Toby's proposals to Ironsides for an end to the paper war resemble the negotiations between France and the allies for ending the War of Spanish Succession: 'Sir, you may talk till Doomsday if you please, but I shall make you no other Reply than Fort *Ad—son*, Fort *Ad—son*'.[11] Toby sets forth peace proposals calling for the surrender of Button's and the Whig wits, assurance of Hereditary Succession to the 'Province of Scandal' for Abel Roper and his heirs, and giving certain rights to 'Sieur *Jacob* [Tonson], Librarian and Stationer to the Town of *Button*'.[12] There is a good deal of similar tomfoolery deriving from the correspondence of paper wars to real ones and ending with the usual complaint that Steele used to be entertaining but now is not.

In her notes to *Englishman*, no. 36, Rae Blanchard describes the gist of the attacks on Steele:

> In these pieces the changes are rung on the same themes, as if they had been drawn up and agreed upon in a conspiracy against him: his Irish birth and obscure parentage, his insolence and ingratitude to the Queen and her ministers; his lack of veracity; his low-life friends; his bad grammar and faulty style; his association with deists; his arrest and imprisonment for debt; his experiments in alchemy; his fame as a writer due to the work of others; his unfitness for political writing; and the forecast that he would not be allowed to take his seat in the Commons.

Steele identifies four of these attacks in the pamphlet that constitutes *Englishman*, no. 57:

> If anybody has leisure enough to read *The Honour and Prerogative of the Queen's Majesty Vindicated – The Importance of the* Guardian *– The Reasons concerning the immediate Demolishing of* Dunkirk *–* They will see the Offences I have committed, and the Resentment of the Authors upon them at large. But a very notable Piece called *Toby's Character of Mr. St—le*, will let the Reader into the whole Occasion of former Anger, and the Increase of my Sins against some People.

The first and third of the titles listed were probably by Defoe, and *Toby's Character* by William Wagstaffe, but they were all published by John Morphew and advertised in the *Examiner*. Hence Steele believed them all to be by Swift, and the attribution fuelled his antagonism.[13]

Attacks on Steele grew in intensity during the course of the *Englishman* (6 October 1713 to 15 February 1714) and climaxed once he published *The Crisis* (19 January 1714) and began his aborted career in Parliament (16 February 1714). Reactions to the *Englishman* might be considered separately from reactions to *The Crisis*. *Another Letter from a Country Whig to Richard Steele, Esq.; on his Defence of his Guardian, August the 7th* (London, 1713) ironically praises Steele for taking up politics rather than virtue and morality in the *Guardian*, and for his boldness in telling the Queen what the nation expects. It finds Steele's attacks on Dunkirk and defence of the *Guardian* both ineffective. The author's efforts to distribute Steele's *Defence* have prompted a torrent of complaint on the familiar pattern of quotation and insult. In December the ghost of John Tutchin, the libellous pamphleteer who had been killed six years earlier, appeared to Steele and urged him not to be like the *Tatler, Spectator*, and *Guardian* but, in the *Englishman*, to be like Tutchin himself.[14] But *A Letter from an English Tory to his Friend in Town. Chiefly Occasioned by the several Reflections on Mr. Steele's Guardian of August the Seventh* (London, 1713) was actually a defence of Steele, as was *To the Author of the Englishman. Written to him on New-Years Day [1714], and Published now for the Benefit of all his Fellow-Members, whether Whigs, Tories, or New Converts.* (1714), a three-page squib suggesting Mortimer as a Harley-like figure to be treated in the *Englishman*.

A more considerable and effective attack on Steele, published in early January 1714, was Swift's *The First Ode of the Second Book of Horace Paraphrased and Addressed to Richard Steele, Esq* (London, 1713 [1714]).[15] Horace's poem was addressed to Gaius Asinius Pollio, a minor public figure and author who spanned the late republic and early years of Augustus. He was writing a history of the civil wars from 60 BC to the Battle of Actium in 31 BC, a time of great Roman bloodshed and, as Horace points out, dangerous to talk about. Steele takes the place of Pollio, his periodicals the place of Pollio's history, the War of Spanish Succession replaces the Civil Wars, and Pollio's tragedies give way to Steele's comedies. In addition to these allusions, Swift adds a rich variety of references to Steele's personal life and literary career. The basic notion is that Steele spends a great deal of effort telling his readers things they already know and makes a great deal of noise advertising his effort. In the second half of the poem, Steele's domestic advice as Isaac Bickerstaffe is compared to his self-centred political posturing. Swift knows what *The Crisis* is going to say, and he can predict what Steele's play-in-progress (*The Conscious Lovers*) will be like, because both works follow the predicable pattern of a writer who has little to say.

Englishman, no. 57 (15 February) is a miscellaneous pamphlet, clearly intended not only to summarize the major threads of the *Englishman*, but to signal a new direction in Steele's propaganda in wake of *The Crisis*, which had been published on 19 January, and as Steele prepared to take his seat as a new member of Parliament (16 February). It reasserts the importance of the Protestant succession and warns of the dangers of the Pretender; it uncovers the policies of the ministry and the principles of the Tory Church that tend to support the Pretender and undercut the revolution settlement, which it sees as the culmination of a process of historical development that serves as a warning against an improper balance of monarch, nobles and people. Clergy as well as politicians must regard the essential unity of Church and State:

> I consider the Church and State as united in just such a Political, as the Soul and Body is in a Natural Constitution; and that the Life, as well as the Health of the whole, depends upon the UNION and Vigour of these essential Parts.[16]

One of his specific concerns was to respond to the attacks of 'Toby', but another was to answer the charge that the Whigs had spread rumours of the Queen's illness, which in turn prompted a run on the bank from which Whig merchants profited. Steele supplies considerable (if tedious) documentary evidence to show that these rumours were spread in the Tory press. Finally he writes a letter to 'Mr. — at Windsor' (called 'Jack' in the letter) defending himself for his positions on Dunkirk and, in *The Crisis*, on the succession, attacking the false religiosity of the 'New Converts' (certainly Oxford, but possibly Bolingbroke and others) in the ministry. He concludes with three wishes: the demolition of the harbour at Dunkirk, the removal of the Pretender from Lorrain, and, finally, 'That his Electoral Highness of *Hanover* would be so grateful to signify to all the World, the perfect good Understanding he has with the Court of *England*, in as plain Terms as her Majesty was pleased to declare she had with that House on her part'. (*Englishman*, no. 57, p. 249). The final wish, with its implication that the Queen may have been mistaken or, still worse, dishonest, became one of the points of attack when Steele was expelled from the House of Commons.

Steele's political position in the *Englishman* was hardly original. His historical account of the development of mixed government, in nos. 25, 28, and 32, derives from the works of Sir William Temple, no. 28 from *Of Heroic Virtue* and no. 32 from his *Essay upon the Original and Nature of Government*.[17] The function of the *Englishman* was political propaganda rather than political philosophy. But it sought to root that propaganda on a theoretical view of mixed government that was supported by an account of its origins and development. It sought as well to blend that view of a restrained and balanced government with a parallel view of a moderate church whose clergy took seriously their duty to guide the consciences of their flock rather than to comment on matters of state. Most particularly, the *Englishman* rejected the doctrine of passive obedience, which implied the illegitimacy of the present government and denied

the right to resist the religious or political tyranny of its successor. It answered
Tory propaganda efforts to yoke the Whigs to Dissenters and freethinkers by
associating the Tories with the French and Catholicism. It identified Whigs and
Hanoverians as the true defenders of the Church and Protestantism against the
Francophile ministry. It served as a consistent and considerable Whig presence
to answer the *Examiner*, and for much of its run it promised and advertized
Steele's forthcoming *The Crisis*.

The Crisis and its Consequences

On October 22, 1713, *Englishman*, no. 8 contained a letter from the publisher:

> As you are an ENGLISHMAN; I desire you to insert this Advertizement in a conspicu-
> ous Manner in your Paper. A Discourse, now ready for the Press, is designed as an
> Antidote against the treasonable Insinuations which are licentiously handed about
> the Town; and is entituled *THE CRISIS*; or a *Discourse plainly shewing, from the most
> authentick Records the just Causes of the late happy Revolution: And the several Settle-
> ments of the Crowns of* England *and* Scotland *on her Majesty; and on the Demise of her
> Majesty without Issue, upon the Most illustrious Princess Sophia, Electress and Dutchess
> Dowager of Hanover and the Heirs of Her Body, being* Protestants; *by both Parliaments
> of the late Kingdoms of* England *and* Scotland; *and that no Power whatsoever can* barr,
> alter, or make void *the same: With some* seasonable remarks *on the Danger of a POP-
> ISH SUCCESSOR. By* Richard Steele, *Esq;.*

The phrase denying that the settlements could ever be changed was deleted from
the title page of the published pamphlet.

The Crisis was again advertised in nos. 9, 10, 12, 13, 14, 22, 23, 32, 36, 46, 47,
and 49. In no. 36 (26 December 1713) an advertizement was inserted that, in
compliance with the wishes of 'several Ladies of Quality', publication was postponed until more women could subscribe. By the time *The Crisis* actually appeared
on 19 January 1714, it had been strongly, even excessively advertised. Whatever
excitement might have been generated by these repeated announcements, the
actual tract, once it appeared, was bound to disappoint. The publisher's description of it was all too accurate: the first half of the tract consisted of passages,
mainly from Parliamentary records, establishing and verifying the Protestant
succession, and these are followed by Steele's urgent and sometimes excessive
warnings against the dangers of a Jacobite Succession.

Steele begins with a rather cheeky dedication 'To the CLERGY of the *Church*
of ENGLAND'. Despite Steele's protestations of the honour and respect in which
he has held the clergy, he tells them that they have used their position to advance
views that have little to do with religion, perhaps out of ignorance of the legal
principles that will be documented in *The Crisis*, principles that ought to have
been 'carefully recommended to the Perusal of young Gentlemen in Colleges'.[18]

Steele had the temerity to propose curricula to Oxford and Cambridge, but he had the further audacity to prescribe, in threatening terms, the content of their sermons, in light of the danger from Catholics and the Pretender:

> It behooves you therefore, Gentlemen, to consider, whether the Cry of the Church's Danger may not at length become a Truth: And as You are Men of Sense and Men of Honour, to exert your selves in undeceiving the Multitude, whenever their affectionate Concern for you may prove fatal to themselves.[19]

Not only does Steele tell the Clergy what the substance of their sermons ought to be, he strongly implies that their position during the Sacheverell incident that the Church was in danger is false. The 'Preface' provides a sketchy historical theory that absolute power at first seemed the natural solution to social disorder but that absolute power in one individual became recognized as tyranny. He supports this view with contemporary quotations.

Beginning the body of his tract, Steele defines liberty as 'the Happiness of Mens living under Laws of their own making by their personal Consent, or that of their Representatives' and goes on to celebrate its beneficial effects and to consider the measures that ensure it. But liberty is presently endangered by the possibility that laws will 'for ever depend upon the Arbitrary Power of a Popish Prince'.[20] Despite the relative recency of the revolution, Jacobite sentiments persist in light of which it is important to present verbatim the sequence of laws relevant to the Protestant Succession that have been enacted by Parliament since 1688. Steele devotes the first sixty percent of *The Crisis* to the repetition of these laws: the Declaration and Bill of Rights, the establishment of the Protestant Succession for both England and Scotland; the oaths of allegiance and abjuration; the 1701 Act of Settlement that specifically established Princess Sophia of Hanover and her line as the successors; the Act of Attainder (1702) that defined James III as a traitor in the wake of the recognition of him as King by Louis XIV; the 1702 Abjuration Oath requiring office-holders, clergy and teachers to declare that William is lawful King and James is not, to recognize the Succession of Anne and, after her, of Princess Sophia; a 1705 Regency Bill detailing the procedures by which the transition from the Stuart dynasty to the Hanovers would take place; the 1707 Union Treaty's articles ensuring that Protestant Succession would take place in Scotland as well as England; further acts of 1708 and 1709, in the wake of James's unsuccessful effort to invade Scotland, which made it treasonable to argue against the legitimacy of the present monarch and the Protestant succession.

All of this did not make for entrancing reading, and it is doubtful that it actually had many readers. But turning the pages and skimming would have revealed some important points. The Tories argued that the collection of documents simply served to show that there was not a crisis, and that the Protestant Succession was safely guarded not only by legal authority but by Parliamentary will. Steele claimed, according to this view, that a Popish Succession was impossible but dangerous.[21] But this put-down misses some of the force of the compilation of legal acts. Although they are to a large degree overlapping, each derives from a particular threat: the Revolution itself; France's breaking of a treaty to recognize the Pretender as King; the death of the Duke of Gloucester and the consequent end of the lineage of Protestant Stuarts; the inclusion of English Succession as one of the issues of the War of Spanish Succession, the Union with Scotland, and the Pretender's subsequent effort to invade. If the Tories claimed that the laws indicate that there is no crisis, the Whigs could claim that the existence of so many drastic laws enacted within a short period of time is itself evidence of danger.

But the explicit argument that there was a crisis came in Steele's commentary in the final two-fifths of the tract. If British dynastic arrangements fail, Britain will be the victim of diverse foreign claims in addition to that of the Pretender, the Duke of Savoy being the most immediate threat. At this point *The Crisis* becomes an assertion that the so-called 'Peace' of Utrecht has failed. England had been saved by the military successes of Marlborough, 'this wonderful Instrument of Providence', but after his removal and the peace of Utrecht 'the House of *Bourbon* is at this Juncture become more formidable, and bids fairer for an Universal Monarchy, and to engross the whole Trade of *Europe*, than it did before the War'.[22] Dunkirk has not been destroyed; France and Austria are still at war; Portugal is in danger, and the Catalans have been betrayed. At home the attitude towards these dangers is one of dangerous neglect and 'a Lethargick Unconcern' as a consequence of 'an Impudent Suggestion of the Church's Danger', despite the 'Treasonable Books' that have attacked the Protestant Succession.[23] His major concern thereafter is to paint a threatening picture of the dire consequences of Catholic rule. The particular danger is the possibility that James III will convert to the Church of England on the grounds that London is worth the *Book of Common Prayer*. In fact, both Oxford and Bolingbroke (independently) were making secret overtures to the Pretender to do just that. But Steele uses the examples of previous Catholic monarchs whose positions moved from tolerance to intolerance, or even from Protestantism back to Rome, once they gained the crown: James II, Louis XIV, Mary Tudor. Massacres in Ireland, Savoy and, especially, France testify to the Papist attitude that no moral restraint should impede the dominance of the Church. Since a number of Catholic heirs are more closely related to Anne than the Electress of Hanover is, recognition of inheritance as the overriding principle of succession would put the Queen's life in danger. Steele's insistence on the danger is intense – virtually hysterical:

> These are some instances of what must ever be expected. No Obligations on our side, no Humanity or Natural Probity on theirs, are of any weight; their very Religion forces them, upon Pain of Damnation, to forget and cancel the former, and to

extinguish all remains of the latter. Good God! To what are they reserved, who have nothing to expect but what such a Religion can afford them?[24]

The one preservation against these dangers was the principle of Protestant Succession embodied in the laws that Steele has presented.

Part documentary history and part political diatribe, *The Crisis* has hardly stood the test of time and was possibly more important as a point around which Whigs could rally and Tories attack than as a sustained political argument. Nonetheless, it managed to unite Whig complaints about the inadequacy of the Treaty of Utrecht, fear of the Pretender, doubts about his legitimacy, rejection of succession by inheritance, and anti-Catholicism. It sought to replace clerical fear of Dissenters and their Low-Church allies with the more dire threat of a Catholic monarch. It hardly added new themes to Whig propaganda, but it took advantage of the opening of Parliament to organize a broad array of issues and direct them specifically at the ministry. To the array of issues it engaged it added the exciting cry of uncertainty and danger. The Tories, having exhausted their agitation over 'the Church in danger', or seen the issue pass in a different form to the Whigs, did not have a response of equally broad scope or high alarm, and their attacks, therefore, had a defensive quality and centred on the particular person of Richard Steele.

But Steele's role in writing *The Crisis* was as a spokesman for the Whig leadership, and the preparation of the tract was a cooperative affair. Although it was not quite a committee document, its components were derived from diverse sources. Steele explained the process of composition in the 'Preface' to his *Apology*:

> The Gentleman mentioned in the following Defence, as giving the first Hint to the Design, I need no longer conceal; it was Mr. [William] Moor[e] of the *Inner Temple*, a man perfectly skilled in the History, the Laws, the Constitution, of this Kingdom, and, in my poor Opinion, as capable of doing eminent Service, where those Qualities are requisite, as any Man in England not already employed ... When the *Crisis* was written Hand in Hand with this Gentleman, I, who was to answer for it with my All, would not answer upon our single Judgment, therefore I caused it to be printed, and left one Copy with Mr. *Addison*, another with Mr. *Lechmere*, another with Mr. *Minshull*, and another with Mr. *Hoadly* ... From these corrected Copies (no one of these Gentlemen knowing till this Day that the other had seen it) the Crisis became the Piece it is.[25]

Steele's circumspection and the assistance of a lawyer (who may also have provided the relevant Parliamentary Bills) were not only motivated by concern for factual accuracy but because Steele was aware that he was skirting the line of sedition. He was aware that the Tories would question the validity of his Stockbridge election; the pamphleteers had told him as much. But the process of invalidating elections was relatively cumbersome compared to the swift and effective method of finding him guilty of seditious libel and expelling him from the House (or even sending him to the Tower). Steele's *Crisis* was widely distributed and some counter propaganda was needed before the Tories could go after the author.

The various responses to *The Crisis* can be grouped into two categories: those actually or ostensible concerned with *The Crisis* itself, and those concerned primarily with Richard Steele. Those concerned with Steele often (if they were published after 15 February 1714) comment on the last *Englishman* paper as well. *The Life of Cato the Censor* is a thirty-four-page poem in iambic tetrameter that takes off on Steele's designation of himself as 'censor' in the *Tatler* and elsewhere and on his use of Cato's famous saying the Carthage must be destroyed as motto for the *Englishman*. Parallels between the life of Cato and the life of Steele are not easy to make, but the author suggests that they share a humble background and a love of disputation. Both, of course, are warmongers. Romans, like the English, continued to argue fruitlessly after the war had been won. The conclusion is the people who attack the government 'should be despis'd like poor D—k St—le'.[26] *A Letter from the Facetious Doctor Andrew Tripe at Bath, to the Venerable Nestor Ironside* attacks Steele as Isaac Bickerstaff, although the letter is, of course, addressed to Steele as Nestor Ironside. Like other attacks on Steele, Tripe's letter (possibly written by William Wagstaffe) makes no substantial political points but tries to undermine confidence in the intelligence, competence and sanity of Steele himself. Tripe and others are in a coffeehouse when Bickerstaff enters. He is described, comically and at some length, as addlebrained – seldom speaking truth and seldom believed. He has just published 'a most *Elaborate Treatise*' which shows 'with what Brightness and Vivacity he can abstract *Acts of Parliament*'.[27] Tripe goes on to attack Bickerstaff's ignorance, his vague religion, his dominant wife, his humble background, and his Irish birth.

Jack the Courtier's Answer to Dick the Englishman's Close of the Paper so call'd (London, 1714) comments more specifically on the final *Englishman* paper, defending the ministry, the *Examiner*, and Swift from Steele's attacks. It makes the standard Tory arguments that Steele is not an Englishman at all, that he lacks the appropriate status to criticize a treaty, that he has given up his government positions only for the more lucrative work of a pamphleteer, that the preservation of Dunkirk (soon to be destroyed) was necessary to provision the English garrison there, and that the parliamentary acts quoted by Steele merely show the nation's security about the succession. The point of all these personal attacks, although obviously detrimental to the personal integrity and public authority of Steele himself, was to set him up for the efforts at expelling him from Parliament, which held its first meeting on 16 February 1714.

The Crisis was finally published on 19 January. By 26 January a particularly well-written response appeared. *Remarks on Mr. Steele's Crisis* asserted that the mountain of preparation had, at last, only brought forth a mouse, for there is no real crisis:

> Alas, alas, Mr. *Tatler*, Mr. *Spectator*, Mr. *Guardian*, Mr. *Englishman*, Mr. *Ironside*, Mr *Steele*, where is your wonted Understanding? Whither is that Brightness, that Vivacity of Thought, that Elegancy of Expression, and Accuracy of Judgment fled, that us'd to Distinguish your Writings, and set them apart from the Compositions of other Authors?[28]

The government has already done what is really needed in Steele's demands. His implicit appeal for arms on behalf of the House of Hanover is an apparent call to insurrection. A similarly titled tract complains that Steele is unwarranted in his dedication to the Clergy and unsystematic in his presentation of laws governing succession. He merely presents familiar acts and makes meaningless comments on them. He wants to see how far he can go in attacking the government without suffering legal consequences, and hence writes in a malicious indirection that relies on an unarticulated understanding with his readers.

> He is well acquainted with the Cunning of his Interpreters, who can easily pick out the meaning of the Calumny, when the Author *dares* not speak it quite out, they can raise *Supposition* into *Demonstration*, and know how to construe one *Mood*, and *Tense* by *Another*, more *Positive* and *Declaritive*. [29]

He inconsistently argues that a Popish succession is impossible but dangerous.

The most masterful belittlement of *The Crisis* was Swift's *The Publick Spirit of the Whigs: Set forth in their Generous Encouragement of the Author of the Crisis: with some Observations on the Seasonableness, Candor, Erudition, and Style of that Treatise* (London, 1714), which appeared on 23 February, after the first, organizational meeting of Parliament but before the Queen's speech and the Tory move to expel Steele. As the title and Swift's previous practice both make clear, *The Publick Spirit of the Whigs* has little to say about the substance of *The Crisis* (Swift implies there is little substance to talk about), but a lot to say about the phenomenon of its appearance. Hence he concentrates on its immediately visible characteristics: its excessive advertisement, and its unusual sale by subscription. Swift asserts that the noble subscribers surely have not read it. The language of the title page is dissected in some detail. Swift argues particularly with the term 'discourse' as applied to the parliamentary acts. He asserts ironically that Steele's *Crisis* is a tribute to the Whigs: 'I grant there is nothing material in all this, further than to shew the Generosity of our Adversaries in encouraging a Writer, who cannot furnish out so much as a Title-page with Propriety or common Sense'.[30] As Bertrand Goldgar points out, 'Swift's principal satiric device is to pretend admiration for the generosity of the Whigs, who encourage writers of so little real value to their cause'.[31] According to Swift the author of *The Crisis* would be superior to his fellow Whig hacks 'provided he would a little regard the Propriety and Disposition of his Words, consult the Grammatical Part, and get some Information in the Subject he intends to handle'.[32] This kind of unsubstantial but clever personal attack recurs in *The Publick Spirit of the Whigs*, but the essay is not organized as a personal attack. Instead it is a section-by-section treatment of *The Crisis*. Perhaps Oxford or some other superior had told Swift to organize that way, because he seems quite uncomfortable with this pedestrian manner of approach. He makes fun of Steele's pretensions, in his dedication, to teach the constitution to the clergy, most of whom know more about it that he does. He simply denies that the Protestant Succession is in danger, and hence seems unaware that Harley and Bolingbroke were negotiating with the Pretender. He returns repeatedly to his basic assertion of Steele's stupidity: 'I defy any Man alive to shew in double the Number of Lines, although writ by the same Author, such a complicated Ignorance in History, human Nature, or Politicks, as well as in the ordinary Proprieties of Thought or of Style'.[33]

But as he works through Steele's quotations and citations, he makes a stupid mistake himself. Well into his citation of parliamentary precedents for the Protestant Succession, Steele lists the union with Scotland, quotes several paragraphs of 'An Act for the Union of the Two Kingdoms of England and Scotland',[34] and insists on the importance of the Protestant succession despite the religious differences between the two countries. Swift describes the Scots as 'a poor, fierce Northern People', and complains that the numerous Scottish nobility constitutes 'one of the great and necessary Evils of the Union upon the foot it now stands'.[35] But Scottish nobles were an important source of support for the Tory majority in Parliament, and as the case against Steele was advancing in Parliament, the counter-case against Swift was also under way. But, unlike Steele, whose name appeared on the title page of *The Crisis*, Swift remained anonymous, as usual. Hence on 15 March, 1714, the day on which Steele moved unsuccessfully that the demolition of Dunkirk be investigated, the House of Lords wrote a letter to the Queen condemning *The Publick Spirit of the Whigs* for its remarks on Scotland. The Queen in turn issued a proclamation offering £300 for the discovering of its author. Morphew the publisher and Barber the printer were arrested. Steele's turn was soon to come.

The debate between *The Crisis* and *The Public Spirit of the Whigs* exemplifies not only Swift's personal animosity towards Steele but, at a more profound level, the basic disagreement between Steele and his Tory antagonists about the meaning of 1688. For Steele, the authority of the monarch derived from the consent of the governed, and the people, acting jointly, had the right to replace the monarch when he or she seriously violated their safety or even interests. The difficulty of replacing the monarch acted as a restraint on civic disorder; the possibility of such replacement acted as a deterrent to monarchical excess. But for Tories no such right was structured into or implied by the constitution. The authority of the Crown derived from Divine approval as providentially manifested in history. If extraordinary circumstances required a violent intervention in order to assure the safety of the nation (and especially of the Church), that revolution might be a lesser evil, but it did not flow from the inherent rights of citizens. For Steele, revolution principles were an important protection of civic order; for Tories, Steele's argument undermined the substance and continuity of monarchical rule and opened the way to radical excesses.

Steele and Swift struggled not only over the theory of government but, even more sharply, over the interpretation of history. Each sought to advance the historiography that derived from his political theory. Swift sought the position of historiographer so that he could transmit the truth about the reign of the Queen to future ages. The danger to that truth was the insistence of such Whig writers as Steele that the facts bore quite a different interpretation. A central figure of historical contention was the Duke of Marlborough. For Steele he was the great military figure of modern time, surpassing even Charles XII. He had held the European alliance together against France and had won every battle he fought. But his strategic victories were sacrificed when the Tories agreed to an inadequate peace, and his great accomplishments were answered with ingratitude and ignominy. For Swift he was, despite his military genius (or even because of it) a heartless and avaricious man, willing to sacrifice human life for minor successes, loyal to the Queen only as far as he could gain from her, and insatiably hungry for power. The contrast between Sidney Godolphin and Robert Harley similarly engaged quite different views of the present to be projected to the future – one (take your choice) incompetent and corrupt, the other the saviour of the nation. Swift, in particular, saw power not merely as a means of controlling the experience of the present but of determining its meaning for the future.

Bertrand Goldgar claims that 'if nothing else, *The Publick Spirit of the Whigs* demonstrates once more that Steele was no match for Swift and the other Tory writers'.[36] But within eighteen months Steele was knighted, a member of Parliament once again, and a manager of Drury Lane Theatre, while Swift was in virtual exile in Ireland. Steele's *Crisis* was a significant contribution to efforts to ensure the Hanoverian succession, and to that end, Steele was quite willing to subordinate his personal style and even his rapport with his audience. The result was a tract that provided a useful if dreary collection of Parliamentary acts and an overstated warning of the dangers of a Catholic successor. Swift, in turn, was on the defensive in the broad debate but carried out his defence by direct personal attack. Personal attack, especially in the hands of a master such as Swift, is likely to be wittier and more entertaining than Steele's earnest, unwitty efforts to make an important point about what he perceived as a danger to the nation.

In that sense Goldgar is right that Steele was no match for Swift, but they were playing different games.

Steele's expulsion from Parliament was acted out in an almost mechanical sequence. On 15 February 1714 Steele closed *The Englishman* with its long and controversial final paper. On the next day, Queen Anne's last Parliament opened its last session. The main business of the day was to elect the moderate Tory Sir Thomas Hanmer as Speaker. Steele did not wait to make an impression, and the Tories were equally anxious to ensure it was not a good one. Hanmer was one of the so-called Whimsical Tories who opposed the commercial clauses the previous spring, and the Whigs were anxious to gain converts among them. When Steele rose to support Hanmer's candidacy, catcalls and cries of 'the Tatler' immediately began. Steele praised Hanmer for his role in defeating the commercial clauses. Steele concluded that 'I rise up to do him Honour in some measure, and distinguish my self, by saying, *I wish him our Speaker for that his Inestimable Service to his Country*'.[37] At that point the cry against him grew 'insupportably loud'; Steele compared it to the spectators at a cockfight.[38] The speech immediately generated two publications. The first contains the short speech itself, but the second, somewhat longer, is a parody of Steele's discourse, rambling through a series of supposedly appropriate topics: the prerogative of the people, the glories of the Whigs, their great general Marlborough, their great martyr Guiscard (the attempted assassin of Harley), and the value of a parliamentary army to revive the revolution of the 1640s.[39]

A more sinister (and more accurate) alternative to this public foolery was Defoe's private letter of warning to Oxford written on 19 February:

> The new champion of the party, Mr. Steele, is now to try an experiment upon the Ministry, and shall set up to make speeches in the House and print them, that the malice of the party may be gratified and the Ministry be bullied in as public a manner as possible. If, my lord, the virulent writings of this man may not be voted seditious none ever may, and if thereupon he may be expelled it would suppress and discourage the party and break all their new measures.[40]

Swift's *Public Spirit of the Whigs* appeared on 23 February. On 2 March, the Queen's opening speech to both Houses (written by Oxford) asserted that the insinuation that the Protestant Succession was in danger angered her and that

> There are some who have arrived to that Height of Malice, as to Insinuate, that the *Protestant* Succession is in Danger under my Government. Those who go about thus to Distract the Minds of Men with Imagining Dangers, can only mean to Disturb the Present Tranquility, and to bring real Mischiefs upon us ... Attempts to Weaken my Authority, or render the Possession of the Crown uneasie to me, can never be Proper Means of Strengthen the Protestant Succession.[41]

The Commons, in its response, expressed, in language echoing that of the Queen, its due abhorrence of seditious publishing. Although on 3 March a petition was lodged by James, Earl of Barrymore (in Ireland) and Sir Richard Vernon, complaining of 'an undue Election and Return for the Burrough of *Stockbridge* in the County of *Southhampton*,' the charge of sedition offered a shorter and a surer method of expelling Steele.[42]

Accordingly, on 11 March a lawyer named John Hungerford moved consideration of that part of the Queen's speech that dealt with seditious libel, and he was supported by Auditor Thomas Foley, a relative of Oxford. Steele wrote to his wife that 'Ld Hallifax would not let Me go to the House, but thought it would be better to have the first attack made in my absence.'[43] Steele stayed away on 12 March as well, when Foley presented the formal complaint against *Englishman*, no. 46, *The Crisis*, and *The Englishman: Being the Close of the Paper so Called*. Steele was ordered to appear on 13 March to answer the charges. When he did so, he was met with complaints about his seditious writing from Foley, Edward Harley (Oxford's brother), and various others. James Craggs began to answer in Steele's defence, but the Tories insisted that he do so himself. Accordingly, he insisted that he needed a week to prepare his defence. Foley and Harley insisted that he do so on Monday, but Steele, taking advantage of their strict religious principles, expressed surprise that the pious Harley should 'force any one to incur the Pains of eternal Damnation by breaking the Sabbath-Day, what he must do, if held up to such Terms.'[44] The matter was postponed until Thursday 18 March, a small but encouraging victory for Steele. One possible reason for the delay was to allow time for more Whig MPs to come to London for the trial.[45]

On Monday 15 March, Steele moved that the Queen 'would be pleased to give Directions, That the several Representations of her Ingeniers and Officers who had had the Care and Inspection of the Demolition of *Dunkirk*, and all Orders and Instructions given thereupon, might be laid before the House.'[46] The motion would certainly have saved Steele the trouble of making the Dunkirk argument on his own authority, but voting against the motion made the Tories appear to be uninterested or uncertain of the outcome. The previous question was called by a vote of 214 to 109. The motion seems to have been overconfident, and it confirmed, if confirmation was necessary, that Steele was going to lose the expulsion vote.

Steele's defence, as it unfolded, was a party affair. J. H. Plumb reports that it was organized by Robert Walpole,[47] but Lord Halifax also had a role behind the scenes. On 12 March, Steele had written to his wife that 'I am going to Mr. Walpole's to meet some Freinds, there is nothing that can arise to Me which ought to afflict you, therefore Pray be a Roman Lady and assume a Courage equall to yr Goodnesse. The Q—n is very ill.'[48] Addison had a major role in writing Steele's speech and in supporting him while he gave it. General Stanhope joined

Walpole in speaking in Steele's defence, as did Lord Finch, the brother of Lady Charlotte, whom Steele had defended in *Guardian*, no. 41.

Before Steele spoke in his defence, there was considerable debate as to whether he should defend his accused writings paragraph by paragraph or should make a general address. It was eventually resolved that he should speak generally, but his speech, as he later reported it in *Mr. Steele's Apology for Himself and His Writings; Occasioned by His Expulsion from the House of Commons* (October 1714) fits either model. (One can hardly defend against the accusation of sedition in specific passages without discussing the passages.) At the outset, Steele asserts that the passages in question, written in response to the falsehoods of the *Examiner* and other Tory writings, amounted to no more than a paper war between himself and Swift, that this public dispute between two private persons was outside the scope of parliamentary inquiry, and that 'they must have but a mean Opinion of the Dignity of a *British* House of Commons, who think they will make themselves Parties in either Side of it'.[49] Appropriately enough, three days earlier, the House of Lords had condemned *The Publick Spirit of the Whigs* for its remarks on the Scots and had written to the Queen to that effect. The Queen issued a reward of £300 for discovering the writer. Morphew the bookseller and Barber the printer were arrested.

Steele's consideration of particular passages is dominated by a major argument about the appropriate rules for interpretation in legal and quasi-legal matters: language should be interpreted in its most obvious and literal sense, since there is no way of proving that figurative interpretations were actually intended by the author, who is liable to be punished, rather than projected by the reader who is bent on punishing. Even when language is actually ambiguous, the more innocent interpretation must be adopted. 'That which I shall insist on is this; that if an Author's Words, in the obvious and natural Interpretation of them, have a Meaning which is Innocent, they cannot without Great Injustice be condemned of another Meaning which is Criminal'.[50] Sentences should not be torn from their context so as to appear to mean something quite different from their original meaning. Steele spends considerable time supplying contexts that change the meaning of accused passages. 'It would be very unfair to separate my Words, and to pronounce a Meaning in them, which I have not expressed, when that which I have expressed is a positive Denial of having entertained any such Meaning'.[51] He insists that an author's meaning in a particular passage should be governed by other passages in the same work or even in different works where he expresses an opinion on the same topic.

Armed with these principles, Steele spends considerable time reading passages and elucidating their meaning, and hence their innocent intentions. He points to explanatory contexts and produces parallel or otherwise relevant texts. Not only does he seek to demonstrate the innocence of the passages, he doubtless takes great pleasure in repeating and amplifying points that his accusers have found to be offensive. He uses the occasion to emphasize the key issues that he has been hammering for the past year: the glorious achievements of Marlborough in contrast to the shabby treatment he has received from the Tories; the failure of the French to demolish Dunkirk, both as dangerous in itself and as symptomatic of French perfidy; the failure of the Treaty of Utrecht to bring about peace in Europe, as indicated by a survey of various countries, and therefore the danger of Britain being drawn again into a continental war; the urgent dangers to the Protestant succession and the atrocities committed by Catholic monarchs as a matter of policy. He insists at some length on his respect for the universities and for the clergy, and he produces passages from various works to demonstrate it.

At the end of his address he raises a salient question of authority that ought, perhaps, to have begun his defence. He has been accused of sedition, but he tries to argue that his supposedly seditious acts were mainly his disagreements with Harley over matters of policy. He asks if the House of Commons is the appropriate agency to determine this issue.

> I think I have not offended against any Law in Being: I think that I have taken no more Liberty than what is consistent with the Laws of the Land: If I have, let me be tried by those Laws. Is not the Executive Power sufficiently armed to inflict a proper Punishment on all kinds of Criminals? why then should one part of Legislative Power, take this Executive Power into its own Hands?[52]

Having made this constitutional point, he closes by urging the House not to 'sacrifice a Member of their own Body, to the Resentments of any single Minister'.[53] *The History of the First and Second Session of the Last Parliament*, written with a decided Whig bias and dedicated to Steele, reported that he spoke for three hours 'with such a Temperament of Mind, Modesty, Unconcern, easie and flowing Eloquence, as gave entire Satisfaction, to all who were not inveterately prepossess'd against him'.[54] Steele had defended himself as best he could; thus he withdrew to await the verdict. Addison was sent after him to tell him to remain hidden until after the censure. 'Nothing can happen to [make] my Condition in private the Worse', he wrote to his wife, 'and I have busied myself enough for the publick'.[55]

In the course of his passage-by-passage defence of his writings, Steele had managed to include enough general points and constitutional issues to open the floor to the broader attacks that Robert Walpole and his cohort were to make in consequence. Among that cohort were Horace Walpole, Lord Lumley, Lord Hitchinbroke and Lord Finch. Lord Finch, in his maiden speech, added a strong human interest to the procedures. As the son of the Earl of Nottingham, he was the brother of Lady Caroline, the notorious knotter-in-church whom Steele had defended against the *Examiner*'s attack. Steele himself told the story a few weeks later:

A Gentleman who had chastised a Ruffian for an Insolence towards a Kinswoman of his, was attacked with outrageous Language in that *Assembly*; when his Friend's Name was ill treated from Man to Man, this ingenuous Youth discovered the utmost Pain to those who sat near him, and having more than once said, *I am sure I could fight for him, why can't I speak for him?* at last stood up. The Eyes of the whole Company were upon him, and tho' he appeared to have utterly forgot what he rose up to speak, yet the generous Motive which the whole Company knew he acted upon, procured him such an Acclamation of Voices to hear him, that he expressed himself with a Magnanimity and Clearness proceeding from the Integrity of his Heart, that made his very Adversaries receive him as a Man they wished their Friend.[56]

Lord Finch apparently gave a commendable maiden speech in Parliament.

Robert Walpole's basic tactic was to insist upon the truth and importance of the attacks that Steele had made in the passages under debate. He had defended the Protestant succession and the Constitution and attacked the Pretender and the threat of Catholicism. Steele could only be regarded as seditious by people who shared the positions he attacked. By equating the case against Steele with lack of support for the Hanoverian succession, Walpole sought to weaken the ministry even if it was successful in expelling Steele from Parliament. He argued that Steele should not be accountable to Parliament for his writings as a private individual. He used the occasion of his first speech after his own expulsion from Parliament to mount a wide-ranging and powerful attack on the government.[57] Substantial debate followed Walpole's speech, but although the Whigs had raised questions that may have troubled some Tories in the weeks ahead, Steele's language was condemned by a vote of 245 to 152.[58] The suggestion that he be imprisoned as well as expelled was diverted by the likelihood that his creditors would do that once he was deprived of Parliamentary immunity. His antagonist Edward Harley described him as 'being more than ordinarily generous, out if his Excess of Compassion for the Distress'd'.[59] In fact, creditors resumed their legal efforts to collect his debts. But Steele was anonymously given £3000, presumably to prevent precisely that embarrassment. On 19 March, the day after the vote, Steele wrote to Sir Thomas Hanmer, asking whether the vote in the House precluded legal prosecution and whether his expulsion meant that he could not be elected again in the same term (an issue tested by John Wilkes in 1769). Steele was smarting from the charge of sedition, and doubtless thought that legal action could remove the taint. Hanmer replied that he could not appropriately reply but that the case was now closed and no further action could be taken.

But *The Crisis* and its consequences continued to be debated in print. On 20 March, *The Case of Richard Steele, Esq; Being an Impartial Account of the Proceedings Against Him* provided a straightforward account of events and defended Steele. It expressed some surprise that 'Men of Property' should sacrifice their honour to the interests of men of power.[60] A correspondence between William

Robinson and Thomas Staines dated 16 March defends Steele rather narrowly
from prosecution for inserting an advertisement that maintains that no power
can alter the succession.[61] Steele is roundly attacked in *A Letter to Mr. Steele, Concerning His Crisis* (Edinburgh, 1714), which expresses some surprise that Steele,
an able entertainer, should write highly charged political tracts and opines that
he would better serve his cause by keeping his mouth shut. But Steele is defended
by a letter from 'Tim Tomkins', who characterizes his writings on Dunkirk as
'too noble Instances of an *English* Spirit ever to be forgotten' and rehearses the
familiar atrocities that would follow the installation of the Pretender.[62] Steele
wrote one further Dunkirk tract in July 1714, complaining about the continued
procrastination of the French in destroying the fort and harbour of Dunkirk
and about French construction of an even more dangerous harbour in nearby
Mardyck.[63] But by that time political discourse had shifted to other topics.

The Fall of the Tories

Ten days after closing the *Englishman*, Steele began a new periodical, the *Lover*.
Written in Imitation of the Tatler, which appeared three times a week from 2 February 1714 to 27 May (forty numbers). Like the *Tatler* it observed and commented
upon the niceties of social behaviour. It subsumed these observations under the
headings of love and courtship, and its tone was generally light and playful. For
Steele it probably was a relief from the intensive politicking and *Examiner* exam-
ining of the *Englishman*. It may have reflected Steele's decision at the beginning of
his short Parliamentary career to concentrate his political activity on Parliament.
But continuing to conduct a periodical provided him with a medium if political
developments implied that he should use it, as indeed they did.

The *Lover* is conducted by a pleasant gentleman named Marmaduke Myrtle,
who explains at the outset that Ann Page, the love of his youth, rejected him in
favour of a wealthier man, leaving him to compensate for his loss by learning as
much as he could about love and observing the various relationships of lovers.
The rakery of the age of Charles II cut short his career as a spectator of love, and
he now lives in spacious apartments in Covent Garden, where he observes 'the
Knight-Errantry of this present Age' whose purpose is to ruin as many women as
possible. 'Thus I every day see Innocents abused, scorned, betrayed and neglected
by Brutes, who have no Sense of any thing but what indulges their Appetites.'[64]
Myrtle's Covent-Garden location also identifies him with the theatre, a topic to
which he occasionally returns in the course of his paper. Myrtle, like Mr Spectator, has a club, made up of two widowers, one husband, an old bachelor, a young
man named Mr Severn and Myrtle himself. Severn is the only character to be
delineated in any detail, and even he does not play a significant role in the paper.

Myrtle's first hint of political concern comes in no. 4, which celebrates dancing, an art particularly practiced by the French. The allegorical contention is that French dancing is becoming popular in England, much like the Francophilia of Oxford and other ministers. The 'Master of the Revels' carries in his hand a white wand like that of the Lord Treasurer, and 'he has ordered that the first Person who shall be taken out, is to be the Censor of *Great Britain*'. Steele here predicts his own expulsion from Parliament and blames it on Oxford. As soon as that prediction had come true, the political allegory of the *Lover* became harsher and cruder. Steele sees the Harley family as both the prime sources and main actors in his expulsion. The family included not only Robert Harley himself (here represented as Sir Anthony Crabtree) but also his brother Edward Harley (Zachariah Crabtree), and his brother's father-in-law Thomas Foley (Brickdust), all of whom had spoken significantly against Steele at his Parliamentary trial. In a series of letters that begins on 20 March, two days after Steele's expulsion, Steele depicts the Harley family as the Crabtree family, living, as did the Harleys, in Herefordshire. The series is continued in nos. 14, 16 and 21; its thrust is accurately described by Rae Blanchard:

> The points emphasized in these *Lover* papers are family pride, officiousness, nepotism, and hypocrisy in religion; Oxford's antiquarian tastes in the collecting of old manuscripts; and with particular venom, physical aspects – the dark complexion and enormous scope and bulk of Thomas Foley, 'the accuser', who had introduced the expulsion proceedings.[65]

Number 21 is a bitter letter from Susan Matchless, who complains that the complex financial conniving of the Crabtrees resulted in the loss of her dowry and hence of the fine husband that it was to buy. The allegory refers to the financial manoeuverings of Oxford and especially the establishment of the South-Sea Company. Once she has established her elaborate allegory, Susan can express her anger by harsh personal attack:

> When I reflect upon this Race, especially the Knight himself, I confess my Anger is immediately turned into Mirth; for how is it possible that an ungainly Creature, who has what he is writ in his Face, should impose upon any body? He looks so like a Cheat, that he passes upon People who do not know him from no other Advantage in the World, but that they are ashamed to be govern'd by so silly an Art as Physiognomy.

The nastiness of Steele's personal attack is explained not only by the low level of political discourse general in the age but by Steele's understanding, probably, for the most part correctly, that the source of similar attacks against himself was Oxford. But the attacks of *Lover*, no. 21 have a specific political function as well. The Harleys are depicted as Dissenters who have lately converted to the Church of England but who may move even higher. The mockery of Oxford as a hypocritical Dissenter and occasional conformist was an effort to widen the tension between Bolingbroke and him.

Except for this outburst of political ill-will, the *Lover* concentrates on its announced topic, which essentially is advising perplexed, frustrated or defeated lovers. In no. 3, women who visit Myrtle tell him about 'lovers vagabond', whose character is the opposite of knights-errant and whose purpose is to ruin maidens in distress instead of rescuing them. Saving maidens thus becomes one of Myrtle's defining functions – often exercised through comedy but sometimes seriously moralistic. Myrtle repeats his purpose in no. 32:

> The Task which I have enjoyned my self in these Papers, is to describe Love in all its Shapes: To warn the unwary of those Rocks, upon which so many in all Ages have split formerly, do split still, and will split hereafter, as long as Men and Women shall be what they now are; and to delineate the true and unfeigned Delight, which virtuous Minds feel in the Enjoyment of their lawful and warranted Passions.

This passage serves as the introduction to a paper that distinguishes among sins against God, sins against other people, and sins against oneself, as an answer to the stoic principle that all sins are equal.

A serious warning against the evils of illicit love is the story told in no. 36. Two male slaves on a Maryland plantation, whose owner encourages his slaves to marry and reproduce so that he can have more slaves, have become particularly close friends. One of them is married and has a family, the other is unmarried and attracted to his friend's wife. The married slave goes hunting and, when he returns, finds his wife and friend asleep in each other's arms. His cries of grief wake the couple, and an exchange of grief and guilty remorse follows. The married slave insists that he cannot live when the two people who made his hard life not only endurable but happy have betrayed him. The unmarried slave takes all of the responsibility on his own shoulders and promises the couple that they will be satisfied on the next day. The next day they discover that he has hanged himself. Steele contrasts this sense of honour and remorse to the false gallantry of modern England. The location of the story among slaves in Maryland defamiliarizes the tale of adultery, intensifies the shock of the final suicide and underlines Steele's contrast of universal moral values to English social customs (without quite suggesting that English adulterers should follow the example of the adulterous slave).

Moral values and social customs were a salient concern for the *Lover*, as they had been for the *Tatler*, *Spectator* and *Guardian* before it, and they are specifically applied to topics of love. The periodical's function to provide an alternative to what Steele saw as the shallowness of the Restoration dictates early concern for the contrast between virtue and wit (no. 5, see also no. 37). A similar contrast is the conflict between money and love as reasons for marriage (nos. 9 and

17). The money-love conflict is sometimes an element in a generational conflict between parents and children (nos. 20, 22, 28). Myrtle's letter on women who slander the reputation of others (no. 24) is followed by a paper on the advantages of flattery in the arsenal of courtship (no. 25). Myrtle also provides advice on the importance of politeness in courtship, particularly in the bestowing of favours on others (no. 12). The obvious goal of love is marriage, in which, as Myrtle's visit to a widower in no. 29 illustrates, religion is an important ingredient. But no. 15, which Blanchard believes (on little evidence other than the unique use of Propertius as a motto) is not by Steele,[66] describes three prostitutes who are

> Eminent above the rest for their Charms and Vices. The first can only please Novices; the second seeks only Men of Business, and such of them as are between Fools and Knaves; the third runs through the whole Race of Men, and has Arts enough about her to ensnare them all, as well as Desire enough to entertain them all.

In *Lover*, no. 31 Tom Pip tells us how he fell in love with a young woman because an unfortunate fall from her horse caused her to reveal more parts of her body than are usually displayed. Unfortunately the couple in speaking to her father, unwittingly implied that Pip's unusual knowledge came from other reasons than inadvertent accident, with the result that the daughter was suddenly sent away. In no. 34, Myrtle defends himself, rather awkwardly, from the claim by the Tory *Monitor* that the story of the 'fallen woman' in No. 31 was indecent.

Although Myrtle's residence in Covent Garden, a few blocks from Drury Lane Theatre, would seem to signal frequent attention to cultural matters, especially the stage, their appearance in *The Lover* is infrequent and random. In announcing his attention to make wit and love 'subservient to the Interests of Honour and Virtue' (no. 5), Myrtle praises the treatment of love in Addison's *Cato* and comments on the difficulties of representing virtuous love on the stage (an indication that Steele may have been working on *The Conscious Lovers* during this period). In no. 27, Myrtle's letter to his friend Mr Severn transmitting a recent edition of Latin authors leads to praise of Dr Busby, the legendary master of Westminster School, as an influential educator and to observations on the usefulness of Latin in helping a lover speak as a man of sense and virtue. The paper ends with a puff of Mrs Centlivre's *The Wonder or a Woman Keeps a Secret,* first acted that night at Drury Lane. Susan Centlivre was a notably Whig author, and the published edition of *The Wonder* is dedicated to the Duke of Cambridge (the future George II). No. 33 is devoted to a detailed description of the huge painting by James Thornhill on the ceiling of Greenwich Hospital. In no. 34, Myrtle praises John Gumley's glass gallery, especially as an instance of the 'incredible Improvement our Artificers of *England* have made in Manufacture of Glass in thirty Years time', which, in turn, he sees as an example of the accomplishments of English trade. The final paper of the *Lover* is devoted to two theatrical puffs – of Jo Prince the dancer and, at more length, of Tom d'Urfey, whose play *The Richmond Heiress* would be given for his benefit some eleven days after the date of this paper.

Although the *Lover* does not tell us much about Steele that we would not know from reading the *Tatler*, many of its papers are equal to those of the *Tatler* in quality, and it has the advantage of a much more concentrated thematic organization than any of Steele's earlier periodicals. But, whatever other reasons he may have had for ending the *Lover*, a periodical in which over 70 per cent of the papers are devoted, in one way or another, to the subject of love ought to be ended before the topic has become stale, although Steele hardly exhausted the range. The *Lover* is a pleasant and moderate periodical, neither heavily moralistic nor superficial. For a period of about three weeks (22 April through 10 May), it was accompanied on alternate days by Steele's overtly political paper the *Reader* which, as the title suggests, engaged in paper war with the *Examiner* and its recent sidekick the *Monitor*.

While the *Lover* was spinning out its pleasant social commentary, the political situation was intensifying. Steele's expulsion from Parliament was one of the first actions of a session that promised to be fraught with contention. Its two underlying sources of energy were the uncertain state of the Queen's health, causing fears that she would be succeed by her half-brother rather than by an heir from Hanover, and the growing rift between Oxford and Bolingbroke. On 30 March, Steele sent a dire prediction to his wife:

> According to the Situation of affairs nothing but Divine Providence can prevent a Civil War within [a] few years, and against such disasters there can be no remedy but preparing our minds for the incidents we are to meet with with chearfulnesse.[67]

In fact, he had spent much of the day with Lieutenant-General William Cadogan, to whom he had dedicated the first volume of the *Guardian*. Calhoun Winton suggests that, in a plan contingent on the introduction of the Pretender, Cadogan was to lead a military resistence, in which Steele may have had a role.[68] Given Steele's sense of the seriousness of the situation, the *Lover* may have been a diversionary tactic designed to allay Tory suspicion of the likelihood of armed resistance to the Pretender. In mid-April *The Crisis upon Crisis: A Poem* was published attacking Steele. This long (eighteen-page) verse-couplet poem described, in bad verse and elaborate but insubstantial allegory, the arming of Nestor Ironside for battle and his subsequent withdrawal from the field.[69]

By early April, James had rejected the invitation to become a Protestant in order to become King and wrote letters to that effect to Oxford, Bolinbroke, and the Queen. Neither Oxford or Bolingbroke had courted the Hanovers with the attention that they showed towards James, and as a result they had no fallback position other than to hope the Queen's health improved. Their alliance had been frayed since Oxford's lukewarm support for the Commercial Treaty in the previous Spring and Bolingbroke had taken advantage of Oxford's absence for his son's wedding in September, 1713 to bribe and coerce members of the court, especially the Queen's favourite Lady Masham, to undermine Oxford.[70] Oxford himself was in ill health and drinking heavily. His political dexterity had slowed, even as his acute mind was aware of the difficulties of his situation. Parliament declared that the Protestant Succession was not in danger by very thin margins – in Commons by fifty votes, with the so-called Whimsical Tories (Tories who had opposed the Commercial treaty, led by Sir Thomas Hanmer) voting against the Ministry, in Lords by a vote of twelve.[71] Hanoverian supporters in both parties urged that the Duke of Cambridge, grandson of the Electress Sophia, be allowed to take his rightful place in the House of Lords, in the interests of his father and grandmother. Queen Anne, who had no legal alternative, very reluctantly granted his writ. On this matter, as now on virtually every other, Oxford and Bolingbroke took opposite positions.

Steele began the thrice-weekly *Reader* on Thursday 22 April, the same day as the Tory *Monitor*, but switched its publication dates to Monday, Wednesday and Friday with the third paper. Its purpose was 'chiefly to disabuse those Readers who are imposed upon by the licentious Writers of this degenerate Age' (the *Reader*, no. 2), of which the *Examiner* was the greatest offender.[72] But in no. 3 Steele turns his attention to the *Post Boy* and notices the *Monitor* in no. 4, where he introduces the recurring theme of 'Nonsense to the Conscience', which he describes as occurring 'when the Party has arrived to such a disregard to Reason and Truth, as not to follow it or acknowledge it when it presents it self to him'. He portrays Oxford in the guise of an unnamed leader of the Italian Ghibelins party who is not personally unattractive but also a master of nonsense.[73] In No. 6 Steele defends himself from attack by the *Examiner* and announces (in the third person) that Mr. Steele has collected information for a history of the war in Flanders that will cover the period of Marlborough's command. The *Reader* has papers on the Duke of Cambridge (nos 2 and 7), on the destruction of Dunkirk (no. 5) and on the politically charged topic of the superiority of Portuguese Port to French Claret (no. 8). Otherwise the *Reader* responds in detail to the attacks on Whigs in the *Examiner* and *Monitor*. By the time it closed on May 10, other topics were demanding Steele's attention as a writer.

Primary among these were the interconnections between politics and religion. On 12 May Bolingbroke introduced a 'Bill for Preventing the Growth of Schism', which required all teachers, even private ones, to be authorized by their local Bishop. The Bill was intended effectively to shut down the fine system of education that had developed among Dissenters, a system that was essentially superior to other education available in England. Bolingbroke seems to have intended the Bill as a sop to the 'Whimsical' Tories who supported the

Whig positions on the Commercial Treaty and the Protestant Succession but who were, nonetheless, decided supporters of the Church of England and its interests. But, even more strongly, he intended the Bill as an embarrassment to Oxford, who, although he conformed to the Church, came from a Dissenting background and was educated in precisely such schools. As leader of the Tories, he had to support the Bill or lose the support of his party; as the major figure of a Dissenting family, he must have seen the Bill as anathema. It was, of course, no accident that a solid base of support for the Whigs was the vote of Dissenters. On 1 June, after considerable heated debate, the Bill received its third reading in the Commons and was sent to the Lords. Two days later Steele's response, *A Letter to a Member of Parliament Concerning the Bill for Preventing the Growth of Schism* (London, 1714), appeared. It was perhaps his best, certainly his most principled, political tract.

Steele notes that teachers, under a statute of Charles II, were required to have the authorization of a Bishop, but that Dissenters, in the Act of Toleration of William III, were specifically exempted from that requirement, which is now reimposed by the new Bill.

> This Act therefore, in a stealing and too artful a Manner, takes away the Toleration of Dissenters; for the Force of it is directed to take place in Confirmation of a Law which they are expressly defended against by the said Act of Toleration ... Now, *Sir*, I say, if the Purpose of this Bill be to deprive the Dissenters of the Liberty of receiving Instructors into their Families, or publick School-masters or School-mistresses but under the above-mentioned Restrictions, this Bill is to deprive them of all Right, both Natural, Religious, and Civil.[74]

Steele points out the anomaly that Dissenters in England are attacked by the Bill but Anglicans in Scotland do not have similar requirements to conform to the (Dissenting) Kirk of Scotland.

Steele compares the Bill to the revocation of the Edict of Nantes in France, which terminated the rights of Huguenots to worship. He looks at the Bill under the headings of religious rights and civil rights. The universal right of Protestantism, he argues, is the right to read the Bible, to interpret it and to teach it in accordance with one's own conscience, a right that was protected by the Toleration Act and is denied here: 'it is a Characteristick of Protestant Churches to admit with all Candour the Liberty of studying the Scriptures, and consequently of teaching and being taught by them'.[75] Of course, non-Anglicans should not be allowed to proselytize among Anglicans, but, by the same token, they should be allowed to teach their own faith to their own children. Not to allow them to do so would, over the course of time, eliminate their communion altogether. Movement towards such an outcome would violate civil rights and present a danger to civil order: it would disturb the public peace and lead to abuse by irrationally prejudiced magistrates. It puts the Church of England in the same position as the Catholic Church – having to rely on civil authority rather than religious conviction for its power. Such reliance on legal coercion will ultimately weaken rather than strengthen the Church, and, more immediately, Dissenters would have no motive to resist the possibility of Catholic invasion on behalf of the Pretender if their conscience were equally violated by both Churches. 'If this Bill passes, and the Pretender should come upon our Coast, I would fain know what could move a Dissenter to lift an Hand, or employ a Shilling against Him?'[76] The Bill would encourage many Dissenters to emigrate, and hence no longer to pay tithes to the established Church. Dissenters have done no civil harm that requires the sudden deprivation of their basic human rights. Poor schoolmistresses would be punished for teaching young children their letters. The Bill is an example of using the Church to achieve purely secular ends. If it is passed the Queen should reject it. 'No Man can exert himself on a more worthy, or more important Occasion, than in Opposition to this Bill'.[77] It does not advance the cause of religion and therefore is of no value to the state. Steele concludes with some minor teasing of his expulsion enemies Thomas Foley and Edward Harley, both of whom came from a Dissenting family. (Harley actually voted against the Bill.)

Several characteristics make Steele's *Letter to a Member* an enduringly successful political tract. It engages large issues of great importance – freedom of conscience and the relation of religious to secular authority. In effect the religious disputes of the late seventeenth and early eighteenth centuries involved the question of what it meant to be an established church that was nonetheless Protestant and distinct from the religious control of the state associated with Catholic countries. Steele takes the Protestant position that religious authority essentially derives from conscience and belief, and he criticizes the idea that it is correlative with the authority of the state. But for Steele (and perhaps for us) the idea has a greater urgency. As he recognized, the appeal to religion (from Bolingbroke, a man who was known as a libertine and a freethinker) was a completely cynical gesture of political power, here at the expense of Oxford, whose religiosity seemed genuine, even if much else about him was questionable. What gave the Bill particular urgency for Steele was its duplication of the very principles that he was against in his writings against Catholicism. His argument gains particular force in its absolutely sincerity. This is not the screed of a political hack but the deeply-felt conviction of a complex and sympathetic writer. Before the end of June, Daniel Defoe, Steele's usual antagonist, produced a tract agreeing with his attack on the Schism Bill.[78] George Sewell published a tract in which he argued that Dissenters were, by definition, a danger to the Church and state, and hence the state had the right to protect itself. In particular, parents do not have the right to educate their children as they see fit; the state also has educational rights.[79] The Schism Bill passed in Lords on 15 June by only five votes. But the

Bill was scheduled to go into effect 1 August, the day of Anne's death. It was only occasionally enforced thereafter and was finally repealed in 1719.

Between the introduction of the Schism Bill (12 May) and the appearance of his tract on 3 June, Steele attacked the other side of the religious argument with a publication much closer to hack writing. *The Romish Ecclesiastical History of Late Years* (London, 1714), published on 25 May, was 'professedly design'd to expose the Prophanation of True Religion, by the Artifices of the Church of *Rome*; and the Ambition of all Men, in other Communities, who make a False Zeal for Religion, their Tool, to work their Way to such Ends as Religion most abhors'.[80] Steele only wrote the Dedication to Lord Finch, the Preface, a brief introduction to the 'Ecclesiatical History' itself, and conclusions to Chapters 1 and 2, in which he pretends to present the reports of Cardinal Gaultiero, the 'missionary' to England, regarding the religious and political situation in England:

> The *Tory* accuses the *Whig* of a Design to subvert the Monarchy of ENGLAND; the *Whig* tells the *Tory*, his utmost Endeavour is to introduce absolute and despotick Power in the Sovereign, and destroy the Liberty of the Subject. Certain it is, that neither of these Men aim directly at the Ills of which they accuse each other, that is, they do not design the Abuse of those Sentiments which they profess; for the *Whig* does not aim at *Republicanism*, nor the *Tory* at *Slavery*; but it has been ever observed, that from Aversion to each other, each shuns the opposite Character, till he is reduced to an Absurdity in the prosecution of his own Principles.[81]

But although the Cardinal's fictitious report seems to undercut the political propagandizing in which Steele is presently engaged by accusing both parties of inaccurate extremes, the fact remained that there was a present danger from Catholic attack and, the Cardinal implies, Catholic infiltration. The major danger against which Steele attacks is the false use of religion for secular purposes. The occasion recorded in the 'Ecclesiastical History' is the canonization of saints, which Steele regards as a territorial invasion of Heaven itself. The occasion is primarily an excuse to insist 'That the Clergy have nothing to say to us concerning Government, but as other Men have it, from the Laws themselves'.[82] The tract's mockery of Catholic ceremony, or what it imagined to be Catholic ceremony, fits the anti-Catholicism of Steele's Anglo-Irish tradition. But the real targets of the tract are High Churchmen who uses religion as a political tool.

Another theme that Steele wanted to keep alive was the deception of the French regarding the destruction of Dunkirk. *The French Faith Represented in the Present State of Dunkirk. A Letter to the Examiner, In Defence of Mr. S—le* (London, 1714) is an act of hidden self-defence, where the defender is apparently not Steele but someone acting on his behalf. It is, in effect, a reminder that the French have not really disabled Dunkirk but have built an even stronger harbour a few miles away at Mardyck and connected it to Dunkirk by canal. The dangers presented by Dunkirk remain, and Steele has not been an alarmist: 'I do not defend Mr. *Steele's* Writings against those of your Eminence, any further than it now is evident that he had Reason to fear, and you no Reason to abuse him.'[83] Parliament should vote that Britain is being deceived and that France's building of a new, connected harbour is an infringement of its treaty obligations. Except for the information on Mardick, the pamphlet does not add much that is new. (It quotes extensively from *The Importance of Dunkirk Consider'd*.)

Steele continued to come under attack from Whig pamphleteers during the summer of 1714. Francis Hoffman wrote (and published) a rare comic pamphlet *Two Very Odd Characters, tho the Number be Even*, which contrasts a picture of the Whig 'flesh-fly', shown lying on a page with the title of Steele's periodicals and threatened by the rapier of Powell (presumably Martin Powell, Steele's victim in several *Tatler* papers), in contrast to the industrious Tory Bee, pictured sucking honey from a rose and representing none other than Francis Hoffman himself, the hero of this highly self-referential tract.[84] Two eleborate but nonetheless vicious allegories were published under the name of the eccentric religious writer John Lacy, who almost certainly did not write them. *The Ecclesiastical and Political History of Whig Land, of Late Years* is a confused allegorical mélange that begins with a particularly scandalous biography of Steele.[85] *The Steeleids, or, the Tryal of Wit* is the verse chronicle of the efforts of both Mr Examiner and Mr Steele to make their way to Parnassus amid a crowd of living and mostly dead poets. Eventually Mr Examiner achieves Parnassus because of his truth, while Steele is sent back to the hellish world of pamphleteers. His worst sin seems to have been his praise of Marlborough.[86]

Disputes in the political world were more telling than literary ones. Oxford, although nearly incapacitated, hung on to his position as Lord Treasurer with a tenacity driven primarily by his insistence that Bolingbroke not be allowed to gain power. Bolingbroke, on the other hand, sought a complex alignment of continental alliance that would unite Spain, France and England against Austria (the alignment broke up on the death of Anne), and he continued to conspire with Lady Masham to turn the queen against Oxford, now weakened by neglect of his duties. Oxford joined the 'Whimsicals' in their support of the House of Hanover and joined with the Whigs in accusing Bolingbroke of corruption involving the South-Sea company. To prevent further investigation Queen Anne prorogued Parliament on 9 July, but the charges against Bolingbroke made her hesitant to appoint him treasurer. On 27 July, she regretfully dismissed Oxford as Lord Treasurer. On July 30, her ailing health took a turn for the worse, and she appointed the moderate Hanoverian, Lord Shrewsbury, as Secretary of the Treasury. On 1 August she died.

Whig fears of widespread Jacobite resistance, although not altogether unfounded, were unrealized. Information and invitations were promptly sent to George, and a pro-Whig regency of Lords Justice was formed with Joseph

Addison as secretary. The Duke and Duchess of Marlborough quickly arrived in London after their Dutch exile. Bolingbroke was dismissed as Secretary of State. The Whigs had triumphed. On 18 September, after a slow trip, King George arrived at Greenwich to begin a dynasty that remains in power today. Steele had spent much of that summer preparing his *Apology*, in which he recorded his speech of defence to the House and attacked the Harley-Foley family that had led the prosecution. He was angered that the charge of sedition had compromised his reputation. 'In Defence of Truth', he tells Walpole in the dedication, 'I incurred popular Hatred and Contempt, with the Prospect of suffering the want even of the ordinary Conveniences of Life'.[87] The *Apology* was intended at least to clear that reputation. But with the death of Anne, the loss of Tory Power, and the coming of George to England, the *Apology* became for Steele an excellent way of introducing himself to the new monarch, especially since a major factor in his prosecution was his strong and outspoken defence of the Hanoverian claim to the throne. The *Apology* was published by R. Burleigh on 22 October. Another project by Steele that appeared in October was *The Ladies Library*, published in three volumes by Tonson.

On 15 August, Steele wrote his wife that 'I have been with Cadogan who gives me great hopes of success in the Patent for Farthings; Baron Bothmar dines with Him and He will have me be there'.[88] General Cadogan was an old friend and ally; Baron Bothmar was Hanover's envoy to England and an important advisor of the new King. In a letter of 5 August, he mentioned Steele's particular service to Hanover.[89] The scheme for minting new farthings responded to the country's need for coinage and Steele's avocation as an economic projector. Like so many of Steele's other schemes, it came to nothing in the end. But Steele's connections with Bothmar, the Hanoverians and the Whigs paid off substantially in the next months. Steele's interest in the theatre – as a playwright, as a reformist critic, as a friend and promoter of actors and managers and as a budding entrepreneur in his own 'Censorium' – pointed towards a share in the management of Drury-Lane Theatre, an ambition that the current managers supported because of Steele's useful political connections. Accordingly, the Lord Chamberlain, at that point the Duke of Shrewsbury, issued a licence to Steele, Booth, Doggett, Wilks, and Cibber to form a company of players (Drury Lane). Even before Steele's appointment, Drury Lane was known as a Whig house. (The political, economic, aesthetic and personal complexities of Steele's management role will be the subject of the next chapter of this biography.)

In December, Thomas Pelham-Holles, an ambitious young Peer who had, on the accession of King George, been made Earl of Clare, and who had accumulated the nomination for a number of parliamentary seats, offered Steele a candidacy for Parliament from Boroughbridge, in Yorkshire. Lord Clare was, alas, a model of pre-reform parliamentary management. If a tenant did not vote as Clare ordered, he evicted him. Steele, who prided himself on his independence, was playing a dangerous game by accepting his nomination. Nonetheless, he accepted it. He was given £500 by the King, presumably for election expenses and, in January, set off to contest the election, which he won on 2 February. On 9 April 1715, Steele was presented to the King by the Earl of Clare, and the King knighted him. Henceforth he was Sir Richard Steele.

Steele's propaganda campaign of 1713–14 was dominated by genuine (if exaggerated) worries: that the House of Hanover would not succeed to the British throne but that Britain would instead be ruled by authoritarian, Catholic members of the Stuart family; that the potential achievements of the costly War of Spanish Succession had been sacrificed to a dishonourable peace and were likely to be further diminished by the Francophile tendencies of Bolingbroke; that the Tories were particularly culpable in their failure to recognize and honour the accomplishments of the Duke of Marlborough; that the preservation of religious liberty was essential not only to the personal freedom of British citizens but even to the welfare of the Church of England. Underlying all of these concerns was his sense that Britain was a trading nation and that the preservation, indeed the increase, of trade was a key principle of foreign policy. The pursuit of these principles in the face of Tory opposition and Jacobite threat changed him from a genial if somewhat uncontrolled moral reformer to a political activist who was willing to make significant sacrifices for the Whig cause.

6 THE POLITICS OF THE THEATRE

Richard Steele's career on the London stage after 1714 is characterized by his reformist programme, his efforts to protect the professionalism of the theatre, and his involvement in the arguments of political faction. Despite his ambivalence about the great comic dramatists of the Restoration, he proclaimed himself often and loudly as a reformer of the theatrical scene, and his record as both critic and playwright seemed to verify that intention. But the discrepancy between his pronouncements in *Town-Talk* and *The Theatre* on one hand and the actual repertory of plays at Drury Lane on the other seemed to characterize his reformist claims as hypocrisy, although the one play that he actually did complete for Drury Lane, *The Conscious Lovers*, was saliently moralistic.

Cibber, Wilks and Booth, the actor-managers, knew Steele's economic record too well to entrust him with any financial responsibility for the theatre. But he was nonetheless able to entangle the theatre in his own personal finances. The patent for Drury Lane, once Steele secured it, was an asset which Steele could mortgage, and he did so in his unending quest for solvency. The obvious danger was that Steele might not pay the mortgage and his creditors might take over the patent. The financial and personal implications of this and other problems in Steele's behaviour ultimately resulted in a legal suit which Steele lost, as he did most of the many suits against him concerning financial matters.

Steele was appointed one of the managers of Drury Lane as a reward for his propaganda efforts on behalf of the House of Hanover and the Whigs during 1713 and 1714. He was suspended from the management (1720), via a revocation of the licence and the framing of a new one that did not include him, for a variety of reasons, primary among them was failure to support the Peerage Bill that the ministry proposed. The bill failed and Steele's exclusion from the profits of Drury Lane can be seen as something of an act of revenge. Steele's position was restored when Walpole became Lord Treasurer in April 1721. Even more important than the Peerage Bill as a source of tension between the Duke of Newcastle, then Lord Chancellor, and the Drury Lane managers were their differing views over the power of the crown and the independence of the theatrical company, an issue that was not to be resolved until the draconian Licensing

Act of 1737. Beyond that, Drury Lane was a Whig house after 1714, so that Lincoln's Inn Fields, which opened in 1714, became, reluctantly and by default, a Tory house.[1] The complex intertwinings of Steele's reformist goals, his status as manager of Drury-Lane Theatre, and the politics that reigned within the theatre and outside it require a more detailed and careful explication.

Patent and Licence

Queen Anne's death on 1 August 1714 came when Drury Lane was down for the summer, and hence the mandatory six-week suspension of plays on the death of the monarch had relatively little impact. But it also meant that the theatre's licence to perform, which was coterminous with the life of the monarch who had granted it, had ended. The actor-managers were anxious to supplant William Collier, a Tory lawyer who was the non-acting manager of the theatre and who received a pension of £700 per year. They recognized that in the present circumstances a Whig might be a more useful non-acting manager, and Steele, whom they knew personally, was presently in high favour at court.

> We knew too, the Obligations the Stage had to his Writings; there being scarce a Comedian of Merit, in our whole Company, whom his *Tatlers* had not made better, by his publick Recommendation of them. And many Days had our House been particularly fill'd, by the Influence, and Credit of his Pen. Obligations of this kind from a Gentleman, with whom they all had the Pleasure of a personal Intimacy, the Menagers thought could not be more justly return'd, than by shewing him some warm Instance of their Desire, to have him, at the Head of them. [2]

Steele was thus commissioned to secure the license, and Cibber reports that he did so through the influence of the Marlboroughs, who had just returned to England.[3] A licence was granted to Steele and to the actors Robert Wilks, Colley Cibber, Thomas Doggett, and Barton Booth, dated 18 October 1714.

The licence gave them power to perform 'all Comedys, Tragedies, and all other Theatricall Performances (Musicall Entertainments only excepted) Subject to such Rules and Orders for their good Government therein, as they shall receive from time to time from the Chamberlain of Our Household.'[4] Theatres functioned under the protection and authority of the King, and that authority was carried out through the agency of the Lord Chamberlain, although the nature and limits of his authority were not well defined and were to become a major point of contention in later years. Moreover, the licence remained in effect as long as the King (or his Lord Chamberlain) thought it should. It expired at the death of the king and thus had to be renewed at the beginning of a new reign. Steele and his partners were agreed that a more durable grant was desirable. The expectation was that Steele would continue to be paid the £700 that had been paid to Collier every year.

The desirability of a stronger grant quickly became evident. When Steele secured the license, Drury Lane was the only theatre at which public plays could be seen. But on 18 December 1714, John and Christopher Rich opened a theatre in Lincoln's Inn Fields, and they did so by virtue of a patent they inherited from their father, Christopher Rich, who, in turn had acquired it from Sir William D'Avenant and Thomas Killigrew, to whom it was granted by Charles II. A patent, unlike a license, was not dependent on the will of the King and did not expire upon his death. It was, in a sense, owned by the patentee. It could be bought, sold, and inherited. Christopher Rich had been silenced during the reign of Anne but he possessed a genuine patent, and that, in the view of King George, enabled him to renew productions in a new reign. The possession of a patent by Lincoln's Inn Fields created the anomalous situation in which the major of two companies operated on a flimsy license, while the minor upstart had a solid and more authoritative patent. Because of the political sentiments of many of its plays and because it was so closely connected with court, Drury Lane was identified as a Whig house. Somewhat reluctantly, Lincoln's Inn Fields became a Tory house.

The managers of Drury Lane sought several results by acquiring a patent. When Lincoln's Inn Fields opened, 'seven or eight Actors, in one Day, deserted from us, to the Service of the Enemy'.[5] As an obvious consequence Drury Lane had to postpone plays or mount them with fewer actors than usual. A situation in which rival houses competed not only for audiences but for actors as well was bound to become unstable. Drury Lane appealed to the Lord Chamberlain to insist that the actors return or be silenced. Apparently he did not do so.[6] If on one hand the managers sought the support and protection of the Lord Chamberlain, on the other they wanted to become completely independent of him. They saw the company of actors not as 'the king's servants' but as an autonomous group responding to the demands of its audience rather than of the crown. The actor-managers agreed that Steele should seek the patent and upon receiving it, divide it among them.

Steele's petition justifies the patent on highly moralistic principles:

> That the use of the Theatre has for many years last past been much perverted to the great Scandal of Religion and Good Government.
> That it will require much time to remedy so inveterate an evil, and will expose the Undertaker to much Envy and Opposition.
> That an affair of this Nature cant be accomplished without a lasting Authority.[7]

The patent that resulted from Steele's application might have been written by Steele himself. It emphasizes Steele's political service, stating that the patent is being given to 'Our Trusty and Well-beloved *Richard Steele*, Esq; for the promoting these Our Royal Purposes, not only from his Publick Services to Religion and Virtue, but for his steady Adherence to the true Interest of his Country'.[8] It acknowledges 'the good and faithful Services' that Steele has done, and consequently awards the patent for the term of Steele's natural life plus three additional years. The patent given to D'Avenant and Killigrew by Charles II had no such limited term, and hence was now being used by Rich at Lincoln's-Inn-Field..

The purpose of giving the patent to Steele is clearly to reform the theatre and to improve the moral standards of its performances. At its opening the patent reads as if it had been written by Jeremy Collier. The theatre has offended

> the Sober, Intelligent, and Religious Part of our People; and, by indecent and immodest Expressions, by prophane Allusion to Holy Scripture, by abusive and scurrilous Representations of the Clergy, and by the Success and Applause bestowed on Libertine Characters, it hath given great and insufferable Scandal to Religion and good Manners (*Town-Talk*, no. 6).

What is needed, then, is a new, exemplary theatre 'that, for the future, Our Theatre may be Instrumental to the Promotion of Virtue, and Instructive to Human Life' (*Town-Talk*, no. 6). Collier had specifically reprobated the offensive language, action, and topics of contemporary drama, its use of swearing and cursing, its abuse of religion in general and the clergy in particular, and its willingness to let immoral (if attractive) characters go unpunished.

The patent imposes what seems to have been envisioned as censorship duties on the patent-holder:

> no New Play, or any Old or Revived Play [may] be Acted under the Authority hereby Granted, containing any Passages or Expressions offensive to Piety and good Manners, until the same be Corrected and Purged by the said Governor, from all such Offensive and Scandalous Passages and Expressions (*Town-Talk*, no. 6).

The 'Governor' in question here is clearly Steele and those responsible to Steele. The patent seems to achieve the end sought by Steele and the actor-managers. It does not mention or refer to the authority of the Lord Chamberlain but leaves the responsibility for policing the moral content of plays squarely in the hands of the manager. A year later (20 January 1716) Steele published the patent in *Town-Talk*, a periodical devoted to promoting the interests of Drury Lane Theatre, perhaps as a means of making clear to the public the moral intentions of the theatre and its managers.

Colley Cibber would certainly be considered the most important of the Drury Lane actor-managers, even if he did not trumpet his significance so loudly in his *Apology*, which nonetheless remains an important source for the history of the theatre during the period of Steele's management. An effective comedian who longed to play heroic parts for which he was not suited, he scored a big success as the foppish Sir Novelty Fashion in his own play *Love's Last Shift; or,*

The Fool in Fashion (1696), and went on to play other Restoration fops such as Sir Fopling Flutter in Etherege's *The Man of Mode; or Sir Fopling Flutter* (1676) and Lord Foppinton in Vanbrugh's *The Relapse; or, Virtue in Danger* (1696). He was doubly useful as both playwright and actor, although he wrote little after 1713. With Robert Wilks and Thomas Doggett, he eventually purchased the Drury-Lane company, and the three actors became co-managers. Wilks achieved great popular success as a romantic lead in the plays of Etherege and Farquhar, as well as warhorses by Shakespeare. Cibber describes him as a vain, extravagant and touchy manager, in contrast to the economical comedian Thomas Doggett.[9] Doggett had ceased to play an active role in the management of the company after 1713, partly in reaction to the personality and temperament of Wilks, and partly in response to the introduction of Barton Booth as a new manager. Although he refused to act or manage, he insisted on payment of his share in the company's profits. The case was argued back and forth and eventually went to court, where it was settled in favour of Cibber and the other managers. Barton Booth became a manager almost as a result of popular demand. He had been on the London stage since 1700 and, most recently, had appeared with notable success in the title role of Addison's *Cato*. He was particularly effective in heroic roles, in which he was the successor to the great Thomas Betterton.

The question of how to split up the profits became contentious when Doggett stopped acting but insisted on payment and when the addition of Booth raised the number of managers to four (counting Daggett but not counting the Tory Collier). Cibber describes the complex and sometimes hostile negotiations in detail.[10] Steele was not involved in these negotiations, some of which preceded his joining the management but most of which did not concern him directly. When he took the place of Collier, he also received the £700 that Collier received each year. But the opening of a rival house in Lincoln's Inn Fields cut seriously into the revenues of Drury Lane. Steele's generous response was to agree that an equal share in the profits would substitute for his fixed annual income. This step cost him substantially in the first year of the theatrical rivalry but benefited him in later years (or would have done so if Steele had not mortgaged away his theatrical profits).

The three actor-managers were different in their personalities and, more to the point, in the kinds of roles they could play. Therefore there was little conflict regarding parts in plays. Cibber, thanks in part to the minimal interests of the other managers in the business side of things, took the primary role in scheduling plays, in assigning roles and in conducting rehearsals. Steele was, in effect, the liaison between the company and the community at large. He had extensive political connections and was a familiar figure at court. He was responsible for encouraging members of society to attend the theatre. He was required to write plays for the company (of which he wrote but one) and to meet regularly with the other managers – to participate, in short, in the process of evaluating new plays and hiring new actors. The lawsuit of 1729 between Steele and his fellow managers revealed further duties that were controversial, particularly the obligation to instruct young actors.[11] While it is conceivable that Steele might have helped introduce neophytes to the corpus of plays acted at Drury Lane or that, as the former self-proclaimed Censor-General of Great Britain, he might have given advice on socially accepted behaviour. But he was certainly no actor and would have made no more sense as an instructor of actors than as treasurer of the company. He denied that responsibility but seems to have performed his other duties reasonably well until 1720, when the Lord Chamberlain suspended him, and his ill-health and other interests led to the end of his active participation.

One significant feature of Steele's period as active manager of Drury Lane was his introduction of Addison's *The Drummer*. Steele announced it in the final number of *Town-Talk* as

'delivered, by the Author, to the Governor of the Royal Company of Comedians, under the Seal of Secrecy as to the Name of its Writer; for it seems, though it is thus excellent, the Spirit of it is too fine, and the Characters drawn with too much Delicacy to be attended to by an Audience, who require Violence and Extravagance to awaken them to Delight (*Town-Talk*, no. 9, p. 249).

The Drummer was the only new play acted in 1715–16 and, as Steele predicted, it was not successful. Tonson published it in March, but Tickell did not include it in his posthumous edition of Addison's works of 1721. Steele bought the copyright back from Tonson, who thought that Steele might have deceived him about Addison's authorship, and published it in December 1721, with an informative dedication to Congreve. The play was subsequently picked up by Lincolns-Inn-Fields, where it went successfully into the repertory.

The Failure of Reform

Although Steele appears in the patent as a champion of reform because of 'his Publick Services to Religion and Virtue', and was given authority to censor plays for that same reason, his attitude towards reform reflects an ambivalence and uncertainty that was perhaps widely shared and perhaps explains the continued acting of plays condemned by Collier and, indeed, by Steele himself. As we have seen in Chapter 1, Steele defended Congreve's *The Way of the World* in his poem 'To Mr. Congreve'. Steele did not concentrate on Congreve's relatively inoffensive play but on his works in general, and he made the argument, which was subsequently used by Dennis and others in response to his own attack on Etherege, that in the central characters of his plays Congreve had created plausible but negative examples, so that the audience's perception of their folly and its consequence becomes the governing moral purpose of such plays. Steele tries to hold on to the idea that comedy functions properly to give examples that members of the audience can use to resolve their own moral dilemmas, but in the case of Congreve he is willing to see the comedy as satire and to accept the plays as revealing negative examples.

In discussing *The Country Wife* in *Tatler*, no. 3, Steele somewhat sidesteps the moral issue by historicizing. *The Country Wife* was only occasionally performed in the years before 1709. It was not acted again until 1715, when Steele was a manager of Drury Lane, and was acted relatively regularly thereafter. It was originally performed in 1675, and Steele thus treats it as a picture of social life and behaviours that had changed by 1709.

> The Character of *Horner*, and the Design of it, is a good Representation of the Age in which that Comedy was written; at which Time, Love and Wenching were the Business of Life, and the Gallant Manner of pursuing Women was the best Recommendation at Court (*Tatler*, no. 3).

He sees comedy as exemplary, but as providing examples of social manners rather than morality.

> I cannot be of the same Opinion with my Friends and Fellow-Labourers, the *Reformers of Manners*, in their Severity towards Plays, but must allow, that a good Play, acted before a well-bred Audience, must raise very proper Incitements to good Behaviour, and be the most quick and most prevailing Method of giving Young People a Turn of Sense and Breeding (*Tatler*, no. 3).

In *Tatler*, no. 8, Bickerstaff's friend Eugenius recommends 'the apt Use of a Theatre, as the most agreeable and easie Method of making a Polite and Moral Gentry, which would end in rendring the rest of the People regular in their Behaviour, and ambitious of laudable Undertakings'.

Steele's famous attack on *The Man of Mode* in *Spectator*, nos. 65 and 75 may be less at odds with his tolerance of Congreve and Wycherley than first appears. *The Man of Mode* was first performed one year later than *The Country Wife* and thus could have been similarly regarded as a picture of a distinct historical period. But Steele does not do so, regarding Dorimant instead as 'a direct Knave in his Designs, and a Clown in his Language' (*Spectator*, no. 65). At the beginning of this essay he establishes, as a criterion for evaluation, 'that for which each respective Play is most celebrated', and the *Man of Mode* is reputed to be 'the Pattern of Gentile Comedy' (*Spectator*, no. 65). But the play itself, he insists, is inconsistent with its reputation. 'This whole celebrated Piece', he goes on, 'is a perfect Contradiction to good Manners, good Sense, and common Honesty; and there is nothing in it but what is built upon the Ruin of Virtue and Innocence' (*Spectator*, no. 65). He resumes the attack with vigour in response to a defence of Dorimant by 'a Fine Lady of my Acquaintance' (*Spectator*, no. 75), and concludes that she and he have contrasting notions of what a 'Fine Gentle-man' is. Steele insists that the fine gentleman acts according to socially accepted standards of behaviour. 'What is opposite to the eternal Rules of Reason and good Sense, must be excluded from any Place in the Carriage of a Well-bred Man' (*Tatler*, no. 75). He echoes, in a softer voice, Collier's assertion that 'a fine Gentleman is a fine Whoring, Swearing, Smutty, Atheistical Man'.[12] It is hard to say whether Steele was actively working on *The Conscious Lovers* in 1711; he evidently was in 1713. But he is here establishing the kind of hero he will try to create in Young Bevil – a man whose distinguishing qualities of character con-sist of scrupulous morality rather than social pretence. *Spectator*, no. 51, written in response to the complaint of young woman about salacious language in *The Funeral*, insists that poets write bawdry to compensate for their lack of inven-tion and urges them to create better heroes. 'A Man that is Temperate, Generous, Valiant, Chaste, Faithful and Honest, may, at the same time, have Wit, Humour, Mirth, good Breeding, and Gallantry' (*Spectator*, No. 51). (In addition to its allegedly improper language, *The Funeral* offends reformist neoclassical norms because its villain Sable is not appropriately punished.)[13]

Steele's notions of theatrical reform were more moderate than those of Col-lier, despite their substantial overlap. Although Collier never quite called for the abolition of the theatre altogether, other reformers did so.[14] Running through Steele's dramatic efforts, as a playwright, as a critic, and as a manager, was an effort to preserve the theatre in more-or-less its contemporary form, in the face of radically conservative attack, but this would require some modification of its attacks on conventional values. His evaluation of Dorimant's status as a gentle-man not only echoes the recurrent theme of the *Tatler* and *Spectator* that moral rectitude and social decency are the primary characteristics of a gentleman but seeks to establish criteria that are both secular and universal for evaluating the morality of plays. Such criteria can, on one hand, replace the narrow religious zeal and neo-critical artificiality of Collier and open the play as a whole as a moral subject, rather than concentrating attention on the snippets of language that Collier rather successfully condemns. But, on the other, they reject the implica-tion of much Restoration comedy that moral condemnation of the behaviour it represents is merely hypocritical posturing.

Nonetheless, Steele's reform does seem to require the avoidance of evil, or of actions on the part of positive characters that might give offence to the delicacies of the audience. A performance of *The Scornful Lady* in January 1712 provides the occasion for sharp articulation of Steele's sense of what is outrageous:

> It is so mean a thing to gratify a loose Age with a scandalous Representation of what
> is reputable among Men, not to say what is sacred, that no Beauty, no Excellence in
> an Author ought to attone for it; nay such Excellence is an aggravation of his Guilt,
> and an Argument that he errs against the Conviction of his own Understanding and
> Conscience. Wit should be tried by this Rule, and an Audience should rise against

such a Scene, as throws down the Reputation of any thing which the consideration of Religion or Decency should preserve from Contempt (*Spectator*, no. 270).

Good characters should not insult women and should in general conduct their relations with politeness. Steele's ideal dramatic hero manages to be a distinctive character while adhering to the norms of social convention, in language as well as in behaviour. He must be a man of honour and courage without being a duellist. Beyond avoiding evil and misbehaviour, he must perform significantly positive actions, and these constitute his claims to a kind of heroism – the heroism of ordinary life. Such a character requires a definition of a masculinity that is bourgeois but at the same time appealing.

Steele pursued his reformist intentions in his weekly periodical *Town-Talk*, which ran from 17 December 1715 to 13 February 1716 (nine numbers) and was designed, in large part, to promote interest in the stage. Appearing weekly, *Town-Talk* was longer than the periodicals that appeared several times a week, and each issue ranged over a variety of topics, rather like the early *Tatlers*. It takes the form of weekly letters to a woman in the country, perhaps, as Blanchard suggests, Lady Steele, who has asked the author to report his observations of fashionable life, especially the doings of her cousin Arthur, whose sensible observations and reflections become a major authorial device in the course of the periodical.[15] The anonymous letter-writer and Arthur are members of a group of men and women who meet regularly at the home of Mr Johnson, a man of 'very ample Fortune, and a numerous Family' (*Town-Talk*, no. 3, p. 203), and the development of topics often follows the interests and activities of Arthur and this family. He is eventually taken by the charms of Amorett, 'who is as much more Knowing, as she is more Fair, than the rest of her Sex' (*Town-Talk*, no. 4, p. 210), and the series concludes with his declaration of his passion. Arthur exemplifies Steele's ideal comic hero – charming, sociable, well-behaved, and well-spoken.

Arthur describes the reformist intentions of Drury Lane and the threats to that program caused by the opening of a rival house in Lincoln's Inn Fields:

> But the best Vehicle for conveying right Sentiments into the People, is certainly the Theatre; and I have been credibly informed, that the Sharers in that of *Drury-Lane*, had form'd a Design of Reforming the Present Tast of it, by giving due Encouragement to Men of Abilities, as well by a careful Performance of what they should Act, as a just Recompence for the Purchase of their Works, to engage them steadily and heartily in their Interests. But a New House, finely Gilded, having been opened against them last Winter, they were forced to suspend their Improvement to consult their Safety, which was in very great Danger, by the Loss of many of their Actors, who knew, if they were not excellent, they were necessary. (no. 2, pp. 194–5.)

To prove the point, the letter-writer presents a copy of the Drury Lane patent in no. 6, and adds a comment on the relation of the patent's good intentions to the present and to plans for the future:

> The Indulgence at present given to what is represented there, is a Sufferance which it is to be hoped will be made up to the Audience in future Plays. If every Thing that shall not be represented is not virtuous, let it at least be innocent. This will bring a new Audience to the House; and it is from the Hope of entertaining those, who are at present terrified at the Theatre, that the Sharers must hope for their Success hereafter. (no. 6, p. 232).

Table-Talk presents a full statement of the intentions of Steele and (presumably) his colleagues to transform the theatre along the lines of the reformist programme. Drury Lane seeks to attract new plays that are at least inoffensive but at best embody the combination of charm and virtue that Steele proposes. Such plays will, without turning off those who come to plays by Dryden, Wycherley, Congreve, Etherege and Vanbrugh, attract a new audience, largely bourgeois, that had been, as Steele puts it, 'terrified at the Theatre'. Such plays, addressed to such an audience, would finally fulfill the justifying function of the stage to motivate its audience to moral behaviour.

But this reform never took place, despite Steele's promises and protestations. A sampling of plays sometimes regarded as morally dangerous shows that they continued to be performed regularly during the period of Steele's active participation in the management of the company (1714–20). Congreve's *Love for Love* was acted four or five times per year, for a total of twenty-seven performances. Vanbrugh's *The Relapse*, to which Collier devoted some twenty-three pages of attack,[16] was not performed at all in 1714–15, the year Steele became manager, but thereafter it too was performed four or five times every year, totalling twenty-two. Wycherley's *The Country Wife* was not performed until May 1715, when it was advertised as not acted for six years. Thereafter it was performed seventeen times before the end of the 1719–20 season. Even Etherege's *The Man of Mode*, which Steele so famously and roundly condemned, was performed fourteen times between 1714 and 1720. An anonymous writer responding to Steele's *The State of the Case* (1720) lists the evidence for the degeneracy of the stage:

> The same lewd Plays being acted and revived without any material alteration, which gave occasion for that universal complaint against the English Stage, of lewdness and debauchery, from all the sober and religious part of the nation; the whole business of Comedy continuing all his time to be the criminal intrigues of fornication and adultery, ridiculing of marriage, virtue, and integrity, the giving a favourable turn to vicious characters, and instructing loose people how to carry on their lewd designs with plausibility and success.[17]

Some of these plays were advertised as being revised, and the most evident example of revision was in Act IV of Vanbrugh's *The Provoked Wife*, where Lord Brute's drunken disguise as a clergyman was changed to his equally drunken disguise as his wife. Nonetheless, the question remains as to why these plays, and others like them, continued to be performed despite Steele's promises of reform. At first, Steele claimed that the rivalry with Lincoln's Inn Fields delayed the reform. But the continued presence of plays that could be regarded as morally questionable suggests a lack of sincerity on Steele's part or his inability to persuade his fellow managers to change their ways. The plays were familiar. They were loved by at least a segment of the theatre-going public. The actors on the whole knew the roles, and they could be mounted with minimal rehearsal time. It was simply more convenient and profitable to continue performing them. Drury Lane, after all, was run as a business enterprise rather than a centre for moral improvement, even if Steele sometimes did justify the theatre in those terms. The choice of plays followed the interests of the audience.

A related issue was the failure of Drury Lane to perform new plays. One of the essential elements of theatrical reform was the provision of plays that not only avoided naughtiness but also addressed the interests and sensibilities of a bourgeois audience and thus expanded the theatre's clientele. But instead of wholesome new dramas, Drury Lane presented not only the offensive old standards but a more extensive programme of farces, afterpieces and pantomimes, precisely the kind of mindless entertainment that Steele had mocked in the *Spectator* (for example, *Spectator*, nos. 14, 22, 36). These grew at Drury Lane in direct response to their introduction at Lincoln's Inn Fields. John Loftis notes a letter of 27 November 1715 from the Earl of Stair, then in Paris, to Steele.[18] Stair wrote in response to Steele's apparent request regarding an English actor named Baxter presently performing in France. Loftis identifies him as an expert in Harlequin roles who had performed in France since 1707 and who in 1716 indeed performed at Drury Lane.[19] The introduction and spread of such performances, however, was not the kind of reform Steele promised from his tenure as manager.

Loftis enumerates two new plays during the season of 1714–15 (one of them by Nicholas Rowe); only one play, Addison's *The Drummer*, in 1715–16; four new plays, including Mrs Manley's *Lucius* which, in a spirit of reconciliation, Steele supported (he wrote the prologue for it, and it was dedicated to him); two again in 1717–18, Cibber's *The Non-Juror* among them; three in 1718–19. In addition, a number of plays that had not been acted for many seasons were dusted off (if not cleaned up), revised and newly mounted. For the actors if not for the audience these may well have seemed like new plays, but they hardly fulfilled the promise of new directions in the theatre. New plays required fairly extensive rehearsals during the day while the actors were often performing other roles at night. They meant setting aside the stock repertoire for three or six nights and giving the profits of the third and sixth night to the playwright. Financially, aesthetically and in terms of time, new plays were a risky venture, and relatively few of the new plays produced stayed in the repertoire.

Much of the complaining about the failure to put on new plays came, of course, from the playwrights themselves, and so can be considered special pleading. But the loudest of this pleading comes from John Dennis, whose appropriately Whig play, *The Invader of his Country* was staged under deliberately unfavourable circumstances, Dennis implies in dedicating the play to the Lord Chamberlain, the Duke of Newcastle. (A critic of the play points out that the actors took the meagre proceeds of Dennis's failed third night and offered him the proceeds of any other night in return.)[20] The basic problem, Dennis and other critics contend, is that Steele, rather than shouldering responsibility for the managing Drury Lane has irresponsibly shifted it to the actors themselves, so that the servants have become the masters. Thus Newcastle must determine

> whether Gentlemen who have great Capacities, who have had the most generous Education, who have all their Lives had the best and the noblest Designs for the Service of their Country, and the Instruction of Mankind, shall have their worthy Labours supported and rendered effectual to the great Ends for which they intended them; or whether they must be sacrific'd to two or three insolent Actors, who have no Capacity, who have no Education, who have not the least Concern for their Country, who have nothing in their Heads or their Hearts but low Thoughts, and sordid Designs; and yet at the same time have so much Pride and so much insupportable Insolence, as to dare to fly in the Face of the greatest Persons in *England*.[21]

Actors, Dennis insists, are uncouth, uneducated mechanicals who manage to memorize a part and can move and speak on the stage but lack the judgment and penetration to evaluate plays and run a theatre.[22] Actors are uneducated and have less knowledge of plays than their predecessors. Learning countless parts by rote makes them incapable of discrimination. Their greed causes them to support popular plays of little merit, rather than meritorious ones. They can be respected as actors but not as gentlemen. The present age lacks the great playwrights and great actors of the past. 'But while the Stage is sinking under you, by the Conduct of your Deputies and your own, you are bragging that they will exalt it higher than those of the *Grecians,* and *Romans*'. Dennis insists at length that Steele has overestimated Cibber, who 'has neither God nor Religion, Relation, Friend, nor Companion, for whom he cares one Farthing'.[23]

Dennis's ranting is, of course, due to his disappointment. His play was postponed, in part because Lincoln's Inn Fields was, at the time, performing the real *Coriolanus*, and because the Drury Lane actors were preparing a lavish production of Dryden's *All for Love* and might reasonably feel that two modern revisions of Shakespeare in a row would be too much of a good thing. When, at last, it was performed, it was (arbitrarily, Dennis argued) closed after only three performances. But behind or below Dennis's ranting is a class issue: actors are workers, but writers are the higher beings who provide what they work upon. Steele therefore becomes a class traitor in giving the power of judgement to actors. As a Knight of the Realm, as a Member of Parliament, and as a writer rather than an actor, he should control those lesser beings who claim to exercise authority over their masters. (Behind this class argument lies the complaint that Steele, a mere political scribbler, should never have been made a knight of the realm and placed in a position of authority that he had no skill to fulfil.) The argument that Steele and his colleagues would make is that there were, in fact, few plays worth producing. The Sophocles of the Enlightenment was not being suppressed because ignorant actors like Cibber, Booth and Wilks were reading his or her play and dismissing it as worthless.

The failure of reform and the consequent arguments with Dennis and other, less vociferous, writers marks a significant, if perhaps temporary, moment in the professionalization of the theatre and of writing more generally. Aside from the reformist moral arguments, Steele and his colleagues asserted that the complexities of running a theatrical company and evaluating the plays that were proposed to it called for an expertise that outsiders simply did not possess. A major achievement of Steele as a manager of Drury Lane was that he left the technical details to the actor-managers, including the choice and scheduling of plays. The essential conflict that Steele faced, indeed that he internalized, was between the stage as a unique arena for the promulgation not simply of moral teaching but of moral example or the stage as a centre of professional acting and performance that had multiple functions from pantomime and farce to the most serious tragedy and even, in the case of Steele, the most moral comedy. The position of Steele and his colleagues was for a professional theatre of high quality, where actors were not dismissed as uneducated workers but recognized as significant artists.

If actors and playwrights are recognized as significant artists, independent of the power of the crown, they become political figures in their own right. Hence the significance of the famous incident at the first performance of Addison's *Cato* when Bolingbroke invited Booth, who acted Cato, to his box and gave him money as a reward for his efforts in fighting a tyrant. Bolingbroke either naively or, much more likely, cunningly conflates the actor, the character in Addison's play, the historical figure and the contemporary political figure for whom he stands. Characters in plays can represent contemporary political figures and comment on contemporary issues, and do so from *Cato* through Gay's *Beggar's Opera* to Fielding's *Pasquin*. When *Henry VIII* was acted at Hampton Court, Steele remarked that 'I was afraid I should have lost all my Actors! For I was not sure, the King would not keep them to fill the Posts at Court, that he saw them so fit for in the Play'.[24] The independent professional theatre becomes an autonomous political site, and it does so, in the eyes of Steele, Cibber, and their colleagues, by virtue of the royal patent. Newcastle's interest in removing Steele was not merely a matter of personal peek; it was, in its own way, an attempt to force him into silence, as he had with Cibber. An independent theatre, dependent as it is on the support of the public, can hardly function as the theatre of moral reform, but it can prove threatening to its theoretical masters in the government.

Steele's Censorium

If the public theatre was an unreliable source of moral teaching, more could be expected from the private performances planned for the Censorium. It was an alternative venture, changing its nature slightly over the ten years of so that the York Building venue remained in Steele's hands, but always focused on a productive use of the space and on providing a supplement to or substitute for other public performances. Its revival in 1715 may have been prompted by Steele's relative freedom from the demands of writing periodicals, but it was certainly stimulated by Steele's recent emergence as a political and cultural insider. Steele's initial intention to gather a select company of Whigs and Tories who would unite in their enjoyment of good music, verse, oratory and useful instruction was dashed by the political antagonisms of 1713–14, to which he himself contributed so energetically. But Sir Richard, patent-holder of Drury Lane, and Member of Parliament, was in a stronger position to gather a cadre of like-minded lovers of art and knowledge. His position as manager of Drury Lane gave him access to the best talents to present whatever he proposed or his audience desired.

Because the Censorium gave Steele the opportunity to demonstrate what public entertainment ought to be, the productions there can be defined most clearly by what they are not. Most emphatically they are not operatic performances. The musical performances that took place there, in addition to the expected orations, songs and instrumental performances, were settings of poetry to music. Thomas Clayton's setting of 'Alexander's Feast', although musically unsuccessful and not sponsored by Steele himself, demonstrated the idea of combining music and poetry to enhance the effect of language rather than overwhelming it. Steele sought to emphasize the power of language in its combination with music, as articulated by Addison in *Spectator*, no. 29. Similarly, Steele sought to avoid the interest in spectacle that, he believed, had infected the theatre and corrupted the taste of its audiences. Although the opera was the worst offender, followed by Lincoln's Inn Fields, Drury Lane itself was not exempted. Spectacle, and consequently its substantial cost, gave way at the Censorium to dramatic readings, recitations and enactments of the classics. Gone were comic dances, pantomimes, farces and afterpieces, although their place was taken by comic poems and speeches, and Steele remained interested in the dance. Although the entertainments included performances, they were not plays themselves. As a manager of Drury Lane, Steele doubtless wanted to provide an alternative rather than a competitor: 'This Project will be to the Stage, what an Under-Plot is to a Play' (*Town-Talk*, no. 4, p. 209). For the most part, therefore, subscribers to the Censorium would have enjoyed non-narrative performances focused on language and avoiding the loose morals of Restoration comedy.

Steele's great room in the York Buildings is called the 'Censorium' in his first reference to it in *Table-Talk* (*Table-Talk*, no. 4). In No. 6 it is called 'Sensorium', but the C-spelling retains much of the meaning of the S-spelling:

> The *Censorium*, every body knows, is the Organ of Sense, as the Eye is of Sight; and it seems more proper to use a Word, which implies *Sensio tantum*, the bare Conception of what is presented to the Spectator, rather than any Name, which, in a Didactick Manner, pronounces what ought to be received or rejected (*Town Talk*, no. 4, pp. 209–10).

Part of the significance of the title is its vagueness of reference, particularly useful to Steele because he too did not always know what was going to be presented there. But it is useful also in its ambiguity. 'Censorium' seems to refer to Isaac Bickerstaff the Censor, who prides himself on the effectiveness of his strictures against social offenders (*Tatler*, no. 162). The self-appointed arbiter of what is proper taste will now, in his specially designed 'room', demonstrate the proper objects of good taste. But the room is also a place of the senses, enjoyed in appropriate moderation, but manifold in their appeals to profitable pleasure. In addition to music and recitation, the Censorium/Sensorium provided lectures and scientific demonstrations, becoming thereby a conduit for liberal knowledge.[25] Founded in part on the model of continental acadamies,[26] it became a significant Enlightenment project, if, in the long run, a commercial failure.

The fact that Steele's great room would only accommodate some 200 people gave gatherings there the feeling of intimacy as well as exclusiveness, making possible a degree of self-referential joking. Steele's spokesman Arthur describes in *Town-Talk*, no. 4 the celebration that took place there on 28 May 1715 in honour of the King's birthday. The Prologue (attributed to Steele by Blanchard) is printed not in no. 4 but in no. 7.[27] It sets forth the basic purposes of the Censorium, especially its effort to make high culture an attribute of the fashionable world: '*Virgil* shall be the Talk of every Beau, / And Ladies lisp the Charms of *Cicero*' (*Town-Talk*, no.7). The Prologue introduces an Ode of very conventional verse, probably set to music, praising the King and his family. The Ode pleases the company at Mr Johnson's, who all wish to become subscribers. Johnson reports that the subscription list is already full. The conversation turns to the 'Comic Heroe', Richard Steele, who is the subject of the 'Epilogue', written by Addison, and spoken very effectively by Robert Wilks. The 'Epilogue' summarizes Steele's biography, emphasizing his projects for the common good. His failure at alchemy is compared to his quixotic efforts to make people virtuous and to bring about the destruction of Dunkirk. He will now seek to convert the Pope. Steele's willingness to laugh at this good-natured humour exemplifies the geniality of the company in his great room. The audience at the Censorium is, of course, duplicated by the gathering at Mr Johnson's, which in turn is reduplicated by the audience of readers.

The Censorium was a manifestation of Steele's efforts to address the public on serious issues, but its self-conscious openness to a broad range of intellectual concerns suggests its purpose was educational as well as moral. It sought to form the genuine person of taste not only by the variety of material one could encounter there but by the congenial audience of fellow seekers after knowledge who would constitute the Consortium audience. It sought to expand the scope of the stage. It sought as well to make money, and in this latter purpose it failed. Little is heard of the Consortium after 1716, but musical concerts were occasionally advertised there in 1717 and 1718. Loftis is certainly right in speculating that Steele was renting space to other artists. A series of scientific lectures took place in 1719, and a satiric account of speeches given there appeared in the *Original Weekly Journal* for 1720.[28] Like the writing of periodicals and the management of Drury Lane, the Censorium was an effort on Steele's part not only to convey a way of life to an audience but to explore the nature of that audience itself and the genres by which it could best be addressed. He seemed to preserve the hope that something might be made of the idea and the space until he moved from London in 1724 and the great room was advertised for rent.

Steele Agonistes

Within the first five years of Steele's patent, serious complaints had emerged about the policies and practices of Drury Lane and about Steele's performance as manager, despite an excellent cadre of actors and a repertory of fine (if sometimes controversial) plays. These came from members of the moral middle class that Steele hoped he could reach, from angry critics such as Dennis who complained about the discrepancy between moral pretence and immoral practice, from playwrights who saw the Drury Lane stage as closed or available only to members of a select inner circle, from audience members who saw a certain sameness in the offerings, despite a large repertoire and a lack of predictability in the price of admission. But they came as well from the Lord Chancellor and his associates, who saw in the behaviour of the managers a deliberate attempt to undermine the authority of the throne.

Steele in particular had promised to reform the theatre, but no such reform had taken place, the same offensive plays continued to be acted, with minor cosmetic alterations. The vitality of the stage itself, its gradual improvement in moral standards and its ability to reach out to new audiences depended on its willingness to mount new plays, especially plays that reflected the moral attitudes of the new intended audience. But such plays were not forthcoming, and even Steele's new play, which was to show the way, had remained unfinished and unacted for years. Steele, the self-styled reformer, had allow this stasis to continue and, to make matters worst, he had, as Dennis complained, assigned four-fifths of his patent to the actor-managers, the very people whom he ought, as patent-holder, to control. This devolution allowed Dennis and other critics to blame Steele for all the faults of the managers. But Steele defended the actor-managers and, in their name, he dared to do battle with the Lord Chancellor. The managers refused to submit plays to the approval of the Master of the Revels and, as we have seen, Steele asserted a virtual independence given him by the patent.

Not only had Steele handed over managerial authority to those who, in the eyes of many, ought to be managed, he had mortgaged his own share of the patent, which he regarded as the equivalent of a freehold of land. In early 1716 Steele mortgaged his share of the patent to Edward Minshull, and seems to have taken sums beyond the large amount he initially borrowed. The mortgage was in turn transferred among various creditors, so that it was unclear how much Steele had paid. Steele's creditors were less than scrupulously honest, and Steele kept less than careful records. The messy affair took years to settle, and the details need not concern us here.[29] What concerned his fellow managers and, ultimately, the Lord Chancellor was the fact that he had so entangled the patent that he now longer seemed to possess what might be called a clear title, and although he made genuine efforts to extricate himself, the process seemed unending. Steele's personal financial irresponsibility was now tied to his role as manager.

To make matters worse, his personal relations with the Duke of Newcastle, who became Lord Chamberlain in 1717, had turned decidedly sour. Thomas Pelham-Holles (1693–1768) had a long and distinguished career in the course of the century, although distinguished more for its persistence than its excellence. In 1715, having recently become Lord Clare, he sponsored Steele's candidacy for Parliament from the borough of Boroughbridge. He and Steele had probably known each other as members of the Hanover Club and as fellow Whigs. Their relationship remained cordial, although Clare was a man who brooked no insubordination and Steele was insistently independent. Clare was Steele's formal sponsor when he was knighted, and Steele dedicated his *Political Writings* to him in early June, 1715, praising him in fulsome terms. Lord Clare became the First Duke of Newcastle in 1715 and Lord Chamberlain in 1717. The Lord Chamberlain was, among other things, responsible for the regulation of the theatres, and it was in that role that Newcastle's power clashed with Steele's independence. One of the Lord Chamberlain's first actions was to offer the managers a new licence in return for the resignation of Steele's patent. Steele refused.

Open hostility began in September 1718, when the Drury Lane actors were scheduled to perform for the King and courtiers at the Great Hall of Hampton Court. The opening performance was Farquhar's *The Beaux Stratagem*, with a Prologue specially commissioned by Newcastle and written by Thomas Tickell.

But Steele, anticipating that a Prologue would be needed for the occasion, wrote one himself, which the actor Wilks had memorized. The question was whose prologue would be used, and the issue was referred to Newcastle, who was hardly a neutral party. Steele recognized that Tickell's prologue would do just as well as an 'Epilogue', so that his own could be read as the prologue. But this eminently sensible suggestion was also rejected by Newcastle. Steele felt the incident not merely as a mix-up but as a calculated insult. He wrote Newcastle a respectful but offended letter on 21 September.[30] He eventually published the Prologue in *Theatre*, no. 12 (13 February 1720). Except for the contretemps with Newcastle, the season at Hampton Court was a success.

More seriously, in March 1719 Steele joined Robert Walpole and others in opposing the Peerage Bill, severely limiting the ability of the monarch to create new peers. The bill was introduced by the Duke of Somerset and supported by Newcastle. It was a manifestation of the serious division within Whig ranks that had broken out in 1717 between Sunderland and Stanhope on one hand and Walpole and Townshend on the other. Steele leaned towards the Walpole side, and certainly did on the Peerage Bill. The dissension among the Whigs created real problems for the patent-holder of Drury Lane. The theatre operated as an extension of government, influencing public opinion by articulating a dominant ideology. One of the major reasons for the assignment of the Drury Lane patent to Steele was the combination of his reliability as a Whig propagandist and politician with his experience as writer of plays and friend to actors. If the Ministry splits, as it did, Steele's presence in the opposition camp gives a particularly political coloration to the territorial battle between the Lord Chamberlain and the actor-managers. If the theatre is under the control of the Lord Chamberlain, it serves the ideological interests of the government in power; if it is under the control of the patent holder, the government could no longer speak confidently from the stage. The potential conflict was made more serious by Steele's mortgaging of the patent, leaving the possibility of control, as least theoretically, to whomever ended up owning it. Steele's opposition to the Peerage Bill was articulated in the four numbers of *The Plebeian*, which will be discussed in the next chapter. In the end the Sunderland-Stanhope forces lost, as, on 14 April 1719, the bill was put off to the next session rather than facing a third reading in Lords that would send it to a hostile commons, where it was finally defeated on 8 December 1719.

The next significant step in the antagonism between Steele and Newcastle was Colley Cibber's dedication of his play *Ximena* to Steele on 29 September, after the Bill was withdrawn from Lords but before it was reintroduced in Commons. Cibber praised Steele in extravagent terms, celebrating the remarkable ability of the *Tatler* to turn out a theatrical audience and emphasizing his independence and his willingness to sacrifice for the general good 'in the restless Office of a

Patriot', especially in his periodical essays and tracts. A man bent on service of his country, Cibber warned, must 'enslave those talents to the will and dominion of some great Leader in the stage' or else be 'treated at best as a mutineer'.[31] Steele's antagonists accused him falsely of taking credit for work actually done by Addison, but Cibber reminds his audience that Steele had loyally promoted Addison and his work. The dedication was dated 29 September but not published until late October. Newcastle, perhaps properly concerned for the finances of the theatre, demanded its accounts on 8 November. The demand was refused. Newcastle responded to this insubordination by silencing Cibber. On 19 December 1719, he wrote Steele, Wilks and Booth requiring them 'immediately to Dismiss Mr. Colley Cibber from Acting at the Theatre in Drury Lane, and from being in any ways concern'd in the management of the said Playhouse'.[32]

Steele rightly interpreted this move as an assertion of new authority by Newcastle, who seemed to be testing the limits of his power over the theatre. Hence Steele immediately reacted with what, within the limits of courtly etiquette, could only be interpreted as an outraged letter.

> Your Grace has obliged me, this Evening, with an opportunity, I have long wished for, of showing How devoted I am to your Service; but I wish for Your sake, rather than my own, that you had given me any other occasion for manifesting this unreserv'd inclination for your Person and Character, than that of bearing Oppression from you ... Mr Cibber is a Principall Actor, and many Familyes (as well as my Property) are concern'd in His Appearance on the Stage. I hope your Grace, in the determination of this proceeding, will give way to your own Temper, which, I know, must be diverted from its natural Bent, when you offer an Injury. [33]

Newcastle reacted to Steele's protestation by refusing to correspond with him further. Cibber interpreted Newcastle's sharp position as a punishment for his dedication of *Ximena*. Steele saw it as a punishment for publicly siding with the opposition on the Peerage Bill. (Steele had published *A Letter to the Earl of Oxford, Concerning the Bill of Peerage* on 8 December. The Bill was debated in Parliament in the same day, and Steele joined Walpole in speaking against it.)

Thereafter, the moves on both sides were carefully calculated as they unfolded in January 1720 and Steele found his opportunities closed off. In the end, he had no recourse other than public opinion. On 2 January, he began his periodical the *Theatre*, in which he addressed not only the issue of the appropriate management of the stage but other issues as well, particularly, in the later papers, the problems of the South-Sea Company. (For the present, I will concern myself with the theatrical papers of the *Theatre*, leaving the others to the next chapter, which will examine Steele's direct political activities.) On 17 January he wrote separate letters to four Privy Councellors (Stanhope, Craggs, Parker and Argyle) urging them to interdict Newcastle's threat to go to law over the patent and to silence the theatre. But Newcastle had sought the advice of the Attorney-General regarding the legalities of the patent, and, it seems, had based his course of action on that advice. Sir Thomas Pengelly the Prime Sergeant, on 20 January ruled that the licence (rather than the patent) could indeed be revoked. Hence Steele's petition to the King on 22 January, which he presented in the presence of Newcastle, was, like his other efforts to avoid the inevitable, doomed to failure. Two days later the King revoked the licence, and two days after that Newcastle suspended performances at Drury Lane. Steele's only recourse, having been forbidden to correspond with Newcastle, was to write him a public letter, which was published in *Theatre*, no. 8 (26 January 1720). In it Steele recounts the history of the patent, the injuries he has suffered, and the harm done to the sixty families under his protection. Fortunately, he did not have to worry long on their behalf, for on the next day a new license, exclusive of Steele's patent was issued to Cibber, Wilks and Booth. Steele, assuming a connection between the licence and the patent, had been outwitted by Newcastle's separation of the two, so that the licence could be granted to the other managers, leaving Steele with a patent that would be useless unless he could gather another company and find another theatre. (More dangerous was the fact that the patent, heavily mortgaged, now had no monetary value or income.)

Steele's *Theatre* (twenty-eight numbers, appearing twice weekly from 2 January 1720 to 5 April 1720) and his pamphlet *The State of the Case between the Lord-Chamberlain of His Majesty's Household and the Governor of the Royal Company of Comedians* (published on 9 March) are the main texts Steele wrote regarding this crisis. The *Theatre* announces that it is written by Sir John Edgar, at that point the name of the character who became Sir John Bevil in *The Conscious Lovers*. He is an older man whose interest has been reawakened in plays by the influence of his son, whose friend Sophronia, like Mr Johnson in *Town-Talk*, keeps a house where conversation on matters of culture, and especially the theatre, is commonplace. 'Deviation from Reason and good Sense is there the only Error, and uninstructed Innocence is pity'd and assisted, while studied Faults, and assumed Singularities are banish'd and discountenanc'd'.[34] Sophronia and her three female companions define good taste, which may not conform to the taste of the town. In his second number Edgar announces that he will write to improve the theatre but may take up other topics on the grounds that all the world is a stage.

Despite this genteel beginning and the predominately feminine cast of characters, the *Theatre* is a highly contentious paper, and particularly so on the government of Drury Lane. In no. 7 Edgar wonders at the unpopularity of Cibber, and attributes it to his performance of villainous roles. But thereafter the paper becomes allegorical. Newcastle is attacked by means of the cunning but false behaviour of Cardinal Wolsey. Edgar defends Steele's sharing of the patent:

> The Patentee therefore, in my humble Opinion, did like a wise Man, and a great Politician, in becoming but a Sharer and Director, with relation to the Expense, and reserving the Character of Governor only with Regard to the Morality of the Stage.

He recollects the story of a rich landowner who gives a rather barren Field 'to one who had more Art and Industry, than Stock and Cattle'. The tenant invents a glass beehive which attacks crowds of onlookers. The landowner demands his field back, along with the beehive the tenant has constructed. The tenant refuses, and the landowner tries to take it by force, getting severely stung in the process. The landowner of course is Newcastle, and the industrious tenant is Steele.

The next paper (no. 8) is introduced by Edgar who praises Steele and prints his otherwise undeliverable letter to Newcastle. Among other things, Steele had requested information on Newcastle's legal adviser, and, in no. 9, Edgar identifies him as Sir Thomas Pengelly by means of puns and makes a great deal out of the association of 'pen' with 'lie'. A lawyer who is paid to injure the reputation and livelihood of others is like the apothecaries in plays who dispense poison for money. Steele continues his assault in no. 10, where he wonders whether subjects of the king are secure in their property by his protection. Steele's treatment of the issue of theatrical government is less focused thereafter. Nos. 11 and 12 respond to Dennis's attack in the first two parts of *The Character and Conduct of John Edgar*, and no. 13 provides Steele's undelivered Prologue at Hampton Court and continues the attack on Newcastle by representing Drury Lane as a school where boys and girls are taught lessons of morality. Other than an attack on French pantomime in no. 21, the other main papers on the theatre are no. 15, on the death of John Hughes, and no. 28 (the final paper).

John Hughes, long a friend of Steele, managed to be friendly with most of the literary figures of Queen Anne's London. A semi-invalid, he wrote poems, translated Eloise and Abelard, collaborated on periodicals and wrote plays. He was also a musician and occasionally advised Steele on the music proposed for the Censorium.

> His Head, Hand or Heart was always employ'd in something worthy Imitation; his Pencil, his Bow-string, or his Pen, each of which he us'd in a Masterly manner, were always directed to raise and entertain his own Mind, or that of others, to a more cheerful Prosecution of what was noble and virtuous (*Theatre*, no. 15).

He died in the evening, after his play *The Siege of Damascus* was premiered at Drury Lane, and he knew the success of the play before he died. The audience was particularly moved by the hero's contemplation of death in a speech patterned after Cato's soliloquy in Addison's play. Hughes was like his hero in patience and virtue. Despite his chronic ill-health, he retained a cheerful disposition. He was an example of the extraordinarily good ordinary man.

In his final paper, Steele identifies his own situation with that of every citizen who is subject to an oppressive government:

> I took for my Defence the only Method a friendless Man could, to wit, a Method for showing that my Case was that of every Subject in these Dominions. My powerful, unprovok'd Adversaries wanted Wit enough, in their Anger, to reflect, that a generous People have always a Concern for the Oppress'd, and Detestation of Oppressors (*Theatre*, no. 28).

He contends that his harsh treatment of the Duke of Newcastle was warranted by the Duke's harsh treatment of him. In a burst of perhaps justified self-pity he exclaims that Readers should consider the *Theatre* as 'written by a Man neither out of Pain in Body or Mind; but forced to suspend the Anguish of both ... and that for no other Reason but pursuing what he thought just' (*Theatre*, no. 28). Steele did, however, take some comfort from the temporary success of his fish-pool project and his forthcoming new play (which, at this point, he was planning to publish rather than bring to the stage).

A week before the *Theatre* closed, Steele published a pamphlet on the dispute with Newcastle, *The State of the Case between the Lord Chamberlain of His Majesty's Household and the Governor of the Royal Company of Comedians.* As in Steele's other arguments throughout the controversy, he here assumes that his possession of a patent implies that he also has a licence, and that depriving him of his licence in effect deprives him of his patent as well. He attacks Newcastle in strong terms: 'My Lord Chamberlain has, contrary to Law and Justice, dispossessed me of my Freehold in a manner as injurious to the King his Master, as to me his Fellow-Subject'.[35] He argues that the patent is inalienable and dismisses the position that laws do not properly apply to actors. Steele cites the legal opinions of Sir Francis Pemberton, Sir Edward Northey, and Sir Thomas Parker, prominent legal authorities, on the validity of patents and the legitimacy of actors. The patent given to Steele is stronger than that given by Charles II to D'Avenant because it was given for a specific term – Steele's life plus three years – and it was given for services rendered to the crown. Steele liberally calculates the financial loss he incurred as a result of Newcastle's arbitrary action as £9,800 and insists that Newcastle acted for no other reason than to ruin Steele.

> All this is done against a Man, to whom Whig, Tory, Roman-Catholick, Dissenter, Native, and Foreigner, owe Zeal and Good-will for good Offices endeavour'd towards every one of them in their Civil Rights, and their kind Wishes to him are but a just Return.[36]

Steele's pathetic tone is derived in part from his genuine sense of pain, but it also reflects the untenable position in which Newcastle had placed him. The chronology of events reveals the unfolding of a careful plan plotted by Newcastle and Pengelly and the feckless efforts by Steele to seek one recourse after another, only to be reduced at last to meaningless threats and demeaning self-pity. What is clear is that Steele's politics were the primary reason for his loss of Drury Lane. Newcastle's initial attack was against Cibber, and one of the complaints against Steele was that he had, by assigning shares in his patent to them, allowed the actors too much unchecked power. But Steele was removed by closing the licence that included him and issuing a new one to the actors themselves. Perhaps Newcastle felt that he could more effectively control the policies of Drury Lane by doing so directly, rather than relying on an intermediary patentee. The more probable reasons, however, seem to be revenge on the audacious Steele for his insubordination on the Peerage Bill and fear that an independent theatre, led and protected by a disloyal manager, could not be easily controlled by the government.

Steele's aggressive defence sparked considerable controversy. On 15 February 1720, between nos. 13 and 14 of the *Theatre*, an *Anti-Theatre* began to appear, and it ran until the end of Steele's paper. It initially announces that Sir John Edgar, Steele's persona, has agreed to combat, but by no. 4 it fears that Edgar will not fight. Falstaffe, the persona of the anti-theatre, observes that Edgar's language is weak in meaning; he 'seems to have a respect for the *sound* of his words, without considering what *ideas* to affix to them'.[37] The stage, he claims, has been moral in the past, but that was under careful supervision – the kind of supervision, he goes on to imply, that is possible now that Steele has been removed. The rich man (i.e., Newcastle) who tried to take the beehive in *Theatre*, no. 7 appears to be uninjured. In fact, a newly constituted Drury Lane is going forward, and Steele is irrelevant. English plays are as indecent as the French because poets and players conform to the worst tastes of the town simply in order to make money.

Two days earlier (13 February), a probably fictitious Andrew Artlove published the first of three weekly letters on the case in *Applebee's Original Weekly Journal*[38]. He claims that Edgar

> has spent nearly two-thirds of his Twelve Papers in the most fulsome and impudent praise of himself that ever was published by any Author in the world; and in the rest, he advances such ridiculous falsehoods as are obvious to the meanest capacity.[39]

His major falsehood is his assertion that the British stage is superior to that of the ancients or of the French.

The longest, most detailed, and most effective attack on Steele and defence of Newcastle is *The State of the Case between The Lord Chamberlain of His Majesty's Houshold, and Sir Richard Steele, as represented by that Knight, Re-stated, In Vindication of King George, and the most Noble the Duke of Newcastle*.[40] One has to read fairly far into the title to distinguish it from Steele's *The State of the Case*, but the content could not be more different. Steele, the author argues, misrepresents punishment for an offence as an illegal invasion of his rights and property. The offence that Steele has committed has been his complete failure to reform the stage, since the same plays that have been found offensive are still being performed. Steele would argue that eliminating the offensive plays would destroy the stage.

> To this I reply, that it is certainly impracticable to reform the Stage by making use of those very Plays which have all along corrupted it; and that it is much better there should be no Stage at all, than a Stage that can only be supported by the teaching of Vice, Irreligion, and Prophaneness.[41]

Careful comparison shows that Steele's claim that his patent is superior to or even different from D'Avenant's is completely spurious. The King is well within his right to issue a new licence that excludes Steele. If Steele wants to use his patent, he can found a new company. The Lord Chamberlain has not violated Steele's patent because that patent was not exclusive. The claim that the action against Steele was politically motivated is simply dismissed. Steele of course had his supporters but they are fewer and weaker than those on the other side. Many of them direct their attack at Dennis – a more public and less dangerous target than Newcastle.[42]

Steele's journalistic campaign had more-or-less died by April, 1720, although in May he wrote Henry Pelham, Newcastle's brother, threatening to petition the King or to seek further legal remedy. Nothing came of the matter, beyond a petition to the King in February 1721, but by that point the situation had changed dramatically.[43] The issue was resolved even more clearly than it began by means of political alliance. During the entire controversy, as the following chapter shows, Steele sided with Walpole not only on the Peerage Bill but, even more significantly, in his negotiations to respond to the collapse of the South-Sea company. In early February 1721, Craggs and Stanhope died. Power shifted to Walpole, and on 3 April 1721, he became Chancellor of the Exchequer and First Lord of the Treasury. On 2 May, Newcastle issued orders to the Drury Lane managers to account to Steele for his past and future earnings, essentially restoring him to his position as co-director.

But Steele no longer played an active role in the management of the theatre. He was beset by a variety of other duties and his health was not good. Beginning on 27 January 1720, the managers had deducted £5 from Steele's pay, and continued to do so even after his restitution as manager. On the next day, Steele wrote to them insisting that they could not act without his authority as manager and licence-holder. They acted anyway and claimed in a later lawsuit regarding Steele's salary that 28 January 1720 was the date on which he ceased to play an active role as a manager. But Steele had one more contribution for Drury Lane.

On 22 November 1722 his long-delayed play, now called *The Conscious Lovers*, was performed with great popular success.[44]

The Conscious Lovers

The Conscious Lovers had undergone a long gestation before its triumphant and profitable premier on 7 November 1722. In January 1713, Berkeley had written to John Percival that Steele was writing a play, and there is no other candidate than *The Conscious Lovers*.[45] Swift's 'First Ode of the Second Book of Horace Paraphras'd' (1714) describes Steele work-in-progress in terms close enough to the finished text to imply that Swift had seen it or that Steele had talked it up at Button's Coffee House:

> And when thou'st bid adieu to cares,
> And settled Europe's grand affairs,
> 'Twill then, perhaps, be worth thy while
> For Drury Lane to shape thy style:
> To make a pair of jolly fellows,
> The son and father, join to tell us,
> How sons may safely disobey,
> And fathers never should say nay,
> By which wise conduct they grow friends
> At last – and so the story ends.[46]

John Loftis speculates that the development of *The Conscious Lovers* began several years earlier than these references by Berkeley and Swift, that Steele is himself the 'young poet' to whom Steele refers in *Tatler*, no. 182 who has the outlines of a play that Bickerstaff has seen:

> There are, I find, to be in it all the Reverend Offices of Life, such as Regard to Parents, Husbands, and honourable Lovers, preserved with the utmost Care; and at the same Time that Agreeableness of Behaviour, with the Intermixture of pleasing Passions as arise from Innocence and Virtue, interspersed in such a Manner, as that to be charming and agreeable shall appear the natural Consequence of being virtuous.[47]

The description certainly fits Steele's goals for *The Conscious Lovers*, but it is general enough to fit his other plays as well. Loftis notes later references that might be interpreted as referring to *The Conscious Lovers*: a 1716 note to his wife hoping that he could finish a long-delayed project, and a 1717 letter hoping that he can ready the play for production the following winter.[48] There are further references in 1719–20, especially Steele's own *Theatre*, that suggest the play was nearly finished.

Loftis plausible suggests that the play was substantially drafted, as Berkeley said, after Steele laid down the *Spectator* in December 1713, but that Steele put it aside in order to take up the *Guardian* and his subsequent political writings. He is likely to have taken it up again in 1715 or 1716. (His role as non-acting manager of Drury Lane implied that he would serve the theatre by writing plays.) The play was virtually finished by 1720, when Steele in *Theatre*, no. 28 stated that he would publish it, since he could not get it performed, given his dispute with Newcastle. When Steele regained his status at the theatre (and his income) in May 1721, the path was clear for the production of the play. Steele's completion of the play was thus delayed, in the first instance, by his propagandizing and, in the second, by the disfavour of the Lord Chamberlain.[49] Steele always had a number of projects going simultaneously, and doubtless found it difficult to concentrate on his play for extended periods. But he may have also become the victim of his own puffing. He had characterized his work in progress, especially in *Tatler*, no. 182, as morally and socially exemplary, showing what plays should be like and how people should act. His pretentious comments would, he must have recognized, assure a hostile response from critics such as John Dennis. Even if his play was not as innovative as he thought, his thought in itself made him hesitant to go forward. His public role as a literary critic, even if a limited one, and as a social moralist meant that his play would be subject to high and definite expectations on the part of its audience.

The play was brought to the stage in early November 1722, after a chorus of excessive notices in the newspapers, including the announcement that 'it is thought by some excellent Judges to be the best Comedy that ever appear'd on the English Stage'.[50] Such hyperbole prompted John Dennis's *A Defence of Sir Fopling Flutter, A Comedy Written by Sir George Etheridge*, which argues that "tis the Business of a Comick Poet to cure his Spectators of Vice and Folly, by the Apprehension of being laugh'd at; 'tis plain that his Business must be with the reigning Follies and Vices'.[51] Exemplary comedy, such as Steele proposed, was not comedy at all, and *The Conscious Lovers* was therefore a fraud. The one genuinely comic element of the play, the scenes between the servants Tom and Phillis, was apparently improved by Cibber, who acted Tom and also took the lead role in mounting the play at a point when Steele was ill.[52] Notwithstanding the critical controversy it sparked even before its first performance, *The Conscious Lovers* was an extraordinary success, running for eighteen nights, earning more money for Drury Lane than any previous play, and earning £500 from the King for Steele's dedication.

Although it is no longer possible to share the enthusiasm of early audiences for the play, it remains an interesting and significant failure. Its structure is commendable even if its plot is not. (The plot follows closely the *Andria* of Terence, which, in turn, was adopted from a lost play of Menander. The transposition from the Mediterranean world centuries before Christ to eighteenth-century London creates some of the play's improbabilities.) The structure is driven by a series of generational tensions, by gender relations among two contrasting families, one landed and one moneyed, and by consequent conflicts of class and values. Sir John Bevil and his son, the landed family, are characterized by the reverse of the traditional comic antagonism between fathers and sons. They have very tender feelings for each other, and the tension between them comes from their fear of offending the other, as we are told by Sir John's loyal servant Humphrey. Humphrey's function in the play as a friend to both father and son and as a useful device for exposition contrasts to Davus in Terence's play, who is the main agent of the plot. Out of affection for his father, Young Bevil has promised not to marry without his father's permission, promising, in effect, to marry whomever his father has chosen. And his father has made such a choice – Lucinda, the daughter of Mr Sealand, a wealthy merchant. Although Lucinda turns out to be an attractive and reasonably sensible young lady, Bevil has no intention of marrying her. Without his father's knowledge he has fallen in love with Indiana, an English orphan whom he has rescued from threatening circumstances in France and brought to London, where he has set up her and her aunt in an apartment; there he visits her, but without any sexual impropriety. In fact, he does not even tell her that he loves her because he is technically engaged to Lucinda and feels bound by his promise to his father. Although he leaves Indiana with considerable uncertainty about his intentions, she correctly believes that they are honourable. (Her aunt does not.) At the beginning of the play an incident at a masquerade has revealed both to Sir John and to Sealand that Bevil is interested in a mysterious woman, but the nature of the relationship is as mysterious as the identity of the woman.

Bevil can sustain this uncertain and even deceptive relationship because he knows that Lucinda has no interest in marrying him, and for much the same reason. She is in love with his friend Myrtle, a decent man in every respect other than his intense jealousy. Since he knows that Lucinda is engaged to Bevil, he is suspicious of his friend, despite Bevil's assurances that neither he nor Lucinda has any intention of marrying the other. This jealousy leads Myrtle to challenge Bevil to a duel, thus prompting the famous scene in Act IV, scene 1, where Bevil is successful in persuading Myrtle that killing each other is not a good idea. (Steele declared that the play was written for the sake of this scene, which allowed him once again to attack the institution of duelling.) Lucinda is also courted by Cimberton, the only character among the high-class lovers who can be described as comic in the sense articulated by Dennis. He is promoted by Lucinda's mother, Sealand's second wife, but he is a coxcomb, interested in the wealth Lucinda will bring and interested in her breeding capabilities. He investigates these in a scene in which he surveys her, as she complains, 'like a Steed at Sale'.[53]

But the Sealand generational plot has another twist. Sealand had a first wife whom he left behind with their infant daughter when he returned from the Indies to England. The wife and daughter, travelling back on a different ship, were captured by pirates. The wife died, but the daughter was brought to France and raised by a French family. When the family died, the family heir had sinister designs on Indiana, and she was rescued from these by Bevil. But because Seal-and had, somewhat inexplicably, changed his name after the loss of his wife and daughter, the discovery of Indiana's heritage is conveniently delayed until the last act, where it provides the sentimental climax of the play. (Indiana, having long repressed her feelings amid her uncertainties, discovers her father and erupts in tears, as did most of her eighteenth-century audience.) So the generational plot of the Bevils is seconded by the rather different lost-child plot of the Sealands. Steele intensified Terence's lost-child plot to make it both more moral and more sentimental if less plausible.

Steele had an ambivalent attitude towards parent–child relations. On one hand he felt that parents were right more often than not and that they deserved the respect and love of their children. On the other hand, he felt that parents should not arbitrarily impose their will in the case of such identity-determining issues as the choice of a mate. The situation in *The Conscious Lovers* is complicated by the fact that Bevil has consciously given Sir John authority over whom he should marry. A major and compelling criticism of the play is that Bevil leaves Indiana in a position of painful uncertainty regarding his intentions and suppresses his own presumably powerful feelings of love and desire, even though he is an adult male in possession of an independent fortune and hence perfectly able, despite his father's objection, to marry the orphan he has promised to protect. In effect, therefore, there is relatively little at stake in the generation plot of the Bevils. If worst comes to worst, Bevil will be unable to fulfil his promise to his father by marrying Lucinda.

As most commentators have noted, Steele has not only reversed the usual antagonism between father and son, he has also reversed the traditional comic hierarchy of love-plots. In Restoration comedy the principle pair of lovers is the witty pair, and serious lovers, if any, are relegated to secondary status. Here the serious lovers are primary, and the only witty lovers are the tertiary pair – Bevil's servant Tom and Lucinda's servant Phillis. Their love-games are witty in themselves and at the same time a satire on the apparent inability of aristocratic lovers to be sincere. Tom and Phillis are the jolly couple, pretending to be hesitant about marriage. Unlike the other couples, their relationship is not threatened by rivals. Love plots require intrigue, and here the schemers are Bevil and Lucinda, who deceive their fathers but, in another reversal in this play of reversals, deceive them into thinking they are serious in their plans to marry each other when they are only buying time until their real love affairs can lead to marriage.

In addition to generations within families and to lovers, the third defining element of structure in *The Conscious Lovers* is class. Immediately following the scene in which Bevil persuades Myrtle that duelling would be, in their case, not only immoral but inappropriate to the circumstances, Sir John and Sealand meet in a scene that is, both in plot and in didactic significance, central to the play. Sir John is motivated by his concern that his son not marry into a socially unworthy family; Sealand is concerned that his daughter not marry a morally unworthy man. When Sir John mentions the relative importance of 'Genealogy and Descent', Sealand mocks them in terms that recall the comic dismissal of Cimberton's interest in breeding: his father only talked of the genealogy and descent of his dogs. He does not object to Bevil's family; "tis his Morals, that I doubt'. The problem this issue creates for Sir John is that he does not know the real nature of Bevil's relations to Indiana. He therefore can defend his son only in general terms. Whatever his offences with the mystery woman, 'my Son, Sir, is, in the Eye of the World, a Gentleman of Merit' (IV.ii, 65–6). But Sealand will have none of it. He has seen, although he does not quite put it in those terms, plays by Vanbrugh and others (including Steele) in which the wife is abandoned while the husband chases after other pursuits. He has, he explains, lost a wife and daughter already. He will not have his remaining daughter abused by a husband whose real affections lie with his mistress rather than his wife. He will investigate this relationship for himself by visiting Bevil's mysterious woman, and this resolution effects the resolution of the play.

The difference in class translates into a difference of morals. For Sir John, Bevil's decent and genteel behaviour testifies to qualities that make him worthy of Sealand's daughter. Aristocratic status, in effect, covers minor sexual dalliances. The noble gentleman is a man of his word, which is why Bevil's adherence to his promise to his father is so important to both of them, and a man of his word can be trusted in his marital contract, whatever his sexual experience may have been before marriage. Sealand sees the notion of aristocratic integrity as a myth whose truth needs to be suspected and tested. Real daughters may experience real pain if fathers anxious for a title trust in the insecurity of sexual constancy. Therefore he insists on the test that will determine whether the unknown Indiana is a danger to Lucinda. Of course she would be, in a peculiarly unexpected way, since she turns out to be loved by the virtuous and honest Bevel and turns out as well to be Sealand's daughter. The scene in which this revelation takes place is so moving, or at least so histrionic, that it obscures the more likely and more problematic alternative: what if Indiana was as innocent and Bevil as virtuous but she was not Sealand's daughter? What if she was, as advertised, an orphan emerging from piracy with no claim to protection other than the fact that Bevil has, so to speak, adopted her? For all Sealand's claim to reject the claims of breeding for those of virtue, the play is resolved when the lost orphan turns out to be his daughter.

One of the salient characteristics of Steele's attitude towards class is that he wants to have it both ways. He wants to preserve both the gentility and politeness of the aristocracy and the enterprise and openness of the bourgeoisie. That conflict and his efforts to reconcile it are at the heart of *The Conscious Lovers*. The locus of those efforts lies in competing notions of what it means to be a gentleman. A gentleman was a man of some status in society who enhanced that status by good manners, gallantry towards women and, if need be, personal courage. Myrtle's challenge to Bevil derived from his notion of gentlemanly behaviour, but Bevil's refusal to fight manifested a different idea of the gentleman. For Steele the gentleman is a man in control both of himself and of his situation. His status as a gentleman derives ultimately from his inner virtue. His goodness and politeness make him attractive to other characters, and the consonance of his actions and his principles (his sentiments in the eighteenth-century sense) theoretically gives his advice particular power. The force of his character and his effect on other characters makes him an exemplar for members of the audience, who ought to be converted along with the other characters. Bevil as the exemplary gentleman serves as an antidote to Dorimant, whom Steele saw as a poisonous model of the fine gentleman. Steele's gentleman rejects the idea of duelling. Steele's gentleman, unlike Dorimant, is chaste and respectful towards women. Steele's gentleman, as far as possible, preserves and enhances the movement of his family through time. Bevil is intended as the epitome of such a gentleman.

But it is precisely that role that critics of Steele's play found most objectionable. The criticism of John Dennis, the most intelligent of Steele's antagonists, is rooted in rigid classicism. He dislikes *The Conscious Lovers* and considers it something of a fraud because it violates the basic principles of comedy. Comic plays should be funny, and they are funny by ridiculing vice, not by introducing 'a Joy too exquisite for Laughter'.[54]

> When Sir *Richard* says, that any thing that has its Foundation in Happiness and Success must be the Subject of Comedy, he confounds Comedy with that Species of Tragedy which has a happy Catastrophe. When he says, that 'tis Improvement of Comedy to introduce as Joy too exquisite for Laughter, he takes all the Care he can to shew, that he knows nothing of the Nature of it; of Comedy.[55]

This generic offence has its roots in Bevil's exemplary character. A nearly faultless character can hardly be funny, and Bevil certainly isn't. But there are other problems with such a character that are independent of Dennis's narrow concept of genre.

Exemplary characters such as Bevil do not have the inner conflict that drives dramatic plots, and they do not have much external conflict either. Bevil may offend his father if he turns out to be pre-engaged to Indiana and thus unable to wed Lucinda, but that should not be an offence that breaks their friendship. There seems to be a tension, perhaps even a contradiction, between being exemplary and being sympathetic. The sympathetic, indeed pathetic character of the play, the one with inner conflicts we can understand, is Indiana, but in other respects she is too underdeveloped to be much more than a conduit for emotions. An exemplary character such as Bevil is superior to the audience. It is that very superiority that makes him exemplary but, at the same time that distances him from us. We are unlikely to feel much kinship with such a person, even if we admire him. But the danger is that we will not admire him, that we will see him instead as stuffy, pretentious and hypocritical. 'The Character therefore of young *Bevil*', Dennis complains, 'is not an Image of any thing in Life, and especially in common Life, as every thing in Comedy ought to be, but the Phantom of a feverish Author's Brain, as several of the other Characters likewise are'.[56] Dennis is harshly perceptive as well about the absurdity of the incidents of the play and the awkwardness of its language, which he describes as 'too often *Hibernian*'.[57]

Defenders of Steele similarly base their arguments on Bevil's exemplary character, his representation of the qualities of the ideal gentleman: 'In short, if polite Language, noble Sentiments, and the subjecting every Passion to the Law of Reason, are the essential Parts of a fine Gentleman, *Bevil*'s is a perfect Character'.[58] For Victor, Dennis's claim that comedy should only be concerned with vicious characters is like claiming 'that a Baudy-house is a fitter Place for the Improvement of Virtue, than a Church'.[59] Dennis's criticism, however cogent, seems to have been overwhelmed by the audience's discovery that comedy could move them deeply. The pleasures of that experience make quibbles about inconsistence and dramatic theory seem irrelevant. *The Conscious Lovers* dominated the stage for the rest of the century. Although it now seems a less interesting play than *The Tender Husband* and even *The Funeral*, it was Steele's crowning success.[60]

Two Stages of Retirement

Steele's active role as a manager of Drury Lane Theatre effectively ended in late January 1720, when a licence was issued to Cibber, Wilks and Booth excluding him. When his status was restored in May 1721, his income from the theatre continued but he did not return to the management. In 1720, the other managers deducted £5 daily (when there were performances) from his share of the profits, and they continued to do so after his reinstatement. In the lawsuit that eventuated from this deduction they argued that they were paying themselves an appropriate salary for the work that Steele did not do as manager. Steele had two large and complex financial problems to resolve regarding his management of Drury Lane. He had to be paid the various moneys owed him by the actor-managers, especially for the time he was excluded from the management. That situation was compounded by the fact that Doggett, who had been paid his share since 1714, was, by 1721, out of the picture, so that the profits were now divided among four managers rather than five. Since Steele had mortgaged his one-fifth share, the additional one-twentieth was a new source of income.

Steele, Cibber, Wilks and Booth drew up articles of agreement in September 1721 dividing up the property, providing an appropriate settlement on Steele's inheritors and insisting that no party could mortgage, sell or distribute his share, an obvious response to Steele's irresponsibility in doing precisely that. On 7 December 1721 he wrote separate but similar letters to Wilks, Booth and Cibber reproaching them, as his longtime friends, for withholding money from him that he was due as manager and patent-holder. The language of the letters is somewhat unclear as to the nature of the money Steele felt was owed him. It is not clear at what point Steele became aware that the actor-managers were skimming from his profits. On 4 September 1725 Steele, through his attorney David Scurlock (his wife's cousin), began a suit for the recovery of the sums, by now quite considerable, that had been withheld from him. Cibber in his *Apology* claims that Steele had been told several years earlier that this was the case.

> It must be observed then, that about two, or three Years, before the Suit was commenc'd, upon *Sir Richard's* totally absenting himself, from all Care, and Management of the Stage (which by our Articles of Partnership he was equally, and jointly oblig'd with us, to attend) we were reduc'd to let him know, that we could not go on, at that Rate; but that if he expected to make the Business a *sine Cure*, we had as much Reason to expect a Consideration for our extraordinary Care of it; and that during his Absence, we therefore intended to charge ourselves at a Sallary of 1 £. 13s. 4d. every acting Day (unless he could show us Cause , to the contrary) for our Menagement: To which, in his compos'd manner, he only answered; That to be sure, we knew what was fitter to be done, than he did; that he always had taken a Delight, in making us easy, and had no Reason to doubt of our doing him Justice.[61]

Cibber's account is not entirely credible. It seems doubtful that Steele, after a composed response that said, in effect, that he trusted them completely, should suddenly claim that he had been bilked. Steele's suit against the managers was brought on 4 September 1725; the managers brought a countersuit, but it was not until 17 February that the combined suits came to a hearing, The court decided in favor of the managers on the matter of the special compensation, but it found that Steele was owed £1,062 in back profits. There the matter rested. Steele died in 1729, and the theatre paid his surviving daughter his share of the profits for three years.

The second problem Steele had to resolve was the mortgage on his share. He had mortgaged it to Edward Munshall in 1716, and Minshall had further assigned portions to his own creditors. A year later a further deed of assignment, in effect a virtual sale, was drawn up and held by Robert Wilbraham, Minshall's attorney. By 1722 Steele thought he had redeemed the deed and sued Wilbraham to get it back. The case was evidently settled out of court, but a year later a creditor of a creditor of Minshall made demands of Steele that led to a further drain on his profits. In 1724 Steele's income from the theatre was turned over to David

Scurlock, his legal trustee, to pay his creditors, and an indenture was drawn up including Steele, the actor-managers, Steele's creditors, and Scurlock. After a lifetime of financial mismanagement, Steele had arranged his affairs so that his estate would be clear for his heirs. In the summer of 1724, he retired to Wales.

Steele's final theatrical effort consisted of several fragments of plays that he had begun by 1723 but not completed before his death.[62] *The School of Action* is the longest of these fragments; *The Gentleman* has only one scene.[63] 'Action' in *The School of Action* refers to acting, and the plot revolves around the efforts of a lively young man (Mr Severn), assisted by his learned and solemn friend Mr Humber, to coax a young lady from her crotchety guardian by disguising his acting school as an inn where various spectral figures, played by actors, plague the guardian. The lively young man seems modelled on Steele himself and his learned friend on Addison. Less than half the play was written, and the fragments explore the various elements of the plot – the daughter and her family, the tricks played on the stingy guardian, the candidates auditioning for the acting school, the revelation of the theatrical hoax by neighbours. It is not clear how Steele intended to fit these pieces together, and that may well have been the problem that stalled him as he moved into retirement. But he may have been stalled as well by the deteriorating condition of his health. 'The *Gentleman*', the other fragment printed by Aitken, is an incomplete scene in which servants take on their masters' identities and pleasures at a neighbouring tavern while their masters are at the theatre. Further memoranda and summaries describe ideas for unwritten plays.[64]

If Steele's theatrical career as a playwright and manager is judged rather a failure, it is in part because the goals he proposed for the theatre were far too unrealistic and ambitious. The kind of reform he sought would have required strong and persistent commitment on the part of playwrights and actors, as well as the development of a new kind of audience, anxious to see plays that provide moral instruction as well as entertainment. If we look at his accomplishments without measuring them by these goals, they are still at best mixed but nonetheless more significant than when measured by his own ambitions.

It is tempting to regard Steele's career as manager of Drury Lane Theatre as one of a number of failures that plagued him after the accession of George I in 1714. Certainly Newcastle and his allies were correct that he had failed to produce the reform he had promised and the patent had recognized. But by other standards of success, he at least held his own and possibly advanced. The quality of plays and acting remained very high, although few new plays were incorporated into the repertoire. He turned over the active management of the stage to professionals where, in his view, it belonged. And he protected those professionals as much as he could from what he saw as the intrusive power of the Lord Chamberlain. He took the side of the actors and their audience against the moral rigidity of those reformers who, like the author of the hostile *State of the Case*, insisted that no stage was better than a corrupt one. But at the same time as he sympathized personally with the actor-managers and saw their professional leadership as the most important element of the theatre's success, he also sympathized with the reformers. The best he could realistically hope for in face of these conflicting principles was a series of compromises and partial successes that would in turn surely conflict with his grandiose statements of change. He was plagued as well by an apparent shortage of effective new plays that embodied the values of a new audience of merchants and traders. In the end he had to write one himself.

Beyond the financial and managerial details of Steele's conflict with the actor-managers in 1725–7, there was an inherent conflict in their roles. Steele presented himself to the court and to the public as a theatrical reformer, but the managers were professional men of the theatre, interested in pleasing their audiences in the most effective manner, not in promulgating a particular moral code that, in the long run, seemed against their interest. That conflict between reform and the market echoes the ambivalence of Steele himself, who praised Congreve and *The Country Wife* but attacked *The Man of Mode*. It is the conflict between moral rectitude and entertainment. It is just possible to look at Steele's reformist programme as a front for his more serious purpose of preserving the theatre as an arena for the spread of Whig culture. The few new plays produced were Whig in sentiment, sometimes in response to particular situations. In defending his play *The Invader of His Country*, John Dennis claimed it was particularly appropriate because of invasion threats from Sweden and Spain.[65] The identification of Drury Lane with the Whigs was complete during Steele's tenure as manager. In that sense he had done what he had been appointed to do. But the conflict within the Whig party, as we have seen, paralleled the quarrel between Steele and Newcastle over the governance of the theatre. The intersection of conflict over reform with political conflict gave Steele's years as manager of Drury Lane their particular character.

But Steele was caught by other conflicts, less intellectual and more practical. A dominant characteristic of his life was his overcommitment to political causes and moneymaking schemes. This was the case for the last ten years of Steele's London life, and it certainly affected his concentration on the reform of the stage. His financial position remained precarious, his wife had separated from him for several years and died soon after returning, and his health deteriorated to the point where he was often incapacitated. Steele's multiple non-theatrical concerns during these years become the subject of our final chapter.

7 THE FINAL DECADE (1715–24)

By April 1715, Steele's fortunes had shifted dramatically after his exclusion from the House in 1714. He had been elected to Parliament, made manager of Drury Lane Theatre and given a patent for it, been given various sinecure appointments (Deputy Lieutenant of County Middlesex and Surveyor of the Royal Stables at Hampton Court) and been knighted. These offices on the whole represented an expansion of his work as the major Whig propagandist. His notion of using membership in Parliament as the basis for authority as a political writer was now realized. His role as manager and patentee of Drury Lane assured continued Whig control over the stage. His status as baronet gave him a position of dignity that the slurs and cavils of Tory propaganda could not obscure. He had, to all appearances, a happy and growing family. Admittedly, he was still irresponsible in his financial dealings, but he had in all other respects established a firm basis for continuing success. Nonetheless, he was not fully successful. His wife was away in Wales for most of the remaining years of their marriage and died soon after her return. Few of his children survived. His career as theatre manager ended in a dispute with his fellow managers over his failure to fulfil what they saw as his responsibilities. His project for a ship to bring live fish to London collapsed after a promising beginning. He continued to write and speak on political matters, but sometimes found himself at odds with the leaders of his party. After long battles with gout, his health gave way. He managed to put his finances in order and retire to his wife's property in Wales in 1724. His public life was over.

One factor in this decline, I suspect, was that the multiplicity of his activities and concerns precluded adequate attention to any one. During the period between April 1709 when the *Tatler* started and February 1714 when the *Englishman* closed, Steele had been heavily involved in writing periodicals, and this gave regularity and discipline to his literary life that seemed absent once he took on such a variety of official functions. During the years of the *Tatler*, *Spectator* and *Guardian* he was, for the most part, on the outside of political power, seeking to get in. He saw the route to power as lying in the conversion of his audience to a Whig ideology that combined courtly manners and learning with bourgeois energy and openness. But after 1715 the ingredients of the Whig party began to seem unstable, with the climax coming in the split between Walpole and Pulteney on one side and Stanhope and Sunderland on the other (April 1717), followed by the collapse of the South-Sea Bubble in September 1720 and the consequent emergence of Walpole. As a Member of Parliament and as a propagandist, Steele was involved in many of the intra-party disputes, and, particularly after the defeat of the 1715 Jacobite rebellion, he began to take independent positions on specific issues rather than follow the dictates of party leaders. While the decade was one of personal and physical decline, he achieved commendable accomplishments in a number of areas.

Lady Steele

In mid-November 1716, Lady Steele left her husband and children and travelled to her family property in Wales in order to oversee the management of her late mother's estate, especially the collection of rent from her tenants. There is every reason to believe that she did attend to these functions, but there is every reason short of direct evidence to be suspicious of her journey. It was an inconvenient time for such a journey. Steele had suffered a debilitating attack of the gout during the previous spring. Their daughter Molly (Mary) was ill with what shortly turned out to be the smallpox. The children were put out to nurse, and Steele was left to manage as best he could: 'We had not when you left us an Inch of Candle a pound of Coal or a bit of meat in the House. But we do not want now.'[1] The Steeles' second son Richard had died some time since 28 March 1714, the last time he is mentioned in the letters.[2] When, on 13 December 1716, Steele comments on each of the children before providing news of political developments, Richard is not mentioned.[3] Silence about the death of his son is just one of the mysterious lacunae in Steele's otherwise frequent correspondence.

   That silence tempts speculation about the real circumstances surrounding Lady Steele's departure and about the real reasons for it. No doubt her estate needed supervision, and the collection of rents would benefit from having an interesting party present. She and Sir Richard seem to have made a pact to improve the financial situations on both sides of the family in order to assure the security of their children. He was scheduled to take a trip to Scotland for the Commission for Forfeited Estates, and although the trip did not take place at that time, it would have seemed to her a good occasion for tending to her family business. She may well have plunged into severe grief over Richard's death, and her busy husband not have noticed or may have been unable to assuage it. Steele's drinking may also have been a source of concern. On 16 February 1717 he wrote (and this is the text of the entire letter), 'Dear Prue[,] Sober or not, I am Ever Yours, Richard Steele.'[4] Despite the tone of comic tenderness, this is hardly a note that is likely to convince a sensitive wife to return to her errant husband. Not only is Steele guilty of writing under the influence, the letter seems an instance of his dubious displays of affection, partly intense and sincere, but partly a habit of speech, not entirely convincing to his wife.

She may have found her husband's sexual interests in her excessive or distasteful. In September or October 1717, after ten or eleven months of separation, Steele wrote in some exasperation in response to her complaint of his coldness:

> As to the coldnesse on the Subject I answer very sincerely that Your Ladyship's coldnesse to me as a Woman and as a Wife has made me think it necessary to Supresse the expression of my Heart towards You, because it could not end in the pleasures and enjoyments I ought to expect from it, and which You oblig'd Me to Wean my self from, till I had so much money &c and I know not what impertinence.[5]

Her insistence on his financial reform grew tiresome to him. 'Therefore in the name of God have done with talk of money, and don't let me lose the right I have in a Woman of Wit and Beauty, by eternally turning Her self into a Dun.'[6] But these outbursts are exceptions to the usual tone of appreciation and flattery with which he writes her, as if trying to cajole her into coming back to him sooner rather than later. He uses the children also as lures, writing often about their attractive and lively qualities. But despite his obvious interest in her return, he never overtly insists that she come back. The tone of his correspondence presents a patina of consistent affection and flattery (which he knew she liked), occasionally broken by anger or impatience.

She urges him to withdraw from the labour and ingratitude of public life, and he promises to curtail his activities in order to support his family. 'My Wife and my Children are the objects that have wholly taken up my Heart ... You are the Head of Us and I stoop to a female reign as being naturally made the Slave of Beauty.'[7] He assures her that her estate can be set aside as an investment and that the money he will allow her and the children will be more than the estate can bring.[8] She quarrels vehemently with members of her own family about money matters and resents what she sees as their ungenerous behaviour. 'I am ty'd here for my childrens good, for some time, and can see nothing but behaviour very odious to me; it has given me vapours to a vast degree.'[9] Shortly before her return to London, Steele tells her that he is outraged at 'the Treatment you tell me you receive, as being affronted and called Fool to your Face, by rude Blockheads'. He promises things will improve: 'you never will be with relations, who are often apt to think your being in the world is an injury'.[10] It may well have been this last blow-up that brought her to London.

Lady Steele was clearly caught in a dilemma. On one side was a husband who, despite his obvious affection, was an unstable source of support and a wavering source of companionship; on the other side was a family which seems hostile and rude. In the middle was a woman who was to a degree dependent on both husband and family and who sought to make her children independent of the kind of trap in which she now was caught. An alternative reading sees her as caught in a trap of her own making. She was a handsome woman, if Godfrey Kneller's portrait, printed as the frontispiece to the second volume of Aitken's *Life of Richard Steele*, is an accurate depiction. But she also seems a highly sensitive one, with perhaps an elevated sense of what was due her. She was shy in social situations, in contrast to her gregarious husband. If she repeatedly urged Sir Richard to withdraw from thankless public activities, it was because she herself preferred a life of quiet comfort. The combination of shyness and pride may well have come across as a social haughtiness that, in turn, led to the envy and dislike of her family. It was possibly the hostility of her family that brought her back to London rather than her desire to return to her husband. She may have feared another pregnancy, but she became pregnant, and that pregnancy probably contributed to her death.

She arrived back in London in December 1717. In April 1718 she and Steele spent a disastrous few weeks with John Sansome, an old but unreliable friend of Steele. Tensions had arisen over his self-imposed role in the Fish Boat project, and Steele left when he threatened violence to Lady Steele. It was apparent at this point that Lady Steele was pregnant. On 26 December, Lady Steele died. On the next day, Steele wrote a brief letter to her cousin Alexander Scurlock announcing that 'my Dear and Honour'd Wife departed this life last night'.[11] She was buried in Westminster Abbey on 30 December. The simple inscription on her grave has been effaced by time but was recorded by John Nichols and included in his edition of Steele's correspondence. She was forty years old.

Of the Steeles' four children, only one, Elizabeth, lived to become a mature adult. Richard (born 1710) died sometime between 1714 and 1716; Eugene (born 1712) died in 1723; Mary (born 1713) died of tuberculosis in 1730, one year after her father. Elizabeth (born 1709) was reportedly beautiful and, as the inheritor of her father's fortune, now cleared of debt, rich. She was much sought-after as a wife and eventually married John Trevor, a Welsh judge, in 1732. He succeeded to the title of Lord Trevor in 1753 and died in 1764. They had two children–a stillborn child in 1733 and a daughter, Diana Marie (1744), who was mentally defective and died in 1778. But Lady Trevor remained close to the family of her elder half-sister Elizabeth Ousley Aynston, Steele's natural daughter, who married William Aynston in 1720. Her daughter Katherine married a Welshman surnamed Thomas and became a companion to Lady Trevor, who paid for the education of her sons. She gave one of those sons the letters from Steele to her mother that are the basis of these pages. (They in turn were sold to John Nichols and published in 1787.)

Steele and the Jacobites

When Steele began the second series of *The Englishman* on 11 July 1715, he had a clear and announced purpose – to make clear that the previous ministry was guilty of treason for aiding the French King. Sir Thomas Burnet's *The Necessity of Impeaching the Late Ministry, In a Letter to the Earl of Halifax* (London: J. Roberts, 1715) proposed the step indicated in the title. As soon as the new Parliament met, in March, Robert Walpole moved an address that indicated the government's intentions to take measures against the late ministry, and the government began preparing its case. In the course of doing so, it certainly turned to Steele, the leading Whig propagandist, for support. Steele wrote to Lord Clare on 25 May to enumerate the sums he had expended in the Whig cause and to ask for financial support for his new periodical. Steele's friends in the Godolphin ministry were either dead (Wharton, Halifax) ill (Somers, Sunderland), or had little power (Marlborough).[12] Despite his quarrels with the Oxford–Bolingbroke ministry, Steele was not inclined to seek revenge. Nonetheless, he was willing to conduct the periodical if properly paid, as he explained to Lord Clare:

> In one word, My Lord, the purpose of this letter is to lay my dissatisfactions before You, and to declare on what foundation I will enter the lists. I cannot turn so much time that Way and be supported by assistants equall to the Work for lesse than 1000 l. a Year. And before I enter upon the Argument I hope to receive 500 l. or be excused from so painfull, so anxious, and so Unacceptable a Service.[13]

Soon after he began *Englishman* II, Steele wrote again to Lord Clare, complaining that he had not been paid and threatening not to continue.[14] The sum was finally paid to Steele's assistant Leonard Welsted on 27 August.[15] What Steele's letter to Clare made abundantly clear was how distasteful to him was the task of vilifying a political opponent and criminalizing a political difference.

The accession of George I did not allay the political hostilities of recent years but merely rearranged them. Although the English were hostile to a Catholic monarch, they were more than restive under a foreign one. In the spring of 1715 popular unrest was widespread and vehement,[16] and much of it centered upon the Duke of Ormond, whose loyalty and military accomplishments, despite his role in the 1712 campaign, in which he replaced Marlborough as British commander-in-chief but failed to act against the French, made him a popular Tory figure, a stand-in for the Pretender. In May Steele allowed his name to be used as author of *An Account of the State of the Roman Catholic Religion throughout the World* (by Benjamin Hoadly). Blanchard attributes the preface to Steele; in it Steele attacks the Schism Act and asserts the intelligibility and goodwill of Christianity. The publication on 2 June 1715 of Steele's *Political Writings*, a collection of tracts from 1712 through 1714, served as a reminder of the evils of the Oxford administration. On 20 June *The Report of the Secret Committee* laid out the case, such as it was, against Oxford, Bolingbroke, Ormond, and such lesser participants as Matthew Prior. Steele used the report as the basis for the case he laid out in *The Englishman*.

The Englishman began, on 11 July 1715, by focusing its attack sharply on Robert Harley, Earl of Oxford, who was taken to the Tower on charges of treason on 12 July, accompanied by anti-government rioting. Steele immediately connects the charges against him with his well-known manipulative character: 'Upon the whole of his Conduct, it will appear that the great Skill of his Life may be comprehended in the single Rule of *undermining Wisdom with Cunning, and overbearing Honesty with Impudence*' (*Englishman*, Series 2, no. 1). Steele's second step is to define treason in a way that encompasses Oxford's misdeeds by turning to the Treason Act of Edward III and asserting that 'Treasonable Thoughts manifested by and exerted into an Action, an open or overt Action, that is, an Action which expresses and discovers deliberate Malice or Design in the Heart, constitute the Crime of Treason by this Act (*Englishman*, Series 2, no. 2). In no. 8 he points out the considerable latitude allowed to Parliament in the interpretation of treason and quotes the sixteen treason articles brought against Harley. Steele metaphorically uses the term 'Parracides' to describe Oxford, Bolingbroke, Strafford, and others in the Tory ministry whom he wants to attaint. But he insists that the major crime with which he is concerned is the Treaty of Utrecht and that the total responsibility for the treaty and its violations of the constitution lies with Oxford, the others, whom Oxford engaged by skillfully playing on their personal ambitions, serving merely as fronts or agents (no. 6). When, in no. 9, he turns to the case of Henry St. John, Viscount Bolingbroke, he has an easier task. Bolingbroke's womanizing (which Steele casts as disrespect for the Queen) and his flight into France virtually make the case for his disloyalty by themselves. 'This Gentleman is now well known to have withdrawn himself from the Justice of the Nation, and while his Country is employed in prosecuting his Crimes in *England*, he is adding to the Number of them in *France*' (*Englishman*, Series 2, no. 9). Steele pursues the attack on Bolingbroke in no. 19 (12 September).

But Steele has greater difficulty in making the case against the Duke of Ormond. James Butler, Second Duke of Ormond had been Chancellor at Oxford when Steele was a student there. When Steele left Oxford to join the army, 'he cock'd his Hat, and put on a broad Sword, Jackboots, and Shoulder-Belt, under the Command of the unfortunate Duke of *Ormond*'.[17] In 1704 Steele dedicated *The Lying Lover* to Ormond. Steele's uncle Gascoigne had been secretary to the present Duke's father. Beyond these personal connections, Ormond was a charming man with a long and distinguished military record. His 'treason' consisted in his replacing Marlborough as allied commander in 1712 and carrying out the controversial 'restraining orders' issued by Bolingbroke that required him not to fight the French, to hide from the Dutch his orders not to fight the

French, and to cooperate with the secret revelation to the French that he was not going to fight them. Clearly there was treachery involved here, but the question was whether Ormond was simply obeying legitimate orders or whether he had grounds to question them. The fact that Ormond was Tory – even Jacobite – in his politics did not make his case any more sympathetic.

In *Englishman*, no. 10, Steele describes him as

> the only Person concerned in the Report who can possibly move Pity in those who read his Story; and tho' the Facts against him are very strong, yet such is the Indulgence towards him, that Men are more inclined to Pity than Condemn him, for having done them.

Steele generously considers the arguments on Ormond's behalf:

> but all the Arguments which the Good-nature or Wit of his Well-wishers could, or can form for him, are answer'd by his Grace's Flight into *France*; his Flight to the Conversation of that Secretary who betrayed his Honour, and whose Accomplice he cannot but appear by this Action (*Englishman*, Series 2, no. 10).

Clearly Steele's generous and partial comments on Ormond had gone beyond his brief, and they were corrected by the insertion of a letter, almost certainly not by Steele, in the next paper. This letter quotes extensively from the *Report*, and lays out the damaging facts against Ormond in a way that Steele had not. Steele gives the articles of impeachment against Ormond a month later in no. 21 (21 September, 1715).

In contrast to the characters of the 'Parracides', Steele presents a positive portrait of the Duke of Marlborough on 19 August. But the positive qualities of Marlborough, as Steele presents him, empower Steele's attack on the ingratitude of the Tories: 'the sacrificing of the Duke of *Marlborough*, was the *Open Deed* which convinced all discerning Men of their intended Treason' (*Englishman*, Series 2, no. 12). The descriptions of the various accused politicians serves as the exemplification of Steele's more general points, and these general points in turn serve Steele well when, after the Earl of Mar unfurled the Stuart banner on the Braes of Mar (6 September), the Jacobite rebellion began in earnest. Steele insists that the Treaty of Utrecht was a betrayal that allowed the French to support James in his efforts to mount an attack on British soil. By negotiating that weak and unfavourable treaty, the 'Parracides' had, probably intentionally, created conditions for the present rebellion. The rebellion proved the seriousness and criminality of their offense. Even before Mar raised his standard, Steele argued against 'the Usurpation of Power in Secular Matters' (*Englishman*, Series 2, no. 14) and insisted that liberty of conscience is an essential principle of Protestantism. Steele follows up this religious principle by attributing the success of Tory propaganda to the ignorance of the populace – those who do not think for themselves. Such people turned to their parsons and their landlords as authorities, and the result was the violent agitation that followed the Sacheverell decision. Churchmen tend to act in their own narrow self-interest when there should be unity in the interests of church and state: 'two Relations of the same Society, and not as two Divisions or Denominations of Men among Us' (*Englishman*, Series 2, no. 17). For Steele the root of loyalty lay in basic Whig principles. In no. 22 he makes the familiar argument that the purpose of government lies in the welfare of the people, and that government that seriously endangers that welfare can be resisted. He argues that this is the principle behind the revolution of 1688, but even present citizens who feel that revolution was unjustified still have an obliga-tion to support King George, who ascended the throne in a peaceful and legal way rather than by conquest (as obviously would be the case of James III were his rebellion to succeed).

The last dozen or so papers in the second series of *The Englishman* are, with few exceptions, concerned with Jacobites and Catholicism rather than with the impeachable offenses of Oxford, Bolingbroke, Ormond, and others. Although effective in aggregate, these are among the least original, most derivative of the *Englishman* papers, and one suspects that Steele had Welsted, Burnet, or some other assistant put them together.[18] no. 26 follows Dr. Higden, a converted nonjuror, in arguing that the English have a responsibility to be faithful to the reigning monarch and to obey his laws, as various references to past monarchs indicate. In no. 27 a contributed letter uses the history of monarchs since Charles II to explain why, despite the demonstrated legitimacy of the present govern-ment, there has been a revolution against it. no. 28 acutely observes that the death of Louis XIV has prevented massive French intervention on behalf of Mar and the Jacobites. Another contributed letter (from Shute Barrington) stresses Catholic rigidity and intolerance, its opposition to reform and its hostility to England, as demonstrated by a series of horror stories. A letter in no. 29 attacks the comments of Cardinal Pool that Protestants are worse than Moslems. Not to be outdone, Steele goes on to compare Catholicism unfavorably to Islam on various doctrinal positions.

A letter in no. 30 consists of passages from [Richard Willis,] *An Address to those of the Roman Communion in England* (1700). Nos. 31 and 32 provide documents connecting the 'parricides' to the Jacobite revolution: the coming of the Pretender had in effect been predicted by George's comments against a sepa-rate peace in *Bothmar's Memorial* (1711); Godolphin's 1710 letter to Queen Anne resigning, as requested, his post as Lord Treasurer specifically warns of the danger of the Pretender. 'Convert Hearty', a former Jacobite, argues closely that one's oath of allegiance is determined by Parliament and cannot be set aside by an oath to Pretender (No. 33); no. 34 argues against the general principle that oaths taken to the present government are invalid and need not be observed.

no. 35 attacks the clergy who explicitly or implicitly support the Pretender. no. 36 complains about newspapers that show respect to the rebels (as Steele was shortly to do himself), and no. 37 consists of a sermon by Benjamin Hoadly showing the dangers of the Pretender. The final paper condemns the indifferent man who does not concern himself with party disputes and is therefore indifferent to the fate of his country.

The Englishman closed when its propaganda functions had ended. The impeachment trials were over, and the Jacobites had been defeated at Preston and Sheriffmuir on 17 November. Whig propaganda now shifted to Addison who, although generally more moderate as a propagandist, took a harder line in the *Freeholder* about the captured Jacobite rebels than Steele had done in *The Englishman*. Steele, probably gratefully, shifted to the theatrical and social criticism in *Town Talk* (17 December 1715–13 February 1716). Steele had resumed *The Englishman* reluctantly, agreeing to publicize the Report on treason, and he justified the prosecution by moving from abstract consideration of the nature of treason to the character and behaviour of those accused. The outbreak of the Jacobite rebellion gave his periodical greater purpose and concentration. Here the deployment of papers on various aspects of the subject was professional and effective. The one break in Steele's consistent support for the ministry was his defence of the Duke of Ormond, and that moment of independence was a sign of things to come. *The Englishman* was undertaken to meet limited and changing goals. When it met those goals, it was closed, with perhaps no one happier than its author.

But his relations to the Jacobites had one more turn. In *Town-Talk* for 13 January (no. 5), Steele deviates from social to political news and concerns himself with the 'Declaration' of the Pretender, which he claims to have acquired from a prostitute at the Drury Lane Theatre, who herself received it from her client Viscount Bolingbroke. Steele responds in a long letter, signed 'R. S.'. It begins with the familiar Whig principle that 'the Basis of all Government is the Good of the People governed; and that all Incidents of a State must be rectified by that single Rule, and no other'. One way or another (and Steele provides several alternatives), the Pretender's claim to the throne is illegitimate, and his ascension to it would be followed by the dire punishments associated with Catholic power, in contrast to the mild and condign punishments suffered by the Jacobite rebels. He prints the Pretender's Declaration, which asserts (among other things) that James III is the legitimate and lawful monarch, whom Queen Anne would have preferred on the throne, had she not died prematurely, that he has wide popular support among the people, that the present ruling family consists of German-speaking foreigners, that the present government is run by a faction, and that the rights and privileges of the Scots must be restored. Steele, of course, denies each point. *Table-Talk* no. 5 is the longest of the periodical, and Steele liked it enough to recast it, in a less mocking, more moderate style, as a pamphlet with the 'Declaration' and the answer on facing pages.

Steele had earlier written *A Letter from the Earl of Mar to the King before His Majesty's Arrival in England* (London: Jacob Tonson, 1715) in response to Mar's September 6 raising of the Jacobite standard. It makes the obvious case that Mar, with whom Steele passed 'some agreeable Hours at different times in his Company',[19] has presently acted in ways that are inconsistent with his past. Mar now rebels on behalf of James III but has sworn that James III has no title to the throne. He provided faithful service to Queen Anne but now claims that her title was illegitimate. Liars such as Mar are contrasted to honest Non-jurors (non-jurors in contrast to conjurers). He is now in a state of rebellion. The mendacity of his behaviour replicates the falseness of the claim he is supporting.

The surprising shift in Steele's attitude towards the defeated Jacobites occurs on 9 February 1716, when the six Scottish Lords captured at Preston were condemned to death. Steele was present at the parliamentary trial and reported it in *Town-Talk*, no. 9. In the previous paper he had given a dismissive description of the Pretender: 'There is no Air in his Motion, Sense in his Discourse, or Dignity in his Aspect' (*Town-Talk*, no. 8) He intensifies the description in no. 9 by calling him an 'Indolent Invader', a man with neither the personal energy nor magnetism to lead a potent rebel army. He 'comes into their Camp like a Spy, and goes out of it like a Deserter'. Steele then shifts to Westminster Hall, with a solemn account of the officers in their uniforms who are gathered for the sentencing.

> You must form to yourself, how every Heart would beat, during the awful Silence and Suspence of so many Persons assembled to hear nothing but a Sentence of Death pronounced against such a Number of Peers, who stood now Disabled and Unarmed beseeching Mercy, One by One, and acknowledging they deserved it not: Their Quality, Change of Condition, the Vigour of their Days, and the present Inability to offend further, pleaded very strongly to a good-natured, and generous People, who are quick to Anger, but slow to Revenge (*Town-Talk*, no. 9).

Steele walks the line between an outright plea for mercy and a willingness to go along with the government's harsh sentence. He sees the prisoners not as criminals but as unfortunate men misled by misplaced and outdated loyalties. His description seems intended to scorn the man whose deceptions brought them to this pass.

Strong efforts were made to gain a reprieve, and Steele was instrumental in making them. On 22 February the wives of the condemned Lords presented petitions to Parliament, as did Steele, who spoke strongly and at length on their behalf. In order to forestall a vote, Walpole moved a postponement until 1 March, when the sentences would have been carried out. It passed by only seven votes. On the next day, Lords Derwentwater and Kenmure were beheaded. Two others escaped from the Tower, and Parliament passed an act releasing the final three in 1717.[20] Steele had begun as loud opponent of James III, Catholicism, Jacobites, and the rebellion, but he ended as an advocate of mercy. Walpole and others were nervous at the independence this showed. Accordingly, Steele was attacked and belittled in *St. James's Post* of 2 March as 'Cavaliero Risko Chalybeski' and, along with the other advocates of mercy, charged with taking bribes from the enemy.[21] Steele responded in *A Letter to a Member, &c. concerning the Condemn'd Lords* (6 March 1716).

Steele repeats the substance of his speech before Parliament, in which he argues that impeachment is inappropriate in this case. The condemned Lords had surrendered to the King, hoping, perhaps, that he would pardon them, By bringing an impeachment against them, Parliament was making it impossible for the King to do an act of kindness even if he wanted to do it: 'so that this Circumstance of the Impeachment hurt the Prerogative in its most amiable Instance, that of Forgiveness, and robb'd the Subject of the most valuable Effect of it, the receiving that Forgiveness ...'[22] Turning to his own case, Steele ironically notes that he is now suffering the same kind of personal attack that he suffered two years before on behalf of the King. In response to the charge of bribery, he insists that 'if I have made my self Cheap, I am sure I have not made my self Mercenary'.[23] Steele knew, and Walpole's hired writer apparently did not, that the danger of a moralistic attack such as the *Journal's* charge of bribery lay in the likelihood that it would foster a still more moral defence. Steele distinguishes sharply between judgments that are essentially aesthetic and those that are moral.

> It is not for me to say how I write , or speak; but it is for me to say, I do both honestly; and when I threw away some Fame for Letters and Politeness, to serve the nobler Ends of Justice and Government, I did not do it with a Design to be as negligent of what should be said of me, with relation to my Integrity in Support of those Ends. No; Wit and Humour are the Dress and Ornament of the Mind; but Honesty and Truth are the Soul it self, and the Difference in a Man's Care for his Reputation for one and the other is just in the Proportion that being Robb'd bears to being Murder'd.[24]

However successful this moral defence may be against the charge of bribery, it does little to answer the underlying rhetoric of that change. Steele's defence of the Jacobites cannot easily be reconciled with his attack against them, and Steele's assertions about the prerogative of the Monarch or the integrity of writers do little to reconcile two logically incompatible positions. But the essence of Steele's position is that such narrowly conceived logic is inappropriate to the human complexities of politics. In the last analysis, Steele implies, humanitarian sympathy is more appealing politically than literal legality.

> I have never talked of Mercy and Clemency, but for the sake if my King and Country, in whose Behalf I dare to say, That to be afraid to forgive is as low as to be afraid to

punish; and that all the noble Geniuses in the Art of Government have less owed their Safety to Punishment and Terror, than Grace and Magnanimity.[25]

Steele's anti-Jacobite writings may well be those he had in mind when he admitted that he 'threw away some Fame for Letters and Politeness'. Occasionally they rise to the level of argumentative sharpness and rhetorically resounding (if not original) principle, and they are absolutely scintillating when compared to many tracts by other authors, but on the whole they are relatively predictable. They encapsulate a nexus of concerns on Steele's part, however, and they direct them towards a political problem of real urgency. Steele's Whig principles called for a mixed government where power was shared rather than concentrated in the person of an omnipotent monarch. The result of such sharing would be freedom for the subjects whose interests would be represented, directly or indirectly, in such a government. Jacobite principles, in contrast, called for a centralized state where power lay almost exclusively with the King, as in the case of the France of Louis XIV. A shared government ought to be able to assure intellectual and religious liberty to its citizens. To do so, the government should be secular, for if, as in Catholic France, it becomes an arm of the state – or the state becomes an arm of the church – the result is legal persecution against Jews and Protestants. Steele has no real fear that Britain will become a nation of Catholics, or even a nation persecuted by Catholics, but he does fear the comparable (if not equivalent) zealotry of the high church Tories, and hence his anti-Jacobite comments often have as a subtext the toleration of Dissenters and, to a limited degree, even Catholics within a state that is essential secular. Steele's attack on Jacobitism unites his political and religious liberalism, and his urging of clemency towards the condemned lords derives from this essential moderation.

Steele had one more encounter with Jacobites before his retirement. Steele almost certainly wrote two numbers for *Pasquin*, a pro-Walpole periodical that was edited by his friend George Duckett and Nicholas Amhurst. These are in response to the Atterbury plot and, more specifically, in response to its defence in *The True Briton*. Walpole's ascendency eliminated any chance of Tory power, and Atterbury, the Bishop of Rochester and witty friend of Pope and Swift, was the most prominent Tory and proponent of the Stuart dynasty. Out of desperation, he and a handful of co-conspirators plotted the return of James from Italy and the consequent triumph of the Tories. The scheme was a failure virtually from the outset. The French Regency was uninterested in imposing James on the British, and they discovered evidence of Atterbury's plans, which they reported to Walpole.[26] Steele joined Walpole on a Parliamentary committee that prepared an address to the King complaining of the Jacobite conspiracy.[27] The evidence before the House, which tried Atterbury in a bill of Attainder, consisted primarily of coded messages that needed decipherment, a process that Swift famously mocked in Book III of *Gulliver's Travels*. Atterbury's speech resounded with wily rhetoric but could not deny either the evidence or the intentions to which it pointed.

Steele's *Pasquin*, no. 46 takes the form of a letter from Atterbury, here called Illington, to *The True Briton*. Illington warns the paper to be more deceitful, circumspect, and hypocritical: 'For which Reason, I take the Liberty to advise, that if you wou'd have what you say regarded, you should not be so sincerely wicked'.[28] It should join Illington in practicing the art of prevarication, 'that is, a Way of seeming to speak the Truth, but keeping a Reserve in your own Heart, as if you had said nothing'.[29] A passage from his own defence is offered as a model for such misdirection. *Pasquin*, no. 51 (26 July 1723) regards *The True Briton*'s attack on Bishops (most of whom were Whigs) as an abuse of liberty of the press. Steele acknowledges Atterbury's intellectual excellence but adds that it is 'join'd with a consummate Hypocrisy and glaring Impudence'. *The True Britain*'s attacks on Walpole, he claims, are just audacious name-calling.

Since Atterbury sailed into exile on 18 June 1723, three weeks before the first and most successful of Steele's *Pasquin* papers, it seems reasonable to ask why they were written. They were, of course, a response to *The True Britain*, and although Atterbury had departed, the echoes of his considerable voice remained. *The True Briton* was a project of the Duke of Wharton (son of the Junto Lord), who later joined the Pretender and converted to Roman Catholicism. Walpole had developed many enemies, and although he was at the height of his power in 1723, he needed to keep up the battle and he was willing to use any literary force to do so, even his nearly-spent ally Sir Richard Steele. Steele's final defence of Walpole may have been even more significant than his attack on Atterbury. His final foray against the Jacobites proved to be his last political writing before his retirement in 1724.

Steele in Parliament

After years of intense and rather blinkered attention to periodicals, Steele found that the accession of George I and his own restored status as a political writer opened a variety of possibilities, many of which he explored. Perhaps the most unlikely was his effort to succeed Dr. Thomas Burnet as Master of Charterhouse. Steele, of course, had graduated from Charterhouse, but the position of Master had traditionally been held by unmarried members of the clergy, and Steele's candidacy was therefore a stretch. Nonetheless, Steele wrote to Sir Thomas Parker, now Lord Chief Justice of the King's Bench and a governor of the Charterhouse, and to Charlotte Clayton, a Woman of the Bedchamber to Princess Caroline. He went so far as to petition the King, in French.[30] The appointment was made elsewhere. But Steele quickly took up his position as manager of Drury Lane Theatre, staged an elaborate celebration of the King's birthday at the Censorium, and, in particular, plunged into his duties as the newly elected Member of Parliament from Boroughbridge, under the patronage of the Earl of Clare (later the Duke of Newcastle).

Steele's career in Parliament was distinctly independent, and his independence was tolerated because he was in other respects a very useful member. Much Parliamentary work was done through ad-hoc committees, and Steele was in high demand as a committeeman and writer. He drafted the Commons' address to the King's opening speech. On the occasion of his being knighted, he presented a Petition of loyalty to the King in which Parliament assured him, with unmistakable reference to the previous ministry,

> that the time is now come, wherein integrity and uprightness shall no longer be distinguished from the true policy; wherein cunning shall no longer pass for wisdom, nor deceitfulness for prudence; but the measures of a wise, just, beneficent, and steady Administration, shall establish the prosperity of these Realms.[31]

He served on a committee to hear petitions of elections (including his own), on a committee to investigate a libel in the *Evening Post*, on committees to write a bill in favour of the Quakers, a Bill to naturalize Protestant aliens, a Bill to naturalize the Palatines in Ireland, and a bill to augment the salaries of poor clergymen. He wrote an Address calling for the suppression of riots, an Address for the deputies of Middlesex, an address on disturbing the peace from the electors of Boroughbridge, and, on 21 January 1716, an address of thanks for the King's speech on the Pretender. Through this flurry of legislative activity a clear pattern emerges – to strengthen the Protestant interest, especially the non-conforming interests, in the face of possible Jacobite attack.

Most of Steele's parliamentary committee work was as Commissioner for Forfeited Estates. The Commissioners were appointed 7 June 1716 'to enquire of the estates of certain traitors, and of popish recusants, and of estates given to superstitious uses, in order to raise money out of them for the use of the public'.[32] Of the thirteen Commissioners, seven were for English, Welsh, and Irish estates and six were for estates of Scottish Peers. Steele was elected to the Scottish group. The salaries were £1000 per annum, but the assignment, especially for Scotland, was not a sinecure. The Commissioners were not allowed to hold other official appointments.[33] One of the Commissioners was stationed in London to interact with Parliament and the judicial system, but there were annual meetings in Scotland, which, for various reasons, Steele often did not attend in the early years – sometimes because of ill-health, and sometimes because his project for a 'Fish Pool' to transport live fish caught at sea back to London, where they could be eaten fresh, demanded his attention. Such was the case in 1716. But Steele worked diligently to acquire funding for the Commission, which was supposed to be supported from the estates it confiscated. But no such confiscations took place in the first year of the Scottish Commission, Robert Walpole, the Chancellor of the Exechequer, was in an abstemious mood, and Steele had not endeared himself by his opposition to the execution of the renegade peers. The Treasury did not agree to pay the salary of the Commissioners (Steele included) until summer 1717. In October, then, Steele travelled to Edinburgh, where he was warmly welcomed as a great British writer, despite Scottish antagonism towards the project that brought him there. In return he gave a very successful dinner at which the guests expressed such effective drunken wit that Steele claimed 'he had learned from them humour enough to form a whole comedy'.[34]

A particular problem faced by the Commission was the hostility of the Scottish Court of Session, combined with the strangeness of Scottish law which governed the cases. Moreover, the families of the convicted naturally tried in every way to evade the loss of property. Clarity was needed through new legislation.[35] Steele helped to draft and present, in January 1718, a report of the Commission to Parliament on the work of the Commission and the need for clearly defined authority, and Parliament accordingly lodged authority in the Commission rather than the Court of Session. In 1718, Steele planned to go again to Scotland (he certainly rented a house there), but was delayed by his 'Fish Pool' project. He attended a plenary meeting on 20 August 1719. In 1719 he intended again to go to Scotland, but only got as far as Wales, where he now had property inherited from his late wife. His salary was accordingly docked £500. Thereafter, he faithfully attended the Scottish meetings until he left the Scottish Commission in 1723.[36]

Beyond his *Englishman* campaign against the Jacobites and his subsequent urging of clemency for the renegade peers, Steele's political writings during the last decade of his activity focused on three major issues: the Septennial Bill, which changed the three-year term for Commons members to seven years; the Peerage Bill, which limited the number of Peers the King could appoint; and the South-Sea Bill and other measures surrounding the collapse of the South-Sea Company in 1720. The first began as a contest with Addison, but Steele soon swung to take the same side. The second ended whatever was left of the Addison–Steele friendship, and Addison died soon after. The third cemented Steele's position in the Walpole faction of Whigs, despite their earlier disagreement over the renegade peers.

The reigning Whigs proposed, in 1716, that the three-year Parliamentary term be extended to seven and that the change begin with the present sitting members. The proposal grew out of Whig uneasiness with the temper of the country in the wake of the Jacobite rebellion and the consequent fear that the Whig majority would be weakened or would disappear in the upcoming election in 1718. But there were long-range issues at play as well. The triennial election cycle meant that the factions and their constituencies were almost always in campaign mode, and a party in power could not assume that it would remain in power for long enough to push through complex legislation. In *Freeholder*, no. 25 (16 March 1716) Addison wrote to set the stage for the Septennial Bill and based his argument on the fickle nature of the English public, as reported by Europeans and as manifested particularly by English inconsistency in negotiations over the treaty with France. Steele drafted a paper in response attacking the Septennial Bill. But the paper, which seemed to begin a new periodical, was never published, and the periodical, which may have been entitled simply *Whig*, never appeared. Steele's anonymous persona praised the *Freeholder* in general but was particularly offended by no. 25, which he called 'a subtle destructive paper'.[37] Steele was offended by Addison's reading of the Utrecht negotiations. The problem, he insisted, was not English inconsistency but the treachery of Oxford, and he could not agree 'that the *one Change more* should extend to what we all fear his discourse aims at, the suspension of the Trienniall Act'.[38]

By the time the Septennial Bill was introduced in April 1716 Steele had changed his mind and spoke on behalf of the bill on both its second reading (24 April) and its third (26 April). Why Steele changed his mind is uncertain. He might have been talked out of his earlier position by any of a number of fellow Whigs, including Addison.[39] But there are solid reasons why he might simply, on further thought, have reversed his position. Although the three-year term seems to a modern more democratic than a seven-year one, the fact is that the real 'electors' to whom M.P.s were beholden were not the (few) people who actually cast votes but the aristocrats, magnates, and overlords, whose power and wealth determined elections. Seven years between elections increased the likelihood that MPs would act in the national interest rather than the interest of their sponsors. As a soldier in the trenches of the pamphlet wars, Steele realized as well as anyone that continued skirmishing drained political energies and forced attention to partisan bickering rather than public policy, and it was this argument that he stressed in his 24 April speech.[40] The first year of Parliament is spent in disputes about elections; the second takes up business 'with a Spirit of Contradiction' against the previous Parliament; and the third is shadowed by fear of the upcoming election. Steele denies that the change of terms for sitting members in the middle of their term is a breach of trust: 'The Trust, Sir, repos'd in us, is that of the Publick Good'. Experience has shown that the triennial term does not serve the public interest.

> Destruction is done with a Blow; But Reformation is brought about by leisurely Advances. All the Mischiefs which can be wrought under the Septennial Act, can be perpetrated under the Triennial; but all the Good which may be compassed under the Septennial, cannot be hoped for under the Triennial.[41]

The Septennial Bill easily passed and remained in effect until 1911.

Steele's participation in the debates leading up to the rejection of the Peerage Bill of 1719 in Commons was more extensive and more significant. Just as the Tory party had split between Bolingbroke and Oxford in 1714, the Whig party in 1717 split between Lord Stanhope and the Earl of Sunderland on one side and Robert Walpole and Lord Townshend on the other. Although Walpole had been a leader in Steele's defence in 1714 (and Steele had dedicated his *Apology* to him), Steele often spoke in Parliament against Walpole's positions. His advocacy of clemency for the condemned Scottish Lords was an open breach. In March 1717 Steele was the only M. P. to speak against a plan proposed by Walpole to reduce the national debt. Later that month he spoke in favour of a bill to relieve Catholics of various burdens, on the grounds of toleration for both Catholics and Dissenters. He subsequently attended a meeting of Whigs called by Newcastle in a vain attempt to reconcile the differences between the two warring camps of Whigs. On 10 April he wrote his wife reporting his speech on behalf of Catholic toleration and giving much more significant news:

> When I had adventured to say this others followed and there is a Bill directed for the releif of the Petitioners. I suppose this may give an Handle to the Fame of my being a Tory, but you may, perhaps, by this time, have heard that I am turned Presbyterian. For the same day in a meeting of an 100 Parliament men I labour'd as much for the Protestant dissenters. Now for the News. Mr. Walpole, Mr. Methuen and Mr. Pulteney have resigned their Offices. Mr. Stanhope is to go into the Treasury. Mr. Addison and Ld Sunderland are to be Secretaryes of State. Ld Townshend is removed from Ld Lt of Ireland. He is to be succeeded by the Duke of Bolton and the Duke of Newcastle to be Ld Chamberlain. We have no money.[42]

There was national rivalry owing to George's dual role as King of England and Elector of Hanover, and there was mutual suspicion between the English ministers and George's German advisors, in whom he had great confidence.[43] The King spoke little English, certainly not enough for complicated diplomatic negotiations. As a result he spoke to his English ministers in whatever language other than English he thought most likely to be understood–French, German, or even Latin. Walpole, for his part, adopted a policy of opposing the government at every opportunity.[44] In addition to the English–German split and the Stanhope–Walpole split, there was further rivalry within the Stanhope–Sunderland faction. Lord Cadogan was close to the German advisors and therefore suspected by Stanhope and Sunderland of seeking still greater power.[45] But the most serious rivalry was between the King and George Augustus, Prince of Wales, his son. The Prince of Wales had tried on several occasions to strike out independently, but the breach was occasioned in particular when Princess Caroline gave birth to a son (November 1717). The King insisted that the Duke of Newcastle be godfather, but the Prince resisted and, at the Christening, insulted him. (Newcastle, himself a testy man, thought the Prince had threatened to fight him.) The quarrel resulted in the Prince's banishment from court and his establishment of Leicester House as a gathering place for a variety of dissidents, including Walpole and Townshend. The King, in turn, insisted that his grandchildren live with him rather than with their parents.

The Peerage Bill can be seen as an immediate consequence of this hostility, and it was, as well, the occasion for a shift in Steele's political allegiance. In December 1717 and January 1718, Steele spoke on behalf of the Supply Bill sponsored by James Craggs, the Secretary of War and friend of Addison. In December 1718 he spoke strongly on behalf of a bill sponsored by Stanhope that offered relief to Dissenters. Up to the introduction of the Peerage Bill Steele's interventions were on behalf of the government and opposed to Walpole's opposition. It was appropriate that this be the case: in a sense; Steele, as patent-holder and manager of Drury Lane Theatre, was a government man. On 28 February 1719 the Duke of Somerset, acting for the government, introduced a Peerage Bill designed to limit the House of Lords to 235 members, allowing the King to appoint only replacements. Although it was seldom discussed in personal terms, the bill would clearly have the effect of limiting the future power of Prince George and the opposition that had gathered around him. In effect he could not appoint peers except in cases where families had died off. The bill had various benefits for the ministry in its efforts to play sides off against each other. By prohibiting the Prince from making appointments that would suddenly change the balance in Lords, Stanhope and Sunderland could make probable their continued power under a new monarch. By gaining the power to appoint thirty-one new peers, they could remedy their weakness in Lords and could determine a sympathetic Parliament for at least a generation. They could, at a stroke, put an end to the pay-for-play bribery among the King's German advisors and mistresses that had determined the creation of new peers.[46] The bill called for the sixteen peers now elected from the pre-Union Scottish peers by the Scottish peers themselves to be replaced by 25 permanent and hereditary peers appointed by the King. In addition, six new English peers would be appointed to preserve the national balance (or, depending on one's point of view, perpetuate the imbalance).

Steele joined Walpole in the opposition and, with Walpole, took a leading role in propaganda against the bill. It is quite possible that Walpole paid him to do so; Steele was in a sense a professional political writer.[47] But he had taken the government's positions in the recent past and could reasonably have expected to be paid by the government for supporting it in this case, had he chosen to offer his services despite his frosty relations with Newcastle and Addison. His convictions lay with the argument against the bill, and he took that position at substantial personal cost. The bill was, as expected, favourably received in Lords, but the hostility it faced in Commons was exacerbated by the powerful propaganda campaign launched by Steele and Walpole. The first and most significant number of Steele's *Plebeian* was dated 14 March 1719. *The Thoughts of a Member of the Lower House, in Relation to A Project for Restraining and Limiting the Power of the Crown in the Future Creation of Peers*, generally attributed to Walpole, appeared within days.[48] These effective tracts were soon answered by Addison in *The Old Whig*, no. 1 (19 March), who directed his arguments generally in favour of the bill and specifically at Steele and the *Plebeian*, and by Lord Molesworth, whose *Letter from a Member of the House of Commons to a Gentleman Without Doors, Relating to the Bill of Peerage Lately brought into the House of Lords*, dated 16 March, purports to give a balanced list of arguments for and against the bill but actually takes a strong position in favor. But these were the first shots in a volley of propaganda on both sides, although the arguments, by eighteenth-century standards, were quite reasonable, dealing, as they did, with complex and important constitutional issues. The fuss raised by the bill led Stanhope to withdraw it from Lords before it could get its third reading on 14 April, only to reintroduce it in the next session.

Four major issues (among lesser ones) were in dispute. (1) The bill ended the monarch's Prerogative to create peers. (2) Beyond the question of the use and abuse of the Royal Prerogative was the question of how the changes to Lords would affect the constitutional balance among the branches of government, particularly between Lords and Commons. (3) On the theory that power follows property, a further imbalance may be created by the redistribution of money and property in the two houses, exacerbated both by the limitation of the size of Lords and by the fact that Commoners could no longer be elevated to the peerage, except in rare cases. (4) A seriously contentious issue was whether the bill, by replacing an elected Scottish peerage with a hereditary one, violated the Union treaty and robbed Scottish peers of an assured right, or corrected a flaw in the treaty by basing both Scottish and English peers on heredity.

The bill recognized the bad feelings remaining from Queen Anne's creation of twelve occasional peers to assure the passage of the Treaty of Utrecht in the House of Lords. Proponents of the bill pointed out that it prevented the Crown and Ministry from stacking Lords with occasional peers in support of particular measures. The increase of Lords under Anne resulted in the terrible Treaty of Utrecht.[49] One could, Addison asserted, hardly claim that constitution is balanced since the King can control the size of Lords.[50] The bill does keep Lords from growing disproportionately (and at the expense of the spiritual peers, who would otherwise lose power as the number of other peers grew). But the King would still have the power to appoint approximately two new peers each year, based on the disappearance of ennobled families, thus allowing him to reward meritorious commoners.[51] And the King has waived his Royal Prerogative to create new Lords, so that the bill does not wrest a privilege from him.[52] But, said the opponents, the bill 'takes away from the King, the brightest Jewel of his Crown, which is the Distribution of Honours, and in effect of Offices too'.[53] The abuse of the Prerogative by creating occasional peers can be prevented by the threat of ministerial impeachment and by requiring a substantial gap of time between the appointment of a new Peer and his first vote.[54] The sudden addition of at least fifteen new peers is a greater stacking of Parliament than under Anne, made worse by the sudden closing of the Peerage. The Bill allows even minors to become peers – and why not women too, since they are more likely to be qualified than minors?[55] The bill prevents the Crown from acting as a referee between the two houses by increasing the number of peers in case of deadlock on vital matters.[56] Lords acts as an important shield and protector of the Crown.[57]

The issue of the Royal Prerogative led to the broader issue of the constitutional balance, and hence actual power, among Monarchy, Lords, and Commons. Proponents insisted that the bill assures a proper balance, and that the Constitution is now out-of-balance because of the King's power to change the membership of Lords. Addison, among others, pointed out that Lords had grown considerably since Elizabeth I.[58] The bill will improve the working of Commons because it will moderate the ambition of Members to become peers, and take their property with them. A smaller House of Lords will mean less property and influence for the body as a whole, and hence the government would not, as opponents contend, become an autocracy.[59] It is clearly in the interest of Commons to have Lords as little under the interest of the Crown as possible. The number is

> great enough to take off the Superfluity of Dignity and Power in that House; great enough to be a Bar against the most fatal Managements of bad Ministers, by the sole Influence of Posts and Profits; and yet not great enough to create any Danger to the Whole, in any other Respect, if it be stop'd at once effectually.[60]

The Patrician insists that opposition to the bill is opposition to the House of Lords in general.[61] But the opponents of the bill argue that the Constitution may be altered only for urgent reasons, and such a reason is not apparent in this case.[62] Indeed, the King's Prerogative is the only check on Lords, the only way Peers can be held accountable. Similarly Ministers could not otherwise be called to account.[63]

> If this Prerogative is taken away, the House of Lords will be a fixed independent Body, not to be called to an account like a Ministry, nor to be dissolved or changed like a House of Commons: The same Men will meet again with the same Resolutions, and probably be heighten'd by Disappointment, and nothing can stand before them.[64]

A smaller Lords gives more power to each peer and hence leads to greater power for factions. In any contest with Commons,

> the Lords would have the advantage of them; because an united constant Body of Men, always acting for the same Interest and Grandeur, and pursuing a continued

Scheme, must be an Over-match for so transitory a Body, and made up of persons of
such different Views and Interests as the House of Commons is.[65]

Since the bill so strongly favours Lords, Lords will never revoke it.[66] Future
reform would thus be impossible. The bill gives too much independence to
Lords, not only from Commons but from the King. 'The Crown is ever to Act
by his Ministers, but an unchangeable House of Peers might Act unaccountably
for themselves'.[67]

A further imbalance is, or is not, created by the redistribution of money and
property between the two houses. Fewer peers will, proponents argue, mean
less aristocratic influence in elections, and an ever-increasing Lords will mean
a concentration of property, and hence power, in one house, which the Bill will
prevent.[68] Opponents such as Steele insist that the limited, unchanging size of
Lords concentrates power and influence strongly in a few important families.
Vacancies will be filled by

the Creatures and Relations of those Peers who have at that time the greatest Influence
in the House, and whose Requests to the Throne will very much resemble Demands
… But another Consequence, of a much higher nature, attending the Limitation of
the Number of Peers, is the Danger there will be of changing the Constitution by this
means into an Aristocracy.[69]

The charge of aristocracy or oligarchy is a powerful and repeated theme of opposing propaganda.

If one line of argument went to the constitutional question of the relative
power of the two Houses, another asked whether the Peerage Bill, with its shift
from an elected to a hereditary peerage constituted a violation of the Union
treaty. Connected to this question was argument over whether that violation
implied the dissolution of the Union altogether. 'The terms of the Union cannot
be revok'd without disuniting the Kingdoms'.[70] Proponents point out that the
increase in Scottish Lords parallels the increase in English Lords, and the shift
from elected to hereditary Scottish Lords makes the manner of selection consistent for all Lords. Elections are simply inappropriate for a House of Peers.[71] The
change from elections to heredity relieves Lords of the indignity of begging for
votes at every election. It is a change in the Union that is clearly allowed by the
Union Treaty itself,[72] and if it is a violation of the Union, it is justified by the
greater good. The same power that made the Union can change it, and justice
to a few Scottish peers should not be allowed to outweigh the general public
good.[73] Opponents insist strongly and repeatedly that the Bill is a violation of
the Union treaty, which guaranteed to the Scottish peers, who relinquished
their place in a Scottish Parliament, an opportunity to be elected to serve in
the new British Parliament and a vote in deciding who should be elected. But
these sixteen representative, elected peers are now to be replaced by twenty-five

hereditary ones. What has happened since the Union to indicate that twenty-five is a more appropriate number of Scottish Peers than the original sixteen?[74] The new peers – political appointments whose issue will continue to serve for generations – will have no constituents and be responsible to no one, not even, as at present, to other peers. England should not violate 'the Rights of Nations for mere private Convenience'.[75]

The arguments for and against the Peerage Bill were accessible to various writers, and there is a great deal of duplication in substance and even language. Part of this may be due to the development of stables of writers associated with particular politicians and propagandists. J. A. Downie has shown the connection between politics and the press in the case of Robert Harley, and B. A. Goldgar has done so for and against Walpole.[76] P. B. J. Hyland argues convincingly that during 1713–4 a number of tracts and periodicals were written, perhaps with Steele's assistance, by friends of Steele and contributors to his work. Hyland cites an October 1713 letter to Walpole from Edward Smith, asserting that Steele housed and fed a 'training college' for some eight or ten students at his house in the York buildings.[77] It seems very likely that the same sort of stable of writers was at work here, either under Walpole directly or under Steele at Walpole's behest. Such a system would explain the duplication of argument at the same time as it complicates the question of attribution.

Similarly complicating was the use of multiple personae by the same author and the use of the same persona by multiple authors. The debate over the Peerage Bill includes writers who claim to be moderate but actually are not. It includes summaries of arguments on both sides. It includes letters to Members of Parliament and letters from Members of Parliament to other Members or to constituents. Letters and essays attributed to Scots express betrayal or welcome the changes. The *Plebeian* and *Old Whig* are answered not only by each other but by various other writers as well. Periodicals as well as pamphlets were active. The case of Richard Steele is instructive.

Plebeian, no. 1, the opposition's opening salvo, is allegedly written in response to dangerous rumours that a Peerage Bill would be brought forth. It then, as we have seen, became the target for both the *Old Whig* and the *Patrician*. The *Old Whig* sets out a series of points in numbered paragraphs and begins by seeming a carefully structured argument, moving from general points to specific examples in the bill. But as it becomes more specific, it becomes more disorganized and random. It is sarcastically rebuked in *Plebeian* no. 2, with, among other things, repetition and expansion of the scarcely veiled references to the homosexuality of the Spartans Steele made in *Plebeian* no. 1.[78] *Plebeian, no.* 3 appeared before the *Old Whig* appeared again. So it commented that slowness was a well-known quality of age and devoted the paper, very short, to a parody speech. The major arguments on both sides had been made in the first paper of each periodical, and the quality as well as civility of the debate declines in later numbers. *Old Whig*, no. 2, in general, is a combination of impatient bickering, name-calling, and quibbling about the details of passages. On the Spartans it comments that 'I am informed there are two or three keen disputants, who will return a proper answer to it, when they have discovered the Author'. It makes a reference to *The Spanish Friar* and 'Little Dicky'. Like the homosexual references, this one seems of studied ambiguity. It might not refer to Steele, but probably was meant to suggest Addisonian belittlement. The persona admits that age has not made him slow but testy.

Plebeian, no. 4, in response, suggests that age has also made the Old Whig forgetful, for he had promised a discussion of the Scottish problem but does not provide one. Steele therefore does, in the form of a letter written by Scottish nobleman who was not one among the elect but an outcast. The letter had appeared a week earlier in the *Honest Gentleman*, a weekly Whig journal, to which Steele was close.[79] Steele may well have written the letter, moving from Scottish sympathies to a Scottish persona, but it is also possible that he used a letter with which he was familiar to vary his tone, to push the Scottish arguments, to tease Addison, and to plug a Whig periodical that was, like his, engaged with the Peerage Bill. What is most unlikely is that the letter was written by a Scottish nobleman. Addison ended *Old Whig*, no. 2 with a partial but probably sincere compliment: *Plebeian* has made the best of a bad case, and 'a good one would shine in his hands'. *Plebeian*, no. 4, in return, concludes by hinting at the authorship of *Old Whig* and by quoting a ringing passage from Addison's *Cato* in defence of inherited rights. Addison died several months later (17 June 1719) without a final reconciliation with Steele.

On May 2, when the Parliamentary session ended, Steele produced *The Joint and Humble Address of the Tories and Whigs Concerning the Bill of Peerage*, a mock address to the King, congratulating him on having survived the session without passage of the Peerage Bill, expressing thanks and wonder at his willingness to relinquish his power to create Peers but contempt and hatred for those who persuaded him to do so, and warning him of the danger of an unchecked House of Lords: 'Let us not, Dread Sir, change certain Protection for possible Oppression. The Crown is ever to Act by his Ministers, but an unchangeable House of Peers might Act unaccountably for themselves'.[80] There are no known tracts by Steele on the peerage issue during the summer of 1719, when Parliament was away. Stanhope and Sunderland were in Hanover, where they concocted a scheme to solidify their power, essentially by making it impossible for anyone to vote them out of office. They intended to reintroduce the Peerage Bill in the next session, but to introduce as well a bill to rescind the Septennial Act which had just been passed in 1716. The change would return Parliament to the pre-revolution period when Parliamentary sessions were indefinite and thus could continue for many years (during which Stanhope and Sunderland expected to remain in office). (The next elections were scheduled to be held in 1722.) Newcastle persuaded them that such an evident play for power was likely to arouse a flood of concern that would sink the Peerage Bill as well, and they withheld it. Parliament met on 23 November, and two days later the Duke of Buckingham introduced the Peerage Bill in Lords.

Steele responded with *A Letter to the Earl of O—d, Concerning the Bill of Peerage*, which appeared on the morning of December 8, the date of the major and decisive debate on the bill in Commons. In addition to its apt timing, it represented perhaps the most audacious manipulation of persona and addressee. It was addressed to Oxford (Robert Harley), who had been released from the Tower and found innocent by Lords, largely because the two houses could not agree on the charges against him. It was Oxford who was most responsible for the Occasional Peers, the ministerial abuse that proponents claimed justified the Peerage Bill. But the same Oxford, now returned to his position in Lords, argued against the Peerage Bill, largely because it would prevent the monarch from rewarding merit. It was Oxford who had called Steele an incendiary, 'not capable of writing or acting any more than nature designed'.[81] Oxford, along with Nottingham, had spoken against the bill when it was first proposed in Lords. Anticipating language later repeated by Walpole, Oxford charged that 'it tended to take away the brightest gem from the crown' and 'would put it out of the power of the crown to reward merit and virtuous actions'.[82] Steele addresses Oxford as a fellow-opponent of the bill and writes in his own person, as one individual to another. He tries to retract some of the hostility he had expressed toward Oxford in 1714 and 1715, claiming that his harsh treatment of Oxford, except for the period after his own expulsion from Parliament, was undertaken reluctantly and out of patriotism. Both publicly and in private he consistently praised Oxford's capacities.

Steele takes up the usual arguments. Unelected peers will not represent the Peerage of Scotland, and withdrawing that power to elect representatives is a violation of the Union Treaty that in effect nullifies the treaty itself: 'The Terms of the Union cannot be revok'd without disuniting the Kingdoms'.[83] If the new peers were to include the sixteen Scots now elected, they would 'climb to Honour through Infamy'.[84] The Prerogative can do no harm if the Ministers act responsibly, but an unchecked House of Lords can do irreversible damage. The bill is an unworthy distraction from more important subjects: 'It is a melancholy Consideration, that under the Pressure of Debts, the Necessities of a War, the Perplexities of Trade, and the Calamities of the Poor, the Legislature should thus be taken up and employ'd in Schemes for the Advancement of the Power, Pride and Luxury of the Rich and Noble'.[85] In the afternoon the bill was debated in Commons. Craggs spoke first for the government, and Steele led the way in opposition, essentially repeating the arguments he had published that morning in his *Letter to Oxford*, and concluding that 'for my part, I am against committing of this bill, because I think it would be committing of sin'.[86] 'The run of the debate', J. R. Plumb notes, 'went with Steele rather than Craggs and by the time Walpole rose to spoke few could have any doubt as to the outcome of the debate'.[87] But Walpole's speech was particularly effective, both in its rhetoric and in its political tactics, and the bill was defeated by a vote of 177 in favour, 269 opposed.

The debate over the Peerage Bill was essentially not a debate about whether Britain would or would not be governed by an oligarchy but a debate about the size and composition of that oligarchy. As C. Jones argues, resistance to the bill derived from resentment of Scottish intrusion and fear of an expanded peerage. He agrees with the opposition Whig argument that the bill would concentrate power in fewer hands: 'If both the repeal of the Septennial Act and the Peerage Bill had succeeded they would undoubtedly have led to a more oligarchic form of government which would have grown stronger at the expense of the royal prerogative'.[88] Steele certainly did not expect a peerage himself as a result of his efforts, but whatever reward Steele might have gained from Walpole, the penalty he suffered from the government was severe. On 25 January 1720, the Lord Chamberlain's warrant suspended performances at Drury Lane. Two days later a new license, exclusive of Steele's patent, was issued to Cibber, Wilks, and Booth. Steele was effectually barred from Drury Lane.

Steele's interest in trade as a source of national and personal wealth, a major theme of the *Tatler* and *Spectator*, continued in his private life. In the winter of 1716–7, he worked with the mathematician William Gilmore, on plans for what he called a 'fish pool', a vessel particularly designed to carry fish in an internal tank of continually replenished water, so that the fish would arrive at the market alive and hence fresh. In January 1718 an old and unreliable friend, John Sansome emerged on the scene and began working on the project. He insisted on joining the partnership but Gilmore (fortunately) declined. The sequence was typical of Steele's naivete in matters that joined finance with friendship. Steele and his wife visited Sansome in an effort to resolve matters, but Sansome threatened violence to Lady Steele. Steele therefore withdrew, and Sansome took the fish-pool partnership to court, but without success.[89]

In March, before the Sansome affair had been resolved, Steele's application for a patent for the fish pool was granted by the attorney general. In June letters patent were granted to Steele for a fourteen-year period, and in August the first fish-pool ship was launched. In September the fish-pool made its first voyage; the total cost, over £1000, was borne by Steele. In November he and Gilmore published *An Account of the Fish Pool*, recounting 'the several Steps and Degrees by which it was brought to its present Perfection',[90] and describing the construction of the vessel. In May 1719 the vessel itself, with several passengers, sailed down the Thames, into the open water, and back with a tankful of fish. At the height of the interest in speculation spurred by the South Sea project, Steele tried (literally and figuratively) to float the fish-pool scheme as a joint stock company and sought to the advice and participation of John Law and Robert Knight, principal drivers of speculation in France and Britain.[91] Despite this early promise, the fish-pool project was not a success. Steele was hardly an effective manager and investor of funds, and the failure of the South-Sea Company had a general negative effect on the many financial schemes that had emerged. Steele sold his patent in the company to a Mr. Dale in the fall of 1720, and by 3 January 1721 a somewhat raucous and even comic meeting of shareholders was held at Steele's York-building rooms for the purpose of denouncing Dale as a fraud and deceit, and complaining that one ever got involved in the scheme. Nonetheless, in April four new vessals were launched at Rotherhithe. But by 1 November 1722 the last vessel was put to port and nothing more was heard of the fish pool. Fish apparently did not enjoy being transported in that way, and they injured or destroyed themselves in collisions with each other and with the sides of the tank, or otherwise they suffered from the roughness of the voyage. Moreover, other fisherman could bring fish to port with equal or better freshness and at lower cost.

Several days after the defeat of the Peerage Bill, while the fish-pool was still in a promising stage and Steele was negotiating unsuccessfully with Newcastle about Drury Lane, Steele published *The Spinster*, a tract supporting the woollen industry.[92] Makers of woollen garments competed with makers of calico, and both competed with foreign makers of silk. There was an issue of what subsidies or tariffs Parliament would give to whom and of what duties would be laid on imported cloth. But a basic concern was fashion and the question of what women would wear, and why. This is the issue to which Steele devotes most of his attention. His persona is a spinster writing on behalf of woollen manufacturers in their dispute with the calico manufacturers. But the real target is the wealthy English lady who dresses from top to toe, as a list of her articles of clothing suggests, in foreign clothes. 'According to this Rule, Foreigners sell this Lady to the Value of a thousand Pounds, where the English sell her to the Value of five'.[93] Steele enumerates the garments and accessories worn by a wealthy woman of fashion and calculates their substantial cost, compared to the cost of English wool. Steele's point is that women do not have to wait on Parliamentary action to support an important cottage industry and the women who make it up. The body-painting Picts Steele described in *Spectator*, no. 41 would fly from these calico-Picts 'as putting themselves in Masquerade only to reduce themselves to their primitive poverty and Nakedness'.[94] Steele raises the relative danger of calico and foreign silk to the English spinsters of wool.

These other clothes, especially calico, were not slow to respond. *The Linen Spinster, in Defence of the Linen Manufactures* comprises a letter written by Jenny

Distaff to her half-sister (Isaac Bickerstaff is apparently their half-brother) point-ing out that most modern ladies are mostly dressed in English garments, rather than the French ones detailed by Steele, that even foreign accessories are imported by English traders, that printed calicoes will maintain the balance of trade on our side, and that the English poor are employed not only in spinning and weaving but also in printing foreign calicoes. Women should not be mistreated for wear-ing calicoes, as apparently happened recently in London. *Tatler* and Bickerstaff references recur throughout. But Steele was supported by *The Female Manufac-turers' Complaint*, addressed to Lady Rebecca Woolpack by a group of women who work in the woollen business. They, and others less fortunate in the profes-sion, have been able to feed their families, but now women have stopped buying wool and wool mixes, so that the shopkeepers have no more work for them to do. Lady Rebecca should consider that her preference for French clothes 'tends to the entire Destruction of the Manufactures of your Country', turning beggars out into the streets and ruining honest traders.[95] Wool should be brought back into fashion. The added 'Epistle to Steele' lists a number of items he has left out of his list of fashionable dress. Despite these pamphlets parliamentary efforts to do something for the wool business were not, in the end, successful.[96]

Steele's most important political involvement in economic matters concerned the South-Sea Bill of 1719–20, the subsequent collapse of the South-Sea Com-pany in September 1720, and Walpole's rescue plan of the following winter. The War of Spanish Succession had been financed in part by bonds, most of which took the form of ninety-nine-year annuities. These had been issued at interest rates that in 1719 looked high. Moreover, since the annuities ran, virtually, for the rest of the century, the government, desperate for resources already, would be squeezed for millions of pounds, unless the debt could be financed at a lower rate, which was precisely (if complexly) what the South-Sea Company sought to do. The Company was founded in 1711 on the model of the East-India Company, to which it was a self-conscious rival, for the purpose of trading with Spanish America. The problem of the company as it first began was that it did not have free trading access to the West Indies, unlike Law's Mississippi company, where the nation actually owned the trading partner. The situation grew still worse in 1718, when war with Spain brought the Spanish–American trade to a halt.

> With its trade at full stop for all to see, the Company became, from sheer necessity, a naked finance corporation; with its wisest heads removed, it was completely exposed to the financial manipulators who had played so large a part in its management from the first; its fortunes were linked, formally and informally, with those of the régime and the government.[97]

To stay alive, the company, inspired by the success of John Law's Mississippi Company in France, offered to take over the national debt at a lower interest rate than the government was then paying. In order to win support, the company distributed large quantities of paper stock as bribes to courtiers, Members of Parliament, and other influential people. The fact that the Bank of England, fearful of losing altogether, bid against the South-Sea Company to take over the debt further seemed to legitimate the Company. Moreover, the Mississippi Company was not only an inspiration, it was a rival. Both the South-Sea Company and the Bank of England tried to stem the flow of capital across the Pas de Calais. At the beginning of 1720 the market value of South-Sea Stock was £130; by April, when the South-Sea Bill passed, it was over £300; by the end of June it was over £1000. The spring and summer of 1720 were seasons of mad stock-jobbing and formed the context for Steele's Fish-Pool Company. But Steele's was only one of nearly two-hundred joint-stock companies that bubbled up during that period.[98] Its demise paralleled that of the South-Sea Company.

Earlier, on 1 February 1720, Steele had published *The Crisis of Property*, which argued, against the South-Sea arguments of Archibald Hutcheson that the original and now costly annuities should be refinanced at a lower rate, that such a proposal is unethical. Steele cuts through the welter of figures and arguments to claim that the annuitants loaned to the government, at considerable risk, for a specific period, at an agreed-upon rate. The government cannot properly now shift the loan to a private company at a lower rate. It cannot ethically put pressure on the annuitants to agree to a scheme so clearly against their own interests. At the root of Steele's concern is the credit of the government. If the government can, after the fact, change the conditions of a loan, on what grounds is the government trustworthy? South-Sea proponents argued that the annuitants were City people who had taken advantage of the government's need (and its consequent willingness to pay) to lock in interest rates that now were impoverishing the country, and hence were milking its landed taxpayers for their own advantage. But Steele would have none of this:

> These Men are not Usurers, are not Extortioners, they are good Citizens, they are Patriots, they lent their Country Money, because they lov'd their Country; they stept out of the Ranks as the *Forlorn Hope of Property*, in Defence of the Land of *England* and its Owners, which Owners had been safe and secure in their Possessions, whatever had befallen these generous Insurers, whose Fortunes fought for 'em.[99]

Steele's tract was answered by *The Crisis of Honesty*, which takes an unfortunately typical position of personal insult and unabashed outrage:

> I will not say how worthy you render your self upon other Occasions of your Place among them; but I can think it no Addition to your Merit, when the Great Council of a Nation are Deliberating upon a Point, whereon the Freedom and Welfare of the Nation absolutely depends; that you should at such a Time, as far as you have any Credit, irritate the People against their Proceedings, by Libelling particular M—ers,

and both by Speaking and Writing, inflame the People against their Representatives, for the greatest Piece of Publick Service that any P—t ever undertook.[100]

The annuitants, he goes on, can hardly complain at getting double their money. The response moves on to global personal assault on Steele, whose work depended on the unacknowledged contributions of Addison and who rejoiced at his death, who attacked John Dennis for his own fault (bad debts), and who was unworthy of late Lady Steele, the best of women:

> She is now no more to pine at your Behaviour; you may now run riot as much as you please, you having nothing now to put you in mind of that Care which every honest Man owes his Family. Your Children are too young to know that you squander away your Substance that should be employ'd for their Support and Education.[101]

Steele's rude antagonist is in turn answered by *Scandal no Argument*. The persona is an Oxford student whose father has put all of his fortune in South-Sea annuities, making the student in some sense a ward of the state. He thanks Steele on behalf of the other annuitants. The attacks on Steele in *The Crisis of Honesty* only make him look better, and the attacks on other annuitants are unwarranted. The issue is one of trust – here trust in the nation's honour: 'Violation of publick Faith, in any the least Degree, tends not to Publick Good, but common Destruction'.[102] Steele was also answered by Sir John Meres, who claimed that Steele had miscalculated, that the annuitants are not at risk, that their funds would not be changed, and that, since the nation's largest debts are in annuities, the nation must be allowed to pay these debts advantageously.[103]

Steele continued to pursue the inequities of the South-Sea scheme in *The Nation a Family*, published on 26 February 1720. Steele's major purpose was to propose that the debt could be more fairly and effectively relieved by a tontine scheme in which shares would be sold to 40,000 people in 4,000 groups of ten each. When one member of the group died, his share would be distributed to the survivors, until no one survives and the remainder is given to the state. The scheme is not wildly irrational but, in the context of the politics of the time, particularly the overwhelming, bribe-driven power of the South-Sea Company, and the plethora of other such suggestions, wildly impractical. But what makes *The Nation a Family* a considerable, even moving contribution to South-Sea propaganda is its general view of the responsibilities of government in financial matters, especially in protecting the interests of annuitants: 'The Legislature has absolutely sold to them those Estates for those Terms; and the Parliament has nothing further to do in this Case, but to protect the Owners, and pay them punctually and honestly'.[104] That responsibility is set in the context of a sharp and accurate understanding of the South-Sea Company and the manipulations of its managers:

> True Policy requires that the Government should be rich, the People in moderate, safe, and comfortable Circumstances: This is far from being our Condition; for the Publick is loaded with Debts, and the generality of the People extremely necessitious, while private Persons, to the Disadvantage of the whole Community, are immoderately Rich, and every Day growing richer by artificial Rumours, whereby self-interested Men affect the publick Funds, and act upon the Hopes and Fears of the People, for their own Gain, tho' to the apparent Hazard of their Country.[105]

Steele's notion of responsible capitalism was, unfortunately, a minority opinion at the time (although soon after shared by John Trenchard and Thomas Gordon, *Cato's Letters*).[106] On 18 February Sir John Vanbrugh wrote to Jacob Tonson reporting the wide enthusiasm for the South-Sea Company and South-Sea Stocks, but he added that

> Sr. R. Steele is grown such a Malcontent that he now takes the Ministry directly for his mark; and treats them (in the House) for some days past in so very frank a manner that they grow quite angry, and 'tis talk'd as if it wou'd not be impossible to see him very soon expelled the House.[107]

Vanbrugh cites in particular Steele's dispute with Newcastle over Drury Lane.

Steele continued his attacks on the South-Sea Company in the pages of *The Theatre*, at the same time as he was pursuing his grievance with Lord-Chancellor Newcastle over his patent at Drury Lane. His first *Theatre* paper on the South-Sea Company (*Theatre*, no. 17) appeared on 27 February, the day after *The Nation a Family*, and argued that the bad credit of the South-Sea Company would infect the government as a whole and that the lowering of interest in South-Sea stocks would lower the circulation of money and hence the wealth of the country. More importantly, he argued in no. 20, the returns thus far paid by the South-Sea Company (not to speak of the bribes, which he does in no. 22) have come from later investors; there is no basis in trade for the income of the company. National participation in the stock, which is now extremely overvalued, is an economic and national danger. In the next number (12 March) he combined his attack on the economic situation with his concern for the theatre, observing that 'as Lust is made the reigning Impulse of the Town, Avarice is the one and entire Passion of the City'. No. 23 emphasizes the inherent injustice of a plan by which the few get rich at the expense of the many, and no. 24 emphasizes the dangers and difficulties of stock-jobbing by illustrative tables. Similar themes are repeated in nos 25 and 27. Almost all of this argument took place before the South-Sea Bill passed the House of Commons at the end of March. On the third reading of the bill, only fifty-five MPs voted against it. The bill was signed by the King on 7 April.[108]

Despite his personal financial mismanagement, Steele's had been the voice of reason and common sense. When he left for Scotland on forfeited-estates business on 1 August 1720, stocks had begun a severe drop.[109] When he returned in November, stocks had collapsed, and he was faced with the task of moderating the anger of Parliament. Although Steele had warned against the company early, often, and cogently, he ultimately sought to divert revenge from the leaders of the company, echoing the pattern he had followed in the case of the recusant Scottish lords. But at the outset he spoke quite sharply on the magnitude of what had happened and on the need to discover what had gone wrong.

> The first who spoke on the side of the question was my quondam colleague (sir Richard Steele) he indeed set the matter in a clear light, by telling us, that a nation of more wealth and greater credit than any in Europe, within less than two years, was reduced to what we see, and too sensibly feel, by a few cyphering cits, a species of men of equal capacity in all respects (that of cheating a deluded people only excepted) with those animals who saved the capitol, who were now to be screened by those of greater figure, for what reason they best know, others were at liberty to judge.[110]

On 21 December, Walpole announced his plan to convert half of the paper capital of the South-Sea Company into equal portions of capital of the Bank of England and the East-India Company.[111] The worst of the crisis had essentially been laid to rest, and nothing was left but the recriminations. These were swift in coming. The Bubble and its collapse came at a seismic shift in British political history. In January 1720 Robert Knight, the cashier of the Company, was scheduled to be examined in the House, but he managed to slip out of London and flee to France. In early February Craggs and Stanhope both died, Stanhope of a stroke, Craggs, the most able and likeable of the Stanhope–Sunderland group, at the age of thirty-five, of smallpox. Sunderland was under investigation by a secret committee, whose report, read to the House on 16 February, outlined in dramatic detail the breadth and depth of the Company's bribery. John Carswell described it as 'an appalling and disheartening document, unique in British parliamentary history'.[112] John Aislabie, Chancellor of the Exchequer, was expelled from the House and sent to the Tower (9 March 1720). Nonetheless Steele spoke on his behalf.[113] Further expulsions followed, and, on the day before his examination, James Craggs Senior, the Postmaster, committed suicide. But two days earlier (15 March) Sunderland had, thanks to the exertions of Walpole, managed to escape condemnation, despite the damning evidence against him. One of the factors in his escape was that Robert Knight was not in the country to confirm that evidence. Steele again spoke on behalf of the condemned man, the Secretary of State to whom he had reported when Gazetteer, over twenty years earlier.[114] Knight himself had been rearrested in Brabant, where local regulations and the lack of specific charges against him kept him from being sent back to England. Many in England were quite happy to have him remain there. During the debates about Knight, Steele argued that he should not be forced back in order to testify against himself.[115] Walpole had solidified his status and begun his rise as Britain's first prime minister. Steele's reward for his help and perspicacity was that his position as manager at Drury Lane was restored.

Steele continued to play an active, if occasional role in Parliament. On 2 June 1721 he spoke on behalf of Sir Theodore Janssen, another South-Sea director. In March 1722 he travelled to Wendover, Buckinghamshire, to canvas voters successfully, but in April the Earl of Sunderland, his patron and supporter in the election, died. The summer and fall were plagued by fears of a Jacobite invasion, but Steele was busy in Scotland during September and preparing *The Conscious Lovers* thereafter. The play opened on 7 November. During 1722–3 Steele served on a parliamentary committee, chaired by Walpole, to compose an address to the King condemning the Jacobite conspiracy, the subject of his final political writing, the *Pasquin* papers of July 1723. But his health was poor, and he began to plan for his retirement, which took place during the summer of 1724. Although he never attended after 1724, he remained an M. P. until his death.

Between 1715 and 1724 Steele had achieved the position he envisioned for himself when he began his political writing during the *Tatler* and *Spectator* years. He was both a Member of Parliament and an author, and he used his position as an author to publicize his views on issues that he thought were important. Britain was a trading nation, and he wrote about trade. Britain was a nation of entrepreneurs, and he was an entrepreneur as well. Partly because of his own nature and partly because the Whigs were now a powerful but divided party, supported by the King, rather than a weak and unpopular one, Steele could take a relatively independent position on issues he cared about. He strongly condemned the causes he saw as dangerous, whether the threat of Jacobitism or the chicanery of stock-jobbers, but he resisted the urge to revenge once the evil had been brought to light. He was magnet for counterattacks, and his personal life made such attacks effective. But he persevered even when he had few allies. The pattern of his best thought was to disregard details and focus on the large issues–the political power of clemency, the constitutional powers of Lords and Commons, the responsibility of national finance to protect its contracts and to act on behalf of the people. Given his independence he was an unpredictable ally, but once he had engaged with an issue, a very useful one.

Richard Steele, Welshman

In the autumn of 1721 Steele worked in Edinburgh with the other Scottish Commissioners for forfeited estates. When he returned in mid-November, he discovered that Thomas Tickell had published Addison's works without his play *The Drummer* and without crediting the acknowledgement that Steele had given for Addison's work. His response was to publish *The Drummer* and to preface it with a letter addressed to William Congreve, a friend of both Steele and Addison, in which he explained the circumstances surrounding the first performance and original publication of *The Drummer*, denied Tickell's implication that he had sought to take credit for works that were Addison's, and pointed out the he had taken the blame for papers whose authorship Addison had wanted concealed. He was clearly offended by Tickell and insisted that the impression Tickell gave of Steele's friendship for Addison was false. He deferred giving an account of Addison's true character 'till I can speak of that amiable Gentleman on an occasion void of Controversy'.[116]

In the early summer of 1722, amid fears of Jacobite invasion, Steele went to Wales on his way the Edinburgh to work on the Commission, and he almost certainly took *The Conscious Lovers* with him. The Jacobite fears intensified in the fall, but the production of Steele's play in November was a great success, although its notion of sentimental comedy was controversial. In the winter of 1722–3, Steele served on a committee, chaired by Walpole, to compose an address to the King condemning the Jacobite conspiracy. He wrote his two *Pasquin* papers on the Jacobites in the summer of 1723. His health was declining: he was no longer conducting significant business with Drury Lane, and Parliament, of course, did not meet in the summer. The *London Journal* of 14 September reported that he was at work on a new play,[117] and he went to Bath in September for his health. Eugene Steele, his only surviving son, died on 20 November. His finances were in their usual tangle. On 30 November *The Weekly Journal* reported that Steele himself was very ill.[118] When he got back to London in better health several months later, he resolved that he was going to retire and devised a plan to clear his estate so that he could leave it debt-free to his two remaining daughters.

He drew up a careful schedule of his debts and his annual income from Drury Lane, which he hoped might be increased in one or both of two ways. He hoped the Drury Lane managers would return to him the money they had siphoned off from his percentage of the income. He also hoped that he would write another play, probably 'The School of Action', which would generate substantial income in light of his success with *The Conscious Lovers*. As it turned out, neither of these projects succeeded. A suit was filed on Steele's behalf for repayment of the money that the actor-managers withheld, but after languishing in courts for several years, it lost. But the plan that Steele developed ultimately worked well. Steele had developed his own sinking fund in which a certain percentage of his income, managed by David Scurlock, his trustee, was dedicated to paying off specific debts over a period of years. Steele, the actor-managers, Steele's creditors, and Scurlock signed an 'indenture quadripartite' on 3 June 1724. At some point that summer, Steele moved to Wales, where he had inherited several properties from his wife, and took up residence in Ty-Gwynn, his farm in Llangunnor, near Carmarthen.[119] There he lived as a semi-invalid until his death on 1 September

1729 at the age of 58. The cause of his death is unknown. He was persistently plagued by the gout, and he may have suffered a stroke while he lived in Wales.[120] His daughter Mary, like Eugene, was sickly and died in April 1730. His daughter Elizabeth was handsome and reputed to be very rich (thus testifying to the success of his sinking fund). She married John Trevor, a Welsh judge, later to become Lord Trevor, on 30 May 1732.

If, during his years in Wales, Steele looked back on his accomplishments, his development of the periodical essay, the success of the *Tatler* and *Spectator*, and the popularity of three of his plays would have stood out. But much of his life and work was devoted to politics, both as a writer and as an M. P. The accession of William and Mary took place when he was in his final year at Charterhouse, and the debates that framed the Bill of Rights and the Toleration Act framed his political orientation as well. William III was Steele's first major cultural hero, celebrated in *The Christian Hero* and elsewhere, and influencing both Steele's specifically political tracts and the often indirect politics of the *Tatler* and *Spectator*. Steele shared a broad view of the advantages of mixed government, which he saw as a uniquely British phenomenon. The key question was the function of the ministers of state. They were, of course, appointed by the crown, but they reported to Parliament on legislative matters and, in Steele's view, were accountable to it for executive matters as well. The exemplary issue here was responsibility for the Treaty of Utrecht. His support for the Septennial Bill and his opposition to the Peerage Bill both stemmed from his concern for the power of the House of Commons as the representative body of the nation. He applied his revolution principles to issues as they emerged, both because he genuinely shared these principles and because he saw them as important talking points in the political debates that took place over specific matters.

Economics was a matter of primary concern to Steele, and also the most complex and conflicted area of his personal life. Colley Cibber clearly measured the distance between Steele's principles and his practice: 'Sir *Richard*, though no Man alive can write better of Oeconomy than himself, yet, perhaps, he is above the Drudgery of practicising it'.[121] Economy meant two things to Steele: the personal and family discipline in financial matters he writes about in the *Tatler* and *Spectator* and the public policy that promoted the circulation of wealth and assured the financial stability of the nation. The two overlap in the figure of the trader whose acquisitive energies are held in check by his concern for the welfare of the country. Hence Steele, in defending those who, during the War of Spanish Succession, invested in government funds, insisted that their motive was public good rather than private profit. Steele saw investment in the family as analogous to investment in trade, with money spent on education returning to the father who spent it. The growth of the family over generations stands in contrast to the static nature of property. But family discipline and financial policy split in cases of excessive greed or where the head of the family allows himself to be buried in a pile of debt – precisely the case of Steele himself. Because Steele was a public figure whose financial irresponsibility was all too well-known, his authority as a teacher and advisor on money and trade was severely undercut.

Steele saw himself as a defender of the faith and supporter of the Church, but for the most part his moral dicta are based on observed experience and historical tradition rather than on scripture. Jenny Distaff, looking into her brother Isaac Bickerstaff's notes observes that 'my Brother deduces all the Revolutions among Men from the Passion of Love' (*Tatler*, no. 10), and Steele's periodical *The Lover* manages, with some stretching to connect a number of topics to love and lovers. But love is only one manifestation of the broad public nature of Steele's moral advice. He needed to reach a general public, and hence his large topics, like love, family values, and attacks on artificiality or social pretension, tended to engage the universal subjective. The universal subjective is reached as well by the emotional force of Steele's anecdotes and stories. All of this operates to create an alternative base for moral behaviour to that of religious faith, although the fact that the conclusions reached are those of faith as well allowed Steele to reassert that he is its defender.

Steele seems to have been a latitudinarian. He looked with suspicion on the Church's authority over political matters. In *Englishman*, Series 1, no. 12 a clerical correspondent, probably a persona of Steele himself, writes with particular clarity about the function of the clergy and the place of the Church in the public sphere:

> where the Declaration of a Deliverer is proclaimed in the Reformed Churches, Singleness of Heart, Simplicity of Manners, Improvement of liberal Science, with all the Charities attending Marriage, Society, and Brotherly Love, are the common Enjoyments of those devoted to Heaven, and those in the Business of the World.

The most prominent manifestation of latitudinarian sentiments was the Bangorian crisis, in which Benjamin Hoadly, Bishop of Bangor, preached a sermon before the King (31 March 1717) on 'The Nature of the Kingdom or Church of Christ', arguing that Christ's comment that his Kingdom is not of this world really means that there is no scriptural authority for the secular and political power of the Church and that the ultimate religious authority is the informed individual conscience. When the sermon was published, there was, of course, a great uproar. There is no evidence that Steele took part in it, although Hoadly was a personal friend and a political ally of long standing. Steele commented on the sermon in a letter to his wife: 'Mr. Hoadly the Bishop of Bangor, has in the sermon for which He is so ill treated, done like an Apostle and asserted the True Dominion established by Our Blessed Saviour'.[122] Steele's liberal religious sentiments paralleled his liberal political ones.

These sentiments were rooted in his character. Although antagonists were happy to demonstrate that his public statements were inconsistent with his private life, in some senses even Steele's personal failures were rooted in what might be called his essentially Whig character. His difficulty in holding on to his money was due in part to his generosity as well as his lack of scepticism. His open and good-hearted character made him an easy target. But, at the same time, he always seemed to find a patron willing to rescue him or a friend willing to give him a loan. His good nature, his concern for others and his gregariousness were well-known, as were his drunkenness and his carelessness. Despite this element of rather messy integrity, there also appeared to be a degree of duplicity in Steele. He attacked the Jacobite rebels, but he urged clemency when they came to trial at the House of Lords. He was a man of piety, a supporter of religion as it impacted ordinary life; but he was an opponent of the High-Church efforts to make the state serve the interests of the Church. During the months leading up to his expulsion from Parliament, he was a fierce enemy of Robert Harley, but his friend before and even after Harley's term in office. He condemned the whole idea of the South-Sea Company but remained a friend of Robert Knight, its Cashier, even after he had fled the country in disgrace. His close companionship with Joseph Addison did not prevent their growing distance from each other and their final debate, unnecessarily bitter, before Addison's death. Steele was a complex, careless, and even uncertain man capable of looking with sympathy on both sides of a question.

He developed the periodical essay at a time of war and dynastic dispute, when, above all, people needed to be reassured about the sense of a national community of which they were members. Having established the basic pattern of speaking in an intimate way with readers about the community to which they belong, Steele could characterize that community to fit his Whig political programme. His specific political arguments – about the demolition of Dunkirk, for example, or the South Sea Company – seem most effective when he draws them out to engage moral and constitutional principles broadly shared by reasonable people on both sides. In doing so, he often looks at and projects the emotional force of the situation, particularly as it impacts on individuals, creating what might be called a politics of sentiment. Beyond the particular set of issues and values that he communicates, he communicates a sense of national coherence. Over the years the values that made up that national sense came, in many cases, to seem commonplace, but in the context of the political divisions between 1708 and 1722 they were often both controversial and uncertain.

Steele is notable both for the indirect propaganda he developed with Addison and for the open partisanship of his own periodicals. He wrote extensively about responsible economics but was famously irresponsible in his own economic affairs. He was a moral writer because, as he admitted, he was not a moral man. He was a strong opponent of dueling who almost killed an adversary in a duel. He was a cheerful and gregarious man who nonetheless suffered from gout and from the death of his wife and several children. A self-proclaimed Englishman, he was born in Ireland and died in Wales. He was not an original political thinker, but he was *un homme engagé* who thought and wrote about a very wide range of issues from a perspective that was liberal and humane, promoting shared government and religious toleration. He wrote prose that was sometimes careless (and Swift's jokes about his solecisms were not entirely off the mark), but his essays often exuded good humour, and reached at times to telling irony or moving pathos. He understood that to be an effective political writer one needed to ground one's political concerns in larger cultural positions and one needed to reach, through indignation or through sympathy, to the hearts of one's readers.

NOTES

Eighteenth-century dates in this book are Old Style, except that 1 January rather than 25 March is regarded as the beginning of the year. References to the text of the *Tatler*, the *Spectator*, the *Guardian*, and the *Englishman* use the issue number; references to the annotations or other editorial material use the page numbers.

Introduction

1. G. Aitken, *The Life of Richard Steele*, 2 vols (London: Isbister, 1889).
2. C. Winton, *Captain Steele* (Baltimore, MD: Johns Hopkins Press, 1964); *Sir Richard Steele, M. P.* (Baltimore, MD: Johns Hopkins Press, 1970).

1 Preparing for Politics

1. *Englishman*, 1st series, ed. R. Blanchard (Oxford: Clarendon Press, 1955), no. 1.
2. *Englishman*, No. 46 (January 19, 1714).
3. Winton, *Sir Richard Steele*, p. 177.
4. I am indebted to Winton, *Captain Steele* for the details regarding Steele's background and early years. Winton corrects details and fills gaps in Aitken, *The Life of Richard Steele*.
5. Richard Steele's petition, which mentions 'Divers losses' as well as 'much sicknesse' and 'a great Charge of Children' is reprinted by Aitken, *The Life of Richard Steele*, vol. 1, p. 15–16.
6. R. Steele, *The Tatler*, ed. D. F. Bond, 3 vols (Oxford: Clarendon Press, 1987), vol. 2, p. 484. All subsequent quotations from the *Tatler* use Bond's edition.
7. *Correspondence of Richard Steele*, ed. R. Blanchard, 2nd edn (Oxford: Clarendon Press, 1968), p. 287.
8. Ibid., pp. 394–5.
9. Ibid., pp. 3–4.
10. For Steele's exertions in drinking Addison 'up to the conversational pitch', see *Correspondence of Richard Steele*, p. 118.
11. 'Thomas Burnet', in *ODNB*.
12. *Correspondence of Richard Steele*, pp. 106–8, 528–9.
13. Ibid., p. 514.
14. See A. Quick, *Charterhouse: A History of the School* (London: James and James, 1990), p. 25.
15. Winton, *Captain Steele*, pp. 39–40.

16. J. Hoppit, *A Land of Liberty? England 1689–1727* (Oxford and New York: Oxford University Press, 2000), p. 195.
17. *Tracts and Pamphlets by Richard Steele*, ed. R. Blanchard (Baltimore, MD: Johns Hopkins Press, 1944), p. 9.
18. *Englishman*, no. 34.
19. *Biographia Britannica*, cited in Winton, *Captain Steele*, p. 38.
20. E. G. W. Bill, *Education at Christ Church College, Oxford 1660–1800* (Oxford: Clarendon Press, 1988), p. 152.
21. R. Steele, *The Theatre*, ed. J. Loftis (Oxford: Clarendon Press, 1962), No. 11.
22. C. Rose, *England in the 1690s: Revolution, Religion, and War* (Oxford: Blackwell, 1999), pp. 137–42.
23. Quoted in the *ODNB* entry for Cutts; Swift's more vicious description of Cutts is his poem 'The Description of a Salamander', in J. Swift, *Complete Poems*, ed. P. Rogers (London: Penguin, 1983), pp. 89–91.
24. Quoted in *ODNB* entry for Cutts.
25. P. Smithers, *The Life of Joseph Addison*, 2nd edn (Oxford: Clarendon Press, 1968), pp. 86–7, 88.
26. For Steele's early relations to Manley, see R. Carnell, *A Political Biography of Delarivier Manley* (London: Pickering and Chatto, 2008), pp. 120–5.
27. D. Manley, *The New Atalantis (1709)*, in *The Selected Works of Delarivier Manley*, ed. R. Carnell (London: Pickering and Chatto, 2005), vol. 2, pp. 116–19.
28. T. Hearne, *Remarks and Collections of Thomas Hearne*, ed. D. A. Rannie, Oxford Historical Society Publications, 34, 11 vols (Oxford: Oxford Historical Society, 1897) vol. 4, p. 325.
29. J. Boswell, *Life of Samuel Johnson LL.D*, ed. G. B. Hill, rev. L. F. Powell, 6 vols (Oxford: Clarendon Press, 1934) vol. 2, p. 449.
30. *Correspondence of Richard Steele*, pp. 9–10.
31. *The Occasional Verse of Richard Steele*, ed. R. Blanchard (Oxford: Clarendon Press, 1952), p. 74.
32. G. D. Lord (ed.), *Poems on Affairs of State: Augustan Satirical Verse, 1660–1714* (New Haven, CT and London: Yale University Press, 1975), p. 601.
33. Quoted in *Occasional Verse of Richard Steele*, p. 76.
34. *Occasional Verse of Richard Steele*, p. 13.
35. Steele, *Tracts and Pamphlets*, pp. 338–9.
36. Manley, *New Atalantis*, p. 116.
37. Steele, *Tracts and Pamphlets*, p. 34.
38. R. Steele, 'The Christian Hero', in Steele, *Tracts and Pamphlets*, p. 49.
39. Steele, *Tracts and Pamphlets*, p. 52.
40. Ibid., pp. 59–60.
41. *The Plays of Richard Steele*, ed. S. S. Kenny (Oxford: Clarendon Press, 1971), p. 4.
42. Ibid., p. 6.
43. D. B. Erskine, *The Companion to the Playhouse*, 2 vols (London, 1764), vol. 1 (unpaginated; dictionary entry under 'Funeral'); C. Dibdin, *A Complete History of the Stage*, 5 vols (London, 1797), vol. 4. pp. 305–10.
44. R. A. Aubin, 'Beyond Steele's Satire on Undertakers', *PMLA*, 64:5 (December 1949), pp. 1008–26.
45. *Correspondence of Richard Steele*, p. 12.

46. Aitken prints the arguments on both sides in the appendix to his Mermaid edition of Steele's plays, *Richard Steele* (1894; New York: Greenwood, 1968), pp. 409–23.

47. *Correspondence of Richard Steele*, p. 14.

48. Winton, *Captain Steele*, pp. 68–9.

49. *The Plays of Richard Steele*, p. 103.

50. Ibid., p. 392.

51. Ibid., p. 115.

52. Cited in R. J. Allen, *The Clubs of Augustan London*, Harvard Studies in English, vol. 7 (Cambridge: Harvard University Press, 1933), p. 43.

53. A readable account of Marlborough's 1704 campaign is D. G. Chandler, *Blenheim Preparation: The English Army on the March to the Danube. Collected Essays* (Staplehurst: Spellmont, 2004); see also G. M. Trevelyan, *England under Queen Anne*, 3. vols (London: Longmans, Green, 1930), vol. 1, pp. 341–401.

54. W. S. Churchill, *Marlborough: His Life and Times*, 6 vols (New York: Charles Scribner's Sons, 1933–8), vol. 4. p. 59.

55. All accounts of the commissioning of *The Campaign*, including Thackeray's in *Henry Esmond*, derive from E. Budgell, *Memoirs of the Life and Character of the Late Earl of Orrery and the Family of the Boyles* (London: W. Mears, 1731), pp. 150–3.

56. *Occasional Verse of Richard Steele*, pp. 14–15.

57. 'The Campaign', ll. 291–2, in *The Miscellaneous Works of Joseph Addison*, ed. A. C. Guthkelch (London: G. Bell, 1914), vol 1, p. 165.

58. S. S. Kenny, 'Two Scenes by Addison in Steele's *The Tender Husband', Studies in Bibliography* 19 (1966), pp. 217–26, suggests on the basis of speech prefaces and unfamiliarity with other details in the play, that Addison wrote the first scenes of Acts III and V.

59. *The Plays of Richard Steele*, pp. 198–9.

60. *Correspondence of Richard Steele*, p. 201; see also Rae Blanchard, 'Richard Steele's West Indian Plantation', *Modern Philology*, 39 (1942), pp. 281–5.

61. F. Rau, 'Steeles Eintritt in den Kit-Cat Club', *Germanisch-romanishe Monatsschrift*, 37 [n.s. 6] (1956), pp. 396–8.

62. *Correspondence of Richard Steele*, p. 201.

63. Kneller's portrait of Lady Steele is reproduced in Aitken, *The Life of Richard Steele*, vol. 2, frontispiece, and in *Correspondence of Richard Steele*, facing p. 310.

2 Creating Whig Culture: the Gazette and the Tatler

1. J. A. Downie, *Robert Harley and the Press: Propaganda and Public Opinion in the Age of Swift and Defoe* (Cambridge: Cambridge University Press, 1979), pp. 103–30; H. L. Snyder, 'Arthur Maynwaring and the Whig Press, 1710–1712', *Literatur als Kritik des Lebens. Festschrift zum 65. Geburtstag von Ludwig Borinski*, ed. R. Haas, H-J. Müllenbrock and C. Uhlig (Heidelberg: Quelle und Mayer, 1975), pp. 120–36.

2. J. O. Richards, *Party Propaganda Under Queen Anne: The General Elections of 1702–1713* (Athens, GA: University of Georgia Press, 1973), p. 54; also W.A. Speck, *Tory and Whig: The Struggle in the Constituencies 1701–1715* (London: Macmillan; New York: St. Martin's, 1970), pages 98–109.

3. The connection of the Scottish raid with the Tories was insistently asserted in *Advice to the Electors of Great Britain: Occasioned by the intended Invasion from France* (London, 1708), usually attributed to Arthur Maynwaring.

4. E. D. Leyburn, 'Swift's View of the Dutch', *PMLA*, 66 (1951), pp. 734–45.

5. 'I lay it down for a Maxim, That no reasonable Person, whether *Whig* or *Tory*, (since it is necessary to use those foolish Terms) can be of Opinion for continuing the War upon the Foot it now is, unless he be a Gainer by it, or hopes it may occasion some new Turn of Affairs at home, to the advantage of his party.' J. Swift, *The Conduct of the Allies*, 'Preface', in *Prose Works*, ed. H. Davis (Princeton, NJ: Princeton University Press, 1951), p. 5.

6. Quoted in Hoppit, *A Land of Liberty?*, p. 233.

7. R. H. Dammers, 'Swift, Steele, and the Palatines', *Ball State University Forum* 18:3 (Summer 1977), pp. 17–22.

8. Hoppit, *A Land of Liberty?*, p. 105.

9. *Tatler*, vol. 3, p. 310.

10. See, in addition to Downie, *Robert Harley and the Press*, B. W. Hill, *Robert Harley: Speaker, Secretary of State and Premier Minister* (New Haven, CT: Yale University Press, 1988).

11. P. Rogers quotes Swift's opinion that Wharton was 'the most universal villain I ever knew', Swift, *Complete Poems*, p. 940.

12. R. W. Achurch, 'Richard Steele, Gazetteer and Bickerstaff' in *Studies in the Eighteenth-Century Periodical*, ed. R. P. Bond (Chapel Hill, NC: University of North Carolina Press, 1957), p. 56.

13. *Correspondence of Richard Steele*, pp. 21–2.

14. P. M. Handover, *A History of the London Gazette 1665–1965* (London: Her Majesty's Stationary Office, 1965), pp. 41–2.

15. R. Steele, 'Apology', in Steele, *Tracts and Pamphlets*, p. 339.

16. *Correspondence of Richard Steele*, p. 23. Blanchard dates the letter in 1707, but J. D. Alsop argues that the proposals were probably made in spring, 1709, when the *Gazette* did begin publishing thrice weekly, 'Richard Steele and the Reform of the *London Gazette*', *Papers of the Bibliographical Society of America*, 80:4 (1986), pp. 455–60.

17. The following paragraph parallels the material, and in some cases the language, of a paragraph in my 'Bibliography and the Shape of the Literary Periodical', *Library*, 6th series, 8:3 (September 1986), p. 234.

18. G. Pollard, 'Notes on the Size of the Sheet', *Library*, 4:22 (1942), pp. 123–4.

19. R. P. Bond, *The Tatler: The Making of a Literary Journal* (Cambridge, MA: Harvard University Press; Oxford: Oxford University Press, 1971), pp. 25–6.

20. Bond, *The Tatler*, pp. 50–9; 220–3.

21. Achurch, 'Richard Steele', p. 58; L. T. Milic, 'Tone in Steele's *Tatler*', in D. H. Bond and W. Reynolds McLeod (eds), *Newsletters to Newspapers: Eighteenth-Century Journalism* (Morgantown, WV: School of Journalism, West Virginia University, 1977), pp. 35–40.

22. Trevelyan, *England Under Queen Anne*, vol, 3, p. 18.

23. Hoppit, *A Land of Liberty?*, p. 120.

24. Bond, *The Tatler*, pp. 52–3.

25. Trevelyan, *England under Queen Anne*, vol. 3, pp. 2–4.

26. The threatening possibilities of Mr Spectator's spying are described in S. Black, 'Social and Literary Form in the *Spectator*', *Eighteenth-Century Studies*, 33:1 (1999), pp. 212–42.

27. On the hoop petticoat, see E. S. Mackie, *Market à la Mode: Fashion, Commodity, and Gender in the* Tatler *and the* Spectator (Baltimore, MD and London: Johns Hopkins University Press, 1997), pp. 104–43; and K. Chrisman, 'Unhoop the Fair Sex: The Campaign Against the Hoop Petticoat in Eighteenth-Century England', *Eighteenth-Century Studies*, 30:1 (Autumn 1996), pp. 3–23.

28. On the uses of coffee-houses for the *Tatler* and *Spectator*, see Allen, *The Clubs of Augustan London*, pp. 201–15; J. Habermas, *The Structural Transformation of the Public Sphere*, trans. T. Burger, with F. Lawrence (Cambridge, MA: MIT Press, 1989), pp. 32–3, 42–3; P. Stallybrass and A. White, *The Politics and Poetics of Transgression* (Ithaca, NY: Cornell University Press, 1986), pp. 94–100, and J. P. Hunter, '"News and New Things": Contemporaneity and the Early English Novel', *Critical Inquiry*, 14 (1988), pp. 501–4.

29. R. Baldick, *The Duel: A History of Duelling* (London: Chapman and Hall, 1965)

30. T. Tickell, in his notes to Addison's *Tatler* contributions, states that Steele 'assisted in this paper' for Nos. 253, 256, 259, 262, and 265; *The Works of the Right Honourable Joseph Addison, Esq*, vol. 2 (London, 1721).

31. I. Italia, *The Rise of Literary Journalism in the Eighteenth Century: Anxious Employment* (London and New York: Routledge, 2005), p. 34.

32. D. F. Bond records a variety of suggestions in his note on *Tatler*, No. 4; Steele, *Tatler*, ed. D. F. Bond, vol. 1, pp. 43–4.

33. Bond, *The Tatler*, p. 67; Winton, *Captain Steele*, p. 123.

34. A. Maynwaring, *History of Hannibal and Hanno in the Second War between Carthage and Rome* (London, 1712.)

35. Sacheverell's sermon and trial and their contexts are described in G. Holmes, *The Trial of Doctor Sacheverell* (London: Eyre Methuen, 1973).

36. B. Hoadly, *Some Considerations Humbly offered to the Right Reverend the Lord Bishop of Exeter* (London, 1709).

37. J. Loftis, *The Politics of Drama in Augustan England* (Oxford: Clarendon Press, 1963), pp. 35–62.

38. Shakespeare, *Henry V*, 'Prologue', l. 7, quoted in *Tatler*, no. 137.

39. Shakespeare, *Julius Caesar*, III.i, ll. 270–3.

40. Virgil, *Aeneid* 1.294–96.

41. T. Eagleton, *The Function of Criticism: From the* Spectator *to Post-Structuralism* (London: Verso, 1984), p. 24.

42. J. Gay, *The Present State of Wit in a Letter to a Friend in the Country* (London, 1711), ed. D. F. Bond, Augustan Reprint Society, series 1: Essays on Wit, No. 3 (Ann Arbor, MI: Augustan Reprint Society, 1947), p. 3.

43. Aitken, *The Life of Richard Steele*, vol. 1, p. 259; Winton, *Captain Steele*, p. 118.

44. Winton, *Captain Steele*, pp. 126–8; Bond, *The Tatler*, pp. 183–7.

45. *Correspondence of Richard Steele*, pp. 29–31.

46. Censor Censorum, *A Condoling Letter to the* Tattler: *on Account of the Misfortunes of Isaac Bickerstaff, Esq; A Prisononer in the --- on Suspicion of Debt* (London, 1710).

47. W. Oldisworth, *Annotations on the Tatler, Written in French by Monsieur Bournelle; and Translated into English by William Wagstaffe*, 2 vols (London, 1710).

48. *The Examiner for the Year 1711, to which is prefix'd a Letter to the Examiner* (London, 1712), p. 66.

49. H. St John, *A Letter to the Examiner* (London, 1710).

50. [W. Cowper], *A Letter to Isaac Bickerstaff, Esq; Occasion'd by the Letter to the Examiner* (London, 1710).

51. *Resistance and Non-Resistance Stated and Decided: In a Dialogue betwixt a* Hotspur-High-Flyer, *a* Canting-Low-Church Man, *and* B—f *Censor of* Great Britain (London, 1710).

52. Bond, *The Tatler*, p. 15.

53. J. Swift, *Journal to Stella*, ed. H. Williams, 2 vols (Oxford 1948), vol. 1. p. 111. H. Davis includes *Tatler*, No. 230 as a contribution by Swift and Nos. 21, 31, 67, 68, 249, and 258 as 'Contributions to the *Tatler* . . . attributed to Swift or containing Hints Furnished by him', in J. Swift, *Bickerstaff Papers*, ed H. Davis (Oxford: Basil Blackwood, 1957), pp. 173–7, 235–47. R. Blanchard summarizes various speculations on Steele's possible *Tatler* contributions in *Correspondence*, p. 34; see also I. Ehrenpreis, *Swift: The Man, his Works, and the Age*, 3 vols (Cambridge, MA: Harvard University Press, 1962–83), vol 2, p. 242.

54. Bond, *The Tatler*, p. 19.

55. *Correspondence of Richard Steele*, p. 33.

56. T. Tickell, 'Preface', *The Works of the Right Honourable Joseph Addison, Esq*, 4 vols (London: Jacob Tonson, 1721), vol 1, p. xii.

57. *Tatler*, vol. 1, p. 3.

58. 'Whatever people do is the mixed material of our page', Juvenal, *Satire 1*, ll. 85–6.

3 The *Spectator*'s Politics of Indirection

1.   Eagleton, *The Function of Criticism*, pp. 9–27.

2.   Habermas, *The Structural Transformation of the Public Sphere*, p. 27.

3.   Ibid., p. 43.

4.   J. A. Downie, 'How Useful to Eighteenth-Century English Studies is the Paradigm of the "Bourgeois Public Sphere"?' *Literature Compass*, 1:18C 022 (2003), pp. 1–19.

5.   B. Cowan, 'Mr. Spectator and the Coffeehouse Public Sphere', *Eighteenth-Century Studies*, 37:3 (2004), pp. 345–66, p. 347.

6.   B. Cowan, *The Social Life of Coffee: The Emergence of the British Coffeehouse* (New Haven, CT: Yale University Press, 2005), pp. 169–92; Cowan also notes efforts to control and regulate coffeehouses.

7.   E.g., 'We, then, should not be too positivist about the public sphere. Its production was largely figurative and rhetorical–discursive–at once invested in the concrete and historical existence of its representative institutions (coffeehouses, newspapers) and simultaneously, as a function of this representation, abstracted from them ... This is not to say that the bourgeois public sphere did not *really exist* in the eighteenth century, but rather that its existence cannot fully be confirmed, or denied, through attempts at the verification of the adherence of eighteenth-century institutions to its tenets'; E. S. Mackie, 'Being Too Positive About the Public Sphere', in D. Newman (ed.), *The* Spectator: *Emerging Discourses* (Newark, DE: University of Delaware Press, 2005), p. 87.

8.   E. S. Mackie (ed.), *The Commerce of Everyday Life: Selections from the* Tatler *and the* Spectator, (Boston, MA: Bedford/St Martins, 1998) p. 3; Mackie develops this argument with greater scope and at greater length in *Market à la Mode*.

9.   L. E. Klein, *Shaftesbury and the Culture of Politeness: Moral Discourse and Cultural Politeness in Early Eighteenth-Century England* (Cambridge: Cambridge University Press, 1994).

10. T. Bowers, 'Universalizing Sociability: *The Spectator*, Civic Enfranchisement, and the Rule(s) of the Public Sphere', in D. Newman (ed.), *The* Spectator: *Emerging Discourses*, pp. 150–74.

11. S. L. Maurer, *Proposing Men: Dialectics of Gender and Class in the Eighteenth-Century Periodical* (Stanford, CA: Stanford University Press, 1998); K. Shevelow, *Women and Print Culture: The Construction of Femininity in the Early Periodical* (London and New

York: Routledge, 1989), pp. 93–145; J. Merritt, 'Originals, Copies, and the Iconography of Femininity in the *Spectator*', in D. Newman (ed.), *The* Spectator: *Emerging Discourses*, pp. 41–58.

12. B. Carey, 'Accounts of Savage Nations: the *Spectator* and the Americas', in D. Newman (ed.), *The* Spectator: *Emerging Discourses*, pp. 129–49.

13. F. Ellis, *Swift v. Mainwaring* (Oxford: Oxford University Press, 1986) provides the texts of both papers, with a useful introduction and annotation.

14. Virtually all discussion of Maynwaring and his role in political propaganda relies on J. Oldmixon, *Life and Posthumous Writings of Arthur Maynwaring* (London, 1715).

15. A. Maynwaring, *Four Letters to a Friend in North Britain, upon the Publishing the Tryal of Dr. Sacheverell* (London, 1710).

16. F. Hare, *The Management of the War; in Four Letters to a Tory-Member* (London: Egbert Sanger, 1711).

17. H.-J. Müllenbrock, *The Culture of Contention: A Rhetorical Analysis of the Public Controversy about the Ending of the War of Spanish Succession, 1710–1713* (Munich: Fink, 1997), pp. 45–50.

18. Tonson was not added as joint publisher until no. 499, but as Steele's long associate he would probably have been consulted.

19. R. Steele with J. Addison, *The Spectator*, ed. D. F. Bond, 5 vols (Oxford: Clarendon Press, 1965), vol. 1, p. xlv. (References to the text of the *Spectator* are by number; references to the editorial material are by volume and page); Aitken, *The Life of Richard Steele*, apportions 274 papers to Addison, 236 to Steele; see vol.1, p. 312.

20. T. Tickell, 'Preface', *The Works of the Right Honourable Joseph Addison, Esq*, 4 vols (London, 1721), vol. 1, p. xiii.

21. Mr Spectator's character and its uses are thoughtfully limned by A. Furtwangler, 'The Making of Mr. Spectator', *Modern Language Quarterly* 38:1 (March 1977), pp. 21–39; see also A. Bony, 'L'Espace du texte: Spatialité de l'essai périodique addisonien', in *Espaces et représentations dans le monde anglo-américain aux XVIIe et XVIIIe siécles* (Paris: Presse de l'Université de Paris-Sorbonne, 1984), pp. 17–34; M. G. Ketcham, *Transparent Designs: Reading, Performance, and Form in the* Spectator *Papers* (Athens, GA: University of Georgia Press, 1985), pp. 11–26, and Black, 'Social and Literary Form in the *Spectator*'.

22. For example, *A Dialogue between Jack High and Will Low: Proper for the perusal of those who have a Right to choose for the ensuing Parliament* (London, 1710); *A Dialogue Betwixt Whig and Tory* (London, 1710); *Resistance and Non-Resistance stated and decided: in a dialogue between a Hotspur-High-Flyer, a Canting-Low-Churchman, and Bickerstaff, Censor of Great Britain* (London, 1710); *Bouchain: In a Dialogue between the late Medley and Examiner* (London, 1711); *A Dialogue between a New Courtier and a Country Gentleman* (London, 1712).

23. J. P. Hunter, *Before Novels: The Cultural Contexts of Eighteenth-Century Fiction* (New York: W. W. Norton, 1990) pp. 12–18.

24. J. E. Evans and J. N. Wall, Jr catalogue and describe the various fictions of the *Tatler* and *Spectator* in *A Guide to Prose Fiction in the* Tatler *and the* Spectator, Garland Reference Library of the Humanities, 71 (London and New York: Garland, 1977).

25. G. Polly, 'A Leviathan of Letters', in D. Newman (ed.), *The* Spectator: *Emerging Discourses*, pp. 105–28.

26. E. Bannet, '"Epistolary Commerce" in the *Spectator*', in D. Newman (ed.), *The* Spectator: *Emerging Discourses*, p. 224.

27. C. Knight, 'The *Spectator*'s Generalizing Discourse', in J. A. Downie and T. N. Corns (eds), *Telling People What to Think: Early Eighteenth-Century Periodicals from* the Review *to* the Rambler (London: Frank Cass, 1993), p. 52; the following paragraphs parallel this text.

28. See, for example, C. S. Lewis, 'Addison', in *Essays on the Eighteenth Century Presented to David Nichol Smith in Honour of his Seventieth Birthday* (Oxford: Clarendon Press, 1945), pp. 1–14; and R. Paulson, *The Fictions of Satire* (Baltimore, MD: Johns Hopkins Press, 1967), pp. 210–12. These draw on E. Legouis, 'Les deux 'Sir Roger de Coverley', celui de Steele et celui d'Addison', *Revue Germanique*, 2:4 (1906), pp. 453–71

29. B. A. Goldgar, *The Curse of Party: Swift's Relations with Addison and Steele* (Lincoln, NE: University of Nebraska Press, 1961), p. 84.

30. *The Spectator*, ed. Bond, vol. 1, p. 97.

31. For attacks on Marlborough during the last years of the war, see M. J. Harris, 'A Study of the Paper War Relating to the Career of the 1ˢᵗ Duke of Marlborough, 1710–12' (PhD dissertation, University of London, 1975).

32. See C. Winton, 'Richard Steele: The Political Writer' (PhD dissertation, Princeton University, 1955; Ann Arbor: University Microfilms), pp. 158–9.

33. Knight, 'The *Spectator*'s Generalizing Discourse', p. 54.

34. The death of Joseph made Charles, the British candidate for the Spanish monarchy, the new Austrian Emperor, and his possession of Spain as well would tip the European balance of power as dangerously toward Austria as Philip's Spanish monarchy would toward France. See Trevelyan, *England under Queen Anne*, vol. 3, pp. 75–88. Among others, Defoe makes the point in *The Succession of Spain Consider'd: Or, a View of the Several Interests of the Princes and Powers of Europe, as the Respect the Succession of Spain and the Empire*. (London:, 1711).

35. [D. Defoe], *An Essay upon Publick Credit: Being an Enquiry how the Publick Credit comes to depend upon the Change of the Ministry, or the Dissolutions of Parliaments ...* (London, 1710), p. 21.

36. On the instability of the Augustans, see M. McKeon, 'Cultural Crisis and Dialectical Method: Destabilizing Augustan Literature', in L. Damrosch (ed.), *The Profession of Eighteenth-Century Literature: Reflections on an Institution*, (Madison, WI: University of Wisconsin Press, 1992), pp. 42–61.

37. R. Blanchard, 'Richard Steele and the Status of Women', *Studies in Philology*, 26:3 (July 1929), pp. 325–55, traces the ambiguities of Steele's attitude towards women.

38. The story of Inkle and Yarico was adopted often in the eighteenth century, with particular attention to its anti-slavery implications. See L. M. Price, *Inkle and Yarico Album* (Berkeley, CA: University of California Press, 1937); F. Felsenstein, *English Trader, Indian Maid: Representing Gender, Race, and Slavery in the New World: An Inkle and Yarico Reader* (Baltimore, MD: John Hopkins University Press, 1999); P. Hulme, *Colonial Encounters: Europe and the Native Caribbean, 1492–1797* (London: Methuen, 1986); and M. Wechselblatt, 'Gender and Race in Yarico's Epistles to Inkle: Voicing the Feminine/Slave', *Studies in Eighteenth-Century Culture* 19 (1989), pp. 197–223. B. Carey considers Inkle and Yarico in the context of other representations of the colonial encounter in the *Spectator*, in 'Accounts of Savage Nations: the *Spectator* and the Americas', in D. Newman (ed.), *The* Spectator: *Emerging Discourses*, pp. 129–49.

39. Steele with Addison, *The Spectator*, ed. Bond, vol. 3, p. 247.

40. Ibid., p. 531, cites Eustace Budgell's story of Addison's reaction in *The Bee*, 1 (February 1733). G. Aitken speculates that *Spectator*, no. 410 was probably by Tickell; *Life* vol. 1, p. 310.

41. A. Müller, 'Putting the Child into Discourse: Framing Children in the *Spectator*', in D. Newman (ed.), *The* Spectator, p. 75; Müller analyses four essays, three of them by Steele, with particular attention to the influence of Locke.

42. Tories as well as Whigs exploited the family-state analogy, most notably in John Arbuthnot's 'John Bull' pamphlets. See J. Arbuthnot, *The History of John Bull*, ed. A. W. Bower and R. A. Erickson (Oxford: Clarendon Press, 1976).

43. I consider the relationship between economic practice and moral principles in 'The *Spectator*'s Moral Economy', *Modern Philology*, 91:2, pp. 161–79.

44. Trevelyan, *England under Queen Anne*, vol. 3, pp. 108–9.

45. Winton makes this suggestion in 'Richard Steele: The Political Writer', pp. 147–9.

46. See, for example, Maynwaring, *Four Letters to a Friend in North Britain*, especially Letter 4; and B. Hoadly, *The Fears and Sentiments of All True Britains; with respect to National Credit, Interest and Religion* (London, 1710).

47. [Defoe], *An Essay upon Publick Credit*, p. 21.

48. P. Backscheider compares Defoe's female embodiments of public credit to Addison's in 'Defoe's Lady Credit', *Huntington Library Quarterly*, 44:2 (Spring 1981), pp. 89–100.

49. J. G. A. Pocock, *The Machiavellian Moment: Florentine Political Thought and the Atlantic Republican Tradition* (Princeton, NJ: Princeton University Press, 1975), pp. 452, 456.

50. Steele with Addison, *The Spectator*, ed. D. F. Bond, vol. 1, p. 352.

51. See R. P. Saller, *Personal Patronage under the Early Empire* (Cambridge: Cambridge University Press, 1982).

52. See Harris, 'A Study of the Paper War'.

53. *The Spectator Inspected; or, a Letter to the Spectator: from an Officer of the Army in Flanders, touching the Use of French Terms, in Relations from the Army, occasion'd by the Spectator of the 8th of Sept. 1711*, (London, 1711), page 7; Bond reprints the same passage in *Spectator*, vol. 2, p.152.

54. *A Spy upon the Spectator. Part I* (London, 1711), p. 15; there was no Part II.

55. *Medley*, no. 23, in Steele, *Tracts and Pamphlets*, p. 65.

56. Steele, 'The Englishman's Thanks to the Duke of Marlborough', in Steele, *Tracts and Pamphlets*, p. 69.

57. Oldmixon, *The Life and Posthumous Works of Arthur Maynwaring*, p. 193. Steele did not resign his Stamp-Office position until June, 1713. The only known example of his anonymous writings between the closing of the *Spectator* and his resignation is his *Letter to Sir M.[iles] W.[arton] Concerning Occasional Peers* (March 1713).

58. *Correspondence of Richard Steele*, p. 279.

4 The *Guardian*, Parliament and Dunkirk

1. Aitken, *The Life of Richard Steele*, vol. 1, p. 361; see Winton, *Captain Steele*, p. 158, and *Correspondence of Richard Steele*, p. 68.

2. B. Rand (ed.), *Berkeley and Percival* (Cambridge: Cambridge University Press, 1914), p. 108.

3. Winton, *Captain Steele*, pages 99–100.

4. *Correspondence of Richard Steele*, p. 284.

5. Ibid., p. 277.

6.   Ibid., p. 278.
7.   Winton, *Captain Steele*, p. 97; Smithers, *The Life of Joseph Addison*, pp. 141–2. Boswell explains Johnson's sources for the story in *Life of Samuel Johnson*, ed. G. B. Hill, rev. L. F, Powell, vol. 4, pp. 52–3, 91. Winton and Smithers based their skepticism on A. L. Cooke, 'Addison vs. Steele, 1708', *PMLA*, 68:1 (March 1953), pp. 313–20, and R. Blanchard, 'Richard Steele's West Indian Plantation', *Modern Philology*, 39:3 (February 1942), pp. 281–5.
8.   *Correspondence of Richard Steele*, pp. 54–5.
9.   Aitken, *The Life of Richard Steele*, vol. 1, pp. 266–7.
10. *Correspondence of Richard Steele*, p. 31.
11. Aitken, *The Life of Richard Steele*, vol. 1, pp. 281–2.
12. Ibid., p. 305.
13. S. Johnson, *An Account of the Life of Richard Savage, Son of Earl Rivers* (London: J. Roberts, 1744), pp. 12–17; G. Aitkin, *Life*, vol. 2, pp. 205–6.
14. *Correspondence of Richard Steele*, p. 242
15. Rand (ed.), *Berkeley and Percival*, p. 106.
16. W. Whiston, *Memoirs of the Life and Writings of Mr. William Whiston, Containing Memoirs of several of his Friends also* (London, 1749), p. 304.
17. J. Woodward, *Select Cases and Consultations in Physick*, ed. P. Templeman (London, 1757), pp. 369–71.
18. R. P. Bond, 'Mr. Bickerstaff and Mr. Wortley', in C. Henderson, Jr, ed. *Classical, Medieval and Renaissance Studies in Honor of Berthold Louis Ullman* (Rome: Edizione di Storia e Letteratura, 1964), vol. 2, pp. 491–504.
19. 1755 letter from Lady Mary Wortley Montague to Lady Bute, quoted in G. Aitken, *The Life of Richard Steele*, vol. 1, p. 333.
20. Rand (ed.), *Berkeley and Percival*, p. 110.
21. J. Loftis, *Steele at Drury Lane* (Berkeley and Los Angeles, CA: University of California Press, 1952), pp. 99–102.
22. *Correspondence of Richard Steele*, pp. 45–7.
23. *Englishman*, ed. Blanchard, p. 426.
24. Rand (ed.), *Berkeley and Percival*, p. 112.
25. Loftis, *Steele at Drury Lane*, p. 107.
26. Smithers, *The Life of Joseph Addison*, p. 262.
27. *Correspondence of Richard Steele*, p. 515.
28. *Wentworth Papers*, quoted in Smithers, *Life of Joseph Addison*, p. 265.
29. P. B. J. Hyland, 'Richard Steele, the Press, and the Hanoverian Succession, 1713–1716', (PhD dissertation, University of Lancaster, 1982), p. 118.
30. *Correspondence of Richard Steele*, p. 488.
31. *Daily Courant* (6 October 1714).
32. Aitken, *The Life of Richard Steele*, vol. 2, pp. 39–42; Winton, *Sir Richard Steele*, pp. 15–20, discusses the copyright issue in some detail.
33. Aitken, *The Life of Richard Steele*, vol. 1, p. 363.
34. R. Steele, *The Guardian*, ed. J. C. Stephens (Lexington, KY: University Press of Kentucky, 1982), pp. 23–4; citations of the *Guardian* will be by number; citations of the introduction and notes will be by page.
35. 'The Publisher to the Reader', *The Guardian*, ed. J. C. Stephens, p. 575.
36. Stephens discusses authorship in detail in *The Guardian*, ed. J. C. Stephens, pp. 17–33.

37. Edward Smith to Robert Harley, October 14, 1713, quoted in Hyland, 'Richard Steele', p. 58.
38. See C. Richardson, *Notices and Extracts Relating to the Lion's Head, which was Erected at Button's Coffee-House, in the Year 1713* (London: Saunders and Otley, 1828).
39. R. H. Hopkins, 'The Issue of Anonymity and the Beginning of the Steele-Swift Controversy of 1713–14: A New Interpretation', *English Language Notes*, 2:1 (September 1964), pp.15–21.
40. *Correspondence of Richard Steele*, p. 70.
41. Ibid., p. 71.
42. Ibid., pp. 72–3.
43. Ibid., p. 74.
44. Ibid., p. 76.
45. Ibid., pp. 76–7.
46. Ibid., p. 77.
47. See P. Hyland, 'Naming Names: Steele and Swift', in P. Hyland and N. Sammels (eds), *Irish Writing: Exile and Subversion* (London: Macmillan, 1991), pp. 13–31.
48. Goldgar, *The Curse of Party*, pp. 118–19; Goldgar's narrative of the breakdown of the Swift–Steele relationship and of their noisier struggles in the fall of 1713 and winter of 1714 is clear and detailed.
49. *Examiner*, 4:2.
50. *The Guardian*, ed. Stephens, p. 660.
51. This single-folio tract was republished in *The Political Writings of Sir Richard Steele* (London, 1715).
52. Steele, *Tracts and Pamphlets*, p. 76.
53. *Reflections on a Paper lately Printed, Entitled, A Letter to Sir Miles Wharton, Concerning Occasional Peers* (London, 1713).
54. *Correspondence of Richard Steele*, pp. 80–1; see also Aitken, *The Life of Richard Steele*, vol. 1, pp.386–90.
55. *Correspondence of Richard Steele*, p. 79.
56. Aitken, *The Life of Richard Steele*, vol. 1, pp. 391–2.
57. Defoe, *Tour through the Whole Island of Great Britain*, quoted in Aitken, *The Life of Richard Steele*, vol. 1, p. 396.
58. Winton, *Captain Steele*, p. 172.
59. Richards, *Party Propaganda under Queen Anne*, pp. 129–53.
60. Quoted in Winton, *Captain Steele*, p. 200.
61. Quoted in Aitken, *The Life of Richard Steele*, vol.1, p. 393.
62. Mackie, *Market à la Mode*.
63. C. Knight, *The Literature of Satire* (Cambridge: Cambridge University Press, 2004), pp. 233–50; the present chapter, focusing on Steele and the political context parallels my earlier focus on the satiric rhetoric of the conflict.
64. D. Defoe, *The Honour and Prerogative of the Queen's Majesty Vindicated and Defended against the Unexampled Insolence of the Author of the Guardian: In a Letter from a Country Whig to Mr. Steele* (London, 1713), p. 8.
65. Ibid., p. 10.
66. Ibid., p. 16.
67. *Examiner*, 4:27.
68. D. Defoe, *Reasons Concerning the Immediate Demolishing of Dunkirk: Being a Serious Enquiry into the State and Condition of that Affair* (London: John Morphew, 1713).

69. J. Toland, *Dunkirk or Dover; or, The Queen's Honour, The Nation's Safety, The Liberties of Europe, and The Peace of the World, All at Stake till that Fort and Port be totally demolish'd by the French*, 2nd edn (London, 1713), p. 10.

70. Steele, *Tracts and Pamphlets*, p. 101.

71. Ibid., p. 109.

72. Ibid., p. 112.

73. Ibid., p. 113.

74. Ibid., p. 121.

75. Ibid., p. 123.

76. Swift, 'The Importance of the Guardian Considered', in *Prose Works*, ed. H. Davis and I. Ehrenpreis (Princeton, NJ: Princeton University Press, 1953), pp. 17–19; *A Letter to Chancellor Middleton* in *Prose Works*, ed. H. Davis, vol.10, pp. 108–10.

77. Swift, *Political Tracts, 1713–1719*, pp. 5–6.

78. Ibid., p. 11

79. Steele, *Tracts and Pamphlets*, pp. 109–10.

80. Ibid., p. 13.

81. Ibid., p. 15.

82. Swift, *Prose Works*, vol. 8, p. 17.

83. *Miscellaneous Works of Dr. William Wagstaffe* (London: J.Bowyer, 1726).

84. *The Character of Richard Steele: With Some Remarks. By Toby Abel's Cousin* (London: John Morphew, 1713), p. 18.

5 The *Crisis* and the Succession

1. *The Englishman. Being a Sequel of the Guardian*, ed. R. Blanchard (Oxford: Clarendon Press, 1955), No. 1, p. 5; further references to the *Englishman* will be parenthetical, by number, to this edition; references to the second series will so indicate.

2. Hyland, 'Richard Steele', p. 75.

3. *Englishman*, ed. Blanchard, p. 405.

4. Hyland, 'Richard Steele', p. 26.

5. G. Hicks, *Seasonable Queries Relating to the Birth and Birthright of a Certain person* (London, 1713).

6. G. Harbin, *The Hereditary Right of the Crown of England Asserted, The History of the Succession since the Conquest Clear'd, and the true English Constitution Vindicated from the Misrepresentations of Dr. Higdin's View and Defence* (London, 1713).

7. G. J. Kolb, 'A Note on "Tristram Shandy": Some New Sources', *Notes and Queries* vol. 196 (1951), p. 227; the Florida edition of *Tristram Shandy*, ed. Melvyn New and Joan New (Gainsville: University Presses of Florida, 1978), vol. 2, p. 953 notes that Steele is a source for neither the English nor the Latin text.

8. R. Lawrence, *Lay-Baptism Invalid* (London, 1712).

9. See for example Maynwaring, *The History of Hannibal and Hanno*.

10. References to the *Examiner* are parenthetical. They use the first series, 6 vols. (London: J. Morphew, 1710–14).

11. *An Invitation to Peace: Or, Toby's Preliminaries to Nestor Ironsides [sic], Set forth in a Dialogue between Toby and his Kinsman* (London, 1714), p. 4.

12. *Invitation to Peace*, pp. 6–7, 7–8.

13. *Englishman*, ed. Blanchard, pp. 445–6.

14. *John Tutchin's Ghost to Richard St—le, Esq.* (London, 1713).

15. For details on the poem's publication history, see Swift, *The Complete Poems*, p. 665. Swift took particular care to keep his authorship unknown.

16. *Englishman*, no. 57, pp. 231–2; because of the length of this number, I will refer to its pages in the Blanchard edition of the *Englishman*. Further references will be parenthetical.

17. *Englishman*, pp. 425, 427.

18. Steele, *Tracts and Pamphlets*, p. 130.

19. Ibid., p. 132.

20. Ibid., pp. 137, 138.

21. E.g., *Remarks upon Mr. Steele's Crisis, Humbly inscribed to the Clergy of the Church of England* (London, 1714).

22. Steele, *Tracts and Pamphlets*, p. 174.

23. Ibid., p. 176.

24. Ibid., p. 178.

25. Ibid., pp. 285–6.

26. *The Life of Cato the Censor: Humbly Dedicated to R. S—le Esq:* (London, 1714), p. 34.

27. *A Letter from the Facetious Doctor Andrew Tripe at Bath, to the Venerable Nestor Ironside* (London, 1714), p. 10.

28. *Remarks on Mr. Steele's Crisis &c. By One of the Clergy*, p. 5.

29. *Remarks on Mr. Steele's Crisis, Humbly Inscribed to the Clergy of the Church of England* (London: Bernard Lintott, 1714), pp. 12–13.

30. Swift, *Prose Works*, vol. 8, p. 35.

31. Goldgar, *The Curse of Party*, p. 145.

32. J. Swift, *Prose Works* vol. 8, p. 32.

33. J. Swift, *Prose Works,* vol. 8, p. 44.

34. Steele, *Tracts and Pamphlets*, pp. 164–5.

35. J. Swift, *Prose Works,* vol. 8, pp. 49, 50.

36. Goldgar, *The Curse of Party*, p. 148.

37. *Mr. Steele's Speech upon the Proposal of Sir Thomas Hanmer for Speaker of the House of Commons*, in Steele, *Tracts and Pamphlets*, p. 214; the text differs slightly from that later reprinted in Steele's 'Apology' (*Tracts and Pamphlets*, p. 293).

38. Steele, *Tracts and Pamphlets*, p. 293.

39. *A Speech Suppos'd to be Spoke by R___ St___l, Esq; At the Opening this Present Parliament. With Some Remarks in a Letter to the Bailiff of St___dge, Very proper to be Bound up with the Crisis* (London, 1714).

40. HMC, *Portland MSS*, vol. 5 (1899), p. 384; reprinted in *Correspondence of Richard Steele*, p. 86.

41. G. F[lint], *The History of the First and Second Session of the last Parliament* (London, 1714), p. 7.

42. *The Case of Richard Steele, Esq; Being an Impartial Account of the Proceedings Against Him* (London, 1714), p. 5.

43. *Correspondence of Richard Steele*, p. 294.

44. F[lint], *The History of the First and Second Session*, p. 29.

45. Hyland, 'Richard Steele', p. 233.

46. F[lint], *The History of the First and Second Session*, p. 30.

47. J. H. Plumb, *Sir Robert Walpole: The Making of a Statesman* (London: Cresset, 1956), p. 190.

48. *Correspondence of Richard Steele*, p. 294.

49. Steele, *Tracts and Pamphlets*, p. 301.

50. Ibid., p. 317.

51. Ibid., p. 307.

52. Ibid., pp. 336–7.

53. Ibid., p. 337.

54. F[lint], *History of the First and Second Session*, p. 34.

55. *Correspondence of Richard Steele*, p. 295.

56. *Lover*, no. 18 ('Tuesday, April 6, 1714), in *Richard Steele's Periodical Journalism*, ed. R. Blanchard (Oxford: Clarendon Press, 1959)p. 67.

57. Plumb, *Sir Robert Walpole*, p. 191; Hyland, 'Richard Steele', pp. 242–4.

58. Winton, *Captain Steele*, p. 203.

59. F[lint], *The History of the First and Second Session*, p. 35.

60. *The Case of Richard Steele*, p. 21.

61. *A Defence of Mr. Steele, in a Letter to a Friend in the Country* (London, 1714).

62. *A Letter to Mr. Steele, Concerning the Removal of the Pretender from Lorrain, Occasion'd by the Crisis. Written by an Englishman* (London: Ferdinand Burleigh, 1714), p. 6.

63. *The French Faith Represented in the Present State of Dunkirk. A Letter to the* Examiner, *in Defence of Mr. Steele* (London: Ferd.Burleigh, 1714), in Steele, *Tracts and Pamphlets*, pp. 257–73.

64. *Lover*, no. 2, in *Richard Steele's Periodical Journalism*, p. 12.

65. *Richard Steele's Periodical Journalism*, p. 275.

66. Ibid., p. 277.

67. *Correspondence of Richard Steele*, p. 299.

68. Winton, *Captain Steele*, pp. 203–4; Winton cites B. Williams, *Stanhope* (Oxford, 1932), p. 144.

69. *The Crisis upon Crisis. A Poem. Being and Advertisement Stuck in the Lion's Mouth at Button's: and Addressed to Doctor S____t*. London: J. Morphew, 1714.

70. Trevelyan, *England under Queen Anne*, vol. 3, p. 260.

71. Ibid., p. 276.

72. Citations of the *Reader* use *Richard Steele's Periodical Journalism*.

73. John Nichols attributed *Reader*, nos. 3 and 4 to Addison, but Blanchard argues persuasively that they are by Steele; *Richard Steele's Periodical Journalism*, p. 293.

74. Steele, *Tracts and Pamphlets*, p. 245.

75. Ibid., p. 246.

76. Ibid., p. 254.

77. Ibid., p. 252.

78. D. Defoe, *A Letter to Mr. Steele, Occasioned by his Letter to a Member of Parliament, Concerning the Bill for Preventing the Growth of Schism. By a Member of the Church of England*. (London: J. Baker, 1714).

79. G. Sewall, *Schism, Destructive of the Government, both in Church and State, Being, A Defence of the Bill, Intitled, An Act for preventing the Growth of Schism. Wherein All the Objections against it, and particularly those in Squire Steele's Letter are fully Refuted* (London, 1714).

80. Steele, *Tracts and Pamphlets*, p. 222.

81. Ibid., p. 232.

82. Ibid., p. 227.

83. Ibid., p. 270.

84. F. Hoffman, *Two Very Odd Characters tho' the Number be Even: Or The Whigg Flesh-Fly and The Industrious Tory Bee* (London, 1714).

85. *The Ecclesiastical and Political History of Whig Land, of Late Years; to which are Prefix'd, The Characters of a Late Ecclesiastical Historian, and of the Author of this History* (London: J. Morphew, 1714).

86. *The Steeleids, or, the Tryal of Wit. A Poem, in Three Cantos* (London: J. Morphew, 1714).

87. Steele, *Tracts and Pamphlets*, p. 279.

88. *Correspondence of Richard Steele*, p. 305.

89. Aitken, *The Life of Richard Steele*, vol. 2, p. 37.

6 The Politics of the Theatre

1. See C. Ramsland, 'Britons Never Will Be Slaves: A Study in Whig Political Propaganda in the British Theatre, 1700–1742', *Quarterly Journal of Speech*, 28 (1942), pp. 393–9.

2. C. Cibber, *An Apology for the Life of Colley Cibber*, ed. B. R. S. Fone (Ann Arbor, MI: University of Michigan Press, 1968), p. 270.

3. Cibber, *An Apology*, p. 271. Steele refers to a meeting with the Duchess of Marlborough in a letter of September 8, 1714; *Correspondence of Richard Steele*, p. 306.

4. Quoted in Aitken, *The Life of Richard Steele*, vol. 2, p. 48.

5. Cibber, *An Apology*, pp. 273–4.

6. Loftis, *Steele at Drury Lane*, p. 42.

7. *Correspondence of Richard Steele*, p. 524.

8. R. Steele, *Town-Talk*, no. 6, in *Richard Steele's Periodical Journalism 1714–16* (Oxford: Clarendon Press, 1959), p.229; further citation of this journal will be parenthetical.

9. Cibber, *An Apology*, pp. 238–9.

10. Ibid., pp. 256–9.

11. Loftis, *Steele at Drury Lane*, p. 58.

12. J. Collier, *A Short View of the Immorality and Profaneness of the English Stage: Together with the Sense of Antiquity upon this Argument* (1698; New York: AMS Press, 1974), p. 143.

13. R. D. Hume, *The Development of English Drama in the Late Seventeenth Century* (Oxford: Clarendon Press, 1976), p. 86; Hume cites *A Comparison of the Two Stages* (1702) as the source of this criticism.

14. R. D. Hume, 'Jeremy Collier and the Future of the London Theatre in 1698', *Studies in Philology* 96:4 (1999), pp. 487–94.

15. *Richard Steele's Periodical Journalism*, p. 300.

16. Collier, *A Short View of the Immorality and Profaneness of the English Stage*, pp. 209–32.

17. *The State of the Case between the Lord Chamberlain of his Majesty's Household, and Sir Richard Steele, as represented by that Knight. Restated, in Vindication of King George, and the Most Noble Duke of Newcastle*; quoted in Loftis, *Steele at Drury Lane*, p. 77.

18. *Correspondence of Richard Steele*, p. 109.

19. Loftis, *Steele at Drury Lane*, pp. 62–3.

20. *A Critick no Wit*, pp. 5–6.

21. J. Dennis, 'Dedication' to *The Invader of his Country*', 1720; in (ed.), *The Critical Works of John Dennis*, ed. E. N. Hooker, 2 vols (Baltimore, MD: Johns Hopkins Press, 1943) vol 2, pp. 76–7.

22. See *The Characters and Conduct of Sir John Edgar, Call'd by Himself Sole Monarch of the Stage in Drury Lane; and his three Deputy-Governors* (1720), in *The Critical Works of John Dennis*, vol. 2. pp. 181–92.

23. *The Critical Works of John Dennis*, vol. 2, p. 189.

24. Cibber, *An Apology*, p. 300.

25. In a manuscript version of *Town-Talk*, no. 4 preserved among the Blenheim papers, Steele explicitly included science and its mechanical applications among the subjects canvassed there: 'All Works of Invention, All the Sciences, as well as mechanick Arts will have their turn in entertaining this Society'. (*Richard Steele's Periodical Journalism*, p. 302.)

26. Loftis, *Steele at Drury Lane*, pp. 99–101.

27. *Richard Steele's Periodical Journalism*, p. 306.

28. Loftis, *Steele and Drury Lane*, pp. 113–14.

29. The details are, as far as can be known, summarized in Aitken, *The Life of Richard Steele*, vol 2, pp. 95–106; see also Loftis, *Steele at Drury Lane*, pp. 91–8.

30. *Correspondence of Richard Steele*, pp.129–30.

31. C. Cibber, 'Dedication to *Ximena*' (1719) (rpt. in *The Theatre, by Sir Richard Steele; to which are added, The Anti-Theatre; The Character of Sir John Edgar; Steele's Case with the Lord Chamberlain; The Crisis of Property, with the Sequel, Two Pasquins, &c.*, ed. J. Nichols (London, 1791)), p. 318.

32. *Correspondence of Richard Steele*, p. 146.

33. Ibid., pp. 146–7.

34. R. Steele, *The Theatre*, ed. J. Loftis (Oxford: Clarendon Press, 1962), no. 1, p. 3; further references will be parenthetical.

35. Steele, *Tracts and Pamphlets*, p. 595.

36. Ibid., p. 608.

37. *Anti-Theatre*, no. 2, in, *The Theatre*, p. 220.

38. *A Full Consideration and Confutiation of Sir John Edgar. By Sir Andrew Artlove, Knight and Baronet. In Three Letters to Mr. Applebee*, reprinted in *The Theatre*, ed. Nichols pp. 427–41.

39. *The Theatre*, ed. Nichols, p. 429.

40. *The State of the Case between The Lord Chamberlain of His Majesty's Houshold, and Sir Richard Steele, as represented by that Knight, Re-stated, In Vindication of King George, and the most Noble the Duke of Newcastle.* (London: J. Applebee, 1720); reprinted in *Theatre*, ed. Nichols, pp. 468–509.

41. *The Theatre*, ed. Nichols, p. 486.

42. Steele's defenders include *An Answer to a Whimsical Pamphlet called The Character of Sir John Edgar, &c.* (11 February 1720); reprinted in, *The Theatre*, ed. Nichols pp. 369–82; and apparently a tract that has not survived, *A New Project for the Regulation of the Stage* (see Loftis, *Steele at Drury Lane*, pp. 165–6; Loftis discusses the journalistic controversy in more detail, pp. 159–80.

43. *Correspondence of Richard Steele*, pp. 153–4.

44. In a deposition in the 1727 suit between Steele and the actor-managers, Steele claimed that the play made £2536.3s.6d. in its eighteen-night initial run (Loftis, *Steele at Drury Lane*, p. 193).

45. Rand (ed.), *Berkeley and Percival*, p. 106.

46. J. Swift, *Complete Poems*, ed. P. Rogers, pp. 157–8.

47. Loftis quotes this passage, *Steele at Drury Lane*, p. 187, but I use the text of the Bond edition.

48. Loftis, *Steele at Drury Lane*, pp. 189–90; *Correspondence of Richard Steele*, pp. 314–15, 361.

49. Loftis, *Steele at Drury Lane*, pp. 183–93.

50. Quoted in *The London Stage*, ed. E. L. Avery, 5 vols (Carbondale, IL: Southern Illinois University Press, 1960–8), vol. 2, p. 691.

51. *The Critical Works of John Dennis*, p. 248.

52. See Aitken, *The Life of Richard Steele*, vol. 2, pp. 277, 314.

53. *The Conscious Lovers* in *The Plays of Richard Steele*, III.294.

54. R. Steele, 'Preface', *The Conscious Lovers*, in *The Plays of Richard Steele*, p. 298.

55. J. Dennis, *Remarks on a Play, Call'd The Conscious Lovers, a Comedy*, in *The Critical Works of John Dennis*, vol. 2, p. 259.

56. *The Critical Works of John Dennis*, vol. 2, p. 271.

57. Ibid., vol. 2, p. 274.

58. B. Victor, *An Epistle to Sir Richard Steele, On his Play, call'd, The Conscious Lovers* (London: W. Chetwood, et al, 1722), p. 15.

59. Victor, *Epistle to Richard Steele*, p. 17.

60. The various contemporary arguments about *The Conscious Lovers* and the responses by Dennis are summarized in Loftis, *Steele at Drury Lane*, pp. 195–213.

61. Cibber, *An Apology*, p. 287.

62. Loftis, *Steele at Drury Lane*, p. 231.

63. The plays were included in G. Aitken in his 1894 Mermaid edition of Steele's plays.

64. See Loftis, *Steele at Drury Lane*, pp. 235–7.

65. *The Critical Works of John Dennis*, vol. 2, pp. 162–5.

The Final decade (1715–24)

1. *Correspondence of Richard Steele*, p. 316.

2. Ibid., p. 298.

3. Ibid., p. 318.

4. Ibid., p. 327.

5. Ibid., p. 381.

6. Ibid., p. 370.

7. Ibid., p. 354.

8. Ibid., p. 361.

9. Ibid., p. 328.

10. Ibid., pp. 378–9.

11. Ibid., p. 386.

12. Ibid., p. 103.

13. Ibid., p. 102.

14. Ibid., p. 105.

15. Ibid., pp. 310–11.

16. See Hyland, 'Richard Steele', pp. 280–83.

17. Steele, *The Theatre*, ed. J. Loftis, no. 11, p. 49; future references to this edition will be parenthetical.

18. For speculation as to the roles of Thomas Burnet, Ambrose Philips and John Harris in the second series of *The Englishman*, see Hyland, 'Richard Steele', pp. 50–1.

19. Steele, *Tracts and Pamphlets*, p. 361.

20. Winton, *Sir Richard Steele*, p. 78.

21. Steele, *Tracts and Pamphlets*, pp. 403–4.
22. Ibid., p. 408.
23. Ibid., p. 411.
24. Ibid., p. 412.
25. Ibid., p. 415.
26. Hoppit, *A Land of Liberty?* p. 411.
27. Winton, *Sir Richard Steele*, p. 225.
28. Steele, *Tracts and Pamphlets*, p. 611.
29. Ibid., p. 611.
30. *Correspondence of Richard Steele.*, pp. 106–8, 528–9.
31. Ibid., p. 526.
32. Aitken, *The Life of Richard Steele*, vol 2, p. 94.
33. Ibid., p. 153.
34. Ibid., *Life*, vol. 2, p. 155; no date for this event was given in Aitken's source.
35. Winton, *Sir Richard Steele*, pp. 125–7.
36. The work of the Commission for Forfeited Estates is described in M. D. Sankey, *Jacobite Prisoners of the 1715 Rebellion: Preventing and Punishing Rebellion in Early Hanoverian Britain* (Burlington, VT and Aldershot: Ashgate, 2005), pp. 130–56; see also D. Szechi, *1715: The Great Jacobite Rebellion* (New Haven, CT and London: Yale University Press, 2006), pp. 230–4.
37. A discussion of Steele's draft essay and its text appear in R. Blanchard (ed.), *Richard Steele's Periodical Journalism*, pp. 330–2; the essay is summarized in G. Aitken, *The Life of Richard Steele*, vol. 2, p. 82–3.
38. *Richard Steele's Periodical Journalism*, p. 332.
39. Winton, *Sir Richard Steele*, p. 83.
40. The speech was published, along with several others, in London and Dublin in 1716 and is reprinted in Steele, *Tracts and Pamphlets*, pp. 417–8.
41. Steele, *Tracts and Pamphlets*, p. 418.
42. *Correspondence of Richard Steele*, p. 339.
43. W. Michael, *England under George I*, vol. 2: *The Quadruple Alliance*, trans. A. and G. E. MacGregor (1939; New York: AMS, 1970), pp. 270–1.
44. Plumb, *Sire Robert Walpole* (London: Cresset, 1956), pp. 248–9.
45. Michael, *England under George*, vol. 2, pp. 276–7.
46. Ibid., pp. 282–3.
47. E. A. and L. Bloom, 'Steele in 1719: Additions to the Canon', *HLQ*, 31:2 (February 1968), p. 126.
48. R. Walpole, *Thoughts of a Member* (London, 1719); E. R. Turner, 'The Peerage Bill of 1719', *English Historical Review*, vol, 28, no 110 (April 1913), pp. 243–59 refers to *Thoughts* as 'by Sir Robert Walpole, one of the best things he ever published' (p. 250), but the *English Short Title Catalog* attributes it to John Trenchard.
49. *Patrician*, no. 1. The *Patrician* was a three-paper series appearing weekly and responding, as the name implies, to *The Plebeian*.
50. J. Addison, *The Old Whig*, no. 1, para. 5. Addison numbers the paragraphs of his first *Old Whig*.
51. R. Molesworth, *Letter from a Member of the House of Commons to a Gentleman without Doors, relating to the House of Lords* (London, 1719).
52. *Patrician*, No. 2.
53. Walpole, *Thoughts of a Member*, p. 18.

54. *Further Reasons against the Peerage-Bill* (London, 1719).
55. R. Steele, *Letter to O—d concerning the Bill of Peerage* (London: J. Roberts, 1719); reprinted in Steele, *Tracts and Pamphlets*, p. 531.
56. *Pleibian*, No. 2, in Steele, *Tracts and Pamphlets*, pp. 476–7.
57. Walpole, *Thoughts of a Member*, p. 9.
58. *Old Whig*, No. 1, para. 16.
59. *Old Whig*, No. 1, paras. 23, 30; *Patrician*, No. 2.
60. *Considerations Concerning the Nature and Consequences of the Bill now depending in Parliament, Relating to the Peerage of Great-Britain. In a Letter from one Member of the House of Commons to another* (London: J. Roberts, 1719), p.15.
61. *Patrician*, No. 3.
62. *Moderator*, No. 1 (London: J. Roberts, 1719); there were no further numbers.
63. *Further Reasons against the Peerage-Bill* (London: J. Roberts, 1719); Bloom and Bloom, 'Steele in 1719', pp. 145–51, attribute this essay to Steele, but the similarities suggest to me that *Further Reasons* and *Plebeian* come from the same stable of authors rather than the same man.
64. Walpole, *Thoughts of a Member*, p. 11.
65. R. Steele, *Plebeian*, No. 2, in *Tracts and Pamphlets*, p. 479.
66. R. Steele, *Plebeian*, No. 1, in *Tracts and Pamphlets*, p. 468.
67. R. Steele, *The Joint and Humble Address of the Tories and Whigs Concerning the Bill of Peerage*, in *Tracts and Pamphlets*, p. 499; there are no surviving copies of the original tract, and hence R. Blanchard uses the text from Abel Boyer, *The Political State of Great Britain*, May 1719, XVII, 490–3, which is the same as a holograph among the Blenheim papers.
68. *Six Questions, Stated and Answered, upon which the whole Force of the Arguments for and against the PEERAGE-BILL, depends* (London: J. Roberts, 1719); *Patrician*, No. 1.
69. Steele, *Plebeian*, No. 1, in *Tracts and Pamphlets*, p. 461.
70. R. Steele, *Plebeian*, No. 4, in *Tracts and Pamphlets*, p. 528.
71. *Letter from a Member of the House of Commons.*
72. *Patrician*, No. 2.
73. *Letter from a Member of the House of Commons.*
74. Steele, *Plebeian*, No. 1, in *Tracts and Pamphlets*, p. 463.
75. Steele, *Plebeian*, No. 4, in *Tracts and Pamphlets*, p. 491.
76. Downie, *Robert Harley and the Press*; B. A. Goldgar *Walpole and the Wits* (Lincoln, NE: University of Nebraska Press, 1976).
77. Hyland, 'Richard Steele', pp. 56–9.
78. On the Spartans Steele uses as his source Niels Krag (or, in Steele's English, Nic. Crags), *De Republica Lacedaemoniorum* as an authority, with a possible pun on Addison's friend James Craggs. Crags was described as 'a person of great Boldness and Industry ... but not so happy in his Judgment'; *Tracts*, p. 466. James Craggs, as a member of government, loyally supported the bill, which he privately opposed. In addition to the references in the *Plebeian*, the only other evidence that Addison and Steele were homosexuals is Pope's remark to Spence that they were hermaphrodites, first published in J. Spence, *Observations, Anecdotes, and Characters*, ed. J. M. Osborn, 2 vols. (Oxford: Clarendon Press, 1966).
79. Bloom and Bloom, 'Steele in 1719', pp. 140–1. The Blooms claim that Steele wrote the letter and discuss it in detail, pp. 140–5.
80. *Tracts and Pamphets*, p. 499.

81. Quoted in Downie, *Robert Harley*, p. 188.
82. Quoted in W. Michael, *England under George I*, vol 2, p. 284; cf. Walpole, *Thoughts of a Member*, p. 18.
83. Steele, *Tracts and Pamphlets*, p. 528.
84. Ibid.,, p. 530.
85. Ibid.,, p. 535.
86. Ibid.,, p. 546; Blanchard uses the text of William Cobbett, *Parliamentary History*.
87. Plumb, *Sir Robert Walpole*, p. 280.
88. C. Jones, '"Venice Preserv'd; or a Plot Discovered": The Political and Social Context of the Peerage Bill in 1719', in *A Pillar of the Constitution*, ed. C. Jones (London: Hambleton, 1989), p.105.
89. The details of the Sansome imbroglio are narrated in Aitken, *The Life of Richard Steele*, vol. 2, pp. 161–79.
90. Steele, *Tracts and Pamphlets*, p. 426.
91. *Correspondence of Richard Steele*, pp. 139–42.
92. R. Steele, *The Spinster: In Defence of the Woollen Manufactures* No. 1 (London: J. Roberts, 1719), in *Tracts and Pamphlets*, pp. 547–56.
93. Steele, *Tracts and Pamphlets*, p. 553.
94. Ibid., p. 555.
95. *The Female Manufacturers' Complaint: Being the Humble Petition of Dorothy Distaff, Abigail Spinning-Wheel, and Eleanor Reel, &c. Spinsters, to the Lady Rebecca Woollpack. With a Respectful Epistle to Sir R— S—l, concerning some Omissions of the utmost Importance in his Lady's Wardrobe. By Monsieur de Brocade of Paris* (London: W. Boreham, 1720), p. 15.
96. Aitken, *Life of Richard Steele*, vol. 2, p. 209.
97. J. Carswell, *The South Sea Bubble* (London: Cresset, 1960), p. 76.
98. Hoppit, *A Land of Liberty*, p. 336.
99. R. Steele, *The Crisis of Property* (London, W. Chetwood, 1720), reprinted in *Tracts and Pamphlets*, p. 565.
100. *The Crisis of Honesty. Being an Answer to the Crisis of Property. In a Letter to Sir R— S—* (London: A. Moore, 1720), p. 7.
101. *The Crisis of Honesty*, p. 26.
102. *Scandal no Argument. An Oxford Annuitant's Letter to Sir Richard Steele, In Answer to the Crisis of Honesty. With Reasons why Guardians should not expose their Wards to Sale, and pay their own Debts out of their Estates, being a short View of the South-Sea Affair yet depending* (London: W. Boreham, 1720), p. 19.
103. Sir J. Meres, *The Equity of Parliaments and the Publick Faith Vindicated; In Answer to the Crisis of Property, and Address'd to the Annuitants*, 2nd edition, corrected (London, 1720).
104. *The Nation a Family: Being the Sequel of the Crisis of Property: Or a Plan For the Improvement of the South-Sea Proposal* (London: W. Chetwood, 1720), reprinted in *Tracts and Pamphlets*, p. 578.
105. Steele, *Tracts and Pamphlets*, p. 581.
106. J. Trenchard and T. Gordon, *Cato's Letters*, in *London Journal* (1720–3); ed. R. Hamowy, 2. vols (Indianapolis, Indiana: Liberty Fund, 1995).
107. Quoted in Aitken, *The Life of Richard Steele*, vol. 2, pp. 239–40.
108. J, Carswell, *The South-Sea Bubble*, p. 127.
109. Ibid., p. 170.

110. Thomas Broderick to Lord Middleton, in W. Coxe's *Walpole Correspondence*, quoted in *Parliamentary History,* W. Cobbett (ed.), vol. 7, p. 686.
111. J. Carswell, *The South-Sea Bubble*, p. 213.
112. Ibid., p. 240.
113. *Parliamentary History* (ed. W. Cobbett), vol. 7, p. 752.
114. Ibid., pp. 759–60.
115. Ibid.
116. *Correspondence of Richard Steele*, p. 516.
117. Aitken, *The Life of Richard Steele*, vol. 2, p. 293.
118. Winton, *Sir Richard Steele*, p. 228.
119. Ibid., p. 232.
120. Aitken, *The Life of Richard Steele*, vol. 2, p. 320.
121. Cibber, *An Apology*, p. 289.
122. *Correspondence of Richard Steele*, p. 356.

WORKS CITED

Primary Sources

Addison, J., *The Old Whig* (Dublin: Zachariah Jenkins, 1719).

—, *The Works of the Right Honourable Joseph Addison, Esq*, vol. 2 (London, 1721).

—, *The Miscellaneous Works of Joseph Addison*, ed. A. C. Guthkelch, 2 vols (London: G. Bell, 1914).

—, *The Works of the Right Honourable Joseph Addison, Esq*, vol. 2 (London, 1721).

—, *The Freeholder*, ed. J. Leheny (Oxford: Clarendon Press, 1979).

Another Letter from a Country Whig to Richard Steele, Esq.; on his Defence of his Guardian, August the 7th (London: John Morphew, 1713).

Arbuthnot, J., *The History of John Bull*, ed. Alan W. Bower and Robert A Erickson (Oxford: Clarendon Press, 1976).

Bouchain: In a Dialogue between the late Medley and Examiner (London: A. Baldwin, 1711).

Budgell, E., *Memoirs of the Life and Character of the Late Earl of Orrery and the Family of the Boyles* (London: W. Mears, 1731).

Burnet, T., *The Necessity of Impeaching the Late Ministry, In a Letter to the Earl of Halifax* (London: J. Roberts, 1715).

The Case of Richard Steele, Esq; Being an Impartial Account of the Proceedings Against Him (London, 1714).

Censor Censorum, *A Condoling Letter to the* Tattler: *on Account of the Misfortunes of Isaac Bickerstaff, Esq; A Prisononer in the — on Suspicion of Debt* (London, 1710).

The Character of Richard Steele: With Some Remarks. By Toby Abel's Cousin (London: John Morphew, 1713).

The Character of the Tatler (London, 1710).

Cibber, C., *An Apology for the Life of Colley Cibber*, ed. B. R. S. Fone (Ann Arbor: University of Michigan Press, 1968).

Collier, J., *A Short View of the Immorality and Profaneness of the English Stage: Together with the Sense of Antiquity upon this Argument* (1698; New York: AMS Press, 1974).

Considerations Concerning the Nature and Consequences of the Bill now depending in Parliament, Relating to the Peerage of Great-Britain. In a Letter from one Member of the House of Commons to another (London: J. Roberts, 1719).

[Cowper W.], *A Letter to Isaac Bickerstaff, Esq; Occasion'd by the Letter to the Examiner* (London, 1710).

The Crisis of Honesty. Being an Answer to the Crisis of Property. In a Letter to Sir R— S— (London: A. Moore, 1720).

The Crisis upon Crisis. A Poem. Being and Advertisement Stuck in the Lion's Mouth at Button's: and Addressed to Doctor S—t (London: J. Morphew, 1714).

A Critick no Wit: or, Remarks on Mr. Dennis's Late Play, called the Invader of his Country. In a Letter from a School-Boy to the Author (London, 1720).

Croxall, S., *An Original Canto of Spencer: Design'd as Part of the Fairy Queen, but never Printed. Now made Publick, by Nestor Ironside, Esq;* (London: A. Baldwin, 1714).

The Daily Courant.

A Defence of Mr. Steele, in a Letter to a Friend in the Country (London, 1714).

[Defoe, D.], *An Essay upon Publick Credit: Being an Enquiry how the Publick Credit comes to depend upon the Change of the Ministry, or the Dissolutions of Parliaments ...* (London, 1710).

Defoe, D., *The Succession of Spain Consider'd: Or, a View of the Several Interests of the Princes and Powers of Europe, as the Respect the Succession of Spain and the Empire.* (London, 1711).

—, *The Honour and Prerogative of the Queen's Majesty Vindicated and Defended against the Unexampled Insolence of the Author of the Guardian: In a Letter from a Country Whig to Mr. Steele* (London, 1713)

—, *Reasons Concerning the Immediate Demolishing of Dunkirk: Being a Serious Enquiry into the State and Condition of that Affair* (London, 1713).

—, *A Letter to Mr. Steele, Occasioned by his Letter to a Member of Parliament, Concerning the Bill for Preventing the Growth of Schism. By a Member of the Church of England.* (London: J. Baker, 1714).

Dennis, J., *The Critical Works of John Dennis*, ed. E. N. Hooker, 2 vols (Baltimore: Johns Hopkins Press, 1943).

A Dialogue between Jack High and Will Low: Proper for the perusal of those who have a Right to choose for the ensuing Parliament (London, 1710).

A Dialogue between a New Courtier and a Country Gentleman (London, 1712).

A Dialogue Betwixt Whig and Tory (London, 1710).

The Ecclesiastical and Political History of Whig Land, of Late Years; to which are Prefix'd, The Characters of a Late Ecclesiastical Historian, and of the Author of this History (London: J. Morphew, 1714).

The Examiner for the Year 1711, to which is prefix'd a Letter to the Examiner (London, 1712).

The Examiner, 6 vols, first series (London: J. Morphew, 1710–14).

The Female Manufacturers' Complaint: Being the Humble Petition of Dorothy Distaff, Abigail Spinning-Wheel, and Eleanor Reel, &c. Spinsters, to the Lady Rebecca Woollpack. With a Respectful Epistle to Sir R— S—l, concerning some Omissions of the utmost Importance in his Lady's Wardrobe. By Monsieur de Brocade of Paris (London: W. Boreham, 1720).

F[lint], G. *The History of the First and Second Session of the last Parliament* (London, 1714).

Further Reasons against the Peerage-Bill (London: J. Roberts, 1719).

Gay, J., *The Present State of Wit in a Letter to a Friend in the Country* (London, 1711), ed. D. F. Bond, Augustan Reprint Society, series 1: Essays on Wit, no. 3 (Ann Arbor, MI: Augustan Reprint Society, 1947).

[Gildon, C.], *A Comparison between the Two Stages, with ... some critical remarks on the Funeral ... and others*. London, 1702.

Harbin, G., *The Hereditary Right of the Crown of England Asserted, The History of the Succession since the Conquest Clear'd, and the true English Constitution Vindicated from the Misrepresentations of Dr. Higdin's View and Defence* (London, 1713).

Hare, F., *The Management of the War; in Four Letters to a Tory-Member* (London, 1711).

Hearne, T., *Remarks and Collections of Thomas Hearne*, ed. D. A. Rannie, Oxford Historical Society Publications, 34, 11 vols (Oxford: Oxford Historical Society, 1897).

Hicks, G., *Seasonable Queries Relating to the Birth and Birthright of a Certain Person* (London, 1713).

Hoadly, B., *Some Considerations Humbly offered to the Right Reverend the Lord Bishop of Exeter* (London, 1709).

—, *The Fears and Sentiments of All True Britains; with respect to National Credit, Interest and Religion* (London: A. Baldwin, 1710).

Hoffman, F., *Two Very Odd Characters tho' the Number be Even: Or The Whigg Flesh-Fly and The Industrious Tory Bee* (London, 1714).

An Invitation to Peace: Or, Toby's Preliminaries to Nestor Ironsides [sic], Set forth in a Dialogue between Toby and his Kinsman (London: Mr. Lawrence, 1714).

Jack the Courtier's Answer to Dick the Englishman's Close of the Paper so call'd (London, 1714).

John Tutchin's Ghost to Richard St—le, Esq. (London: J, Morphew, 1713).

Lawrence, R., *Lay-Baptism Invalid* (London, 1712).

A Letter from an English Tory to his Friend in Town. Chiefly Occasioned by the several Reflections on Mr. Steele's Guardian of August the Seventh (London: E. Smith, 1713).

A Letter from the Facetious Doctor Andrew Tripe at Bath, to the Venerable Nestor Ironside (London, 1714).

A Letter to Mr. Steele, Concerning His Crisis (Edinburgh: Robert Freebairn, 1714).

A Letter to Mr. Steele, Concerning the Removal of the Pretender from Lorrain, Occasion'd by the Crisis. Written by an Englishman (London: Ferdinand Burleigh, 1714).

The Life of Cato the Censor. Humbly Dedicated to R. S—le Esq: (London, 1714).

The Linen Spinster, in Defence of the Linen Manufactures, &c. To be Continued as Mrs. Rebecca Woolpack gives Occasion (London: J. Roberts, 1720).

Manley, D., *The Selected Works of Delarivier Manley*, ed. R. Carnell and R. Herman, 5 vols (London: Pickering and Chatto, 2005), vol. 2, *The New Atlantis*, ed. R. Carnell.

[Maynwaring, A.], *Advice to the Electors of Great Britain: Occasioned by the intended Invasion from France* (London, 1708).

Maynwaring, A., *Four Letters to a Friend in North Britain, upon the Publishing the Tryal of Dr. Sacheverell* (London, 1710).

—, *History of Hannibal and Hanno in the Second War between Carthage and Rome* (London, 1712).

Meres, J., *The Equity of Parliaments and the Publick Faith Vindicated; In Answer to the Crisis of Property, and Address'd to the Annuitants*, 2nd edition, corrected (London, 1720).

Moderator, No. 1 (London: J. Roberts, 1719).

Molesworth, R., *Letter from a Member of the House of Commons to a Gentleman Without Doors, Relating to the Bill of Peerage Lately brought into the House of Lords.* (London, 1719).

Nichols, J. (ed.), *The Lucubrations of Isaac Bickerstaff, Esq*, 6 vols (London: C. Bathurst, J. Buckland, J. Rivington, etc., 1786).

— (ed.), *The Spectator*, 8 vols (London: Payne, Rivington, Davis, Longman, Dodsley, etc., 1788–9).

— (ed.), *The Lover and Reader, to which are prefixed The Whig-Examiner, and a Selection from the Medley* (London: John Nichols, 1789).

— (ed.), *The Theatre, by Sir Richard Steele; to which are added, The Anti-Theatre; The Character of Sir John Edgar; Steele's Case with the Lord Chamberlain; The Crisis of Property, with the Sequel, Two Pasquins, &c.* (London: John Nichols, 1791).

— (ed.), *The Town Talk, The Fish Pool, The Plebeian, The Old Whig, The Spinster, &c.* (London: John Nichols, 1789).

Oldisworth, W., *Annotations on the Tatler, Written in French by Monsieur Bournelle; and Translated into English by William Wagstaffe*, 2 vols (London, 1710).

Oldmixon, J. (ed.), *Life and Posthumous Writings of Arthur Maynwaring* (London, 1715).

The Patrician (London: J. Roberts, 1719).

Poems on Affairs of State: Augustan Satirical Verse, 1660–1714, ed. G. D. Lord (New Haven, CT and London: Yale University Press, 1975).

Reflections on a Paper lately Printed, Entitled, A Letter to Sir Miles Wharton, Concerning Occasional Peers (London: John Morphew, 1713).

Remarks on Mr. Steele's Crisis, &c. By One of the Clergy. In a Letter to the Author (London: B. Berrington and E. Smith, 1714).

Remarks upon Mr. Steele's Crisis, Humbly inscribed to the Clergy of the Church of England (London: Bernard Lintott, 1714).

Resistance and Non-Resistance stated and decided: in a dialogue between a Hotspur-High-Flyer, a Canting-Low-Churchman, and Bickerstaff, Censor of Great Britain (London, 1710).

St John, H., *A Letter to the Examiner* (London, 1710).

Scandal no Argument. An Oxford Annuitant's Letter to Sir Richard Steele, In Answer to the Crisis of Honesty. With Reasons why Guardians should not expose their Wards to Sale, and pay their own Debts out of their Estates, being a short View of the South-Sea Affair yet depending (London: W. Boreham, 1720).

Sewall, G., *Schism, Destructive of the Government, both in Church and State, Being, A Defence of the Bill, Intitled, An Act for preventing the Growth of Schism. Wherein All the Objections against it, and particularly those in Squire Steele's Letter are fully Refuted* (London, 1714).

Six Questions, Stated and Answered, upon which the whole Force of the Arguments for and against the PEERAGE-BILL, depends (London: J. Roberts, 1719).

The Spectator Inspected; or, a Letter to the Spectator: from an Officer of the Army in Flanders, touching the Use of French Terms, in Relations from the Army, occasion'd by the Spectator of the 8th of Sept. 1711, (London, 1711).

A Speech Suppos'd to be Spoke by R_____ St____l, Esq; At the Opening this Present Parliament. With Some Remarks in a Letter to the Bailiff of St___dge, Very proper to be Bound up with the Crisis (London: John Morphew, 1714).

A Spy upon the Spectator. Part I (London: John Morphew, 1711).

The State of the Case between the Lord Chamberlain of his Majesty's Household, and Sir Richard Steele, as represented by that Knight. Restated, in Vindication of King George, and the Most Noble Duke of Newcastle (London: John Applebee, 1720).

Steele, R. (ed.), *Poetical Miscellanies, Consisting of Original Poems and Translations. By the best hands. Publish'd by Richard Steele* (London: Jacob Tonson, 1714).

— (ed.), *The Ladies Library. Written by a Lady. Published by Mr. Steele*, 3 vols (London: Jacob Tonson, 1714).

—, *The Political Writings of Sir Richard Steele* (London, 1715).

—, *Richard Steele* [Plays], ed. G. A. Aitken (1894; rpt. New York: Greenwood, 1968).

—, *Tracts and Pamphlets*, ed. R. Blanchard (Baltimore: Johns Hopkins Press, 1944).

—, *The Occasional Verse of Richard Steele*, ed. R. Blanchard (Oxford: Clarendon Press, 1952).

—,*The Englishman*, ed. R. Blanchard (Oxford: Clarendon Press, 1955).

—, *Richard Steele's Periodical Journalism 1714–16*, ed. R. Blanchard (Oxford: Clarendon Press, 1959).

—, *The Theatre*, ed. J. Loftis (Oxford: Clarendon Press, 1962).

—, with J. Addison, *The Spectator*, ed. D. F. Bond, 5 vols. (Oxford: Clarendon Press, 1965).

—, *Correspondence of Richard Steele*, ed. R. Blanchard, 2nd edn (Oxford: Clarendon Press, 1968).

—, *The Plays of Richard Steele*, ed. S. S. Kenny (Oxford: Clarendon Press, 1971).

—, *The Guardian*, ed. J. C. Stephens (Lexington, KY: University Press of Kentucky, 1982.

—, *The Tatler*, ed. D. F. Bond. 3 vols (Oxford: Clarendon Press, 1987).

The Steeleids, or, the Tryal of Wit. A Poem, in Three Cantos (London: J. Morphew, 1714).

Swift, J., *Journal to Stella*, ed. H. Williams, 2 vols (Oxford: Clarendon Press, 1948).

—, *Political Tracts 1711–1713*, ed. H. Davis (Princeton, NJ: Princeton University Press, 1951).

—, *Political Tracts 1713–1719*, ed. H. Davis and I. Ehrenpreis (Princeton, NJ: Princeton University Press, 1953).

—, *Bickerstaff Papers*, ed. H. Davis (Oxford: Basil Blackwood, 1957).

—, *Complete Poems*, ed. Pat Rogers (London: Penguin, 1983).

Thoughts of a Tory Author, Concerning the Press: With the Opinion of the Ancients and Moderns, about Freedom of Speech and Writing. And an Historical Account of the Usage it has met with from both Parties in England (London: A. Baldwin, 1712).

To the Author of the Englishman. Written to him on New-Years Day [1714], and Published now for the Benefit of all his Fellow-Members, whether Whigs, Tories, or New Converts (n.p., 1714).

Toland, J., *Dunkirk or Dover; or, The Queen's Honour, The Nation's Safety, The Liberties of Europe, and The Peace of the World, All at Stake till that Fort and Port be totally demolish'd by the French*, 2nd edn (London, 1713).

Trenchard, J. and T. Gordon, *Cato's Letters* (in *London Journal*, 1720–3), ed. R. Hamowy, 2. vols (Indianapolis, Indiana: Liberty Fund, 1995).

Victor, B., *An Epistle to Sir Richard Steele, On his Play, call'd, The Conscious Lovers* (London: W. Chetwood, et al, 1722).

Wagstaffe, W., *Miscellaneous Works of Dr. William Wagstaffe* (London: J. Bowyer, 1726).

Walpole, R., *Thoughts of a Member of the Lower House, in Relation to A Project for Restraining and Limiting the Power of the Crown in the Future Creation of Peers* (London, 1719).

Secondary Sources

Achurch, R. W., 'Richard Steele, Gazetteer and Bickerstaff', in R. P. Bond (ed.), *Studies in the Eighteenth-Century Periodical* (Chapel Hill, NC: University of North Carolina Press, 1957).

Aitken, G., *The Life of Richard Steele*, 2 vols (London: Isbister, 1889).

Allen, R. J., *The Clubs of Augustan London*, Harvard Studies in English, vol. 7, (Cambridge: Harvard University Press, 1933).

Alsop, J. D., 'Richard Steele and the Reform of the *London Gazette*', *Papers of the Bibliographical Society of America*, 80:4 (1986), pp. 455–60.

Aubin, R. A., 'Beyond Steele's Satire on Undertakers', *PMLA*, 64:5 (December 1949), pp. 1008–26.

Backscheider, P., 'Defoe's Lady Credit', *Huntington Library Quarterly*, 44:2 (Spring 1981), pp. 89–100.

Baldick, R., *The Duel: A History of Duelling* (London: Chapman and Hall, 1965).

Bannet, E., '"Epistolary Commerce" in *The Spectator*', in D. Newman (ed.), *The* Spectator: *Emerging Discourses*, pp. 220–47.

Bill, E. G. W., *Education at Christ Church College, Oxford 1660–1800* (Oxford: Clarendon Press, 1988).

Biographia Britannica: or, The Lives of the Most Eminent Persons who have flourished in Great Britain and Ireland, 6 vols. (London: J. Walthoe, T. Osborne, H. Whitridge, and others, 1763).

Black, S., 'Social and Literary Form in the *Spectator*', *Eighteenth-Century Studies*, 33:1 (1999), pp. 212–42.

Blanchard, R., 'Richard Steele and the Status of Women', *Studies in Philology*, 26.3 (July 1929), pp. 325–55.

—, 'Richard Steele's West Indian Plantation', *Modern Philology*, 39 (1942), pp. 281–85.

Bloom, E. A. and L., 'Steele in 1719: Additions to the Canon', *HLQ*, 31:2 (February 1968), pp. 123–51.

Bond, R. P., 'Mr. Bickerstaff and Mr. Wortley', in C. Henderson, Jr (ed.), *Classical, Medieval and Renaissance Studies in Honor of Berthold Louis Ullman* (Rome: Edizione di Storia e Letteratura, 1964), vol.2, pp. 491–504.

—, *The Tatler: The Making of a Literary Journal* (Cambridge, MA: Harvard University Press; Oxford: Oxford University Press, 1971).

Bony, A., 'L'Espace du texte: Spatialité de l'essai périodique addisonien', in *Espaces et représentations dans le monde anglo-américain aux XVIIe et XVIIIe siécles* (Paris: Presse de l'Université de Paris-Sorbonne, 1984), pp. 17–34.

Boswell, J., *Life of Samuel Johnson LL.D.*, ed. G. B. Hill, rev. L. F. Powell, 6 vols (Oxford: Clarendon Press, 1934–60).

Bowers, T., 'Universalizing Sociability: *The Spectator*, Civic Enfranchisement, and the Rule(s) of the Public Sphere', in D. Newman (ed.), *The Spectator: Emerging Discourses*, pp. 150–74.

Carey, B., 'Accounts of Savage Nations: the *Spectator* and the Americas', in D. Newman (ed.), *The Spectator: Emerging Discourses*, pp. 129–49.

Carnell, R., *A Political Biography of Delarivier Manley* (London: Pickering and Chatto, 2008).

Carswell, J. *The South Sea Bubble* (London: Cresset, 1960).

Chandler, D. G., *Blenheim Preparation: The English Army on the March to the Danube. Collected Essays* (Staplehurst: Spellmont, 2004).

Chrisman, K., 'Unhoop the Fair Sex: The Campaign Against the Hoop Petticoat in Eighteenth-Century England', *Eighteenth-Century Studies* 30:1 (Autumn 1996), pp. 3–23.

Churchill, W. S., *Marlborough: His Life and Times*, 6 vols (New York: Charles Scribner's Sons, 1933–8).

Cobbett, W., *The Parliamentary History of England from the Earliest Period to the Year 1803*, 36 vols (London: Longman, Hurst, Rees, Orme and Brown, etc., 1811), Vol. 7, *A.D. 1714–1722*.

Cooke, A. L., 'Addison vs. Steele, 1708', *PMLA*, 68:1 (March 1953), pp. 313–20.

Cowan, B., 'Mr. Spectator and the Coffeehouse Public Sphere', *Eighteenth-Century Studies*, 37:3 (2004),   .

—, *The Social Life of Coffee: The Emergence of the British Coffeehouse* (New Haven, CT: Yale University Press, 2005).

Dammers, R. H., 'Swift, Steele, and the Palatines', *Ball State University Forum*, 18:3 (Summer 1977), pp. 17–22.

—, *Richard Steele* (Boston: Twayne, 1982).

Davis, L. J., *Factual Fictions: The Origins of the English Novel* (New York: Columbia University Press, 1983).

Dibdin, C., *A Complete History of the Stage*, 5 vols (London, 1797).

Downie, J. A., *Robert Harley and the Press: Propaganda and Public Opinion in the Age of Swift and Defoe* (Cambridge: Cambridge University Press, 1979).

—, 'How Useful to Eighteenth-Century English Studies is the Paradigm of the "Bourgeois Public Sphere"?' *Literature Compass* 1:18C 022 (2003), pp. 1–19.

Eagleton, T., *The Function of Criticism from the* Spectator *to Post Structuralism* (London and New York: Verso, 1984)

Ehrenpreis, I., *Swift: The Man, his Works, and the Age*, 3 vols (Cambridge, MA: Harvard University Press, 1962–83).

Ellis, F., *Swift v. Mainwaring* (Oxford: Oxford University Press, 1986).

Erskine, D. B., *The Companion to the Playhouse*, 2 vols (London, 1764).

Evans J. E. and J. N. Wall, Jr, *A Guide to Prose Fiction in the* Tatler *and the* Spectator, Garland Reference Library of the Humanities, 71 (London and New York: Garland, 1977).

Felsenstein, F., *English Trader, Indian Maid: Representing Gender, Race, and Slavery in the New World. An Inkle and Yarico Reader* (Baltimore, MD: John Hopkins University Press, 1999).

Furtwangler, A., 'The Making of Mr. Spectator', *Modern Language Quarterly*, 38:1 (March 1977), pp. 21–39

Goldgar, B. A., *The Curse of Party: Swift's Relations with Addison and Steele* (Lincoln, NE: University of Nebraska Press, 1961).

—, *Walpole and the Wits* (Lincoln, NE: University of Nebraska Press, 1976).

Habermas, J., *The Structural Transformation of the Public Sphere: An Inquiry into a Category of Bourgeois Society*, trans. T. Burger, with the assistance of F. Lawrence (Cambridge, MA: MIT Press, 1989).

Handover, P. M., *A History of the London Gazette 1665–1965* (London: Her Majesty's Stationary Office, 1965).

Harris, M. J., 'A Study of the Paper War Relating to the Career of the 1st Duke of Marlborough, 1710–12' (PhD dissertation, University of London, 1975).

Hill, B. W., *Robert Harley: Speaker, Secretary of State and Premier Minister* (New Haven, CT: Yale University Press, 1988).

Holmes, G., *The Trial of Doctor Sacheverell* (London: Eyre Methuen, 1973).

Hopkins, R. H., 'The Issue of Anonymity and the Beginning of the Steele-Swift Controversy of 1713–14: A New Interpretation', *English Language Notes*, 2:1 (September 1964), pp.15–21.

Hoppit, J., *A Land of Liberty? England 1689–1727* (Oxford and New York: Oxford University Press, 2000).

Hulme, P., *Colonial Encounters: Europe and the Native Caribbean, 1492–1797* (London: Methuen, 1986).

Hume, R. D., *The Development of English Drama in the Late Seventeenth Century* (Oxford: Clarendon Press, 1976).

—, 'Jeremy Collier and the Future of the London Theatre in 1698', *Studies in Philology* 96:4 (1999), pp. 487–94.

Hunter, J. P., '"News and New Things": Contemporaneity and the Early English Novel', *Critical Inquiry*, 14 (1988): 501–4.

—, *Before Novels: The Cultural Contexts of Eighteenth-Century Fiction* (New York: W. W. Norton, 1990).

Hyland, P. B. J., 'Richard Steele, the Press, and the Hanoverian Succession, 1713–1716', (PhD dissertation, University of Lancaster, 1982).

—, 'Naming Names: Steele and Swift', in Paul Hyland and Neil Sammels (eds), *Irish Writing: Exile and Subversion* (London: Macmillan, 1991), pages 13–31.

Italia, I., *The Rise of Literary Journalism in the Eighteenth Century: Anxious Employment* (London and New York: Routledge, 2005).

Johnson, S., *An Account of the Life of Richard Savage, Son of Earl Rivers* (London: J. Roberts, 1744).

Jones, C., '"Venice Preserv'd; or a Plot Discovered": The Political and Social Context of the Peerage Bill in 1719', in *A Pillar of the Constitution*, ed. C. Jones (London: Hambleton, 1989), pp. 79–112.

Kenny, S. S., 'Two Scenes by Addison in Steele's *The Tender Husband*', *Studies in Bibliography*, 19 (1966), pp. 217–26.

Ketcham, M. G., *Transparent Designs: Reading, Performance, and Form in the* Spectator *Papers* (Athens, GA: University of Georgia Press, 1985).

Klein, L. E., *Shaftesbury and the Culture of Politeness: Moral Discourse and Cultural Politeness in Early Eighteenth-Century England* (Cambridge: Cambridge University Press, 1994).

Knight, C. A., 'Bibliography and the Shape of the Literary Periodical', *Library* 6th ser. 8:3 (September 1986), pp. 232–48.

—, 'The *Spectator*'s Generalizing Discourse', in J. A. Downie and T. N. Corns (eds), *Telling People What to Think: Early Eighteenth-Century Periodicals from* The Review *to* The Rambler (London: Frank Cass, 1993), pp. 44–57.

—, 'The *Spectator*'s Moral Economy', *Modern Philology*, 92:2 (November 1993), pp. 161–79.

—, *Joseph Addison and Richard Steele: A Reference Guide, 1730–1991* (New York: G. K. Hall, 1994).

—, *The Literature of Satire* (Cambridge: Cambridge University Press, 2004).

Kolb, G. J., 'A Note on "Tristram Shandy": Some New Sources', *Notes and Queries*, vol. 196 (1951), p. 227.

Legouis, E., 'Les deux 'Sir Roger de Coverley', celui de Steele et celui d'Addison', *Revue Germanique*, 2:4 (1906), pp. 453–71.

Lewis, C. S., 'Addison', in *Essays on the Eighteenth Century Presented to David Nichol Smith in Honour of his Seventieth Birthday* (Oxford: Clarendon Press, 1945), pp. 1–14.

Leyburn, E. D., 'Swift's View of the Dutch', *PMLA*, 66 (1951), pp. 734–45.

Loftis, J., *Steele at Drury Lane* (Berkeley and Los Angeles, CA: University of California Press, 1952), pp. 99–102.

—, *The Politics of Drama in Augustan England* (Oxford: Clarendon Press, 1963).

The London Stage, ed. E. Avery and others, 5 vols (Carbondale, IL: Southern Illinois University Press, 1960–8).

Mackie, E. S., 'Being Too Positive About the Public Sphere', in D. Newman (ed.) *The* Spectator: *Emerging Discourses* (Newark, DE: University of Delaware Press, 2005), pp. 81–104.

—, (ed.), *The Commerce of Everyday Life: Selections from the* Tatler *and the* Spectator, (Boston: Bedford/St. Martins, 1998).

—, *Market à la Mode: Fashion, Commodity, and Gender in the* Tatler *and the* Spectator (Baltimore, MD and London: Johns Hopkins University Press, 1997).

Maurer, S. L., *Proposing Men: Dialectics of Gender and Class in the Eighteenth-Century Periodical* (Stanford, CA: Stanford University Press, 1998).

McKeon, M., 'Cultural Crisis and Dialectical Method: Destabilizing Augustan Literature', in L. Damrosch (ed.), *The Profession of Eighteenth-Century Literature: Reflections on an Institution* (Madison, WI: University of Wisconsin Press, 1992), pp. 42–61.

—, *The Secret History of Domesticity: Public, Private, and the Division of Knowledge* (Baltimore, MD: Johns Hopkins Press, 2005.

Merritt, J., 'Originals, Copies, and the Iconography of Femininity in *The Spectator*', in D. Newman (ed.) *The* Spectator: *Emerging Discourses*, pp. 41–58.

Michael,W., *England under George I*, vol. 2: *The Quadruple Alliance*, trs. A. and G. E. MacGregor (1939; rpt. New York: AMS, 1970).

Milic, L. T., 'Tone in Steele's *Tatler*', in D. H. Bond and W. R. McLeod (eds), *Newsletters to Newspapers: Eighteenth-Century Journalism* (Morgantown, WV: School of Journalism, West Virginia University, 1977), pp. 35–40.

Müllenbrock, H-J., *The Culture of Contention: A Rhetorical Analysis of the Public Controversy about the Ending of the War of Spanish Succession, 1710–1713* (Munich: Fink, 1997).

Müller, A., 'Putting the Child into Discourse: Framing Children in the *Spectator*', in D. Newman (ed.), *The* Spectator, pp. 59–80.

Newman, D. (ed.), *The* Spectator: *Emerging Discourses* (Newark: University of Delaware Press, 2005).

Paulson, R., *The Fictions of Satire* (Baltimore, MD: Johns Hopkins Press, 1967).

Plumb, J. H., *Sir Robert Walpole: The Making of a Statesman* (London: Cresset, 1956).

Pocock, J. G. A., *The Machiavellian Moment: Florentine Political Thought and the Atlantic Republican Tradition* (Princeton, NJ: Princeton University Press, 1975).

Pollard, G., 'Notes on the Size of the Sheet', *Library*, 4.22 (1942), pp. 123–4.

Polly, G., 'A Leviathan of Letters', in D. Newman (ed.), *The* Spectator: *Emerging Discourses*, pp. 105–28.

Price, L. M., *Inkle and Yarico Album* (Berkeley, CA: University of California Press, 1937).

Quick, A., *Charterhouse: A History of the School* (London: James and James, 1990).

Ramsland, C., 'Britons Never Will Be Slaves: A Study in Whig Political Propaganda in the British Theatre, 1700–1742', *Quarterly Journal of Speech*, 28 (1942), pp. 393–9.

Rand, B. (ed.), *Berkeley and Percival* (Cambridge: Cambridge University Press, 1914).

Rau, F., 'Steeles Eintritt in den Kit-Cat Club', *Germanisch-romanishe Monatsschrift*, 37 [n.s. 6] (1956), pp. 396–98.

Richards, J. O., *Party Propaganda Under Queen Anne: The General Elections of 1702–1713* (Athens, GA: University of Georgia Press, 1973).

Richardson, C., *Notices and Extracts Relating to the Lion's Head, which was Erected at Button's Coffee-House, in the Year 1713* (London: Saunders and Otley, 1828).

Rose, C., *England in the 1690s: Revolution, Religion, and War* (Oxford: Blackwell, 1999).

Saller, R. P., *Personal Patronage under the Early Empire* (Cambridge: Cambridge University Press, 1982).

Sankey, M. D., *Jacobite Prisoners of the 1715 Rebellion: Preventing and Punishing Rebellion in Early Hanoverian Britain* (Burlington, VT and Hampshire: Ashgate, 2005).

Shevelow, K., *Women and Print Culture: The Construction of Femininity in the Early Periodical* (London and New York: Routledge, 1989).

Smithers, P., *The Life of Joseph Addison*, 2nd edition (Oxford: Clarendon Press, 1968).

Snyder, H. L., 'Arthur Maynwaring and the Whig Press, 1710–1712' *Literatur als Kritik des Lebens. Festschrift zum 65. Geburtstag von Ludwig Borinski*, ed. R. Haas, H-J. Müllenbrock and C. Uhlig (Heidelberg: Quelle und Mayer, 1975), pp. 120–36.

Speck, W. A., *Tory and Whig: The Struggle in the Constituencies 1701–1715* (London: Macmillan; New York: St. Martin's, 1970).

Spence, J., *Observations, Anecdotes, and Characters*, ed. J. M. Osborn, 2 vols (Oxford: Clarendon Press, 1966).

Stallybrass, P., and A. White, *The Politics and Poetics of Transgression* (Ithaca, NY: Cornell University Press, 1986).

Sterne, L., *The Life and Opinions of Tristram Shandy, Gentleman*, ed. M. New and J. New (Gainsville: University Presses of Florida, 1978–84).

Szechi, D., *1715: The Great Jacobite Rebellion* (New Haven, CT and London: Yale University Press, 2006).

Thackeray, W. M., *The History of Henry Esmond, Esq.* (London: Smith, Elder, 1852).

Trevelyan, G. M., *England under Queen Anne*, 3 vols (London: Longmans, Green, 1930).

Turner, E. R., 'The Peerage Bill of 1719', *English Historical Review*, 28: 110 (April 1913), pp. 243–59.

Wechselblatt, M., 'Gender and Race in Yarico's Epistles to Inkle: Voicing the Feminine/Slave', *Studies in Eighteenth-Century Culture*, 19 (1989), pp. 197–223.

Whiston, W., *Memoirs of the Life and Writings of Mr. William Whiston, Containing Memoirs of several of his Friends also* (London, 1749).

Williams, B., *Stanhope* (Oxford, 1932).

Winton, C., 'Richard Steele: The Political Writer' (PhD dissertation, Princeton University, 1955; Ann Arbor: University Microfilms).

—, *Captain Steele* (Baltimore, MD: Johns Hopkins Press, 1964).

—, *Sir Richard Steele, M.P.* (Baltimore, MD: Johns Hopkins Press, 1970).

Woodward, J., *Select Cases and Consultations in Physick*, ed. P. Templeman (London, 1757).

INDEX

Steele's major periodicals (*Tatler*, *Spectator*, *Guardian*, and *Englishman*) and his play *The Conscious Lovers* are separately indexed; other works appear under the author's name.